Jehovah's Kingdom

Jehovah's Kingdom

The Messenger of the Covenant
Brings Good News

L.A. Pressnall

Copyright © 2009 by L.A. Pressnall.

Library of Congress Control Number: 2009911798
ISBN: Softcover   978-1-4415-9809-7
                Ebook   978-1-4500-0221-9

All rights reserved. No part of this book may be reproduced or transmitted in any form or by any means, electronic or mechanical, including photocopying, recording, or by any information storage and retrieval system, without permission in writing from the copyright owner.

This book was printed in the United States of America.

To order additional copies of this book, contact:
Xlibris Corporation
1-888-795-4274
www.Xlibris.com
Orders@Xlibris.com
71790

PREFACE

A Message from God

Ancient Bible prophecies are being fulfilled. Our Heavenly Father, Jehovah, has sent forth his messenger of the covenant prophesied in the book of Malachi. The messenger urges all people to become reconciled to God. As a loving Father, Jehovah welcomes with open arms every person who loves him and is earnestly seeking him. 2 John, verse 3, "There will be with us undeserved kindness, mercy and peace from God the Father and from Jesus Christ the Son of the Father, with truth and love." (Isaiah 49:6) (Malachi 3:1 and Malachi 4:5,6) (Acts 17:24-31) (2 Corinthians 5:16-20)

Christ Rules Over A New World

A righteous new world is being established here on earth through God's Son, and our King, Christ Jesus. When the fulfillment of a prophecy occurs, it does not have to be made physically apparent to us here on earth. Many prophecies are fulfilled on a spiritual level, and not visible to the naked eye. What Jehovah causes to actually occur with a fulfillment, usually does not correlate with our sometimes long-standing and preconceived expectations. That being the case, our own spirituality needs to be sharply honed, in order to grasp the facts and truths until everything is made manifest. The only help for this is a close relationship with Almighty God, Jehovah, that is based on truth. Truth is not usually very hard to understand, but sometimes it can be very hard for us to accept. (Matthew 6:10) (Romans 15:11-13) (Ephesians 3:14-21) (2 Peter Chapter 3, all verses) (Revelation 11:15-18)

Babylon the Great is Scripturally Identified

Our actions toward others and our relationship with God are being closely examined. This is the "great and fear-inspiring day of Jehovah." As prophesied, this is his day of accounting with all people. It is the day of righteous retribution, proper punishment brought by Almighty God upon ungodly persons, those doing willful harm to others and to the earth.

Jehovah's Witnesses bear special accountability to God because they call themselves by his holy name. In God's judgment, those at the head of this international organization have been measured against the highest standards (scriptural standards) for their teaching and example to others, and are found to be lacking. (James 3:1) Many of these individuals have left Jehovah's loving and compassionate ways. It is for personal gain, prominence and its corrupting influence of power and control over others, that they have manipulated God's holy scriptures to subdue loyal members. In doing this, they have failed their scriptural commission to shepherd God's people with tenderness, as Jesus would. (Jeremiah 23:1-4) (Acts 20:29,30) (Revelation 17:5,6)

They were also under scriptural command to prove themselves faithful to God to the end of the last days. They were to remain steadfast and true to Jehovah in all of their conduct, and look to him alone for provision and protection. Instead, they have forsaken God by seeking material wealth, as well as security through political fortification from the nations. In the eyes of God they have committed spiritual prostitution. For this, Almighty God Jehovah denounces them. They are Babylon the Great. (Isaiah 30:1-16) (Malachi 4:5,6) (Matthew 24:45-51) (Revelation Chapter 18) (Revelation 19:1,2)

Revelation 18:4, **"Get out of her, my people**, if you do not want to share with her in her sins, and if you do not want to receive part of her plagues. For her sins have massed together clear up to heaven, and **God has called her acts of injustice to mind.** (Quoted from the New World Translation of the Holy Scriptures, published by the Watchtower Bible and Tract Society.)

CONTENTS

Date   Page

Prayer 2
Bible Prophecy..3
Jesus Christ..4
Our Relationship with God 4
The Day of Salvation 5
Jehovah's Holy Name 5
Babylon the Great...6
Journal History...8
Journal Key...10
Faith 11
JOURNAL 15
June 1 ....Jehovah's Presence: Midnight 15
June 4 ....Departure: Fleeing from Babylon 15
June 6 ....Jehovah's Holy Name: "I Shall Prove To Be,"
                  Chosen to be Jehovah's Messenger:
                  Consecrated to God...15
June 7 ....Commandment: Sabbath, Rosie: Unfaithful
                  Jerusalem, Advice: Patience, Circuit Overseer:
                  Kingdom hall talk given, Galatians 5:22:
                  Fruitage of the spirit, Prophecy:
                  But by my spirit, Angel: Sent forth,
                  Prophecy: Two women coming forth 16
June 8 30
June 9 ....Zion Gives Birth: Spiritual children, Jehovah's
                  Kingdom: Praise Jehovah! His kingdom
                  has come! Revealed: Sequence of events,
                  Rosie: People coming 30
June 10 ....Mother: A mother is merciful and gentle...............32
June 13 ....Seventy Years: Insincere fasting, Angel: Sword
                  coming, Jehovah's Kingdom: Established
                  on earth NOW, Revealed: Jehovah's other
                  chosen servant, Vision: Friend 40

June 16	**Angel:** Sword will pass over us, **Advance Warning:** Expelled, false accusations, **Earlier Decision:** Innocent of charges, **Kingdom Power:** Clearly visible, **Circuit Overseer:** Thanked for journal	43
June 17	**First Meeting with Elders:** In my home, **Bram:** Shout in triumph, **Bram:** Two families chosen	50
June 18	**Angel:** Time moving forward, **Second meeting with Elders:** Justice, **Bram:** Susan attends, **Given:** Lamentations for the unfaithful organization	54
June 19	**Given:** Habakkuk, no law or justice in organization	63
June 20	**Invitation From Friends:** Leaving the organization, not leaving Jehovah, **Given:** Bearing up under reproach, **Given:** Coming of Elijah	68
June 21	**Message:** Marry, Elijah/Elias anagram, Elisha anagram, **Prophecy:** Zion in labor pains	73
June 22	**Third Meeting with an Elder:** A form of godly devotion, **Scriptures:** Indicated by Jehovah, **Prophecy Fulfillment:** Little city	76
June 23	**Parallel Events:** Jesus' day; our day, **Fourth Meeting with Elders:** Shepherd the flock tenderly	80
June 26	**New Covenant:** June 27, 1989, **Bram:** Jehovah went over the land, **Angel:** We recall the sword is coming, **Jehovah's Denunciation Comes:** In a windstorm, **Discovery:** Awake Magazine cover – death's head, **Rosie:** It must come true, **Discovery:** Awake article on Zechariah, **Jehovah Sent These People to Me:** Precious friends	84
June 27	**Fifth Meeting With Elders:** At new Kingdom hall, **Given:** They have denied Jehovah, **Questioned:** Jehovah directing me with holy spirit, **Accused:** Remaining silent, **Scriptures:** Reading from the Bible, **Given:** Reproving with full authority,	

	Bram: We were killed, **Disfellowshipped:** False accusations, judged guilty, **Portent:** Face of Christ, **Given:** See the Son of man, **Under the Earth:** Three days 90
June 28-29	**Bram:** Greetings from heaven above, **Given:** Start a fire, **Given:** Your mouth a fire, **Given:** Burning anger, **Given:** Chosen lady with children 94
June 30	**Denunciation:** Sent in mail, **Overview Of The Week:** June 26 to June 30, **Bram:** Mailing 96
July 2	**Instructions:** Write down the vision, **Instructions:** Raise a signal 98
July 3	**Commandment:** "You will seek," **Commandment:** "Seek! seek where Jehovah is residing," **Phone Call:** Words being burned 104
July 4	 119
July 6	**Phone Call:** Babylon the Great 141
July 7	 141
July 8	 142
July 9	**Given:** I am sending him 143
July 10	 146
July 12	**Prayer Answered:** Not without results, **Definition of Faith:** Realities though not beheld, **Advance Warning:** Being lied to 148
July 14	**Ministry of the Reconciliation:** Give you as a covenant, **Now Is The Day Of Salvation!:** This is Jehovah's day!, **Rosie:** A good work is started, **Phone Call From My Sister, Dawn:** Relationship with God 156
July 15	**Staff Pleasantness:** Lisa, **Staff Union:** Leon 163
July 22	**Conversation With My Sister, Dawn:** Truthfulness of Bible teachings 165
July 27	**Conversation With My Sister, Dawn, Before A Family Get Together:** Prayer, **Jehovah Is Our Resting-place:** Fly away and reside, **Scriptural References In Connection With Jehovah's Denunciation On The Organization**

	Known As Jehovah's Witnesses: We are Jehovah's Faithful Witnesses, **Denunciation Structure:** Their own translation of the Bible, **JEHOVAH'S DENUNCIATION:** Yours is the kingdom, O Jehovah	166
August 4		187
August 5	**Presence:** Sabbath prayer, **Past Events In My Life:** Angel, Truth, Image, Vision, Message, Message, My prayer, Sent forth, Escape from captivity, Persecution from Satan, Message, Prayer answered, Attempted abduction, Intruder, Circuit overseer's visit to our congregation, Jehovah's presence, Prophetesses, Zion, Message, Onward-sweeping tempest, Disfellowshipped for exposing wrongdoing in the organization, Portent, Jehovah's denunciation mailed out, Warning in advance, Given in advance, Angelic presence, Message, Message, Presence of more than one, Our needs were met, Help from Jehovah	187
August 12		204
August 28		208
September 1	**Prayer:** Jehovah has taken action!, **Prayer:** Circle of the earth, **Forest, Wilderness, Mountain, Tower**	216
September 2		221
September 4	**Rosie:** Originating with God	222
September 5	**My Prayer:** Jehovah, Almighty God, Rock of my Heart	222
September 14	**Jesus Christ:** Wisdom	228
September 19	**Zion:** Leon and Lisa, **Two Witnesses**, Elisha/Helisaie anagram	231
September 24	**Given:** Worth waiting for, **Jehovah's Will:** Emotional adjustment, **Attitude Refinements:** Mildness and self-control, **Message:** It is later than you think	250
September 27	**Liberty:** Symbolism	261

September 30...**Today:** Prophet to the nations..................................270
October 1..........**Commissioned:** Do not be afraid, for I am
with you, **Encounter:** Daniel Sydlik, **Adam
and Eve:** Replacement father, replacement
mother, **A Lion Cub Judah Is:** Leon......................272
October 3..........**Advance Warning:** Bad news, **Message:** Soon........289
October 4..........**Message:** Prepare to meet you master,
A Lion Cub Judah Is: Leon, **Two Olive
Trees:** Two anointed ones, **Lion of
Judah:** Greek, **Message:** Compassion,
Jehovah's Desire: Exclusive devotion,
Highest Attributes of Jehovah: Love,
wisdom, justice, power..289
October 7 ....**Anointed:** Two witnesses, **Persecution:** Praying.......306
October 7/8 .....**Midnight, Event:** A "book" 313
October 9..323
October 10..326
October 11........**Message:** Find yourself in a book, **Message:**
Do not underestimate what God can do,
Rosie: The harvest is ripe, **Adam and Eve:**
Everlasting life, **My Prayer:** Forgiveness,
Previous Event: Permission to "read,"
Angel: Being corrected 326
October 15........**Message:** Let your faith grow great, **Message:**
Expect a miracle, **Message:** We are with you
in this, **Message:** Bringing in the royal family,
soon!, **Prayer:** Children, **Vision:** Rebuilding
of Jerusalem, **Zion:** Lisa, **Complete:** Journal,
Manuscript: Handwritten book, **Tablet:**
Write it upon a tablet, **Friend of God:**
Referred to as "friend," **Test:** Likened to
Abraham, **Message:** Leon's spiritual awareness,
Message: Remember the crown!, **Message:**
I will go with him, **Message:** Tomorrow, **My
Response:** Jehovah is our support and
strength, **Jehovah's Holy Name:** "I Shall
Prove To Be," **Jehovah's Faithful Witnesses:**
Our new name 346

REFERENCE MATERIAL ACKNOWLEDGEMENT

New World Translation of the Holy Scriptures, © 1961, 1981, and 1984 by Watch Tower Bible and Tract Society of Pennsylvania, revised 1984, published by Watchtower Bible and Tract Society of New York, Inc., International Bible Students Association, Brooklyn, New York, U.S.A. (All scriptures are quoted from this version of the Bible, unless otherwise noted.)

Authorized (King James) Version of the Holy Bible, © 1958, The National Publishing Co., published by the National Bible Press, Philadelphia, Pennsylvania, U.S.A.

Good News Bible, The Bible in Today's English Version, Old Testament © American Bible Society, 1976, New Testament © American Bible Society, 1966, 1971, 1976, Maps © United Bible Societies, 1976, published by American Bible Society, New York, U.S.A.

The Living Bible, Paraphrased, ©1971 by Tyndale House Publishers, published by Tyndale House Publishers, Wheaton, Illinois, U.S.A.

Insight on the Scriptures, © 1988 by Watch Tower Bible and Tract Society of Pennsylvania, International Bible Students Association, published by Watchtower Bible and Tract Society of New York, Inc., International Bible Students Association, Brooklyn, New York, U.S.A.

"All Scripture Is Inspired Of God And Beneficial," © 1963 by Watch Tower Bible and Tract Society of Pennsylvania, published by Watchtower Bible and Tract Society of New York, Inc., International Bible Students Association, Brooklyn, New York, U.S.A.

The Truth That Leads To Eternal Life, © 1968 by Watch Tower Bible and Tract Society of Pennsylvania, published by Watchtower Bible and

Tract Society of New York, Inc., International Bible Students Association, Brooklyn, New York, U.S.A.

Watch Tower Magazine, © Watchtower Bible and Tract Society, New York, U.S.A.

Awake! Magazine, © Watchtower Bible and Tract Society, New York, U.S.A.

Thirty Years A Watchtower Slave, © June 1971 by W. J. Schnell, (Direction Books) U.S.A.

Liberty: The Statue and the American Dream, © 1985 by L. Allen, Statue of Liberty Ellis Island Foundation with the cooperation of the National Geographic Society, New York, New York, U.S.A.

JEHOVAH'S KINGDOM

1 Chronicles, Chapter 29

11. Yours, O Jehovah, are the greatness and the mightiness and the beauty and the excellency and the dignity; for everything in the heavens and in the earth is [yours]. Yours is the kingdom, O Jehovah, the One also lifting yourself up as head over all. 12. The riches and the glory are on account of you, and you are dominating everything; and in your hand there are power and mightiness, and in your hand is [ability] to make great and to give strength to all. 13. And now, O our God, we are thanking you and praising your beauteous name.

14. "And yet, who am I and who are my people, that we should retain power to make voluntary offerings like this?

(Prayer)

Great is YOUR LOVE for us, JEHOVAH.

YOUR WISDOM is beyond knowing.

YOUR JUSTICE is perfect.

YOUR POWER knows no boundary.

To you, JEHOVAH, belong our deepest love and our highest loyalty. With you, JEHOVAH, there are abundant mercy and complete forgiveness.

From heaven you have sent your Son, to teach us your righteous ways. Strengthen our hearts, please, that we may grow in our faith toward you and our goodness toward others.

Heavenly Father, JEHOVAH, we seek to find your will for us. And we ask forgiveness for all our sins, through your holy Son, Jesus Christ. Amen.

> That people may know that you, whose name is
> JEHOVAH,
> you alone are the Most High over all the earth.
> (Psalm 83:18)

Revelation 11:15-18, . . . "The kingdom of the world did become the kingdom of our Lord and of his Christ, and he will rule as king forever and ever" . . . "We thank you, Jehovah God, the Almighty, the One who is and who was, because you have taken your great power and begun ruling as king. But the nations became wrathful, and your own wrath came, and the appointed time for the dead to be judged, and to give their reward to your slaves the prophets and to the holy ones and to those fearing your name, the small and the great, and to bring to ruin those ruining the earth."

Bible Prophecy

All Bible prophecy is true. On many occasions prophecy finds dual or even multiple fulfillments at later dates in history. When this occurs, these prophecies are said to establish prophetic patterns or parallels. For example, a prophecy may have a fulfillment in the prophet's day, again in Jesus' day and again in the present, or a future day. This is the case today. Jehovah has endowed a present day person with Elijah's spirit. There are other prophecies, as well, being fulfilled for the very first time now, and some that are yet to be fulfilled. (Isaiah 52:7) (Isaiah 60:1-3) (Malachi 3:1-4) (Revelation 11:3,4) (Revelation 12:5,6)

In Elijah's day, his successor was granted a twofold portion of Elijah's spirit. This is actually a twofold portion of God's holy spirit. When a person is endowed with Elijah's spirit, it does not mean that this person is Elijah himself. It means that a double blessing of holy spirit—strength of courage, and great zeal for Jehovah—enabled both Elijah, and later his successor, Elisha, to accomplish the work God had given them to do. (2 Kings 2:9,15) (Malachi 4:5,6)

John the Baptist was likewise endowed with Elijah's spirit. He was God's messenger sent forth in Jesus' day to direct people's hearts back to their Heavenly Father, to get ready for God a prepared people. (Malachi 4:5,6) (Luke 1:17) (John 1:19-21)

The present-day messenger will also, through God's holy spirit, light the spiritual path home to our loving Heavenly Father, Jehovah. As a loving Father, God welcomes with open arms every person who loves him and is earnestly seeking him. Today's messenger is sent forth with the commission to encourage and assist God's people. This includes the many, many people who have become exhausted and weakened by the pressures put on us by this world. In the days ahead, Jehovah will comfort us and prove out that salvation is not owing to personal ability in any of us. In truth, it is the power of God's holy spirit which gives us the strength we need to stand true during these trying times. (Isaiah 49:6) (Isaiah 60:1-3) (Malachi 3:1 and Malachi 4:5,6) (Acts 17:24-31) (2 John 3) (Revelation 3:10)

God's messenger of the covenant is also acquainted with personal weakness and repeated failure, as well as affliction. God demonstrates through the power of his love and holy spirit that he can correct and refine, and raise up a prophet from anyone willing to learn. It is truly love and wisdom from God that instructs our hearts, and makes it possible to become a person ready and approved by God. To Jehovah belong the glory and praise for this. (Isaiah 49:7-13) (Jeremiah 6:27) (Hebrews 12:1-11) (1 Peter 5:10)

Jesus Christ

Almighty God, Jehovah, sent his only-begotten Son, Jesus Christ, to earth. Over two thousand years ago, Christ came to live among us and teach us by his example. The accounts in the Bible of his life and the lives of his apostles help us to see how to conduct ourselves while living in these difficult days. Christ taught us that by learning God's ways and living in harmony with him with faith and endurance, we can have everlasting life. (Matthew 10:22) (John 3:16-21) (John 17:3) (1 John 2:2,3)

Through Christ, we can find peace and comfort in our hearts, and forgiveness, because he was willing to offer up his life in our behalf. The blood from his sacrificial death cleanses us of our sins, and makes it possible to become reconciled to our loving Heavenly Father, Jehovah. (John 14:6,27) (2 Corinthians 7: 10) (Colossians 3:15) (Hebrews 9:24)

Our Relationship with God

In order to have a right and true relationship with our merciful Heavenly Father, we need to give careful thought to some fundamental questions. What is at the core of our relationship with Almighty God? Is it based on truth? Is truth really that important? Is truth important to God, himself? Is our own self-awareness important? How does our current relationship with God look, under close inspection? If we could see ourselves through God's eyes, what would we see? Do we have the courage to look carefully at the person we have become? Are we open to correction from God if we are wrong? Can we make room in our hearts for a God greater than we have ever imagined, whose wisdom and understanding far surpass our own?

Do we give recognition to Jehovah's holy name in prayer? Do we acknowledge Jesus Christ as the only means by which we may approach our Heavenly Father? Is our conduct honorable at all times, especially when we are under great stress and temptation? When tempted, do we run to God in prayer for strength? (Malachi 4:5,6) (Matthew 6:9) (John 14:6) (2 Timothy 3:1-5) (2 Peter 3:7) (Revelation 11:18)

The Day of Salvation

This is the Day of Salvation. Cruelty and oppression are passing away. The end of suffering is in sight. The earth will soon be cleansed and restored, and loved ones will be resurrected. However, at the same time, this is the Day of Judgment. God's "great and fear-inspiring day" is at hand. He is bringing destruction to those doing willful harm. This is righteous retribution, proper punishment brought by Almighty God on ungodly persons. God is destroying all evil, but he shows great mercy on those who love him and walk in his ways. (Malachi 4:5,6) (Revelation 21:3,4)

God has given us the Bible to guide us. As we read, he will assist us through his holy spirit if we come to him in prayer with a humble, open attitude, and a heartfelt desire to accept his ways and abide by them. He is merciful and generous to all. And he will help us to understand that he truly knows what is best for us. (Luke 11:9,10) (2 Timothy 3:16)

Jehovah's Holy Name

At Luke 11:2 Jesus says to his disciples: "Whenever you pray, say, 'Father, let your name be sanctified. Let your kingdom come.'" The scriptures show that the name of Jesus' Father and our Father is Jehovah, which in Hebrew is YHWH (Yahweh). To sanctify means to "make holy." In our hearts, we are to make God's personal name holy. This holy name is very important to God himself, because it represents everything that he stands for. Through our use of his name, we become mindful and thoughtful of everything he means to us. (Psalm 83:18) (Psalm 91:14-16) (Proverbs 18:10)

It is of the utmost importance to show reverence to our Creator by honoring his holy name. When we sanctify God's name in our hearts, there is no mistaking who we recognize as supreme. When we specifically call on Jehovah by name, there is no question who we are praying to. Our recognition and acknowledgement of his holy name is more important than whether we are able to correctly spell or pronounce it. Jehovah knows that at this time we are imperfect and have only partial knowledge. He will give us a more complete and perfect understanding of his great name, in his own time. (Exodus 20:2,7) (Matthew 6:9) (John 17:25,26) (1 Corinthians 13:12,13) (2 Timothy 2:25,26) (Revelation 14:1)

We want to worship Almighty God Jehovah in spirit and truth, on his terms. This is very different from worshipping God according to tradition or doctrine simply because this is the way we were raised in a particular religion, and it is familiar and therefore comfortable for us. (Psalm 83:18) (Mark 7:7,8) (John 4:24) (John 17:3-8)

Babylon the Great

Jehovah's Witnesses bear special accountability to God because they call themselves by his holy name. In God's judgment, those at the head of this international organization have been measured against the highest standards (scriptural standards) for their teaching and example to others. (James 3:1) At one time, they were a spiritually clean people that had an approved standing before God. However, many individuals, especially those at the head of the organization, have left Jehovah's loving and compassionate ways. It is for personal gain, prominence and its corrupting influence of power and control over others, that these individuals have fabricated lies and manipulated God's holy scriptures to subdue members. In doing this, they have failed their scriptural commission to shepherd God's people with tenderness, as Jesus would. (Jeremiah 5:26-31) (Jeremiah 23:1-4)

Through deception and intimidation, they subvert truth and justice. They prophesy in falsehood. They are the modern-day equivalent to the false-hearted Pharisees, religious leaders of Jesus' day. Jesus said: "Woe to you, scribes and Pharisees, hypocrites! because you resemble whitewashed graves, which outwardly indeed appear beautiful but inside are full of dead men's bones and of every sort of uncleanness. In that way you also, outwardly indeed, appear righteous to men, but inside you are full of hypocrisy and lawlessness." Consequently, these individuals and the organization itself have lost Jehovah's holy spirit. (Matthew 23:27,28)

In accord with prophetic parallels from the past, those at the head of the organization of Jehovah's Witnesses have become like the unfaithful kings of Israel who were denounced by the prophets of the Old Testament. Due to the extreme degree of their unfaithfulness to God, the organization is also likened to the pharaoh of Egypt who enslaved the Israelites, and the king of Babylon who led them into captivity.

Jeremiah 5:26-31, **For among my people there have been found wicked men.** They keep peering, as when birdcatchers crouch down. They have set a ruinous trap. It is men that they catch. As a cage is full of flying creatures, so their houses are full of deception. That is why they have become great and they gain riches. They have grown fat; they have become shiny. They have also overflowed with bad things. No legal case have they pleaded, even the legal case of the fatherless boy, that they may gain success; and the judgment of the poor ones they have not taken up.
"Should I not hold an accounting because of these very things," is the utterance of Jehovah, "or on a nation that is like this should not my soul avenge itself? An astonishing situation, even a horrible thing, has been brought to be in the land: The prophets themselves actually prophesy in falsehood; and as for the priests, they go subduing according to their powers. **And my own people have loved it that way; and what will you men do in the finale of it?"**

The governing body, the "anointed" at the head of this organization, were in a covenant relationship with Jehovah. He had given them special honor and dignity, the privilege of bearing his holy name, and they were under his protection, as a faithful wife would be. He was, in fact, their "husbandly owner." (Jeremiah 31:32) As such, they were under scriptural injunction to faithfully continue to look to him for guidance and protection in these critical last days. Instead, out of greed they have sought material wealth and security. And, out of fear of man, they have "given their hand" to the nations, for political fortification. (Lamentations 5:5,6) By these actions they have, in effect, denied their faith. They have denied Jehovah. By consorting with the nations, they have committed spiritual prostitution, a very great sin in the eyes of God. Their honor compromised, Jehovah has denounced the organization of Jehovah's Witnesses. It has become the infamous Babylon the Great, the great harlot of the book of Revelation. (Matthew Chapter 23, all verses) (Isaiah 30:9-12) (Revelation 17:5,6) (Revelation 19:1-3)

Isaiah 30:1-3, Woe to the stubborn sons, is the utterance of Jehovah, those disposed to carry out counsel, but not that from me; and to pour out a libation, but not with my spirit, in order to add sin to sin; those who are setting out to go down to Egypt and who have not inquired of my own mouth, **to take shelter in the stronghold of Pharaoh and to take refuge in the shadow of Egypt!** And the stronghold of Pharaoh must become even for you men a reason for shame, and the refuge in the shadow of Egypt a cause for humiliation.

Revelation 18:4, **"Get out of her, my people,** if you do not want to share with her in her sins, and if you do not want to receive part of her plagues. For her sins have massed together clear up to heaven, and God has called her acts of injustice to mind.

Journal History

"Let God be found true." (Romans 3:4) This journal chronicles events from the year 1989. Initially, these journal entries were in the form of notes I was making to myself as I witnessed the unfolding of extraordinary events around me. The hand of God was clearly indicated on these events, and this became even more obvious to me in the ensuing months. (Jeremiah 1:7) (Jeremiah 29:11-14) (Matthew 6:33) (Luke 11:9) (Hebrews 11:6)

It was at a later date that Jehovah made it clear to me that I was to make this information available to others. In order for my notes to make sense to anyone besides myself, I had to go back into the journal and clarify and expand on what I had written. The greatest care has been given to detail and accuracy. It has been a labor of love and years to bring it to this point of readability to others. Hopefully, I have caught all of my typing errors, and corrected all other mistakes from my first edition of this journal. Please let me know if you find any I missed here.

With this journal type of format, sometimes there are abrupt shifts to the next day or event, or the scriptures shift in focus to different subjects.

By expanding on my notes, occasionally I was able to improve the flow of thought. The journal also did not lend itself to chapter headings or any other form of subdivision. I think the most natural place for readers to pause is at the end of one topic and the beginning of another. However, there are sections that should be read even one scripture or paragraph at a time, meditated on, and thoroughly researched.

In 2009, as I bring this journal to the light of public inspection, we see tremendous upheaval in the world on every level. The nations are truly in anguish and fear, "not knowing the way out" of the problems they themselves have caused. (Luke 21:25,26) The death and devastation caused by war, crime, disease, famine, and all other forms of suffering, staggers the mind. Even many Bible skeptics are now ready to read the Bible and look to God for help.

Jehovah has made many promises to us in the Bible, including the establishment of his righteousness here on earth and the end of all evil. Every one of us should devote close attention to the faithful outworking of these promises. We should familiarize ourselves with the prophecies regarding the last days, because they are upon us. We should inspect the scriptures with a fresh eye, because there is much more going on around us than we perceive, visually. Truly, this is the real reason for the global upheaval. The god of this system of things, Satan, along with his demons, does not want to relinquish his hold on the earth. (2 Corinthians 4:4) They are fighting with everything they have, especially their influence on people's minds and hearts. Daily, evil surpasses itself.

When the fulfillment of a prophecy occurs, it does not have to be made physically apparent to us here on earth. Many prophecies are fulfilled on a spiritual level, and not visible to the naked eye. What Jehovah causes to actually occur with a fulfillment, usually does not correlate with our sometimes long-standing and preconceived expectations. That being the case, our own spirituality needs to be sharply honed, in order to grasp the facts and truths until everything is made manifest. The only help for this is a close relationship with Almighty God, Jehovah, that is based on truth. Truth is not usually very hard to understand, but sometimes it can be very hard for us to accept. (Matthew 6:10) (Romans 15:11-13) (Ephesians 3:14-21) (2 Peter Chapter 3, all verses) (Revelation 11:15-18)

JOURNAL KEY:

[ ] Brackets such as these [enclosing words] in my journal denote my writings and clarifications, to keep them clearly separated from actual scripture.

Notes Notes made in my journal by others are bordered.

! This means that this thought or scripture is very important to me.

→ This means that this thought or scripture should be given careful consideration.

Recall: This means that as I think back or dwell on a thought it recalls to my mind a related thought or scripture.

Research: This denotes the source for the information. The subject heading is ***Bold, Italicized and Capitalized.*** The research material is *italicized.*

Event: Identifying subheadings are often added to distinguish it from surrounding material.

Given: Jehovah has **given** me scriptures to include in the journal.

Message: Jehovah has sent me **messages**, which I have included in the journal.

→ Jeremiah 1:4-9 Good News Bible (1976), The Lord said to me, "I chose you before I gave you life, and before you were born I selected you to be a prophet to the nations."

I answered, "Sovereign Lord, I don't know how to speak; I am too young."

But the Lord said to me, "Do not say that you are too young, but go to the people I send you to, and tell them everything I command you to say. Do not be afraid of them, for I will be with you to protect you. I, the Lord, have spoken!"

Then the Lord reached out, touched my lips, and said to me, "Listen, I am giving you the words you must speak."

→ Psalm 83:18 King James Bible (1958), That men may know that thou, whose name alone is JEHOVAH, art the most high over all the earth.

→ Psalm 18:6-9a New World Translation (1984), In my distress I kept calling upon Jehovah, and to my God I kept crying for help.

Out of his temple he proceeded to hear my voice, and my own cry before him for help now came into his ears.

And the earth began to shake and rock, and the foundations of the mountains themselves became agitated, and they kept shaking back and forth because he had been angered.

Smoke went up at his nostrils, and fire itself from his mouth kept devouring; coals themselves blazed forth from him.

And he proceeded to bend the heavens down and descend.

→ Isaiah 60:1,2 New World Translation (1984), Arise, O woman, shed forth light, for your light has come and upon you the very glory of Jehovah has shone forth. For, look! darkness itself will cover the earth, and thick gloom the national groups; but upon you Jehovah will shine forth, and upon you his own glory will be seen.

→ **Faith is the assured expectation of things hoped for, the evident demonstration of realities though not beheld. (Hebrews 11:1)**

2 Timothy 2:2, And the things you heard from me with the support of many witnesses, these things commit to faithful men, who, in turn, will be adequately qualified to teach others.

[This chapter of Isaiah was given to me by Jehovah. It describes the spiritual work he has given me. I am to bring back to Jehovah his faithful people. I have also been given "for a light of the nations," that all people seeking Jehovah and his righteousness might find him.]

Isaiah Chapter 49 all verses, Listen to me, O you islands, and pay attention, you national groups far away. Jehovah himself has called me even from the belly. From the inward parts of my mother he has made mention of my name. And he proceeded to make my mouth like a sharp sword. In the shadow of his hand he has hidden me. And he gradually made me a polished arrow. He concealed me in his own quiver. And he went on to say to me: "You are my servant, O Israel, you the one in whom I shall show my beauty."

But as for me, I said: "It is for nothing that I have toiled. For unreality and vanity I have used up my own power. Truly my judgment is with Jehovah, and my wages with my God." And now Jehovah, the One forming me from the belly as a servant belonging to him, has said for me to bring back Jacob to him, in order that to him Israel itself might be gathered. And I shall be glorified in the eyes of Jehovah, and my own God will have become my strength. And he proceeded to say: "It has been more than a trivial matter for you to become my servant to raise up the tribes of Jacob and to bring back even the safeguarded ones of Israel [faithful worshippers of Jehovah still in the organization]; I also have given you for a light of the nations, that my salvation may come to be to the extremity of the earth."

This is what Jehovah, the Repurchaser of Israel, his Holy One, has said to him [Lisa] that is despised in soul, to him that is detested by the nation, to the servant of rulers: "Kings themselves will see and certainly rise up, and princes, and they will bow down, by reason of Jehovah, who is faithful, the Holy One of Israel, who chooses you."

This is what Jehovah has said: "In a time of goodwill I have answered you, and in a day of salvation I have helped you; and I kept safeguarding you that I might give you as a covenant for the people, to rehabilitate the land, **to bring about the repossessing of the desolated hereditary possessions, to say to the prisoners, 'Come out!' to those who are in the darkness, 'Reveal yourselves!'** By the ways they will pasture, and on all beaten paths their pasturing will be. They will not go hungry, neither will they go thirsty, nor will parching heat or sun strike them. For the One who is having pity upon them will lead them, and by the springs of water he will conduct them. And I will make all my mountains a way, and my highways themselves will be on an elevation. Look! These will come even from far away, and, look! these from the north and from the west, and these from the land of Sinim."

Give a glad cry, you heavens, and be joyful, you earth. Let the mountains become cheerful with a glad outcry. For Jehovah has comforted his people, and he shows pity upon his own afflicted ones.

But Zion [Lisa] kept saying: "Jehovah has left me, and Jehovah himself has forgotten me." Can a wife forget her suckling so that she should not pity the son of her belly? Even these women can forget, yet I myself shall not forget you. Look! Upon my palms I have engraved you. Your walls are in front of me constantly. Your sons have hurried up. The very ones tearing you down and devastating you will go forth even from you. Raise your eyes all around and see. They have all of them been collected together. They have come to you. "As I am living," is the utterance of Jehovah, "with all of them you will clothe yourself just as with ornaments, and you will bind them on yourself like a bride. Although there are your devastated places and your desolated places and the land of your ruins, although now you are too cramped to be dwelling, and those swallowing you down have been far away, yet in your own ears the sons of your bereaved state will say, 'The place has become too cramped for me. Do make room for me, that I may dwell.' And you will for certain say in your heart, 'Who has become father to these for me, since I am a woman bereaved of children and sterile, gone into exile and taken prisoner? As for these, who has brought them up? Look! I myself had been left behind alone. These—where have they been?'"

This is what the Sovereign Lord Jehovah has said: "Look! I shall raise up my hand even to the nations, and to the peoples I shall lift up my signal. And they will bring your sons in the bosom, and upon the shoulder they will carry your own daughters. And kings must become caretakers for you, and their princesses nursing women for you. With faces to the earth they will bow down to you, and the dust of your feet they will lick up; and you will have to know that I am Jehovah, of whom those hoping in me will not be ashamed."

Can those already taken be taken from a mighty man himself, or can the body of captives of the tyrant make their escape? But this is what Jehovah has said: "Even the body of captives of the mighty man will be taken away, and those already taken by the tyrant himself will make their escape. And against anyone contending against you I myself shall contend, and your own sons I myself shall save. And I will make those maltreating you eat their own flesh; and as with the sweet wine they will become drunk with their own blood. And all flesh will have to know that I, Jehovah, am your Savior and your Repurchaser, the Powerful One of Jacob.

JOURNAL

June 1, 1989

Jehovah's Presence: [As it was approaching midnight of May 31, 1989, I was told in advance to prepare myself spiritually, mentally and physically. Jehovah then descended from on high. He transferred his approval from the governing body of the organization to me. By the light of his holy spirit, he has instructed me and I am sent forth with a message for all people.]

June 4, 1989 Sunday

Departure: [We fled "Babylon." We left the worldwide organization known as the Watchtower Bible and Tract Society, Jehovah's Witnesses, headquartered in Brooklyn, New York, U.S.A.]

June 6, 1989

Psalm 78:49,50 NWT (1984), He went sending upon them [the organization of Jehovah's Witnesses] his burning anger, fury and **denunciation** and distress, **deputations of angels [having authority from Jehovah] bringing calamity.** He proceeded to prepare a pathway for his anger. He did not hold back their soul from death itself; and their life he handed over even to the pestilence.

[Jehovah's denunciation is upon the organization of the Watchtower Bible and Tract Society, Jehovah's Witnesses.]

Jehovah's Holy Name: [Jehovah's holy name means "I Shall Prove To Be What I Shall Prove To Be," "I AM THAT I AM," "He Causes to Become." Jehovah will "cause to become" or "prove" to be true, every promise he has made to his people. Jehovah is calling his faithful people to come out of the spiritual darkness of the apostate organization of Jehovah's Witnesses, and come to the light of his holy spirit.]

Chosen To Be Jehovah's Messenger: [Lisa: Consecrated to God; one of many members of God's earthly and heavenly spiritual family of kindred spirits. As spiritual persons we are of the same "kind" as our heavenly family members in our reverence for Jehovah.]

June 7, 1989

Commandment: Jeremiah 17:24,25a, "And it must occur that, if you strictly obey me," is the utterance of Jehovah, "to bring in no load through the gates of this city on the sabbath day and to sanctify the sabbath day by not doing on it any work, there will also certainly enter in by the gates of this city kings with princes. [These are specific instructions from Jehovah. We must take great care to follow them faithfully.]

Numbers 28:25, And on the seventh day you should hold a holy convention. No sort of laborious work must you do.
[The sabbath begins each Saturday at the setting of the sun, and continues to the setting of the sun on the next day, Sunday. This is to be regularly observed.]

Isaiah 32:12-20, Beat yourselves upon the breasts in lamentation over the desirable fields, over the fruit-bearing vine. Upon the ground of my people [within the organization] merely thorns, spiny bushes come up, for they are upon all the houses of exultation, yes, the highly elated town [the governing body of the organization of Jehovah's Witnesses, the Watchtower Bible and Tract Society]. **For the dwelling tower itself has been forsaken, the very hubbub of the city has been abandoned; Ophel** [a prominent hill; the organization headquarters has been abandoned by Jehovah] **and the watchtower themselves have become bare fields**, for time indefinite the exultation of zebras, the pasture of droves; until upon us the spirit is poured out from on high, and the wilderness will have become an orchard, and the orchard itself is accounted as a real forest.

And in the wilderness justice will certainly reside, and in the orchard righteousness itself will dwell. And the work of the true righteousness must become **peace**; and the service of the true righteousness, quietness and **security** to time indefinite. And my people must dwell in a peaceful abiding place and in residences of full confidence and in undisturbed resting-places. And it will certainly hail when the forest goes down and the city [unfaithful organization] becomes low in an abased state.

Happy are you people [faithful worshippers of Jehovah in the door-to-door ministry still within the organization] **who are sowing seed** alongside all waters, sending forth the feet of the bull and of the ass. [But, there are "thorns" (lies) upon all the "houses of exultation" in the "fruit-bearing vine," the unfaithful governing body of the organization. Therefore, Jehovah has abandoned them to their own unrighteous ways. A faithful remnant of its members will see this, and do likewise.]

Jeremiah 50:9, For here I am arousing and bringing up against Babylon [the organization] a congregation of great nations from the land of the north [heaven], and they will certainly array themselves against her. From there she will be captured. One's arrows are like those of a mighty man causing bereavement of children [members who leave the organization], who does not come back without results.

Isaiah 43:14,18,19, This is what Jehovah has said, the Repurchaser of you people, the Holy One of Israel: "For your sakes I will send to Babylon and cause the bars of the prisons to come down, and the Chaldeans [an earlier people that occupied an area in Babylon] in the ships with whining cries on their part."

Do not remember the first things, and to the former things do not turn your consideration. Look! I [Jehovah] am doing something new. Now it will spring up. You people will know it, will you not? Really, through the wilderness I shall set a way, through the desert rivers.

Jeremiah 50:8,28, Take your flight out of the midst of Babylon, and go forth even out of the land of the Chaldeans, and become like the leading animals before the flock.

There is the sound of those fleeing and those escaping from the land of Babylon to tell out in Zion the vengeance of Jehovah our God, the vengeance for his temple.

Jeremiah 50:14-30, "Array yourselves against Babylon on every side, all you who are treading the bow. Shoot at her. [Expose her sins.] Spare no arrow, for it is against Jehovah that she has sinned. Shout a [spiritual] war cry against her on every side. [Make known her unfaithful deeds.] She has given her hand. Her pillars have fallen. Her walls have been torn down. For it is the vengeance of Jehovah. Take your vengeance on her. Just as she has done, [the angels] do to her. [Jehovah will render retribution for her wrongdoing. It is our responsibility to speak out the truth as we make ready to leave the organization. Warn others of Jehovah's coming vengeance as we leave.] Cut off the **sower** from Babylon, and the one handling the sickle in the time of harvest. Because of the maltreating sword they will turn each one to his own people, and they will flee each one to his own land.

"Israel is a scattered sheep. Lions [those taking the lead in the organization] themselves have done the dispersing. In the first instance the king of Assyria has devoured him, and in this latter instance Nebuchadrezzar the king of Babylon has gnawed on his bones. Therefore this is what Jehovah of armies, the God of Israel, has said, 'Here I am turning my attention upon the king of Babylon and upon his land in the same way that I turned my attention upon the king of Assyria. And I will bring Israel [faithful worshippers of Jehovah still in the organization] back to his pasture ground, and he will certainly graze on Carmel, and on Bashan; and in the mountainous region of Ephraim, and of Gilead his soul will be satisfied.'"

"And in those days and at that time," is the utterance of Jehovah, "the error of Israel will be searched for, but it will not be; and the sins of Judah, and they will not be found, for I shall forgive those whom I let remain."

"Against the land of Merathaim—come up against her and against the inhabitants of Pekod. Let there be a massacre and a devoting to destruction close upon them," is the utterance of Jehovah, "and do according to all that I have commanded you. There is the sound of war in the land, and a great breakdown. [A "congregation of great nations from the land of the north" (Jehovah's armies in heaven, the angels, cut down and break the unfaithful organization of Jehovah's Witnesses. Faithful members need to get out of her and stand at a safe distance when this occurs.) "will certainly array themselves against her." Jeremiah 50:9] O how the forge hammer of all the earth has been cut down and gets broken! O how Babylon has become a mere object of astonishment among the nations! I have laid a snare for you and you have also been caught, O Babylon [unfaithful organization], and you yourself did not know it. **You were found and also taken hold of, for it was against Jehovah that you excited yourself.**

"Jehovah has opened his storehouse, and he brings forth the weapons of his denunciation. For there is a work that the Sovereign Lord, Jehovah of armies, has in the land of the Chaldeans. Come in to her from the farthest part. Open up her granaries. Bank her up, just like those making heaps, and devote her to destruction. May she not come to have any remaining ones. Massacre all her young bulls. May they go down to the slaughter. Woe to them, for their day has come, the time for their being given attention!

"There is the sound of those fleeing and those escaping [faithful worshippers of Jehovah are urged to leave the organization] from the land of Babylon to tell out in Zion the vengeance of Jehovah our God, the vengeance for his temple.

"Summon against Babylon archers, all who are treading the bow. Encamp against her all around. May there prove to be no escapees. **[Jehovah gives his command to the angels.] Pay back to her according to her activity. According to all that she has done, do to her. For it is against Jehovah that she has acted presumptuously, against the Holy One of Israel."**

John 14 all verses, "Do not let your hearts be troubled. Exercise faith in God, exercise faith also in me [Jesus]. In the house of my Father there are many abodes. Otherwise, I would have told you, because I am going my way to prepare a place for you. Also, if I go my way and prepare a place for you, I am coming again and will receive you home to myself, that where I am, you also may be. And where I am going you know the way."

Thomas said to him: "Lord, we do not know where you are going. How do we know the way?"

Jesus said to him: "I am the way and the truth and the life. No one comes to the Father except through me. If you men had known me, you would have known my Father also; from this moment on you know him and have seen him."

Philip said to him: "Lord, show us the Father, and it is enough for us."

Jesus said to him: "Have I been with you men so long a time, and yet, Philip, you have not come to know me? He that has seen me has seen the Father also. How is it you say, 'Show us the Father'? Do you not believe that I am in union with the Father and the Father is in union with me? The things I say to you men I do not speak of my own originality; **but the Father who remains in union with me is doing his works.** Believe me that I am in union with the Father and the Father is in union with me; otherwise, believe on account of the works themselves. Most truly I say to you, He that exercises faith in me, that one also will do the works that I do; and he will do works greater than these, because I am going my way to the Father. Also, whatever it is that you ask in my name, I will do this, in order that the Father may be glorified in connection with the Son. If you ask anything in my name, I will do it.

"**If you love me, you will observe my commandments; and I will request the Father and he will give you another helper to be with you forever, the spirit of the truth, which the world cannot receive, because it neither beholds it nor knows it. You know it because it remains with you and is in you.** I shall not leave you bereaved. I am coming to you. A little longer and the world will behold me no more, but you will behold me, because I live and you will live. **In that day you will know that I am in union with my Father and you are in union with me and I am in union with you.** He that has my commandments and observes them, that one is he who loves me. In turn he that loves me will be loved by my Father, and I will love him and will plainly show myself to him."

Judas, not Iscariot, said to him: "Lord, what has happened that you intend to show yourself plainly to us and not to the world?"

In answer Jesus said to him: "If anyone loves me, he will observe my word, and my Father will love him, and we shall come to him and make our abode with him. He that does not love me does not observe my words; and the word that you are hearing is not mine, but belongs to the Father who sent me.

"While remaining with you I have spoken these things to you. But the helper, the holy spirit, which the Father will send in my name, that one will teach you all things and bring back to your minds all the things I told you. I leave you peace, I give you my peace. I do not give it to you the way that the world gives it. Do not let your hearts be troubled nor let them shrink with fear. **You heard that I said to you, I am going away and I am coming back to you. If you loved me, you would rejoice that I am going my way to the Father, because the Father is greater than I am. So, now I have told you before it occurs, in order that, when it does occur, you may believe.** I shall not speak much with you anymore, for the ruler of the world is coming. And he has no hold on me, but, in order for the world to know that I love the Father, even as the Father has given me commandment to do, so I am doing. **Get up, let us go from here.**"

Jeremiah 17:19-27, This is what Jehovah has said to me: "Go, and you must stand in the gate of the sons of the people by which the [unfaithful] kings of Judah [governing body and others taking the lead] enter in and by which they go out, and in all the gates of [unfaithful] Jerusalem [the rest of the organization]. And you must say to them, 'Hear the word of Jehovah, you kings of Judah and all Judah and all you inhabitants of Jerusalem, who are entering in by these gates. This is what Jehovah has said: "Watch out for your souls, and do not carry on the sabbath day any load that you must bring in through the gates of Jerusalem. And you must bring no load out of your homes on the sabbath day; and no work at all must you do. And you must sanctify the sabbath day, just as I commanded your forefathers; but they did not listen or incline their ear, and they proceeded to harden their neck in order not to hear and in order to receive no discipline."'

"'"And it must occur that, if you strictly obey me," is the utterance of Jehovah, "to bring in no load through the gates of this city on the sabbath day and to sanctify the sabbath day by not doing on it any work, there will also certainly enter in by the gates of this city kings with princes, sitting on the throne of David, riding in the chariot and upon horses, they and their princes, the men of Judah and the inhabitants of Jerusalem; and this city will certainly be inhabited to time indefinite. And people will actually come from the cities of Judah and from round about Jerusalem and from the land of Benjamin and from the lowland and from the mountainous region and from the Negeb, bringing whole burnt offering and sacrifice and grain offering and frankincense and bringing thanksgiving sacrifice into the house of Jehovah.

"'"But if you will not obey me by sanctifying the sabbath day and not carrying a load, but there is a coming in with it through the gates of Jerusalem on the sabbath day, I will also set a fire ablaze in her gates, and it will certainly devour the dwelling towers of Jerusalem and will not be extinguished."'"

Jeremiah 22:5-9, "'But if you will not obey these words, by myself I do swear,' is the utterance of Jehovah, 'that this house will become a mere devastated place.'

"For this is what Jehovah has said concerning the house of the king of Judah, 'You are as Gilead [Galeed, meaning "Witness Heap"] to me, the head of Lebanon. Assuredly I shall make you a wilderness; as for the cities, not one will be inhabited. And I will sanctify against you those bringing ruin, each one and his weapons; and they must cut down the choicest of your cedars [those taking the lead in the organization; even those of the "anointed" who have become unfaithful] and cause them to fall into the fire. And many nations will actually pass along by this city and say one to the other: "On what account did Jehovah do like this to this great city?" And they will have to say: "On account of the fact that they left the covenant of Jehovah their God and proceeded to bow down to other gods [or men they look up to as "gods"] and to serve them."'

Jeremiah 23:6-8, "In his days [faithful] Judah will be saved, and [faithful] Israel itself will reside in security. And this is his name with which he will be called, Jehovah Is Our Righteousness."

"Therefore, look! there are days coming," is the utterance of Jehovah, "and they will no more say, 'Jehovah is alive who brought the sons of Israel up out of the land of Egypt,' but [the obedient of Jehovah will say], 'Jehovah is alive who brought up and who brought in the offspring of the house of Israel out of the land of the north and out of all the lands to which I [Jehovah] have dispersed them, and they will certainly dwell on their own ground."

Psalm 118:23-29, This has come to be from Jehovah himself; it is wonderful in our eyes. This is the day that Jehovah has made; we will be joyful and rejoice in it. Ah, now, Jehovah, do save, please! Ah, now, Jehovah, do grant success, please! Blessed be the One coming in the name of Jehovah; we have blessed you people out of the house of Jehovah. Jehovah is the Divine One, and he gives us light. Bind the festival procession with boughs, O you people, as far as the horns of the altar. You are my Divine One, and I shall laud you; my God—I shall exalt you. Give thanks to Jehovah, you people, for he is good; for his loving-kindness is to time indefinite.

Psalm 119:18,19,38 NWT (1984), **Uncover my eyes**, that I may look at the wonderful things out of your law. I am but an alien resident in the land. Do not conceal from me your commandments.

Carry out to your servant your saying that tends to the fear of you.

Rosie's Notes: Isaiah 3:8,9,12-14, For [unfaithful] Jerusalem has stumbled, and [unfaithful] Judah itself has fallen, because their tongue and their dealings are against Jehovah, in behaving rebelliously in the eyes of his glory. The very expression of their faces actually testifies against them, and of their sin like that of Sodom they do tell. They have not hidden it. Woe to their soul! For they have dealt out to themselves calamity.

As for my people, its task assigners are dealing severely, and mere women [like Elaine, an elder's wife, who is verbally abusive to Jehovah's afflicted ones in one congregation (this type of situation is occurring in other congregations as well)] actually rule over it. O my people, those leading you on are causing you to wander, and the way of your paths they have confused.

Jehovah is stationing himself to contend and is standing up to pass sentence upon peoples. Jehovah himself will enter into judgment with the elderly ones [elders and others taking the lead in the organization] of his people and its princes.

"And you yourselves [unfaithful ones in the organization] have burned down the vineyard. What was taken by robbery from the afflicted one is in your houses."

Zechariah 1:13, And Jehovah proceeded to answer the angel who was speaking to me, with good words, comforting words.

Isaiah 40:1, "Comfort, comfort my [loyal] people," says the God of you men. [Comfort for Tina, a new member of one congregation, who is mild and gentle, and others like her.]

! Jeremiah 28:6-9, Yes, Jeremiah the prophet proceeded to say: "Amen! Thus may Jehovah do! May Jehovah establish your words that you have prophesied by bringing back the utensils of the house of Jehovah and all the exiled people of Babylon to this place! However, hear, please, this word that I am speaking in your ears and in the ears of all the people, as regards the prophets that happened to be prior to me and prior to you from long ago, they also used to prophesy concerning many lands and concerning great kingdoms, of war and of calamity and of pestilence. **As regards the prophet that prophesies of peace, when the word of the prophet comes true the prophet whom Jehovah has sent in truth will become known.**"

Advice: [Patience is being advised here. Jehovah is sending me advice through Rosie. I am considering this advice as I continue with this journal, writing down what Jehovah is indicating to me.]

Jeremiah 29:10-13, For this is what Jehovah has said, "In accord with the fulfilling of seventy years at Babylon [Recall: Seventy years of insincere fasting, 1919-1989] I shall turn my attention to you [faithful] people, and I will establish toward you my good word in bringing you back to this place.'

"'For I myself well know the thoughts that I am thinking toward you," is the utterance of Jehovah, "thoughts of peace, and not of calamity, to give you a future and a hope. And you will certainly call me and come and pray to me, and I will listen to you.'

"'**And you will actually seek me and find me, for you will search for me with all your heart.**'

Circuit Overseer: [Recently, the Circuit Overseer, James Thatcher, gave a talk at the Kingdom Hall in Lancaster, Wisconsin, U.S.A. In reference to me, he used the word "completeness." Jehovah has completed a work in me. He has trained me and given me instruction to make me useful and ready to help others.]

Galatians 5:22, Fruitage of the spirit:
 Love
 Joy
 Peace
 Long-suffering
 Kindness
 Goodness
 Faith
 Mildness
 Self-control

! Psalm 137:4 Good News Bible (1976), How can we [faithful worshippers of Jehovah still in the organization] sing a song to the Lord in a foreign land ["Babylon," the organization]?

! Jeremiah 36:28, Take again for yourself [Lisa] a roll, another one, and write on it all the first words that proved to be on the first roll, which Jehoiakim the king of Judah burned up. [Later in this journal I will include the scriptures which Jehovah directed me to send in a denunciation against the organization bearing his name, Jehovah's Witnesses. It will turn out that those taking the lead in the organization instruct members to burn it.]

Zechariah 3:4, Then he answered and said to those standing before him: Remove the befouled garments from upon him, and he went on to say to him: "See, I have caused your error to pass away from upon you, and there is a clothing of you [Lisa] with robes of state."

Isaiah 61:10, Without fail I shall exult in Jehovah, my soul will be joyful in my God. For he has clothed me with the garments of salvation; with the sleeveless coat of righteousness he has enwrapped me, like the bridegroom who, in a priestly way, puts on a headdress, and like the bride who decks herself with her ornamental things.

Prophecy: Isaiah 49:18, Raise your eyes all around and see. They have all of them been collected together. They have come to you. "As I am living," is the utterance of Jehovah, "with all of them you will clothe yourself just as with ornaments, and you will bind them on yourself just like a bride."

Zechariah 4:1,6, And the angel who was speaking with me proceeded to come back and wake me up, like a man that is awakened from his sleep.

Accordingly he answered and said to me: "This is the word of Jehovah to Zerubbabel [a faithful worshipper of Jehovah; descendant of King David], saying, 'not by a military force, nor by power, but by my spirit,' Jehovah of armies has said. [Rosie and Lisa do not have powerful connections or high-ranking relatives in the organization. It is Jehovah's holy spirit that has verified to the Circuit Overseer, James Thatcher, and the others with him, the person Jehovah has chosen to do this work.]

Angel: [An angel woke me from my sleep, and reference was made to Siloam. My eyes were opened, and I was "sent forth."]

John 9:7, [Jesus] said to him: "Go wash in the pool of Siloam" (which is translated 'Sent forth'). And so he went off and washed, and came back seeing.

Haggai 2:3, Who is there among you that is remaining over who saw this house [worldwide organization of Jehovah's Witnesses] in its former glory? And how are you people seeing it now? Is it not, in comparison with that, as nothing in your eyes?

Luke 18:8, I tell you, he will cause justice to be done to them speedily. Nevertheless, when the son of man arrives, will he really find the faith on the earth? [The answer is yes.]

Malachi 3:16, At that time those in fear of Jehovah spoke with one another, each one with his companion, and Jehovah kept paying attention and listening. And a book of remembrance began to be written up before him for those in fear of Jehovah and for those thinking upon his name.

Prophecy: Zechariah 5:9, Then I raised my eyes and saw, and here there were two women [Rosie and Lisa] coming forth, and wind [spirit] was in their wings. And they had wings like the wings of the stork. [The name of this bird is the feminine form of the Hebrew word for "loyal one; one of loving-kindness"] And they gradually raised the ephah [a container] up between the earth and the heavens. [They took the ephah, with the woman "Wickedness" sitting in the midst of it, to where she was deposited in her place in Shinar (Babylon). (Zechariah 5:8,11)]

Luke 7:16-28, Now fear seized them all, and they began to glorify God, saying: "A great prophet has been raised up among us," and, "God has turned his attention to his people." And this news concerning him spread out into all Judea and all the surrounding country.

Now John's disciples reported to him about all these things. So John summoned a certain two of his disciples and sent them to the Lord to say: "Are you the Coming One or are we to expect a different one?" When they came up to him the men said: "John the Baptist dispatched us to you to say, 'Are you the Coming One or are we to expect another?'" In that hour he cured many of sicknesses and grievous diseases and wicked spirits, and granted many blind persons the favor of seeing. Hence in answer he said to the two: "Go your way, report to John what you saw [with spiritual eyes] and heard: the blind are receiving sight, the lame are walking, the lepers are being cleansed and the deaf are hearing, the dead are being raised up, the poor are being told the good news. And happy is he who has not stumbled over me."

When the messengers of John had gone away, he started to say to the crowds concerning John: "What did you go out into the wilderness to behold? A reed being tossed by the wind? What, then, did you go out to see? A man dressed in soft outer garments? Why, those in splendid dress and existing in luxury are in royal houses. Really, then, what did you go out to see? A prophet? Yes, I tell you, and far more than a prophet. This is he concerning whom it is written, "Look! I am sending forth my messenger before your face, who will prepare your way ahead of you."

1 Corinthians 4:1,7,11, Let a man so appraise us [Rosie and Lisa] as being subordinates of Christ and stewards of sacred secrets of God.

For who makes you to differ from one another? Indeed, what do you have that you did not receive? If now, you did indeed receive it, why do you boast as though you did not receive it?

Down to this very hour we continue to hunger and also to thirst and to be scantily clothed and to be knocked about and to be homeless.

2 Chronicles 16:9, For, as regards Jehovah, his eyes are roving about through all the earth to show his strength in behalf of those [faithful worshippers of Jehovah] whose heart is complete toward him. You [those taking the lead in the organization] have acted foolishly respecting this, for from now on there will exist wars against you.

! Zechariah 7:9, This is what Jehovah of armies has said, **"With true justice do your judging; and carry on with one another loving-kindness and mercies." [We must take great care here: These are very important instructions from Jehovah.]**

Psalm 139 all verses, O Jehovah, you have searched through me, and you know me. You yourself have come to know my sitting down and my rising up. You have considered my thought from far off, and you have become familiar even with all my ways. For there is not a word on my tongue, but, look! O Jehovah, you already know it all. Behind and before, you have besieged me; and you place your hand upon me. Such knowledge is too wonderful for me. It is so high up that I cannot attain to it. Where can I go from your spirit, and where can I run away from your face? If I should ascend to heaven, there you would be; and if I should spread out my couch in Sheol, look! you would be there. Were I to take the wings of the dawn, that I might reside in the most remote sea, there, also, your own hand would lead me. And were I to say: "Surely darkness itself will hastily seize me!" Then night would be light about me. Even the darkness itself would not prove to be too dark for you, but night itself would shine just as the day does; the darkness might just as well be the light. For you yourself produced my kidneys; you kept me screened off in the belly of my mother. I shall laud you because in a fear-inspiring way I am wonderfully made. Your works are wonderful, as my soul is very much aware. My bones were not hidden from you when I was made in secret, when I was woven in the lowest parts of the earth. Your eyes saw even the embryo of me, and in your book all its parts were down in writing, as regards the days when they were formed and there was not yet one among them. So, to me how precious your thoughts are! O God, how much does the grand sum of them amount to! Were I to try to count them, they are more than even the grains of sand. I have awaked, and yet I am still with you. O that you, O God, would slay the wicked one! **Then even the bloodguilty men will certainly depart from me, who say things about you according to their idea; they have taken up your name in a worthless way—your adversaries [the organization calling themselves by God's holy name, Jehovah's Witnesses, but who fail to show love and kindness to Jehovah's "sheeplike" ones, the meek and mild-tempered members in the organization].** Do I not hate those who are intensely hating you, O Jehovah, and do I not feel a loathing for those revolting against you? With a complete hatred I do hate them. They have become to me real enemies. Search through me, O God, and know my heart. Examine me, and know my disquieting thoughts, and see whether there is in me any painful way, and lead me in the way of time indefinite.

Zechariah 4:12-14, Then I answered the second time and said to him: "What are the two bunches of twigs of the olive trees that, by means of the two golden tubes, are pouring forth from within themselves the golden liquid?" So he said to me: "Do you not really know what these things mean?" In turn I said, "No, my lord." Accordingly he said: "These are the two anointed ones [Lisa, and another person to be later identified by Jehovah] who are standing alongside the Lord of the whole earth."

Zechariah 9:12,17a, Return to the stronghold [Jehovah], you [faithful worshippers of Jehovah still in the organization] prisoners of the hope. Also, today I am telling you, I shall repay to you, O woman [Lisa], a double portion. For O how great his goodness is.

Zechariah 10:3, Against the [unfaithful] shepherds my anger has grown hot, and against the goatlike leaders [in the organization] I shall hold an accounting; for Jehovah of armies has turned his attention to his drove [his "sheeplike" ones], the house of [faithful] Judah, and has made them like his horse of dignity in the battle.

June 8, 1989

Psalm 78:49,50, He went sending upon them [unfaithful ones in the organization] his burning anger, fury and denunciation and distress, deputations of angels bringing calamity. He proceeded to prepare a pathway for his anger. He did not hold back their soul from death itself; and their life he handed over even to the pestilence.

June 9, 1989

Proverbs 24:27b, Afterward you [Lisa] must also build up your household. [Lisa is commanded to provide spiritual "food" for Jehovah's faithful people.]

Proverbs 14:1a, The truly wise woman has built up her house. [Lisa has provided the spiritual "food." It is Jehovah's words of truth in this journal.]

Zion Gives Birth: Isaiah 66:8, Who has heard of a thing like this? Who has seen things like these? Will a land be brought forth with labor pains in one day? Or will a nation be born at one time? For Zion [Lisa] has come into [spiritual] labor pains as well as given [spiritual] birth to her sons. [In Isaiah 66:8,9, Zion is a literal woman. Jehovah's "woman" has given "birth" to spiritual "children" this day.]

Jehovah's Kingdom: [**Praise Jehovah! His kingdom has come!** Jehovah's denunciation, consisting of scriptures from the New World Translation of the Holy Scriptures, which Jehovah directed to be recorded verbatim and published, needs to be mailed out to the headquarters, as well as all branch offices of the organization of Jehovah's Witnesses.]

Jeremiah 6:21,22, Therefore this is what Jehovah has said: "Here I am setting for this people [the organization] stumbling blocks, and they will certainly stumble over them, fathers and sons together; the neighbor and his companion—they will perish."
This is what Jehovah has said: "Look! A people is coming from the land of the north, and there is a great nation that will be awakened from the remotest parts of the earth.

Revealed: [A sequence of events: "Zion," a woman living in the present day has spiritually "given birth" to spiritual "children."

Jehovah's denunciation will be sent out to Babylon the Great, which is the organization known as the Watchtower Bible and Tract Society, also known as Jehovah's Witnesses.]

Ezekiel 9 all, And he proceeded to call out in my ears with a loud voice, saying: "Have those giving attention to the city come near, each one with his weapon in his hand for bringing ruin!"

And, look! there were six men coming from the direction of the upper gate that faces to the north, each one with his weapon for smashing in his hand; and there was one man in among them clothed with linen, with a secretary's inkhorn at his hips, and they proceeded to come in and stand beside the copper altar.

And as regards the glory of the God of Israel, it was taken up from over the cherubs over which it happened to be to the threshold of the house, and he began calling out to the man that was clothed with the linen, at whose hips there was the secretary's inkhorn. And Jehovah went on to say to him: "Pass through the midst of the city, through the midst of [unfaithful] Jerusalem, and you must put a mark on the foreheads of the [faithful ones] men who are sighing and groaning over all the detestable things that are being done in the midst of it."

And to these others he said in my ears: "Pass through the city after him and strike. Let not your eye feel sorry, and do not feel any compassion. Old man, young man and virgin and little child and women you should kill off—to a ruination. But to any man [person] upon whom there is the mark do not go near, and from my sanctuary you should start." So they started with the old men that were before the house. And he said further to them: "Defile the house and fill the courtyards with the slain ones. Go forth." And they went forth and struck in the city [the organization].

And it came about that, while they were striking and I was left remaining, I proceeded to fall upon my face and cry out and say: "Alas, O Sovereign Lord Jehovah! Are you bringing to ruin all the remaining ones of Israel while you are pouring out your rage upon Jerusalem?"

So he said to me: "The error of the house of [unfaithful] Israel and [unfaithful] Judah is very, very great, and the land is filled with bloodshed and the city is full of crookedness; for they have said:

'Jehovah has left the land, and Jehovah is not seeing.' And as for me also, my eye will not feel sorry, neither shall I show compassion. **Their way I shall certainly bring upon their own head."**

And, look! the man clothed with the linen, at whose hips there was the inkhorn, was bringing back word, saying: "I have done just as you have commanded me."

[The man with the secretary's inkhorn was doing a "marking" work.] Compare: Exodus 12:23, Then when Jehovah does pass through to plague the Egyptians and does see the blood upon the upper part of the doorway and upon the two doorposts, Jehovah will certainly pass over the entrance, and he will not allow the ruination to enter into your houses to plague you.

[When the Israelites were slaves in Egypt, they were to mark with blood the upper part of the doorway and the two doorposts of their houses. Similarly, the man with the secretary's inkhorn today spiritually "marks" Jehovah's faithful ones, among those taking the lead as well as among their membership in the organization, and spares them from the ruination. **They are already marked.**

Then Jehovah's "six men" (angelic armies) from the "north" strike Babylon the Great, the organization of Jehovah's Witnesses.

The marked ones are tested by fire and survive; a remnant.

There is a signal given to the nations to seek Jehovah.

The nations become a sanctified offering to Jehovah.

Then a restoration work begins.]

Rosie's Notes: People coming to worship Jehovah:

Those [faithful] people in the organization—a remnant, they are "natural Israelites"

Those [faithful] people disfellowshipped by the organization—the dispersed ones, they are "Samaritans"

Those never involved in the organization—the nations, they will not believe a prophet of calamity.

June 10, 1989

! Revelation Chapter 18 all verses, After these things I saw another angel descending from heaven, with great authority; and the earth was lighted up from his glory. And he cried out with a strong voice, saying: "She has fallen! Babylon the Great [the Watchtower Bible and Tract Society, known as Jehovah's Witnesses] has fallen, and she has become a dwelling place of demons and a lurking place of every unclean exhalation and a lurking place of every unclean and hated bird! For because of the wine of the anger of her fornication all the nations have fallen victim, and the kings of the earth committed fornication with her, and the traveling merchants of the earth became rich due to the power of her shameless luxury."

And I heard another voice out of heaven say: "**Get out of her, my people**, [speaking to faithful worshippers of Jehovah in the organization, not to the people in the churches of Christendom, as Jehovah's Witnesses teach] **if you do not want to share with her in her sins, and if you do not want to receive part of her plagues. For her sins have massed together clear up to heaven, and God has called her acts of injustice to mind.** Render to her even as she herself rendered, and do to her twice as much, yes, twice the number of the things she did; in the cup in which she put a mixture put twice as much of the mixture for her. To the extent that she glorified herself and lived in shameless luxury, to that extent give her torment and mourning. For in her heart she keeps saying, 'I sit a queen [the unfaithful governing body of the organization believes that Jehovah is still their "husbandly owner," that he would not abandon them, that they might become a "widow"], and I am no widow, and I shall never see mourning.' That is why in one day her plagues will come, death and mourning and famine, and she will be completely burned with fire, because Jehovah God, who judged her, is strong.

"And the kings of the earth who committed fornication with her and lived in shameless luxury will weep and beat themselves in grief over her, when they look at the smoke from the burning of her, while they stand at a distance because of their fear of her torment and say, 'Too bad, too bad, you great city, Babylon you strong city, because in one hour your judgment has arrived!'

"Also, the traveling merchants of the earth are weeping and mourning over her, because there is no one to buy their full stock anymore, a full stock of gold and silver and precious stone and pearls and fine linen and purple and silk and scarlet; and everything in scented wood and every sort of ivory object and every sort of object out of most precious wood and of copper and of iron and of marble;

also cinnamon and Indian spice and incense and perfumed oil and frankincense and wine and olive oil and fine flour and wheat and cattle and sheep, and horses and coaches and slaves and human souls. Yes, the fine fruit that your soul desired has departed from you, and all the dainty things and the gorgeous things have perished from you, and never again will people find them.

"The traveling merchants of these things, who became rich from her, will stand at a distance because of their fear of her torment and will weep and mourn, saying, 'Too bad, too bad—the great city, clothed with fine linen and purple and scarlet, and richly adorned with gold ornament and precious stone and pearl, because in one hour such great riches have been devastated!'

"And every ship captain and every man that voyages anywhere, and sailors and all those who make a living by the sea, stood at a distance and cried out as they looked at the smoke from the burning of her and said, 'What city is like the great city?' And they threw dust upon their heads and cried out, weeping and mourning, and said, 'Too bad, too bad—the great city, in which all those having boats at sea became rich by reason of her costliness, because in one hour she has been devastated!'

"Be glad over her, O heaven, also you holy ones and you apostles and you prophets, because God has judicially exacted punishment for you from her!"

And a strong angel lifted up a stone like a great millstone and hurled it into the sea, saying: "Thus with a swift pitch will Babylon the great city be hurled down, and she will never be found again. And the sound of singers who accompany themselves on the harp and of musicians and of flutists and of trumpeters will never be heard in you again, and no craftsman of any trade will ever be found in you again, and no sound of a millstone will ever be heard in you again, **and no light of a lamp will ever shine in you again, and no voice of a bridegroom and of a bride will ever be heard in you again**; because your traveling merchants were the top-ranking men of the earth, for by your spiritistic practice all the nations were misled. Yes, in her was found the blood of prophets and of holy ones and of all those who have been slaughtered on the earth."

Luke 2:25-35, And, look! there was a man in Jerusalem named Simeon, and this man was righteous and reverent, waiting for Israel's consolation, and holy spirit was upon him. Furthermore, it had been divinely revealed to him by the holy spirit that he would not see death before he had seen the Christ of Jehovah. Under the power of the spirit he now came into the temple; and as the parents brought the young child Jesus in to do for it according to the customary practice of the law, he himself received it into his arms and blessed God and said: "Now, Sovereign Lord, you are letting your slave go free in peace according to your declaration; because my eyes have seen the means of your saving, that you have made ready in the sight of all the peoples, a light for removing the veil from the nations and a glory of your people Israel." And its [the child's] father and mother continued wondering at the things being spoken about it. Also, Simeon blessed them, but said to Mary its mother: "Look! This one is laid for the fall and the rising again of many in Israel and for a sign to be talked against (yes, a long sword will be run through the soul of you yourself), in order that the reasonings of many hearts may be uncovered."

! Jeremiah 6:13-15, "For from the least one of them even to the greatest one of them, every one [taking the lead in the organization] is making for himself unjust gain; and from the prophet even to the priest, each one [of the governing body] is acting falsely. And they try to heal the breakdown of my people lightly, saying, 'There is peace! There is peace!' when there is no peace. Did they feel shame because it was something detestable that they had done? For one thing, they positively do not feel any shame; for another thing, they have not come to know even how to feel humiliated. Therefore they will fall among those who are falling; in the time that I must hold an accounting with them they will stumble," Jehovah has said.

1 Thessalonians 5:3, Whenever it is that they are saying: "Peace and security!" then sudden destruction is to be instantly upon them just as the pang of distress upon a pregnant woman; and they will by no means escape. [The Watchtower Bible and Tract Society, known as Jehovah's Witnesses, have long pointed the finger at the nations, prophesying that it is they who say: "Peace and security!" and that Jehovah then brings sudden destruction upon them. But Jehovah shows us from the scriptures, by describing the organization in such accurate detail, that it is they themselves, Jehovah's Witnesses, who

are saying it, **not the nations**. The organization claims to have a spiritual "paradise," peace and security right now, believing that they are under Jehovah's protection. To their great surprise sudden destruction will be instantly upon them.

Truly, all the nations are living in darkness, and fearful things are coming their way as a result of their own greed, corruption and violence which continues to devastate many lives and ruin the earth itself. But, their suffering is not the same as what must come upon the unfaithful people who call themselves by Jehovah's own name; the ones who do deliberate harm to his own "sheeplike" ones. Jehovah is judging and condemning the organization of Jehovah's Witnesses for the wickedness and evil of their own actions.]

Zechariah Chapter 2 all verses, especially v.6, And I proceeded to raise my eyes and see; and, look! there was a man, and in his hand a measuring rope. So I said: "Where are you going?"

In turn he said to me: "To measure [faithful] Jerusalem [Lisa], in order to see what her breadth amounts to and what her length amounts to [to what extent justice resides in her]."

And, look! the angel who was speaking with me was going forth, and there was another angel going forth to meet him. Then he said to him: "Run, speak to the young man over there, saying, 'As open rural country Jerusalem will be inhabited, because of the multitude of men and domestic animals in the midst of her. And I myself shall become to her,' is the utterance of Jehovah, 'a wall of fire all around, and a glory is what I shall become in the midst of her.'"

"Hey there! Hey there! [This is repeated twice for emphasis, due to its importance.] Flee, then, you people, from the land of the north," is the utterance of Jehovah. [In this instance this scripture refers to Rosie and her two children. Jehovah is telling us through this scripture that they are to come down from where she lives to where I am living (Lancaster, Wisconsin, U.S.A.), and from there, with my two children, the six of us are to leave this northern area.]

"For in the direction of the four winds of the heavens I have spread you people abroad," is the utterance of Jehovah.

"Hey, there, Zion! Make your escape, you who are dwelling with the daughter of Babylon [the organization]. For this is what Jehovah of armies has said, 'Following after the glory he has sent me to the nations that were despoiling you people; for he that is touching you is touching my eyeball. For here I am waving my hand against them, and they will have to become spoil to their **slaves** [faithful worshippers in the organization are held as slaves by lies and intimidation].' And you people will certainly know that Jehovah of armies himself has sent me.

"Cry out loudly and rejoice, O daughter of Zion; for here I am coming, and I will reside in the midst of you," is the utterance of Jehovah. "And many nations will certainly become joined to Jehovah in that day, and they will actually become my people; and I will reside in the midst of you." And you will have to know that Jehovah of armies himself has sent me to you. And Jehovah will certainly take possession of [faithful] Judah as his portion upon the holy ground, and he must yet choose [faithful] Jerusalem. Keep silence, all flesh, before Jehovah, for he has aroused himself from his holy dwelling.

Hebrews Chapter 2 all verses, especially v.10, That is why it is necessary for us to pay more than the usual attention to the things heard by us, that we may never drift away. For if the word spoken through angels proved to be firm, and every transgression and disobedient act received a retribution in harmony with justice; how shall we escape if we have neglected a salvation of such greatness in that it began to be spoken through our Lord and was verified for us by those who heard him, while God joined in bearing witness with signs as well as portents and various powerful works and with distributions of holy spirit according to his will?

For it is not to angels that he has subjected the inhabited earth to come, about which we are speaking. But a certain witness has given proof somewhere, saying: "What is man, that you keep him in mind, or the son of man that you take care of him? You made him a little lower than angels; with glory and honor you crowned him, and appointed him over the works of your hands. All things you subjected under his feet." For in that he subjected all things to him God left nothing that is not subject to him. Now, though, we do not yet see all things in subjection to him; but we behold Jesus, who has been made a little lower than angels, crowned with glory and honor for having suffered death, that he by God's undeserved kindness might taste death for every man.

For it was fitting for the one for whose sake all things are and through whom all things are, in bringing many sons to glory, to make the Chief Agent [Jesus] of their salvation perfect through sufferings. For both he who is sanctifying and those who are being sanctified all stem from one, and for this cause he is not ashamed to call them "brothers," as he says: "I will declare your name to my brothers; in the middle of the congregation I will praise you with song." And, again: "I will have my trust in him." And again: "Look! I and the young children, whom Jehovah gave me."

Therefore, since the "young children" are sharers of blood and flesh, he also similarly partook of the same things, that through his death he might bring to nothing the one having the means to cause death, that is, the Devil; and that he might emancipate all those who for fear of death were subject to slavery all through their lives. For he is really not assisting angels at all, but he is assisting Abraham's seed. Consequently he was obliged to become like his "brothers" in all respects, that he might become a merciful and faithful high priest in things pertaining to God, in order to offer propitiatory sacrifice for the sins of the people. For in that he himself has suffered when being put to the test, he is able to come to the aid of those who are being put to the test.

Hebrews Chapter 3 all verses [abbreviated here], For this reason, just as the holy spirit says: "Today if you people listen to his own voice, do not harden your hearts as on the occasion of causing bitter anger, as in the day of making the test in the wilderness, in which your forefathers made a test of me with a trial, and yet they had seen my works for forty years. For this reason I became disgusted with this generation and said, 'They always go astray in their hearts, and they themselves have not come to know my ways.' So I swore in my anger, 'They shall not enter into my rest.'"

Beware, brothers, for fear there should ever develop in any one of you a wicked heart lacking faith by drawing away from the living God; but keep on exhorting one another each day, as long as it may be called "Today," for fear any one of you should become hardened by the deceptive power of sin.

For who were they that heard and yet provoked to bitter anger? Did not, in fact, all do so who went out of Egypt under Moses? Moreover, with whom did God become disgusted for forty years? Was it not with those who sinned, whose carcasses fell in the wilderness? But to whom did he swear that they should not enter into his rest except to those who acted disobediently? So we see that they could not enter in because of lack of faith.

Hebrews Chapter 4 all verses, Therefore, since a promise is left of entering into his rest, let us fear that sometime someone of you may seem to have fallen short of it. For we have had the good news declared to us also, even as they also had; but the word which was heard did not benefit them, because they were not united by faith with those who did hear. For we who have exercised faith do enter into the rest, just as he has said: "So I swore in my anger, 'They shall not enter into my rest,'" although his works were finished from the founding of the world. For in one place he has said of the seventh day as follows: "And God rested on the seventh day from all his works," and again in this place: "They shall not enter into my rest."

Since, therefore, it remains for some to enter into it, and to those to whom the good news was first declared did not enter in because of disobedience, he again marks off a certain day by saying after so long a time in David's psalm "Today"; just as it has been said above: "Today if you people listen to his own voice, do not harden your hearts." For if Joshua had led them into a place of rest, God would not afterward have spoken of another day. **So there remains a sabbath resting for the people of God.** For the man that has entered into God's rest has also himself rested from his own works, just as God did from his own.

Let us therefore do our utmost to enter into that rest, for fear anyone should fall in the same pattern of disobedience. For the word of God is alive and exerts power and is sharper than any two-edged sword and pierces even to the dividing of soul and spirit, and of joints and their marrow, and is able to discern thoughts and intentions of the heart. And there is not a creation that is not manifest to his sight, but all things are naked and openly exposed to the eyes of him with whom we have an accounting.

Seeing, therefore, that we have a great high priest who has passed through the heavens, Jesus the Son of God, let us hold onto our confessing of him. For we have as high priest, not one who cannot sympathize with our weaknesses, but one who has been tested in all respects like ourselves, but without sin. **Let us, therefore, approach with freeness of speech to the throne of undeserved kindness,**

that we may obtain mercy and find undeserved kindness for help at the right time.

Philemon 25, The undeserved kindness of the Lord Jesus Christ be with the spirit you people show.

Titus 3:13,14, Carefully supply Zenas, who is versed in the Law, and Apollos [faithful Christians] for their trip, that they may not lack anything. But let our people also learn to maintain fine works so as to meet their pressing needs, that they might not be unfruitful. [Loyal worshippers of Jehovah "carefully supply" other faithful ones in the organization with this spiritual information in order for them to see their "pressing need" to leave. And each of these is to "maintain fine works" by reaching out to others and urging them into action, as well.]

Mother: [A mother is merciful and gentle. Recall: Shepherd the flock tenderly, implore his "sheep" and entreat them gently, as a mother would.]

"Feed my lambs." (John 21:15)

June 13, 1989

Seventy Years: [Seventy years of insincere fasting of the organization, 1919-1989. This corresponds with the original 70 years in Babylonian captivity in 607 BC. (Zechariah 7:3-7)]

Angel: [Night before last, I was given a message from an angel of Jehovah: "There is a sword coming. Your souls will be safe through this. Gabrielle (Lisa's daughter, who's safety has recently been threatened) will be safe."] Jeremiah 31:2, **This is what Jehovah has said: "The people made up of survivors from the sword found favor in the wilderness, when Israel [Lisa] was walking to get his repose."** [We (Rosie and I) went on a walk to meditate. We were given this scripture.]

Recall: [Zion is giving birth to children NOW. (I was told this on the evening of June 9th.)] Jeremiah 31:9b, And as for Ephraim [in this instance, Rosie], he is my firstborn [first to believe].

Jehovah's Kingdom: [Jehovah's kingdom has been established on the earth NOW.]

Jeremiah 31:21, Set up road marks for yourself. Place signposts for yourself. Fix your heart upon the highway, the way that you will have to go. Come back, O virgin of Israel. Come back to these cities of yours. [At this time, Rosie is to "come back" to Lancaster, then Lisa is to "come back to these cities" of Iowa, and bring all of the children.]

! Jeremiah 31:22b NWT (1984), For Jehovah has created a new thing in the earth: A mere **female** will press around an able-bodied man [the governing body of the organization].
[Rosie had been concerned. She had not believed Jehovah would use a woman. Jehovah has assured her that a woman is being used for this work.]

Jeremiah 31:33, "**For this is the covenant that I shall conclude with the house [descendants or "children"]** of Israel [Lisa] after those days," is the utterance of Jehovah. "I will put my law within them, and in their heart I shall write it. And I will become their God, and they [faithful worshippers of Jehovah coming out of the organization] **themselves will become my people.**"

Jeremiah 31:4, Yet shall I rebuild you [Lisa] and you will actually be rebuilt, O virgin of Israel. You will yet deck yourself with your tambourines and actually go forth in the dance of those who are laughing.

Jeremiah 3:19, And I myself [Jehovah] have said, 'O how I proceeded to place you among the sons and to give you the desirable land, the hereditary possession of the ornament of the armies of the nations!' And I further said, '"My Father!" you people will call out to me, and from following me you people will not turn back.'

Jeremiah 3:18, In those days they will walk, the house of Judah alongside the house of Israel, and together they will come out of the land of the north into the land that I gave as a hereditary possession to your forefathers.

Isaiah 42:1-4, Look! My servant, on whom I keep fast hold! My chosen one, whom my soul has approved! I have put my spirit in him. Justice to the nations is what he will bring forth. He will not cry out or raise his voice, and in the street he will not let his voice be heard. No crushed reed will he break; and as for a dim flaxen wick, he will not extinguish it. In trueness he will bring forth justice. He will not grow dim nor be crushed until he sets justice in the earth itself; and for his law the islands themselves will keep waiting. [The primary fulfillment of many prophecies occurred in Jesus' day. However, many of these prophecies have a secondary application in the present day, in parallel events with the people Jehovah is now using.]

Revealed: [Jehovah's other chosen servant here (Isaiah 42:1-4) is Leon Wurzer.]

Isaiah 42:5-7, This is what the true God, Jehovah, has said, the Creator of the heavens and the Grand One stretching them out; the One laying out the earth and its produce, the One giving breath to the people on it, and spirit to those walking in it: **"I myself, Jehovah, have called you [Lisa] in righteousness, and I proceeded to take hold of your hand.**

Vision: [I was given a vision from Jehovah when I first became a true worshipper and dedicated my life to Jehovah in 1979: Jehovah and I were walking down a very long road together, hand in hand, and he called me "Friend."]

Isaiah 42:5-7 continued, And I shall safeguard you and give you as a covenant of the people, as a light of the nations, for you to open the blind eyes, to bring forth out of the dungeon the prisoner, out of the house of detention those sitting in darkness."

[These prophecies will be fulfilled shortly. Jehovah has chosen me to do this work. He has taught me his laws and his ways. He has opened my eyes to his denunciation of the Watchtower Bible and Tract Society, known as Jehovah's Witnesses; those who call themselves by his holy name, but do not walk in his ways. I will be used to bring "prisoners" out of "the house of detention." He has fortified me to stand "upright;" to take a stand for righteousness.]

Jeshurun: [Meaning "Upright One," an affectionate term for Israel. (Isaiah 44:2) Jehovah has called Lisa Pressnall to give her "for a light of the nations" and "as a covenant for the people." (Isaiah 49:6,8) This is a "new thing."]

Jeremiah 31:22b, For Jehovah has created a new thing in the earth: a mere female will press around an able-bodied man [in this instance, Leon Wurzer].

June 16, 1989

Matthew 24:22, In fact, unless those days were cut short, no flesh would be saved; but on account of the chosen ones those days will be cut short.

Isaiah 65:8,9, This is what Jehovah has said: "In the same way that the new wine is found in the cluster and someone has to say, 'Do not ruin it, because there is a blessing in it,' so I shall do for the sake of my servants in order not to bring everybody to ruin. And I will bring forth out of Jacob an offspring and out of Judah the hereditary possessor of my mountains; and my chosen ones must take possession of it, and my own servants will reside there.

1 Peter 2:9-19, But you are "a chosen race, a royal priesthood, a holy nation, a people for special possession, that you should declare abroad the excellencies" of the one that called you out of darkness into his wonderful light.

Recall: The first sentence of Jehovah's denunciation:
1 Chronicles 29:11, Yours, O Jehovah, are the greatness and the mightiness and the beauty and the excellency and the dignity; for everything in the heavens and in the earth is yours. Yours is the kingdom, O Jehovah, the One also lifting yourself up as head over all.

1 Peter 2:9-19, continued, For you were once not a people, but are now God's people; you were those who had not been shown mercy, but are now those who have been shown mercy.
Beloved, I exhort you as aliens and temporary residents to keep abstaining from fleshly desires, which are the very ones that carry

on a conflict against the soul. **Maintain your conduct fine among the nations, that, in the thing in which they are speaking against you as evildoers, they may as a result of your fine works of which they are eyewitnesses glorify God in the day of his inspection.**

For the Lord's sake subject yourselves to every human creation: whether to a king as being superior or to governors as being sent by him to inflict punishment on evildoers but to praise doers of good. For so the will of God is, that by doing good you may muzzle the ignorant talk of the unreasonable men. Be as free people, and yet holding your freedom, not as a blind for badness, but as slaves of God. **Honor men of all sorts, have love for the whole association of brothers, be in fear of God, have honor for the king.**

Let house servants be in subjection to their owners with all due fear, not only to the good and reasonable, but also to those hard to please. For if someone, because of conscience toward God, bears up under grievous things and suffers unjustly, this is an agreeable thing.

Recall: [Our speech, conduct and dress should at all times be modest, clean and reasonable.]

For what merit is there in it if, when you are sinning and being slapped, you endure it? But if, when you are doing good and you suffer, you endure it, this is a thing agreeable with God.

In fact, to this course you were called, because even Christ suffered for you, leaving you a model for you to follow his steps closely. He committed no sin, nor was deception found in his mouth. When he was being reviled, he did not go reviling in return. When he was suffering, he did not go threatening, but kept on committing himself to the one who judges righteously. He himself bore our sins in his own body upon the stake, in order that we might be done with sins and live to righteousness. And "by his stripes you were healed." For you were like sheep going astray; but now you have returned to the shepherd and overseer of your souls.

1 Peter 3:1,2,6-8, **In like manner**, you wives, be in subjection to your own husbands, in order that, if any [husbands] are not obedient to the word, they may be won without a word through the conduct of their wives.

As Sarah used to obey Abraham, calling him "Lord." And you have become her children, provided you keep on doing good and not fearing any cause for terror.

You husbands, continue dwelling **in like manner** with them [wives] according to knowledge, assigning them honor as to a weaker vessel, the feminine one, since you are also heirs with them of the undeserved favor of life, **in order for your prayers not to be hindered.**

→ Finally, all of you be like-minded, showing fellow feeling, having brotherly affection, tenderly compassionate, **humble in mind.**

Psalm 16 all verses, Keep me, O God, for I have taken refuge in you. I have said to Jehovah: "You are Jehovah; my goodness is, not for your sake, but to the holy ones that are in the earth. They, even the majestic ones, are the ones in whom is all my delight." Pains become many to those who, when there is someone else, do hurry after him. I shall not pour out their drink offerings of blood, and I shall not carry their names upon my lips. Jehovah is the portion of my [Lisa's] allotted share and of my cup. You are holding fast my lot. The measuring lines themselves have fallen for me in pleasant places. Really, my own possession has proved agreeable to me. I shall bless Jehovah, who has given me advice. Really, during the nights my kidneys [deepest emotions] have corrected me. I have placed Jehovah in front of me constantly.

Recall: [In one of my prayers, I asked Jehovah to assign an angel to be placed in front of me to constantly correct and admonish me to walk modestly with Jehovah; to always have a humble attitude.]

Because he is at my right hand, I shall not be made to totter. Therefore my heart does rejoice, and my glory [tongue] is inclined to be joyful. Also, my own flesh will reside in security. For you will not leave my soul in Sheol. You will not allow your loyal one to see the pit. [Many times Jehovah has sustained me—rescued me from my severe, even "death-dealing" depression, a condition I have suffered from for years. It is Jehovah's strength, not my own, that makes it possible for me to keep going and accomplish the work he has given me.]

You will cause me to know the path of life. Rejoicing to satisfaction is with your face; there is pleasantness at your right hand forever.

Compare: Proverbs 12:28, In the path of righteousness there is life, and the journey in its pathway means no death.

Angel: [I remember the message from Jehovah: A sword will pass over us, and we will have our lives. This means the six of us will be kept safe, including Gabrielle, my daughter. Gabrielle's life has been threatened on more than one occasion, including an attempted abduction at gunpoint.]

Isaiah 54:14,15,17, "You [Lisa] will prove to be firmly established in righteousness itself. You will be far away from oppression—for you will fear none—and from anything terrifying, for it will not come near you. If anyone should at all make an attack, it will not be at my orders. Whoever is making an attack upon you will fall even on account of you."

"Any weapon whatever that will be formed against you will have no success, and any tongue at all that will rise up against you in the judgment you will condemn. This is the hereditary possession of the servants of Jehovah, and their righteousness is from me," is the utterance of Jehovah.

Advance Warning: [From the Circuit Overseer's talk at the Kingdom Hall in Lancaster, Wisconsin, U.S.A.: When James Thatcher referred to me in his talk, he said that I should expect to be expelled from the "synagogue" (the organization). "Everyone who kills you" could refer to my being disfellowshipped by elders in the organization. Jehovah sent me this warning in advance through the Circuit Overseer, who said that they would possibly press charges against me, make false accusations, call me a false prophet, and accuse me of lying or of being an apostate.]

Earlier Decision: [At an earlier time before much of this happened, Jehovah brought to my attention that I should consider what I would do if I were ever wrongly disfellowshipped. I had concluded at that time, that if, through deep meditation and prayer, I knew in my heart that I was innocent of the charges and was still in good standing with Jehovah, that it didn't matter what others said about me or accused me of. Jehovah is my judge. I would trust in him to decide the matter. I would keep on serving him whole-souled to the best of my ability, and in the end he would establish the facts and prove out the truth.

Jehovah was preparing my heart for the false accusations and lies spoken against me when I was later disfellowshipped. He continued to comfort me and strengthen me as all of these heartbreaking things occurred. And I was reassured by Jehovah that at some future point in time he would set matters right.]

Proverbs 12:19-21,25, It is the lip of truth that will be firmly established forever, but the tongue of falsehood will be only as long as a moment. Deception is in the heart of those fabricating mischief, but those counseling peace have rejoicing. Nothing hurtful will befall the righteous one, but the wicked are the ones that will certainly be filled with calamity.

Anxious care in the heart of a man is what will cause it to bow down, but the good word is what makes it rejoice.

Jeremiah 4:5,6,15,16,19, Tell it in Judah, you men, and publish it even in Jerusalem, and say it out, and blow a horn throughout the land. Call out loudly and say: "Gather yourselves together, and let us enter into the fortified cities. Raise up a signal toward Zion. Make provision for shelter. Do not stand still. For there is a calamity that I am bringing in from the north, even a great crash.

For a voice is telling from Dan [Dan means "judge."] and is publishing something hurtful, from the mountainous region of Ephraim.

→ Make mention of it, you [faithful] people, yes, to the nations. Publish it against Jerusalem. [Publish it against unfaithful Jerusalem, the organization of Jehovah's Witnesses. Make it known what they are doing to innocent people. Expose their wrongdoing and their methods.]

Watchers are coming from a land far away, and they will let out their voice against the very cities of Judah.

O my intestines, my intestines! I am in severe pains in the walls of my heart. My heart is boisterous within me. I cannot keep silent, for the sound of a horn is what my soul has heard, the alarm signal of war.

Jeremiah 4:23-26,30,31, I saw the land, and look! it was empty and waste; and into the heavens, **and their light was no more**. [Jehovah has indicated to me that the spiritual light he had given them has gone out among the governing body in the organization.]

Recall: *Awake!* magazine, "Snuffing out the Gospel Light," WBTS June 22, 1989, pages 24-25.

I saw the mountains, and, look! they were rocking, and the hills themselves were all given a shaking. I saw, and, look! there was not an earthling man, and the flying creatures of the heavens had all fled. I saw, and, look! the orchard itself was a wilderness, and the very cities of it had all been torn down. It was because of Jehovah, because of his burning anger.

Now that you are despoiled, what will you do, since you used to clothe yourself with scarlet, since you used to deck yourself with ornaments of gold, since you used to enlarge your eyes with black paint? It is in vain that you used to make yourself pretty. Those lusting after you have rejected you; they keep seeking for your very soul.

[Babylon the Great, the great harlot in the book of Revelation is the Watchtower Bible and Tract Society, Jehovah's Witnesses, not the churches of Christendom as they claim.]

Recall: *The Watchtower* magazine WBTS, August 15, 1940. [The organization claims to have a spiritual "paradise" right now.]

Ezekiel 13:15,16, "'And I will bring my rage to its finish upon the wall and upon those plastering it with whitewash, and I shall say to you men: "The wall is no more, and those plastering it are no more, the [unfaithful] prophets of Israel that are prophesying to [unfaithful] Jerusalem and that are visioning for her a vision of peace, when there is no peace,"' is the utterance of the Sovereign Lord Jehovah.

Jeremiah 4:31 continued, For a voice like that of a sick woman [Lisa] I have heard, the distress like that of a woman giving birth to her first child, the voice of the daughter of Zion who keeps gasping for breath. She keeps spreading out her palms: "Woe, now, to me, for my soul is tired of the killers!"

Recall: Psalm 6:8, Get away from me, all you practicers of what is hurtful [those taking the lead in the organization], for Jehovah will certainly hear the sound of my weeping.

Kingdom Power: [When the son of man is revealed, kingdom power will be clearly visible to those seeking to observe it.]

Recall: Matthew 24:28, Wherever the carcass is, there the eagles will be gathered. [Those with spiritual wisdom are the far-sighted eagles gathering to the true Christ, who has died in the flesh, but is alive in the spirit. His faithful followers discern his invisible presence in kingdom power.]

Circuit Overseer: [Earlier, I was directed by Jehovah to gather my 1986-7 journal and my 1988-9 journal, along with other notes, and give them to the Circuit Overseer, James Thatcher, during his most recent visit to the Lancaster, Wisconsin congregation. I had prayed to Jehovah about my concern as to whether he would believe that Jehovah had chosen me for this work. Jehovah answered me with this scripture.] 1 Timothy 4:4, The reason for this is that every creation of God is fine, **and nothing is to be rejected if it is received with thanksgiving.**

[I distinctly remember that I trembled uncontrollably as I approached Brother Thatcher after one of the Kingdom Hall meetings and handed him my papers asking him to read them. He was very kind, and **thanked me for them**, not knowing at the time what they were about. Later, at the next Kingdom Hall meeting, he acknowledged that Jehovah had chosen me, saying, "Those are the exact words (identifying prophetic scriptures)."

There are those among the faithful worshippers of Jehovah in the organization today who have discerned from the scriptures that Jehovah is sending them a prophet in the last days. Many among them are also aware that the prophet will be a woman. The Circuit Overseer said that a few would believe, a faithful remnant—but that most would not believe, which is also prophesied.]

Recall: Luke 19:44, And they will dash you and your children within you [those taking the lead in the organization and those following after them, when they should have followed Jehovah] to the ground, and they will not leave a stone upon a stone in you, because you did not discern the time of your being inspected.

June 17, 1989

First Meeting With Elders: [Two elders from the Lancaster, Wisconsin congregation arranged to meet with us in my home.]

Before the meeting:

> Bram's Notes: I read Isaiah 44:21,23, Remember these things, O Jacob, and you, O Israel, because you are my servant. I have formed you. You are a servant belonging to me. O Israel (Lisa), you will not be forgotten on my part.
> Joyfully cry out, you heavens, for Jehovah has taken action! **Shout in triumph**, all you lowest parts of the earth! Become cheerful, you mountains, with joyful outcry, you forest and all you trees in it. For Jehovah has repurchased Jacob, and on Israel he shows his beauty.

Recall: *The Watchtower* magazine, WBTS August 15, 1940. [With reference to when Christ returns: **A message of triumph**.]

Jeremiah 50:35,36, "There is a sword against the Chaldeans [earlier inhabitants of Babylon]," is the utterance of Jehovah, "and against the inhabitants of Babylon and against her princes and against her wise ones [governing body of the organization]. There is a sword against the empty talkers, and they will certainly act foolishly. There is a sword against her mighty men, and they will actually become terrified."

Psalm 121 all verses, I shall raise my eyes to the mountains. From where will my help come? My help is from Jehovah, the Maker of heaven and earth. He cannot possibly allow your foot to totter. The One guarding you cannot possibly be drowsy. Look! He will not be drowsy nor go to sleep, he that is guarding Israel. Jehovah is guarding you [Lisa]. Jehovah is your shade on your right hand. By day the sun itself will not strike you, nor the moon by night. Jehovah himself will guard you against all calamity. He will guard your soul. Jehovah himself will guard your going out and your coming in from now on and to time indefinite. [I was praying to Jehovah for the right words to speak and the strength to speak calmly to the elders. He answered me by comforting me with the Psalms.]

Psalm 122 all verses, I rejoiced when they were saying to me: "To the house of Jehovah let us go." Our feet proved to be standing within your gates, O [faithful] Jerusalem. Jerusalem [Lisa] is one that is built like a city that has been joined together in oneness, to which the tribes have gone up, the tribes of Jah [shortened form of Jehovah's name], as a reminder to Israel to give thanks to the name of Jehovah. For there the thrones for judgment have been sitting, thrones for the house of David. Ask, O you people [faithful worshippers of Jehovah], for the peace of Jerusalem. Those loving you, O city, will be free from care. May peace continue within your rampart, freedom from care within your dwelling towers. For the sake of my brothers and my companions I [Jesus] will now speak: "May there be peace within you." For the sake of the house of Jehovah our God I will keep seeking good for you.

Psalm 123 all verses, To you I have raised my eyes, O you who are dwelling in the heavens. Look! As the eyes of servants are toward the hand of their master, as the eyes of a maidservant are toward the hand of her mistress, so our eyes are toward Jehovah our God until he shows us [faithful worshippers of Jehovah] favor. Show us favor, O Jehovah, show us favor; for to an abundance we have been glutted with contempt. Abundantly our soul has been glutted with the derision of those [taking the lead in the organization] who are at ease, of the contempt on the part of the arrogant ones.

Psalm 124 all verses, "Had it not been that Jehovah proved to be for us," let Israel now say, "Had it not been that Jehovah proved to be for us when men rose up against us, [Jehovah's holy spirit indicates that we have his help. And, Jehovah has also given us proof of his help through our journals, and the scriptures he has been giving us.] then they would have swallowed us up even alive, when their anger was burning against us. Then the very waters would have washed us away, the torrent itself would have passed over our soul. Then there would have passed over our soul the waters of presumptuousness. Blessed be Jehovah, who has not given us as a prey to their teeth. Our soul is like a bird that is escaped from the trap of baiters. The trap is broken, and we ourselves have escaped. [We have seen through the lies they have been teaching us, and we are escaping from the organization.] Our help is in the name of Jehovah, the Maker of heaven and earth.

Psalm 125 all verses, Those trusting in Jehovah are like [faithful] Mount Zion, which cannot be made to totter, but dwells even to time indefinite. Jerusalem—as mountains are all around it, so Jehovah is all around his people, from now on and to time indefinite. For the scepter of wickedness will not keep resting upon the lot of the righteous ones, in order that the righteous ones may not thrust out their hand upon any wrongdoing. O do good, O Jehovah, to the good ones, even to the ones upright in their hearts. As for those turning aside to their crooked ways, Jehovah will make them go away with the practicers of what is hurtful. There will be peace upon Israel.

Recall: Zechariah 2:5, "And I myself shall become to her," is the utterance of Jehovah, "a wall of fire all around, and a glory is what I shall become in the midst of her." [We are reassured that we have Jehovah's protection.]

[The scriptures I read to the elders toward the end of the meeting were all from the New World Translation of the Holy Scriptures, which was "Rendered from the Original Languages by the New World Bible Translation Committee," of the Watchtower Bible and Tract Society.]

Habakkuk 3:14 NWT (1984), **With his own rods** you pierced the head of his warriors when they moved tempestuously to scatter me. [Their own "rods," translation of the Bible, were "piercing" their "head."] Their high glee was as of those bent on devouring an afflicted one in a place of concealment.

[During the meeting, I began to realize that these two elders were not showing proper respect to Jehovah for the seriousness of the spiritual matters we were discussing. One elder, Wayne J., told me he didn't want to keep hearing about scriptural and prophetic parallels and patterns. When I described some of the serious problems within the organization involving lack of kindness and justice, particularly found among those taking the lead, he pointed out to me the example from the scriptures of the Israelite people who were destroyed because they were griping against Moses. He was suggesting that I was "griping" against the organization, and that I did not have legitimate concerns. In response to this, I mentioned the example set by Jesus and Paul when they exposed the wrongdoing of the Sanhedrin and Pharisees.

The same elder then brought up a shepherding call he was supposed to have made on our household, and when I reminded him that he hadn't shown up, he laughed. I read this scripture to them.] Jeremiah 23:1-4, "Woe to the shepherds who are destroying and scattering the sheep of my pasturage!" is the utterance of Jehovah.

Therefore this is what Jehovah the God of Israel has said against the shepherds who are shepherding my people: "You yourselves have scattered my sheep; and you kept dispersing them, and you have not turned your attention to them."

"Here I am turning my attention upon you for the badness of your dealings," is the utterance of Jehovah.

"And I myself shall collect together the remnant of my sheep out of all the lands to which I have dispersed them, and I will bring them back to their pasture ground, and they will certainly be fruitful and become many. And I will raise up over them shepherds who will actually shepherd them; and they will be afraid no more, neither will they be struck with any terror, and none will be missing," is the utterance of Jehovah.

[I was asked if I was applying these scriptures to these two elders. I said I was not pointing fingers at individuals, but that this was typical of a problem throughout the organization. I also read this scripture to them.] Lamentations 4:12,13, The kings of the earth and all the inhabitants of the productive land had not believed that the adversary and the enemy [Satan, with his ability to deceive] would come into the gates of Jerusalem. Because of the **sins of her prophets, the errors of her priests** [the sins and errors of the governing body], there were in the midst of her those pouring out the blood of righteous ones.

[The second elder present at this meeting, John G., berated me for this, and told me that I was misapplying the scriptures. He said these scriptures refer to when Babylon was taking Jerusalem captive.

However, this was part of the point that I was making—that it was **because** of the sins and errors of the priests and prophets that Jehovah was angry. Jehovah allowed Jerusalem to be taken captive by Babylon due to their sins against him. I suggested that it could happen again to the present day organization, if Jehovah became angry with those taking the lead, because they were not fulfilling their responsibilities faithfully.

The elder, John G., claimed to be confident because of the building of their new Kingdom Hall and the increase in the congregation. I told the elders that if Jehovah removed his holy spirit from the congregation, they could expect to see a "drying up of rivers," a member loss like that of Christendom, and less and less of the fruitage of the spirit among the congregation, and more of the other spirit—a contaminated spirit.]

> Bram's Notes: Later, after the elders had left, I made these notes. Jeremiah 33:23,24, And the word of Jehovah continued to occur to Jeremiah, saying: "Have you not seen what those of this people have spoken, saying, 'The two families whom Jehovah has chosen, he will also reject them'? And my own people they keep treating with disrespect, so that it should no more continue being a nation before them." This scripture was given after one of the members from the congregation, Dion S., called on the telephone. He said to my mother, "So we are all wrong and you and Bram and Rosie are the only ones who are right?"

June 18, 1989 Sunday

Jeremiah 30:23,24, Look! A windstorm of Jehovah, rage itself, has gone forth, an onward-sweeping tempest. Upon the head of the wicked ones it will whirl. The burning anger of Jehovah will not turn back until he will have executed and until he will have carried out the ideas of his heart. In the final part of the days you people will give your consideration to it.

Angel: [I was given a sense of things moving forward and by the time it arrives, it will be exactly the time. We must not delay in our departure from the organization.]

Jeremiah 51:50, **"You escapees from the sword** [our two families, Rosie's and mine], keep going. Do not stand still. **From far away remember Jehovah [from outside the organization, keep remembering Jehovah's ways],** and may [faithful] Jerusalem herself come up into your heart."

Recall: [This is one of the scriptures Jehovah included in his denunciation.] Jeremiah 18:11, This is what Jehovah has said: "Here I am forming against you [the organization] a calamity and thinking against you a thought. Turn back, please, each one from his bad way, and make your ways and your dealings good."

Second Meeting With Elders:

> Bram's Notes: We had another meeting in our home. This time the same two elders brought Susan B. with them. She would not admit she had done anything wrong. According to her, the only problem was that my mother's pride was hurt. She convinced the elders that that was all it was and they thought that an apology would be sufficient. They did not see the need for discussing the fact that Susan had been lying about my mother to members in the congregation, and it still continued. We went around in circles. One elder, Wayne J., laughed at my mother, and made facial gestures to match his attitude. The other elder, John G., got angry and spoke sharply to her. And now they accuse us of lying. Then they leave us with their lies and shake our hands, giving us the feeling that during the whole meeting they were putting us down.

[We had a second meeting in my home with the two elders. They brought Susan B. with them. Susan and I had been friends for years, but she had begun to spread malicious gossip and lies about me in the congregation for the past several months. One of the rumors she was spreading was that I didn't want my daughter, Gabrielle. Susan was telling others that she would be happy to be given custody of her and raise her. She was also lying about me to my son, Bram, and trying to alienate my friends within the congregation. I had spoken with her privately but she persisted. She and another friend of mine, Enid K., a full-time pioneer (minister), had both already been admonished at the Kingdom Hall because they had been spreading malicious gossip about me out in field service (door-to-door ministry).

As we were discussing the problems, I referred to this scripture.] 1 John 1:9, If we confess our sins, he is faithful and righteous so as to forgive us our sins and to cleanse us from all unrighteousness.

[I was trying to make the point that there needed to be an acknowledgement by Susan B. of the things she had been saying. Susan B. hedged and would not admit the specific statement she had made. I then read this scripture.] Proverbs 6:16-19, There are six things that Jehovah does hate; yes, seven are things detestable to his soul: lofty eyes, a false tongue, and hands that are shedding innocent blood, a heart fabricating hurtful schemes, feet that are in a hurry to run to badness, a false witness that launches forth lies, and anyone sending forth contentions among brothers.

[One elder, Wayne J., said they didn't want to hear the facts—they were not important. I replied that the facts needed to be established. The truth of the matter needed to be determined before an apology would be appropriate. I suggested that since Susan B. was not admitting to the things she had said, the elders could conduct an investigation, because the gossip Susan B. was spreading was widely circulated in the congregation, and she was continuing in her course of action.

The elder, John G., said it was not a judicial matter—that there was no need to investigate the facts. He then read me a scripture about a treacherous and wicked heart, applying it to me. I said the scripture could apply to all of us here, and that we all seemed pretty confident in ourselves. I then quoted this scripture.] 1 Corinthians 10:12, Consequently let him that thinks he is standing, beware that he does not fall.

[John G. became very angry with me. Susan B. said to me, "Do you want me to be disfellowshipped?" And surprisingly (and accurately), Wayne J. answered her, saying, "No, she (myself) wants justice." Wayne then told me that I was hard-hearted because I wouldn't accept an apology. I said I would accept any apology based on truth. The elders thought I should accept any apology. Apparently truth is not a requirement according to them.

I was amazed. I said I would recall this conversation for future reference.

After the meeting with the elders and Susan B., and they had left, Jehovah gave me this scripture.] Revelation 16:5-7, And I heard the angel over the waters say: **"You [Jehovah], the One who is and who was, the loyal One, are righteous, because you have rendered these decisions, because they poured out the blood of holy ones and of prophets, and you have given them blood to drink. They deserve it."** And I heard the altar say: **"Yes, Jehovah God, the Almighty, true and righteous are your judicial decisions."**

Given: Book of Lamentations all verses [abbreviated here], Lamentations 1:22-2:22,

May all their badness come before you, and deal severely with them [the unfaithful organization], just as you have dealt severely with me on account of all my transgressions. For my sighs are many, and my heart is ill.

O how Jehovah in his anger beclouds the [unfaithful] daughter of Zion [Jehovah's Witnesses]! He has thrown down from heaven to earth the beauty of Israel [the organization]. And he has not remembered his footstool in the day of his anger.

Jehovah has swallowed up, he has shown no compassion upon any abiding places of Jacob. In his fury he has torn down the fortified places of the [unfaithful] daughter of Judah. **He has brought into contact with the earth, he has profaned the kingdom and her princes.**

In the heat of anger he has cut down every horn of [unfaithful] Israel. He has turned his right hand back from before the enemy; and in [unfaithful] Jacob he keeps burning like a flaming fire that has devoured all around.

He has trodden his bow like an enemy. His right hand has taken its position like an adversary, and he kept killing all those desirable to the eyes. Into the tent of the daughter of Zion [the organization of Jehovah's Witnesses] he has poured out his rage, just like fire.

Jehovah has become like an enemy. He has swallowed down [unfaithful] Israel. He has swallowed down all her dwelling towers; he has brought his fortified places to ruin. And in the daughter of Judah he makes mourning and lamentation abound.

And he treats his booth [place of shelter; the organization] violently like that in a garden. He has brought his festival to ruin. Jehovah has caused to be forgotten in Zion festival and sabbath. **And in his angry denunciation he shows no respect for king and priest.**

[Among Jehovah's Witnesses, there are those who consider themselves to be "anointed" by Jehovah, to act as the "faithful and discreet slave" described in Matthew 24:45-47, responsible for dispensing spiritual "food," God's truth, to the rest of the "sheeplike" ones in the organization. For faithfully fulfilling this responsibility, they consider their reward from Jehovah to be heavenly life, where they will rule with Christ as kings and priests, and "power of judging" will be given to them. (Revelation 5:10, Revelation 7:4, Revelation 20:4) But the "faithful and discreet slave" has become unfaithful and has fallen away from true worship, leading Jehovah's people astray, and the reward for this is severe punishment. (Matthew 24:48-51)]

Lamentations Chapter 2, continued, Jehovah has cast off his altar. He has spurned his sanctuary. Into the hand of the enemy he has surrendered the walls of her dwelling towers. In the house of Jehovah they have let out their own voice, as in the day of a festival.

Jehovah has thought of bringing the wall of the [unfaithful] daughter of Zion to ruin. He has stretched out the measuring line. He has not turned back his hand from swallowing up. And he causes rampart and wall to go mourning. Together they have faded away.

Her [the organization's] gates have sunk down into the very earth. He has destroyed and broken her bars in pieces. Her king and her princes are among the nations. **There is no law. Her own prophets also have found no vision from Jehovah.**

The older men of the daughter of Zion sit down on the earth, where they keep silence. They have brought up dust upon their head. They have girded on sackcloth. The virgins of Jerusalem have brought their head down to the very earth.

My eyes have come to their end in sheer tears. My intestines are in a ferment. My liver has been poured out to the very earth, on account of the crash of the daughter of my people, because of the fainting away of child and suckling in the public squares of the town.

To their mothers they kept saying: "Where are grain and wine [spiritual "food," God's truth]?" Because of their fainting away like someone slain in the public squares of the city, because of their soul being poured out into the bosom of their mothers.

Of what shall I use you as a witness? What shall I liken to you, O daughter of Zion [**unfaithful organization of Jehovah's Witnesses**]? What shall I make equal to you, that I may comfort you, O virgin daughter of Zion? For your breakdown is just as great as the sea. Who can bring healing to you?

Your [the organization's] own prophets have visioned for you worthless and unsatisfying things, and they have not uncovered your error in order to turn back your captivity, but they kept visioning for you worthless and misleading pronouncements.

At you all those passing along on the road have clapped their hands. They have whistled and kept wagging their head at the [unfaithful] daughter of Jerusalem, saying: **"Is this the city of which they used to say, 'It is the perfection of prettiness, an exultation for all the earth'?"**

At you all your enemies have opened their mouth. They have whistled and kept grinding the teeth. They have said: "We will swallow her down. This indeed is the day that we have hoped for. We have found! We have seen!"

Jehovah has done what he had in mind. He has accomplished his saying, what he had commanded from the days of long ago. He has torn down and shown no compassion. And over you he causes the enemy [Satan] to rejoice. He has made the horn of your adversaries high.

Their heart has cried out to Jehovah, O wall of the daughter of Zion. Cause tears to descend just like a torrent day and night. Give no numbness to yourself. May the pupil of your eye not keep quiet.

Rise up! Whine during the night at the start of the morning watches. Pour out your heart before the face of Jehovah just like water. **Raise to him your palms on account of the soul of your children, who are fainting away because of famine at the head of all the streets.**

See, O Jehovah, and do look to the one to whom you have dealt severely in this manner. Should the women keep eating their own fruitage, the children born fully formed, or in the sanctuary of Jehovah should priest and prophet be killed?

Boy and old man have lain down on the earth of the streets. My virgins and my young men themselves have fallen by the sword. You have killed in the day of your anger. You have slaughtered; you have had no compassion.

As in the day of a festival you proceeded to call out my places of alien residence all around. And in the day of the wrath of Jehovah there proved to be no escapee or survivor; those whom I brought forth fully formed and reared, my enemy himself exterminated them.

Lamentations, continued [abbreviated], Lamentations 4:1-20,
O how the gold that shines becomes dim, the good gold! O how the holy stones are poured out at the head of all the streets!

As for the precious sons of Zion, those who were weighed against refined gold, O how they have been reckoned as large jars of earthenware, the work of the hands of a potter.

Even jackals themselves have presented the udder. They have suckled their cubs. The daughter of my people becomes cruel, like ostriches in the wilderness.

The tongue of the suckling has cleaved to its palate because of thirst. Children themselves have asked for bread. There is no one dealing it out to them.

The very ones that were eating pleasant things [spiritual "food" from Jehovah, the truth] have been struck with astonishment in the streets. The very ones that were being reared in scarlet have had to embrace ash heaps.

The punishment for the error of the daughter of my people also becomes greater than the punishment for the sin of Sodom, which was overthrown as in a moment, and to which no hands turned helpfully.

Her Nazirites were purer than snow; they were whiter than milk. They were in fact more ruddy than corals; their polish was as the sapphire.

Their aspect has become darker than blackness itself. They have not been recognized in the streets. Their skin has shriveled upon their bones. It has become just as dry as a tree.

Better have those slain with the sword proved to be than those slain by famine, because these pine away, pierced through for lack of the produce of the open field.

The very hands of compassionate women have boiled their own children. They have become as bread of consolation to one during the breakdown of the daughter of my people.

Jehovah has accomplished his rage. He has poured out his burning anger. And he sets a fire ablaze in Zion, which eats up her foundations.

The kings [governing body of the organization] of the earth and all the inhabitants of the productive land had not believed that the adversary and the enemy [Satan] would come into the gates of Jerusalem.

Because of the sins of her prophets, the error of her priests, there were in the midst of her those [those taking the lead in the organization] pouring out the blood of righteous ones.

They have wandered about as blind in the streets. They have become polluted with blood, so that none are able to touch their garments.

"Get out of the way! Unclean!" they have called out to them. "Get out of the way! Get out of the way! Do not touch!" For they have gone homeless. They have also wandered about. People have said among the nations: "They will not reside again as aliens.

The face of Jehovah has divided them up. He will not look upon them again. Men will certainly show no consideration even for the priests [governing body]. They will certainly show no favor even to the old men [elders]."

While we yet are, our eyes keep pining away in vain for assistance to us. During our looking about we have looked out to a nation that can bring no salvation. [The governing body of the organization has consorted with the nations for support. And, Jehovah has abandoned them.]

They have hunted our steps so that there is no walking in our public squares. Our end has drawn near. Our days have come to their full, for our end has come.

Swifter than the eagles of the heavens our pursuers have proved to be. Upon the mountains they have hotly pursued us. In the wilderness they have lain in wait for us.

The very breath of our nostrils, **the anointed one of Jehovah [the unfaithful "faithful and discreet slave," the "anointed," which includes the governing body** (Matthew 24:45-51)**], has been captured in their large pit, the one of whom we have said: "In his shade we shall live among the nations."**

Lamentations Chapter 5 all verses,

Remember, O Jehovah, what has happened to us. Do look and see our reproach.

Our own hereditary possession has been turned over to strangers, our houses to foreigners.

We have become mere orphans without a father. Our mothers are like widows.

For money we have had to drink our own water. For a price our own wood comes in.

Close onto our neck we have been pursued. We have grown weary. No rest has been left for us.

To Egypt we have given the hand; to Assyria, in order to get satisfaction with bread.

Our forefathers [governing body] are the ones that have sinned. They are no more. As for us, it is their errors that we have had to bear.

Mere servants have ruled over us. There is no one tearing us away from their hand.

At the risk of our soul we bring in our bread, because of the sword of the wilderness.

Our very skin has grown hot just like a furnace, because of the pangs of hunger.

The wives in Zion they have humbled, the virgins in the cities of Judah.

Princes themselves have been hanged by just their hand. The faces of even old men have not been honored.

Even young men have lifted up a hand mill itself, and under the wood mere boys have stumbled.

Old men themselves have ceased even out of the gate, young men from their instrumental music.

The exultation of our heart has ceased. Our dancing has been changed into mere mourning.

The crown of our head [governing body of the organization] has fallen. Woe, now, to us, because we have sinned!

On this account our heart has become ill. On account of these things our eyes have grown dim,

On account of [unfaithful] Zion's mountain that is desolated; foxes themselves have walked on it.

As for you, O Jehovah, to time indefinite you will sit. Your throne is for generation after generation.

Why is it that forever you forget us, that you leave us for the length of days?

Bring us back, O Jehovah, to yourself, and we [faithful worshippers of Jehovah still in the organization] shall readily come back. Bring new days for us as in the long ago.

However, you have positively rejected us. You have been indignant toward us very much.

June 19, 1989

Given: Book of Habakkuk all verses NWT (1984), The pronouncement that Habakkuk the prophet visioned: How long, O Jehovah, must I cry for help, and you do not hear? How long shall I call to you for aid from violence, and you do not save? Why is it that you make me see what is hurtful, and you keep looking upon mere trouble? And why are despoiling and violence in front of me, and why does quarreling occur, and why is strife carried?

Therefore law grows numb, and justice never goes forth [in the organization of Jehovah's Witnesses]. Because the wicked one [governing body] is surrounding the righteous one [faithful worshippers of Jehovah still in the organization], for that reason justice goes forth crooked.

See, you people, among the nations, and look on, and stare in amazement at one another. Be amazed; for there is an activity that one is carrying on in your days, which you people will not believe although it is related. For here I am raising up the Chaldeans [earlier inhabitants of Babylon], the nation bitter and impetuous, which is going to the wide-open places of the earth in order to take possession of residences not belonging to it. Frightful and fear-inspiring it is. From itself its own justice and its own dignity go forth. And its horses have proved swifter than leopards, and they have proved fiercer than evening wolves. And its steeds have pawed the ground, and from far away its own steeds come. They fly like the eagle speeding to eat something. In its entirety it comes for mere violence. The assembling of their faces is as the east wind, and it gathers up captives just like the sand. **And for its part, it jeers kings**

[unfaithful "faithful and discreet slave"] themselves, and high officials [governing body] are something laughable to it. For its part, it laughs even at every fortified place, and it piles up dust and captures it. At that time it will certainly move onward like wind and will pass through and will actually become guilty. This its power is due to its god [Satan].**

Are you not from long ago, O Jehovah? O my God, my holy One, you do not die. O Jehovah, for a judgment you have set it; and, O Rock, for a reproving you have founded it.

You are too pure in eyes to see what is bad; and to look on trouble you are not able. Why is it that you look on those dealing treacherously, that you keep silent when someone wicked [governing body of the organization] swallows up someone more righteous [faithful worshippers of Jehovah still in the organization] than he is? And why do you make earthling man like the fishes of the sea, like creeping things over whom no one is ruling? All these he has brought up with a mere fishhook; he drags them away in his dragnet, and he gathers them in his fishing net. That is why he rejoices and is joyful. That is why he offers sacrifice to his dragnet and makes sacrificial smoke to his fishing net; for by them his portion is well oiled, and his food is healthful. Is that why he will empty out his dragnet, and does he have to kill nations constantly, while he shows no compassion?

At my guard post I will keep standing, and I will keep myself stationed upon the bulwark; and I shall keep watch, to see what he will speak by me and what I shall reply at the reproof of me.

And Jehovah proceeded to answer me [Lisa] and to say: "Write down the vision, and set it out plainly upon tablets, in order that the one reading aloud from it may do so fluently. For the vision is yet for the appointed time, and it keeps panting on to the end, and it will not tell a lie. Even if it should delay, keep in expectation of it; for it will without fail come true. It will not be late.

"Look! His soul [unfaithful "faithful and discreet slave" of the organization of Jehovah's Witnesses] has been swelled up; it has not been upright within him. But as for the righteous one [faithful worshippers of Jehovah still in the organization], by his faithfulness he will keep living. **And, indeed, because the wine is dealing treacherously, an able-bodied man [the unfaithful "faithful and** discreet slave"] is self-assuming; and he will not reach his goal, he who has made his soul spacious just like Sheol, and who is like death and cannot be satisfied. And he keeps gathering to himself all the nations and collecting together to himself all the peoples. Will not these very ones, all of them, lift up against him a proverbial saying and an alluding remark, insinuations at him? And one will say,

"'Woe to him [the unfaithful "faithful and discreet slave," holding as prisoners by their lies, the faithful worshippers of Jehovah, who do not belong to them, but truly belong to Jehovah] who is multiplying what is not his own—O how long!—and who is making debt heavy against himself! Will not those claiming interest of you rise up suddenly, and those wake up who are violently shaking you, and you certainly become to them something to pillage? Because you yourself [because the unfaithful international organization of Jehovah's Witnesses harmed people from many different countries with their lies] despoiled many nations, all the remaining ones of the peoples will despoil you, because of the shedding of blood of mankind and the violence to the earth, the town and all those dwelling in it.

"'Woe to the one [the unfaithful "faithful and discreet slave"] that is making evil gain for his house, in order to set his nest on the height, so as to be delivered from the grasp of what is calamitous! You have counseled something shameful to your house, the cutting off of many peoples; and your soul is sinning. For out of the wall a stone itself will cry out plaintively, and from the woodwork a rafter itself will answer it.

"'Woe to the one that is building a city by bloodshed, and that has solidly established a town by unrighteousness! Look! Is it not from Jehovah of armies that peoples will toil on only for the fire, and that national groups will tire themselves out merely for nothing? For the earth will be filled with the knowing of the glory of Jehovah as the waters themselves cover over the sea.

"'Woe to the one giving his companion something to drink, attaching to it your rage and anger, in order to make them drunk, for the purpose of looking upon their parts of shame. You will certainly be satiated with dishonor instead of glory.** Drink also, you yourself, and be considered uncircumcised. The cup of the right hand of Jehovah will come around to you, and there will be disgrace upon your glory; because the violence done to Lebanon is what will cover you, and the rapacity upon the beasts that terrifies them, because of the shedding of blood of mankind and the violence done to the earth, the town and all those dwelling in it. Of what benefit has a carved image been, when the former of it has carved it, a molten statue, and an instructor in falsehood? when the former of its form has trusted in it, to the extent of making valueless gods that are speechless?

"'Woe to the one saying to the piece of wood: "O do awake!" to a dumb stone: "O wake up! It itself will give instruction"! Look! It is sheathed in gold and silver, and there is no breath at all in the midst of it. But Jehovah is in his holy temple. Keep silence before him, all the earth!'"

The prayer of Habbakuk the prophet in dirges: O Jehovah, I have heard the report about you. I have become afraid, O Jehovah, of your activity.

In the midst of the years O bring it to life! In the midst of the years may you make it known. During the agitation, to show mercy may you remember.

God himself proceeded to come from Teman [considered a center of wisdom], even a Holy One from Mount Paran. *Selah. [Pause for silent meditation.]*

His dignity covered the heavens; and with his praise the earth became filled.

As for his brightness, it got to be just like the light. He had two rays issuing out of his hand, and there the hiding of his strength was.

Before him pestilence kept going, and burning fever would go forth at his feet.

He stood still, that he might shake up the earth. He saw, and then caused mountains to leap.

And the eternal mountains got to be smashed; the indefinitely lasting hills bowed down. The walkings of long ago are his.

Under what is hurtful I saw the tents of Cushan. The tent cloths of the land of Midian began to be agitated.

Is it against the rivers, O Jehovah, is it against the rivers that your anger has become hot, or is your fury against the sea? For you went riding upon your horses; your chariots were salvation.

In its nakedness your bow comes to be uncovered. The sworn oaths of the tribes are the thing said. *Selah. [Pause for meditation.]* With rivers you proceeded to split the earth.

Mountains saw you; they got to be in severe pains. A thunderstorm of waters passed through. The watery deep gave forth its sound. On high its hands it lifted up.

Sun—moon—stood still, in the lofty abode thereof. Like light your own arrows kept going. The lightning of your spear served for brightness.

With denunciation you went marching through the earth. In anger you went threshing [to beat or to examine exhaustively] the nations.

And you went forth for the salvation of your people, to save your anointed one. You broke to pieces the head one [unfaithful "faithful and discreet slave"] out of the house of the wicked one. There was a laying of the foundation bare, clear up to the neck. *Selah. [Pause for meditation.]*

With his own rods you pierced the head of his warriors when they moved tempestuously to scatter me. Their high glee was as of those bent on devouring an afflicted one [Lisa] in a place of concealment.

Through the sea you trod with your horses, through the heap of vast waters.

I heard, and my belly began to be agitated; at the sound my lips quivered; rottenness began to enter into my bones; and in my situation I was agitated, that I should quietly wait for the day of distress, for his coming up to the people, that he may raid them.

Although the fig tree itself may not blossom, and there may be no yield on the vines; the work of the olive tree may actually turn out a failure, and the terraces themselves may actually produce no food; the flock may actually be severed from the pen, and there may be no herd in the enclosures;

Yet, as for me, I will exult in Jehovah himself; I will be joyful in the God of my salvation.

Jehovah the Sovereign Lord is my vital energy; and he will make my feet like those of the hinds, and upon my high places [level of spiritual understanding Jehovah is providing Lisa] he will cause me to tread.

June 20, 1989

Invitation From Friends:

[We were all invited to Darrell and Ronda Z.'s. They have been very good friends of ours while we've attended this Kingdom Hall. We discussed integrity and faith, searching the scriptures and praying to Jehovah for insight.

We also discussed this scripture.] John 17:3, This means everlasting life, their taking in knowledge of you, the only true God, and of the one whom you sent forth, Jesus Christ.

[We looked at some of the major problems in the organization. Rosie and I told them we were leaving the organization because it had lost Jehovah's holy spirit, but that, by no means, were we leaving Jehovah. They said that they had always considered us to be faithful and honest Christians.

They have been wonderful friends, always to be counted on for smiles and thoughtfulness. Derrall Z. has a wonderful gift in his sense of humor, which is not the same as the wrong kind of practical jokes and irresponsible behavior of at least one of the elders in this congregation, Wayne J.

I have seen Wayne J.'s actions cause distress to one of the new members of the congregation. He was supposed to be leading the way to an out-of-town assembly for several "sisters." We were following him in our own vehicles. He decided to play a racing game with another "brother" from our congregation on the four-lane highway on the edge of the city. This caused one young "sister" who was driving behind him to lose sight of him in traffic. She ended up getting lost on the way to the Assembly Hall. Later, when she finally arrived, she approached Wayne J. about it and asked him why he did it, since he knew she didn't know how to get to the Assembly Hall by herself. She was crying and obviously very upset. Wayne J. laughed it off.

However, Derrall Z., from the same congregation as Wayne J., has not been allowed to become an elder because he once attended a family function of his non-believing family in order to see family members he hadn't seen for a long time. The elders told him that was why he had been held back.

He would have made a wonderful elder. He has a gift for easing a difficult situation with his tactfulness and understanding. And with his knack for the right word at the right time, he can lift the spirits of a person who is troubled.

Darrell asked me if I realized that I could get disfellowshipped if I kept speaking against the organization? I said that I had to speak out and expose serious wrongdoing in the organization, even if it was at personal cost. I mentioned that Jesus and Paul spoke out against the Sanhedrin and the Pharisees, to expose their wrongdoing. I also told Derrall I could not back down and that the time would come when others would also feel the need to take action, regardless of retaliation from the organization. Darrell said he hoped we would come back to them, but that maybe they would be coming to us.

I told them that we loved them all very much. I am going to miss them terribly. Derrall and Ronda have helped me rediscover my own equilibrium and sense of humor, which I badly needed when I was going through some of my saddest days.]

Given: Jeremiah 15:15-21, You yourself have known, O Jehovah, remember me and turn your attention to me and avenge me upon my persecutors. In your slowness to anger do not take me away. Take note of my bearing reproach on account of your own self. **Your words were found, and I [Lisa] proceeded to eat them; and your word becomes to me the exultation and rejoicing of my heart; for your name has been called upon me, O Jehovah God of armies.** I have not sat down in the intimate group of those playing jokes and begun exulting. Because of your hand I have sat down all by myself, for it is with denunciation that you have filled me. Why has my pain become chronic and my stroke incurable? It has refused to be healed. You positively become to me like something deceitful, like waters that have proved untrustworthy.

Jeremiah 3:11, And Jehovah went on to say to me [Lisa]: "Unfaithful Israel [in this instance referring to Rosie] has proved her own soul to be more righteous than treacherously dealing Judah [in this instance referring to Lisa].

[In the past, I have broken my allegiance to Jehovah. And Rosie had been disfellowshipped at one time. My sin was worse than hers. My sin involved treachery because I am in a covenant relationship with Jehovah, and spiritually he is my "husbandly owner." (Isaiah 54:5-8) I broke allegiance back in 1984 when I was spending time with Daniel M. before we were married, who furthermore, was not a worshipper of Jehovah. Rosie and I have both been properly punished and corrected by Jehovah for our grievous wrongdoing. Still, we were required to work hard to be restored to a clean standing in his eyes. Mercifully for us, with Jehovah there is complete forgiveness for our past sins.] [Selah.]

[The punishment I received from Jehovah was appropriate, as with Jehovah, everything always is. Still, I feared for my soul, because my sin was serious. I did not think that I should be allowed to live in the future paradise on earth. But, a friend of mine, Jeff M., a ministerial servant, counseled me at the time and reminded me that all of our actions have built-in consequences which I was experiencing, including feelings of guilt and shame. It is important to fully acknowledge these emotions, because they produce sincere regret. And this helps to firm up our resolve to never repeat the offense. Unlike human judges with limited knowledge of the facts, Jehovah, as Judge, takes everything into consideration in his judgments. His decisions are always right and true. And when Jehovah forgives, he forgives completely.]

Therefore this is what Jehovah has said: "If you will come back, then I shall bring you back. Before me you will stand. **And if you will bring forth what is precious from valueless things, you will become like my own mouth. They themselves will come back to you, but you yourself will not come back to them.**"

[I recall Derrall Z. saying he hoped we would come back to them, but that maybe they would be coming to us.]

Psalm 103:12, As far off as the sunrise is from the sunset, so far off from us he has put our transgressions.

Hebrews 8:12, For I shall be merciful to their unrighteous deeds, and I shall by no means call their sins to mind anymore.

Isaiah 49:2, And he proceeded to make my mouth like a sharp sword. In the shadow of his hand he has hidden me [Lisa]. And he gradually made me a polished arrow. He concealed me in his own quiver.

Matthew 10:40-42, He that receives you receives me [Jesus] also, and he that receives me receives him [Jehovah] also that sent me forth. He that receives a prophet because he is a prophet will get a prophet's reward, and he that receives a righteous man because he is a righteous man will get a righteous man's reward. And whoever gives one of these little ones only a cup of cold water to drink because he is a disciple, I tell you truly, he will by no means lose his reward. [Darrell and Ronda Z. had invited us to their home. We discussed important spiritual matters. At one point, Ronda literally gave our little children (Sunshine, Elee Jo, and Gabrielle) cups of water when they were thirsty. She and Darrell were concerned for our spiritual well-being, not at all considering this scripture about a reward for their acts of kindness.]

Matthew 11:10, This is he concerning whom it is written, "Look! I myself am sending forth my messenger before your face, who will prepare your way ahead of you!"

Research: Insight On The Scriptures, volume 2, page 695 WBTS (1988), **Prophet:** *A prophet suffers great reproach, mockings and even physical mistreatment. Those receiving a prophet favorably, however, were blessed with spiritual and other blessings.*

Matthew 10:24-31, A disciple is not above his teacher, nor a slave above his lord. It is enough for the disciple to become as his teacher, and the slave as his lord. If people have called the householder [Jesus] Beelzebub [referring to Satan, the ruler of demons], how much more will they call those [Jehovah's prophets] of his household so? Therefore do not fear them; for there is nothing covered over that will not become uncovered, and secret that will not become known. What I tell you in the darkness, say in the light; and what you hear whispered, preach from the rooftops. And do not become fearful of those who kill the body but cannot kill the soul; but rather be in fear of him that can destroy both soul and body in Gehenna. [Jehovah has indicated that I will be mistreated as Jesus and the apostles were. Today's events hold secondary significance in the outworking of Jehovah's will in comparison to the suffering Jesus experienced, but "precious in the eyes of Jehovah is the death of his loyal ones." (Psalm

116:15) The present day "Pharisees," those taking the lead in the organization, will try to "kill" me. I am advised, "Have no fear."]

[One of the elders, John G., wants me to attend the assembly this Saturday because the talks are going to be about the deceptive abilities of Satan to draw us away from the true worship of Jehovah. By this he is suggesting that I have been overreached by Satan. Recall: The Circuit Overseer gave me advance warning that the elders would "expel me from the synagogue," disfellowship me from the organization, believing that I have been drawn away from true worship. Yet, in truth, they are the ones who are being deceived by Satan. He has the ability to cloud the minds of those who do not continue to walk in Jehovah's righteous ways.]

Given: [I was told of the "coming" of the prophet Elijah, the spirit of Elijah, actually Jehovah's holy spirit operating in a present day messenger chosen by Jehovah.]

Matthew 11:11b-15, But a person that is a lesser one in the kingdom of the heavens is greater than he is. But from the days of John the Baptist until now the kingdom of the heavens is the goal toward which men press, and those pressing forward are seizing it. For all, the Prophets and the Law, prophesied until John; and if you want to accept it, He himself is Elijah [meaning: "My God is Jehovah"], who is destined to come. **Let him that has ears listen.**

Habakkuk 3:4, As for his brightness, it got to be just like the light. He [Jehovah] had two rays issuing out of his hand, and there the hiding of his strength was.

Habakkuk 3:12-14, With denunciation you [Jehovah] went marching through the earth. In anger you went threshing the nations.
And you went forth for the salvation of your people, to save your anointed one. You broke to pieces the head one out of the house of the wicked one. There was a laying of the foundation bare, clear up to the neck!
With his own rods [their own translation of the Bible], you [Jehovah] pierced the head [governing body of the organization] of

his warriors when they moved tempestuously to scatter me. Their high glee was as of those bent on devouring an afflicted one in a place of concealment [my home].

June 21, 1989

Message: [I was given a message from Jehovah. I was given the word, "Marry."]

Psalm 16:11b, Rejoicing to satisfaction is with your face; there is pleasantness at your right hand forever.

Ephesians 2:19,20, Certainly, therefore, you are no longer strangers and alien residents, but **you are fellow citizens of the holy ones and are members of the household of God**, and you have been built up upon the foundation of the apostles and prophets, while Christ Jesus himself is the foundation cornerstone.

Isaiah 62:4, No more will you [Lisa] be said to be a woman left entirely; and your own land will no more be said to be desolate; but you yourself will be called My Delight Is in Her, and your land Owned as a Wife. **For Jehovah will have taken delight in you, and your own land will be owned as a wife.**

Zechariah 3:2, Then the angel of Jehovah said to Satan: "Jehovah rebuke you, O Satan, yes, Jehovah rebuke you, he who is choosing **Jerusalem!** Is this one [Lisa] not a log snatched out of the fire?"

Isaiah 49:7, This is what Jehovah, the Repurchaser of Israel, his Holy One, has said to him that is despised in soul, to him that is detested by the nation, to the servant of rulers: "Kings themselves will see and certainly rise up, and princes, and they will bow down, by reason of **Jehovah, who is faithful, the Holy One of Israel, who chooses you [Lisa].**

Jeremiah 6:27, "I have made you a metal tester, among my people, one making a thorough search; and you [Lisa] will take note and you must examine their way."

Research: Aid To Bible Understanding, page 698 WBTS, **Prophetess:** *A woman telling forth messages from Jehovah. During a period of national weakness and apostasy, Deborah served figuratively as* ***"a mother in Israel."*** *(Judges 5:7)*

Research: Insight On The Scriptures, volume 1, page 711 WBTS (1988), **Elijah:** *(Another spelling of the prophet's name is Elias* [Elias = anagram: contains the name Lisa], *page 466, footnote)* [Lisa is likened to Elijah.] *Jehovah names three other people who are to be anointed, or commissioned to do a work for him, besides Elijah.*

[Today there are also three others besides Lisa anointed; commissioned for a work:

Leon Wurzer: Zechariah 9:9,17a, Be very joyful, O daughter of Zion. Shout in triumph, O daughter of Jerusalem. Look! Your **king** himself comes to you. He is righteous, yes, saved; humble, and riding upon an ass, even upon a full-grown animal the son of a she-ass.

For O how great his goodness is, and how great his handsomeness is!

Bram Lewis: Isaiah 55:4, Look! As a **witness** to the national groups I have given him, as a leader and commander to the national groups.

Rosie Olson: Matthew 11:9, Really, then, why did you go out? To see a prophet? Yes, I tell you, and far more than a **prophet**.]

Research: **Elijah,** *continued: King Ahab, unfaithful to Jehovah, seeks to kill Elijah. In fear, Elijah prays to die. An angel prepares Elijah for a long journey to Mount Horeb where Jehovah speaks to him in a display of power (wind, earthquake and fire) and shows him he still has work to do, and that he is not the lone worshipper. There is a faithful remnant of 7,000 people. Elijah appoints his successor, Elisha* [Elisha = anagram: contains the name Lisa]. *Elisha becomes his attendant.*

Recall: [In the talk given by the Circuit Overseer at the Lancaster Kingdom Hall, he mentioned a faithful remnant, and that three others besides myself are commissioned (anointed).]

Elijah again meets Ahab who has illegally seized Naboth's vineyard. Ahab has allowed his wife Jezebel to use false charges, false witnesses and unrighteous judges to kill Naboth. Elijah foretells that Ahab's blood will be licked by dogs. Elijah announces a similar fate for Jezebel.

Recall: Revelation 16:6, Because they poured out the blood of holy ones and of prophets, and you have given them blood to drink. They deserve it.

The time comes for Elijah to transfer his mantle to Elisha, who has been well trained. Elisha takes up Elijah's official garment and "two parts" in Elijah's spirit, (like a firstborn son's portion); a spirit of courage and of being "absolutely jealous for Jehovah the God of armies."

Prophecy: Isaiah 66:8, Who has heard of a thing like this? Who has seen things like these? Will a land be brought forth with labor pains in one day? Or will a nation be born at one time? For Zion has come into labor pains as well as given birth to her sons.

Jeremiah 31:9, With weeping they will come, and with their entreaties for favor I shall bring them. I shall make them walk to torrent valleys of water, in a right way in which they will not be caused to stumble. For I have become to Israel a Father; and as for Ephraim, he is my firstborn. [In this instance, Rosie is likened to Ephraim, "a firstborn son," because she was first to believe what I was telling her that Jehovah is doing for his people. She acted on her faith and followed Jehovah's lead. This occurred in Prentice, Wisconsin before Rosie moved down to Lancaster, and before we all moved to Iowa.]

Research: ***Elijah,*** *continued: He is now transferred to another prophetic assignment.* [In our day, my first assignment is to deliver Jehovah's denunciation to the organization.] *Elijah now becomes prophet to the king of Judah.*

! *He writes a letter to the king. It is fulfilled shortly thereafter.*

Ecclesiastes 4:13, Better is a needy but wise child [Lisa], than an old but stupid king [unfaithful "faithful and discreet slave"], who has not come to know enough to be warned any longer.

Habakkuk 2:17, Because the violence done to Lebanon is what will cover you, and the rapacity upon the beasts that terrifies them, **because of the shedding of blood of mankind and the violence done to the earth, the town and all those dwelling in it.** [Our King, Christ, of the tribe of Judah, renders judgment in justice from his heavenly judicial court.]

June 22, 1989

Third Meeting With An Elder: [An elder, Larry M., came to my home.]
2 Timothy 3:5, Having a form of godly devotion but proving false to its power; and from these [the organization and those taking the lead in it] turn away. [We discussed my health. I suffer from depression. We also talked about Susan B., Wayne J., John G. and how I felt about recent events. Larry M. summed up the situation by saying that it amounted to nothing more than that my feelings were hurt.]

Jeremiah 26:1-16, In the beginning of the royal rule of Jehoiakim the son of Josiah, the king of Judah, this word occurred from Jehovah, saying: "This is what Jehovah has said, 'Stand in the courtyard of the house of Jehovah, and you [Lisa] must speak concerning all the cities of **[unfaithful] Judah [governing body of the organization] that are coming in to bow down at the house of Jehovah** all the words that I will command you to speak to them. Do not take away a word. Perhaps they will listen and return, each one from his bad way, and I shall have to feel regret for the calamity that I am thinking to execute upon them because of the badness of their dealings. And you must say to them: "This is what Jehovah has said, 'If you will not listen to me by walking in my law that I have put before you, by listening to the words of my servants the prophets, whom I am sending to you, even rising up early and sending them, whom you have not listened to, I will, in turn, make this house like that in Shiloh, and this city I shall make a malediction to all the nations of the earth.'"'"

And the priests and the prophets and all the people began to hear Jeremiah speaking these words in the house of Jehovah. So it came about that when Jeremiah had completed speaking all that Jehovah had commanded him to speak to all the people, then the priests and the prophets and all the people laid hold of him, saying: "You will positively die. Why is it that you have prophesied in the name of Jehovah, saying, 'Like that in Shiloh is how this house will become, and this very city will be devastated so as to be without an inhabitant'?" And all the people kept congregating themselves about Jeremiah in the house of Jehovah.

In time the princes of Judah [Jesus' heavenly judicial court (2 Corinthians 5:10)] got to hear these words, and they proceeded to come up from the house of the king to the house of Jehovah

and to sit down in the entrance of the new gate of Jehovah. And the priests and the prophets [those taking the lead in the organization] began to say to the princes and to all the people: "To this man the judgment of death belongs, because he has prophesied concerning this city just as you have heard with your own ears."

At that Jeremiah said to all the princes and to all the people: "It was Jehovah that sent me to prophesy concerning this house and concerning this city all the words that you have heard. And now make your ways and your dealings good, and obey the voice of Jehovah your God, and Jehovah will feel regret for the calamity that he has spoken against you. And as for me, here I am in your hand. Do to me according to what is good and according to what is right in your eyes. Only you should by all means know that, if you are putting me to death, it is innocent blood that you are putting upon yourselves and upon this city and upon her inhabitants, for in truth Jehovah did send me to you to speak in your ears all these words."

Then the princes and all the people **[Jesus' heavenly judicial court]** said to the priests and to the prophets [those taking the lead in the organization today, who do not heed]: **"There is no judgment of death belonging to this man [Lisa], for it was in the name of Jehovah our God that he spoke to us."**

[Today's priests and prophets, those taking the lead in the organization of Jehovah's Witnesses, carry out the execution of Jehovah's prophet.]

Jeremiah 31:33, "For this is the covenant that I shall conclude with the [faithful] house of Israel **after those days**," is the utterance of Jehovah. **"I will put my law within them, and in their heart I shall write it. And I will become their God, and they themselves will become my people."**

Scriptures: These are a few of the scriptures indicated by Jehovah, to be included in his denunciation of the organization of Jehovah's Witnesses:

Matthew 23:4,5, They bind up heavy loads and put them upon the shoulders of men, but they themselves are not willing to budge them with their finger. All the works they do they do to be viewed by men; for they broaden the scripture-containing cases that they wear as safeguards, and enlarge the fringes of their garments.

Matthew 24:15, Therefore, when you catch sight of the disgusting thing that causes desolation, as spoken of through Daniel the prophet, standing in a holy place, (let the reader use discernment,) then let those in Judea begin fleeing to the mountains.

Jeremiah 5:26-31, For among my people there have been found wicked men. They keep peering, as when birdcatchers crouch down. They have set a ruinous trap. It is men that they catch. As a cage is full of flying creatures, so their houses are full of deception. That is why they have become great and they gain riches. They have grown fat; they have become shiny. They have also overflowed with bad things. No legal case have they pleaded, even the legal case of the fatherless boy, that they may gain success; and the judgment of the poor ones they have not taken up.

"Should I not hold an accounting because of these very things," is the utterance of Jehovah, "or on a nation that is like this should not my soul avenge itself? **An astonishing situation, even a horrible thing, has been brought to be in the land: The prophets themselves actually prophesy in falsehood; and as for the priests, they go subduing according to their powers. And my own people have loved it that way; and what will you men do in the finale of it?"**

Jeremiah 6:21-23, Therefore this is what Jehovah has said: "Here I am setting for this [unfaithful] people **stumbling blocks**, and they will certainly stumble over them, fathers and sons together; the neighbor and his companion—they will perish."

This is what Jehovah has said: "Look! A people is coming from the land of the north, and there is a great nation that will be awakened from the remotest parts of the earth. The bow and the javelin they will grab hold of. It is a cruel one, and they will have no pity. Their very voice will resound just like the sea, and upon horses they will ride. It is drawn up in battle order like a man of war against you [those taking the lead in the organization], O [unfaithful] daughter of Zion."

Jeremiah 22;13, Woe to the one building his house, but not with righteousness, and his upper chambers, but not with justice, by use of his fellowman who serves for nothing, and whose wages he does not give him.

Psalm 12:5, "Because of the despoiling of the afflicted ones, because of the sighing of the poor ones, I shall at this time arise," says Jehovah. "I shall put him in safety from anyone that puffs at him."

Prophecy Fulfillment: Ecclesiastes 9:13-17, Also this I saw as respects wisdom under the sun—and it was great to me: There was a little city, and the men in it were few; and there came to it a great king, and he surrounded it and built against it great strongholds. And there was found in it a man, needy but wise, and that one provided escape for the city by his wisdom. But no man remembered that needy man. And I myself said: "Wisdom is better than mightiness; yet the wisdom of the needy one is despised, and his words are not listened to."

The words of the wise ones in quietness are more to be heard than the cry of one ruling among stupid people.

[Jehovah gave me these scriptures and told me that I had fulfilled this prophecy. When I first moved to Lancaster, Wisconsin from Iowa, I had sent a letter to the organization headquarters in New York, concerning some of the elders in the Kingdom Hall in Iowa City, Iowa U.S.A., a "little city." These elders had been overreached by Satan, a "great king," and were mistreating the flock. (At the time I lived in Iowa City, my level of income was considered "needy," sub-poverty level.) My letter to their headquarters was disregarded and there was no investigation.

And, since then it has been said that a young woman in this congregation committed suicide as the result of harsh treatment by at least one of these elders.]

Psalm 14:6, The counsel of the afflicted one you people would put to shame, because Jehovah is his refuge.

June 23, 1989

Parallel Events: [Events surrounding the last days of Jesus' life on earth have become prophecies that are being fulfilled through parallel events occurring today.

Many other faithful worshippers of Jehovah besides myself have experienced derision, false accusations and finally "death" through disfellowshipping at the hands of present day "Pharisees," those taking the lead in the organization. Today's events hold secondary significance in the outworking of Jehovah's will in comparison to the suffering Jesus experienced, but "precious in the eyes of Jehovah is the death of his loyal ones." (Psalm 116:15)]

Fourth Meeting With Elders: [This meeting also took place in my home.]

[Elders Larry M., John G., and Wayne J. came to my home. During the meeting, I repeated that the mistreatment of the flock by the shepherds, or their allowance of mistreatment by other members of the congregation, is a major issue on a broad scale in the organization. **It is lack of justice.** Those taking the lead in the organization bear special accountability to Jehovah, as they are to shepherd the flock tenderly and not disregard justice. (Acts 20:28,29; Matthew 23:23; Luke 11:42)

I brought up prophetic patterns. Israel, as a nation, suffered for disobedience. Larry disagreed. He said only individuals suffered. I suggested the "Insight On The Scriptures" book could give us an idea of how many people ended up in exile in Babylon. He insisted that only individuals would suffer, and that even if Jehovah became angry, he would not stop using the organization. I said that according to patterns of the past he very well could.

Larry M. said that Jesus was proved righteous by works and asked, "Where are yours?" (My thought here is that Jesus has never needed to be proved righteous by works or by any other means. He is righteous.) My answer to Larry M. was that we had the work of witnessing to them, which we were doing at this very moment; that we had been given the work of warning others. Wayne J. said to Larry M. that I was "teaching" them, which I found curious. Rosie later said that John G. was researching apostasy while Larry was talking to me.

During the meeting, I also said that if responsible ones throughout the organization, right up to the governing body, did not keep the congregation in a clean and approved condition before Jehovah, a contamination could take place.] A little leaven ferments the whole lump. (1 Corinthians 5:6b) [Jehovah could become angry enough to remove his holy spirit from the entire organization. Larry said there would always be a "faithful and discreet slave," and if Jehovah has left the organization, "Where is the faithful and discreet slave?" He said, "Jehovah would continue his light somewhere else."

I said, "That's exactly right."

Larry said, "Where did it go?"

I said, "Jehovah would have continued it somewhere else." Larry M. was baiting me. They were trying to find grounds to disfellowship me. They wanted me to call myself a prophet, so that they would have something to condemn me for.

Then I gave them the list of scriptures Jehovah has given me, which include reference to] Jeremiah 4:23, I saw the land, and, look! it was empty and waste; and into the heavens, and their light was no more.

[It also included] Isaiah 60:1, "Arise, O woman, shed forth light, for your light has come and upon you the very glory of Jehovah has shone forth."

[I said to the elders, "As you three are here in a judicial capacity, I'm asking you to judge me on the basis of the scriptures Jehovah has given me." Larry said Jehovah had given them the same scriptures, acting as though he wouldn't even read them. Then he said, "We're not here as a judicial committee." He was lying. It is very clear to me that they want to disfellowship me.

When those taking the lead in the organization close their ears to Jehovah's truth and righteousness from the scriptures, they are, in effect, resisting Jehovah's holy spirit. Jehovah is **very angry** with them.]

Ezekiel 33:30-33, "And as for you, O son of man, the sons of your people are speaking with one another about you beside the walls and in the entrances of the houses, and the one has spoken with the other, each with his brother, saying, 'Come, please, and hear what the word is that is going forth from Jehovah.' And they will come in to you [Lisa], like the coming in of people, and sit before you as my people; and they will certainly hear your words but these they will not do, for with their mouth they are expressing lustful desires and after their unjust gain is where their heart is going. And, look! you are to them like a song of sensuous loves, like one with a pretty voice and playing a stringed instrument well. And they will certainly hear your words, but there are none doing them. And when it comes true—look! it must come true—they will also have to know that a prophet had proved to be in the midst of them.

Deuteronomy 32:39-42, See now that I—I am he [Jehovah] and there are no gods together with me. I put to death, and I make alive. I have severely wounded, and I—I will heal, and there is no one snatching out of my hand. For I raise my hand to heaven in an oath, and I do say: "As I am alive to time indefinite," if I do indeed sharpen my glittering sword, and my hand takes hold on judgment, I will pay back vengeance to my adversaries and render retribution to those who intensely hate me. I shall intoxicate my arrows with blood, while my sword will eat flesh, with the blood of the slain and the captives, with the heads of the leaders [governing body of the organization] of the enemy.
[Jehovah "arrows" are his denunciation. The "slain" ones are those who have been falsely accused and wrongly disfellowshipped.]

Revelation 16:4-7, And the third one poured out his bowl into the rivers and the fountains of the waters. And they became blood. And I heard the angel over the waters say: "You, the One who is and who was, the loyal One, are righteous, because you have rendered these decisions, because they poured out the blood of holy ones and of prophets, and you have given them blood to drink. They deserve it." And I heard the altar say: "Yes, Jehovah God, the Almighty, true and righteous are your judicial decisions."

Zechariah 9:11,12, Also, you, O woman [Lisa], by the blood of your covenant I will send your prisoners out of the pit [the organization] in which there is no water. Return to the stronghold [Jehovah is our stronghold. (Psalm 91:2)], you prisoners [faithful worshippers of Jehovah still in the organization] of the hope.

Zechariah 4:14, Accordingly he said: "These are the **two anointed ones** who are standing alongside the Lord of the whole earth."

Haggai 2:4,5, "But now be strong, O Zerubbabel [Leon]," is the utterance of Jehovah, "and be strong, O Joshua the son of Jehozadak the high priest [Lisa]."

Zechariah 2:13, Keep silence, all flesh, before Jehovah, for he has aroused himself from his holy dwelling.

Psalm 8:1,2, O Jehovah our Lord, how majestic your name is in all the earth, you whose dignity is recounted above the heavens! Out of the mouth of children and sucklings you have founded strength, on account of those showing hostility to you, so as to make the enemy and the one taking his vengeance desist.

Exodus 29:43-46, And I will present myself there to the [faithful] sons of Israel, and it will certainly be sanctified by my glory, and I will sanctify the tent of meeting and the altar; and I shall sanctify Aaron and his sons for them to act as priests to me. And I will tabernacle in the midst of the sons of Israel, and I will prove to be their God. And they will certainly know that I am Jehovah their God, who brought them out of the land of Egypt [out of the unfaithful organization] that I may tabernacle in the midst of them. I am Jehovah their God.

Exodus 34:8-10, Moses at once hurried to bow low to the earth and prostrate himself. Then he said: "If, now, I have found favor in your eyes, O Jehovah, let Jehovah, please, go along in the midst of us, because it is a stiff-necked people, and you have to forgive our error and our sin, and you must take us as your possession." In turn he said: "Here I am concluding a covenant: Before all your people I shall do wonderful things that have never been created in all the earth or among all the nations; and all the people in the midst of whom you are will indeed see the work of Jehovah, because it is a fear-inspiring thing that I am doing with you."

June 26, 1989

New Covenant: [**Jehovah begins a new covenant with his people tomorrow, June 27, 1989.**]

> Bram's Notes: Jehovah went over the land with his denunciation by literal storm.

Angel: Recall: [We recalled to our minds the message Jehovah has sent us. There is a sword coming, but we will be safe. It will pass over us, and Gabrielle, my daughter, will be safe.]

Jehovah's Denunciation Comes: Isaiah 26:20,21, Go, my people, enter into your interior rooms, and shut your doors behind you. Hide yourself for but a moment until the denunciation passes over. [A very powerful windstorm came. We shut the doors and windows. I was literally in an interior room for a few minutes while Jehovah's denunciation passed over. **I sensed Jehovah coming in the windstorm.** Bram and Rosie both mentioned later that at the time of the windstorm, though being in two different parts of town at the time, they each independently thought the same thing.] For, look! Jehovah is coming forth from his place to call to account the error of the inhabitant of the land against him, and the land [the organization of Jehovah's Witnesses] will certainly expose her bloodshed and will no longer cover over her killed ones. [As the windstorm approached, I felt tranquil. Our children all came inside, and I said, "None of them are missing." I was referring to this scripture.] Jeremiah 23:4, "And I will raise up over them shepherds who will actually shepherd them; and they will be afraid no more, neither will they be struck with any terror, and none will be missing," is the utterance of Jehovah.

Psalm 96:11-13, Let the heavens rejoice, and let the earth be joyful. Let the sea thunder and that which fills it. Let the open field exult and all that is in it. At the same time let all the trees of the forest break out joyfully before Jehovah. **For he has come; for he has come to judge the earth.** He will judge the productive land with righteousness and the peoples with his faithfulness.

Isaiah 26:19, Your dead ones will live. A corpse of mine—they will rise up. Awake and cry out joyfully, you residents in the dust! For your dew is as the dew of mallows, and the earth itself will let even those impotent in death drop in birth.

Deuteronomy 32:39, See now that I—I am he [Jehovah] and there are no gods together with me. I put to death, and I make alive. I have severely wounded, and I—I will heal, and there is no one snatching out of my hand. [Jehovah's denunciation literally swept over the land the day before our "death;" the day that they disfellowshipped us.]

Discovery: Exodus 29:38, And this is what you will offer upon the altar: young rams each a year old, two a day constantly.
Awake! magazine, WBTS July 8, 1989, [On the cover was a death's head. Considering everything that the *Awake!* magazine is supposed to stand for, I was astonished. It brought to my mind "the disgusting thing that causes desolation."] Matthew 24:15,16, Therefore, when you catch sight of the disgusting thing that causes desolation, as spoken of through Daniel the prophet, standing in a holy place, (let the reader use discernment,) then let those in Judea begin fleeing to the mountains.

[The *Awake!* magazine is a constant feature of the organization.]

Daniel 8:9-13, And out of one of them there came forth another horn, a small one, and it kept getting very much greater toward the south and toward the sunrising and toward the Decoration. And it kept getting greater all the way to the army of the heavens, so that it caused some of the army and some of the stars to fall to the earth, and it went trampling them down. And all the way to the Prince of the army it put on great airs, and from him the constant feature was taken away, and the established place of his sanctuary was thrown down. And an army itself was gradually given over, together with the constant feature, because of transgression; and it kept throwing truth to the earth, and it acted and had success.

And I got to hear a certain holy one speaking, and another holy one proceeded to say to the particular one who was speaking: "How long will the vision be of the constant feature and of the transgression causing desolation, to make both the holy place and the army things to trample on?"

[Transgression here would mean that righteous ones were acting unrighteously, even falling away from Jehovah, causing "desolation" to faithful members. The "constant feature" was taken away from the "Prince of the army" of the heavens, and "the established place of his sanctuary," a holy place, was thrown down. In Matthew 24:15, the disgusting thing that causes desolation is standing in a holy place, replacing what is supposed to stand there. Daniel 8:12 mentions that it kept "throwing truth to the earth." Truth has certainly been subverted by the organization, and its publications reflect that fact.]

> Rosie's Notes: Ezekiel 33:33, And when it comes true—look! it must come true—they will also have to know that a prophet himself had proved to be in the midst of them.

Discovery: *Awake!* magazine, [The article on Zechariah was tampered with to mislead the reader.]

Ezekiel 33:2-4,6, Son of man, speak to the sons of your people, and you must say to them,

"As regards a land, in case I bring upon it a sword and the people of the land, one and all, actually take a man and set him as their watchman, and he really sees the sword coming upon the land and blows the horn and warns the people, and the hearer actually hears the sound of the horn but he takes no warning at all, and a sword comes and takes him away, his own blood will come to be upon his own head. The sound of the horn he heard, but he took no warning. His own blood will come to be upon his own self. Now as regards the watchman [Both the *Watchtower* and *Awake!* magazines are supposed to live up to their names. The *Watchtower* is supposed to keep "on the watch" and the *Awake!* magazine is supposed to keep "awake." Jehovah's denunciation warns them that a sword is coming against the organization of Jehovah's Witnesses, but their "watchman," the unfaithful "faithful and discreet slave," does not warn the people about the sword.] in case he sees the sword coming and he actually does not blow the horn and the people itself gets no warning at all and a sword comes and takes away from them soul, for its own error it itself must be taken away, **but its blood I shall ask back from the hand of the watchman himself.**"

[In this article, someone added the words, "those of Christendom." If those words had not been added, alert or **"awake"** readers might have recognized the scriptures were describing the Watchtower Bible and Tract Society, the organization known as Jehovah's Witnesses. Their "watchman," does not warn the people and the "sanctuary," (Daniel 8:11) a holy place (a place where people worship Jehovah) gets thrown down because truth has been thrown down. The people are overreached by the sword, and the blood of the people is going to be asked back by Jehovah, from the hand of the "watchman."]

Recall: [In the talk given by the Circuit Overseer, James Thatcher, at the Kingdom Hall in Lancaster, Wisconsin U.S.A., he likened me to Jeremiah.] Jeremiah 6:27, I have made you a metal tester among my people, one making a thorough search; and you will take note and you must examine their way. [In the ten years I have been a member of the organization, I have associated with five different congregations. I have also had the opportunity to associate with many other members at assembles.

Even from the beginning of my association with his people, Jehovah was causing me to become acutely aware of the many different attitudes among those taking the lead, as well as the attitudes among the rest of the association of spiritual "brothers" and "sisters."

Among those taking the lead I have met several wonderful elders and circuit overseers; very sincere Christians. I count many of them as precious friends. I fervently hope to see them all again, as Jehovah begins calling his "sheeplike" ones to his light. In my journal here, when I make mention of "those taking the lead" in the organization, I am **not referring to these kind and helpful elders and circuit overseers**, although their positions would seem to place them in that category.

What I have discovered during my association with different ones is that "those taking the lead" in the organization are doing just that—**TAKING** the lead, whether Jehovah has **GIVEN** them this **privilege** or not. More and more, over the years that I associated with the organization, I saw what appeared to be a **subtle takeover**. The more aggressive and arrogant personalities were **taking** the lead away from the more cooperative, mild-tempered Christian personalities.

This is not to say that a person's personality cannot change from the first type to the second or from the second type to the first. In fact, a person can simply drift toward the arrogant personality, whereas it takes constant spiritual effort to change to a more mild-tempered personality.] Acts 20:29,30, I know that after my [Jesus'] going away oppressive wolves will enter in among you and will not treat the flock with tenderness, and from among you yourselves men will rise [advance in standing within the organization] and speak twisted things to draw away the disciples after themselves.

[We each need to examine ourselves closely to determine which type of personality we have chosen. We can make the necessary changes to correct wrong tendencies. And if we have strayed—with Jehovah there is complete forgiveness for those of us who sincerely regret our wrongdoing, and seek to put it right. I have needed Jehovah's forgiveness and correction. I have needed to learn and change.

And, we need to look about us and ascertain which of those in the organization are harmed most by the oppressive "wolves." They will usually be the hurt "lambs" among the "sheep."]

Jeremiah 49:20b,21a, Surely the little ones of the flock will be dragged about. Surely on account of them he [Jehovah] will make their dwelling place [the organization of Jehovah's Witnesses] become desolate. At the sound of their falling the earth has begun to rock. There is an outcry! [Although this scripture certainly applies to young children in the congregations, there are many others as well. Wolves are predators, and recognize vulnerability in all its forms: the poor and the weak, the sick and the aged, the physically and emotionally disabled.

We can redouble our efforts to strengthen and encourage each one. More than anything, they need our compassion and loving-kindness (loyal love). We must be so careful to do no harm to any of Jehovah's hurt "lambs." And we must help these individuals to earnestly seek Jehovah himself—his strength and protection—his great compassion and loyal love. Jehovah is calling everyone to him. We cannot leave any faithful worshippers of Jehovah behind.]

Jehovah Sent These People To Me:

[Ronda Z. welcomed us into their home. After we had talked at length, she said: "If it (my work) is from God it cannot be overturned." Afterward, I was given these scriptures. Matthew 10:40-42 [abbreviated here], He that receives a prophet will get a prophet's reward, and whoever gives one of these little ones only a cup of cold water to drink because he is a disciple, I tell you truly, he will by no means lose his reward. (This brought back to my mind that while we were there, Ronda gave our "little ones" drinks of water.)

Darrell Z. said: "Maybe you'll come back to us, but maybe we'll be coming to you." Later, Jehovah gave me this scripture: They themselves will come back to you, but you yourself will not come back to them. (Jeremiah 15:19)

Bethel E. brought Rosie flowers, and offered her sympathy. She told Rosie that no one came to help her when she was ailing.

Ruth F. called on the phone. We were encouraged to stay with Jehovah's Witnesses. She said that the elders have a problem. One problem is between John G. and Marvin F., Ruth's husband. She also said their disfellowshipping was unjust.

Marvin F. said elder, John G., acts like he thinks he is a king. He said that the elder's judicial committee was a kangaroo court. He advised me to remain calm.

Tina O. told me that she does not let others put me down. She said she tells them that I always encourage her spiritually.

Robin F. called on the phone and begged me to stay with Jehovah's Witnesses, and to get to the meetings. She said she loves us and she would come to visit us. She also said she would say something to elder, Larry M. about not disassociating me. She said she knew that I was a very good mother, contrary to Susan B's talk against me in the congregation. She said that Larry M.'s children's behavior shows that Larry has a problem.

Lila J. called me two times. She said: "Jehovah will prove it out." She also said: "Anyone, but not Lisa." (It was hard for her to imagine me being disfellowshipped.)

Jan and Daryl B. called three times long distance from Iowa. Jan was very upset. They urged me to stay with Jehovah's Witnesses.]

Friends: [These people are very precious friends. They are all concerned for my spiritual well-being, and fear for me if I am disfellowshipped. It is difficult leaving my friends behind, knowing that they will be told that I am an apostate, and that I have fallen from good standing with Jehovah. They will not be allowed to contact me in any way.

I will miss them and many others as well that are not mentioned here. I fervently hope that I will see all of them again, and that some day we will all be reunited in worship of Jehovah, as dearly beloved friends and members of Jehovah's vast spiritual family.]

June 27, 1989

Fifth Meeting With Elders: [This meeting took place at the newly built Kingdom Hall in Fennimore, Wisconsin]

Given: [Before the meeting, I was given these scriptures from Jehovah.] Jeremiah 5:12-15,24,25, They have denied Jehovah, and they keep saying, "He is not, and upon us no calamity will come, and no sword or famine shall we see." **And the prophets themselves become a wind, and the word is not in them. That is how it will be done to them.**

Therefore this is what Jehovah, the God of armies, has said: "For the reason that you men are saying this thing, here I am making my words in your [Lisa's] mouth a fire, and this people will be pieces of wood, and it will certainly devour them.

Here I am bringing in upon you men a nation from far away, O [unfaithful] house of Israel," is the utterance of Jehovah, "It is an enduring nation. It is a [heavenly] nation of long ago, a nation whose language you do not know, and you cannot hear understandingly what they speak.

But they [unfaithful ones taking the lead in the organization] have not said in their heart: "Let us, now, fear Jehovah our God, the One who is giving the downpour and the autumn rain and the spring rain in its season, the One who guards even the prescribed weeks of the harvest for us." Your own errors have turned these things away, and your own sins have held back what is good from you people.

Hebrews 1:7, Also, with reference to the angels he says: "And he makes his angels spirits, and **his public servants a flame of fire.**"

[Bram and I were called to a meeting with the judicial committee of three elders who had met with us previously. They had wanted us to meet at the former Kingdom Hall in Lancaster, which would shortly be shut down as they had just built a new Kingdom Hall. Somehow, we all ended up at the Fennimore Kingdom Hall.]

Psalm 2:9,12, "You will break them with an iron scepter, as though a potter's vessel you will dash them to pieces." And now, O kings [governing body of the organization], exercise insight; let yourselves be corrected, O judges [those taking the lead in the organization] of the earth. Serve Jehovah with fear and be joyful with trembling. Kiss the son, that He may not become incensed and you may not perish from the way, for his anger flares up easily. Happy are all those taking refuge in him.

Questioned: [The elders questioned me: "Do you feel Jehovah is directing you personally with holy spirit?" I read this scripture to them:] Jeremiah 22:13, "Woe to the one building his house, but not with righteousness, and his upper chambers, but not with justice, by use of his fellowman who serves for nothing, and whose wages he does not give him." [The elder, John G. asked me what I was insinuating. I gave no response but he said he thought he knew what I was referring to, which was their new Kingdom Hall, and the organization as a whole. He had said at a previous meeting with us that he was confident of their standing with Jehovah because they had just finished building the new Kingdom Hall, and they had an increase in members.]

Accused: [When I was being accused, I told them I would follow the example of Jesus before his accusers. (Mark 14:61) He had remained silent. But because I remained silent and did not deny the accusations, the elder, John G., took my silence as a sign of guilt.]

Scriptures: [I read these scriptures to the elders at the meeting.]

Acts 5:38,39, And so, under the present circumstances, I say to you, Do not meddle with these men [Bram, Rosie, Lisa], but let them alone; (because if this scheme or this work is from men, it will be overthrown; but if it is from God, you will not be able to overthrow them;) otherwise, you may perhaps be found fighters actually against God.

Matthew 27:22-24, Pilate said to them: "What, then, shall I do with Jesus the so-called Christ?" They all said: "Let him be impaled!" He said: "Why, what bad thing did he do?" Still they kept crying out all the more: "Let him be impaled!"

Seeing that it did no good but, rather, an uproar was arising, Pilate took water and washed his hands before the crowd, saying: "I am innocent of the blood of this man. You yourselves must see to it."

Malachi 1:10, "Who also is there among you that will shut the doors? And you men will not light my altar—for nothing. No delight do I have in you [unfaithful elders]," Jehovah of armies has said, "and in the gift offering from your hand I take no pleasure."

Jeremiah 50:35-38, "There is a sword against the Chaldeans [earlier inhabitants of Babylon]," is the utterance of Jehovah, "and against the inhabitants of Babylon and against her princes [those taking the lead] and against her wise ones [governing body]. There is a sword against the empty talkers, and they will certainly act foolishly. There is a sword against her mighty men, and they will actually become terrified. There is a sword against their horses and against their war chariots and against all the mixed company that are in the midst of her, and they will certainly become women. There is a sword against her treasures, and they will actually be plundered. There is a devastation upon her waters [membership], and they must be dried up. For it is a land of graven images, and because of their frightful visions they keep acting crazy."

Given: This scripture was given to me from Jehovah: Titus 2:15, Keep on speaking these things and exhorting and reproving with full authority to command. Let no man ever despise you.

> Bram's Notes: I've been physically sick in the last few days, and I felt terrible. I had a high fever and my back was in pain. That evening we were "killed" spiritually (in their eyes). We were disfellowshipped on a false charge—apostasy. We saw the most spectacular sunset that evening.

[My son, Bram, told me he had a bad headache and a head cold. He felt a piercing pain in his back. He was tired and wanted to sleep. He also had a sore throat and it was difficult for him to talk. He told me he was a little depressed. Still, in this condition, he went to the "slaughter." He and I were disfellowshipped this evening.]

Disfellowshipped: [We were lied to, humiliated by false accusations, judged guilty of apostasy, and thrown out of the organization by the elders. In their eyes we are considered as dead persons.]

Portent: [Tuesday evening, June 27, 1989, After the meeting at which Bram and I were disfellowshipped, both of us saw a portent in the sunset sky. It was truly a marvel. We stopped the car to look at it. The shape of it was brilliantly lit, fiery red and huge. It was a very clear image of the face of Christ. We could see three fourths of his upper face rising up from the horizon. The other part of his face was partially concealed in the dark side of the cloud. I looked for a sword, recalling that he would come with one and to the right of his face, in the clouds, an arm was extending, holding a scepter. The head of the scepter had a strange, unrecognizable configuration.]

Given: [I had been given this scripture before the meeting with the elders: Psalm 2:2-12, The kings [unfaithful "faithful and discreet slave"] of the earth take their stand, and high officials [governing body of the organization] themselves have massed together as one against Jehovah and against his anointed one, saying: "Let us tear their bands apart and cast their cords away from us!" The very One sitting in the heavens will laugh; Jehovah himself will hold them in derision. At that time he will speak to them in his anger and in his hot displeasure he will disturb them, saying: "I, even I, have installed my king upon Zion, my holy mountain." Let me refer to the decree of Jehovah; he has said to me: "You are my son; I, today, I have become your father. Ask of me, that I may give nations as your inheritance, and the ends of the earth as your own possession. You will break them with an iron scepter, as though a potter's vessel you will dash them to pieces." And now, O kings, exercise insight; let yourselves be corrected, O judges of the earth. Serve Jehovah with fear and be joyful with trembling. Kiss the son, that He may not become incensed and you may not perish from the way, for his *anger flares* up easily. Happy are all those taking refuge in him.

Luke 21:25-28, especially verse 27, Also, there will be signs in sun and moon and stars, and on the earth anguish of nations, not knowing the way out because of the roaring of the sea and its agitation, while men become faint out of fear and expectation of the things coming upon the inhabited earth; for the powers of the heavens will be shaken. **And then they will see the Son of man coming in a cloud with power and great glory.** [His face and presence were very powerful. He had a **scepter in his hand**, not a sword, because Christ's glory is that of a king. Later as I dwelled on this, I realized that the head of the scepter was a **flame**.]

[I was also given:] Luke 12:54, Then he went on to say also to the crowds: "**When you see a cloud rising in western parts**, at once you say, '**A storm is coming**,' and it turns out to be so. [The face of Christ was rising from the **western horizon; powerful, and with anger in his eyes**.]

Under The Earth: [I spent the next three days putting a new binding on a book belonging to the Kingdom Hall, which the elders had previously brought to me. I have a bookbinding shop in my basement, so I was working below ground—literally. I finished the book on the third day.]

June 28-29, 1989

> Bram's Notes: My mother was given a scripture about fire. She was also given scriptures on greetings from heaven above.

Given: [I had remained calm during the meeting, even as I warned the elders of Jehovah's anger with them. However, I was concerned that Jehovah might be displeased with me because I also became angry with the elders for their resistance to Jehovah's holy spirit, and their false accusations. I prayed to Jehovah and was given his answer through this scripture.] Luke 12:49, I [Jesus speaking] came to start a fire on the earth, and what more is there for me to wish if it has already been lighted?

Given: Jeremiah 5:14, Therefore this is what Jehovah, the God of armies, has said: "For the reason that you men are saying this thing, here I am making my words in your [Lisa's] mouth a fire, and this people will be pieces of wood, and it will certainly devour them." [I was given this scripture before the meeting with the elders, Tuesday evening.]

Given: Jeremiah 30:23-24, Look! A windstorm of Jehovah, rage itself, has gone forth, an onward sweeping tempest. Upon the head of the wicked ones it will whirl. The burning anger of Jehovah will not turn back until he will have executed and until he will have carried out the ideas of his heart. In the final part of the days you people will give your consideration to it.

Given: 2 John all verses, The older man [Jehovah] to the chosen lady [Lisa] and to her children [Rosie, Bram, and the three children], whom I truly love, and not I alone, but all those also who have come to know the truth, because of the truth that remains in us, and it will be with us forever. There will be with us undeserved kindness, mercy and peace from God the Father and from Jesus Christ the Son of the Father, with truth and love.

I rejoice very much because I have found certain ones of your children walking in the truth, just as we received commandment from the Father. So now I request you, lady, as a person writing you, not a new commandment, but one which we had from the beginning, that we love one another. **And this is what love means, that we go on walking according to his commandments.** This is the commandment, just as you people have heard from the beginning, that you should go on walking in it. For many deceivers have gone forth into the world, persons not confessing Jesus Christ as coming in the flesh. This is the deceiver and the antichrist.

Look out for yourselves, that you do not lose the things we have worked to produce, but that you may obtain a full reward. Everyone that pushes ahead and does not remain in the teaching of the Christ does not have God. He that does remain in this teaching is the one that has both the Father and the Son. If anyone comes to you and does not bring this teaching, never receive him into your homes or say a greeting to him. For he that says a greeting to him is a sharer in his wicked works.

Although I have many things to write you, I do not desire to do so with paper and ink, but I am hoping to come to you and to speak with you face to face, that your joy may be in full measure.

The children [144,000 (Revelation 14:3)] of your sister [heavenly organization], the chosen one, send you their greetings.

June 30, 1989

Denunciation: [I mailed out Jehovah's denunciation Friday after 5:30p.m.]

Overview Of The Week: [This is an overview of the events taking place Monday, June 26 through Friday, June 30, 1989.]

Monday, June 26, [Literally, a windstorm swept through. We sensed Jehovah's presence.]

[This is one of the scriptures given.] Isaiah 26:20, Go, my people, enter into your interior rooms, and shut your doors behind you. Hide yourself for but a moment until the denunciation passes over.

[Jehovah has come to call to account the bad ways and dealings of the unfaithful people who call themselves by his name, Jehovah's Witnesses.]

Tuesday, June 27, [Bram and I were disfellowshipped Tuesday evening. June 27th was the first day of the new covenant. We saw a portent in the western sky: Christ, in a cloud.]

[These scriptures were given:] Luke 12:49,54, I came to start a fire on the earth, and what more is there for me to wish if it has already been lighted.

Then he went on to say also to the crowds: "When you see a cloud rising in western parts, at once you say, 'A storm is coming,' and it turns out so.

Wednesday, June 28, [I was given this scripture.] Psalm 96:11-13, Let the heavens rejoice, and let the earth be joyful. Let the sea thunder and that which fills it. Let the open field exult and all that is in it. At the same time let all the trees of the forest break out joyfully, before Jehovah. For he has come; for he has come to judge the earth. He will judge the productive land with righteousness and the peoples with his faithfulness.

[I was also given the book of 2 John.] 2 John, all verses [abbreviated here], The older man [Jehovah] to the chosen lady [Lisa] and to her children [Rosie, Bram, and the three children].

The children [144,000] of your sister [heavenly organization], the chosen one, send you their greetings.

Jeremiah 30:23,24, Look! A windstorm of Jehovah, rage itself, has gone forth, an onward sweeping tempest. Upon the head of the wicked ones it will whirl.

Thursday, June 29, [I made phone calls to locate places for all of us to live back in Iowa.]

Friday, June 30, [I finished binding the Kingdom Hall book for the elders. The denunciation was mailed out. I was given this scripture.] Zechariah 5:2b, In turn I said: **"I am seeing a flying scroll,** the length of which is 20 cubits, and the breadth of which is 10 cubits." [This is roughly the shape of a business size envelope, which Jehovah's denunciation was mailed out in. The domestic mail had stamps with bees with wings on them, and the foreign airmail stamps had an "Aviator Pioneer" plane on them. These stamps both depicted means of flying; therefore, "a flying scroll."]

Isaiah 40:1-11, "Comfort, comfort my people," says the God of you men. "Speak to the heart of Jerusalem [Lisa] and call out to her that her military service has been fulfilled, that her error has been paid off. For from the hand of Jehovah she has received a full amount for all her sins."

Listen! Someone is calling out in the wilderness: "Clear up the way of Jehovah, you people! Make the highway for our God through the desert plain straight. Let every valley be raised up, and every mountain and hill be made low. And the knobby ground must become level land, and the rugged ground a valley plain, And the glory of Jehovah will certainly be revealed, and all flesh must see it together, for the very mouth of Jehovah has spoken it."

Listen! Someone is saying: "Call out!" And one said: "What shall I call out?"

"All flesh is green grass, and all their loving-kindness is like the blossom of the field. The green grass has dried up, the blossom has withered, because the very spirit of Jehovah has blown upon it.

Surely the people are green grass. The green grass has dried up, the blossom has withered; but as for the word of our God, it will last to time indefinite.

Make your way up even onto a high mountain, you woman [Lisa] bringing good news for Zion. **Raise your voice even with power**, you woman bringing good news for Jerusalem. Raise it. Do not be afraid. Say to the cities of Judah: **"Here is your God."** Look! The Sovereign Lord Jehovah himself will come [He has come!! June 26, 1989] even as a strong one, and his arm will be ruling for him. Look! His reward is with him, and the wage he pays is before him. Like a shepherd he will shepherd his own drove. With his arm he will collect together the lambs; and in his bosom [protective place; close in friendship] he will carry them. Those giving suck he will conduct with care.

Psalm 2:6,9-11, Saying: "I, even I, have installed my king upon Zion, my holy mountain."

"You will break them with an iron scepter, as though a potter's vessel you will dash them to pieces." And now, O kings, exercise insight; let yourselves be corrected, O judges of the earth. Serve Jehovah with fear and be joyful with trembling.

Matthew 5:14, You are the light of the world. A city cannot be hid when situated upon a mountain.

> Bram's Notes: Jehovah's denunciation went out. This is our third year here in Lancaster.

July 2, 1989 Sunday

Zechariah 11:1-14, "Open up your doors, O Lebanon, that a fire may devour among your cedars. Howl, O juniper tree, for the cedar has fallen; because the majestic ones themselves have been despoiled! Howl, you massive trees of Bashan, for the impenetrable forest has come down! Listen! The howling of [unfaithful] shepherds, for their majesty has been despoiled. Listen! The roaring of maned young lions, for the proud thickets along the Jordan have been despoiled.

"This is what Jehovah my God has said, 'Shepherd the flock meant for the killing, the buyers of which proceed to kill them although they are not held guilty. And those who are selling them say: "May Jehovah be blessed, while I gain riches." And their own shepherds do not show any compassion on them.'

"'For I shall show compassion no more upon the inhabitants [organization of Jehovah's Witnesses] of the land,' is the utterance of Jehovah. 'So here I am causing mankind to find themselves, each one in the hand of his companion and in the hand of his king; and they will certainly crush to pieces the land, and I shall do no delivering out of their hand.'"

And I proceeded to shepherd the flock meant for the killing, in your behalf, O afflicted ones of the flock. So I took for myself two staffs. The one I called Pleasantness, and the other I called Union, and I went shepherding the flock. **And I finally effaced three shepherds in one lunar month, as my soul gradually became impatient with them, and also their own soul felt a loathing toward me.** At length I said: "I shall not keep shepherding you. The one that is dying, let her die. And the one that is being effaced, let her be effaced. And as for the ones left remaining, let them devour, each one the flesh of her companion." So I took my staff Pleasantness [Lisa] and cut it to pieces, in order to break my covenant that I had concluded with all the peoples [the organization of Jehovah's Witnesses]. And it came to be broken in that day, and the afflicted ones of the flock who were watching me got to know in this way that it was the word of Jehovah.

Then I said to them: "If it is good in your eyes, give me my wages; but if not, refrain." And they proceeded to pay my wages, thirty pieces of silver.

At that Jehovah said to me: "Throw it to the treasury—the majestic value with which I [Jehovah] have been valued from their standpoint." Accordingly I took the thirty pieces of silver and threw it into the treasury at the house of Jehovah.

[The elders gave me my wages, "thirty pieces of silver." Elder, John G., gave me a check for $15.00 at the Kingdom Hall for putting new binding on their book: $15.00 x 2 (in $.50 silver) = "thirty pieces of silver," "the majestic value with which I [Jehovah] have been valued from their standpoint." The covenant with his people, Jehovah's Witnesses, was broken by Jehovah, by cutting the staff Pleasantness to pieces. Jehovah broke the covenant with his people in Jesus' day by ripping the temple curtain, when Jesus was killed.]

Then I cut in pieces my second staff, the Union [Leon Wurzer], in order to break the brotherhood between Judah and Israel.

Jeremiah 49:20-22, Therefore hear, O men, the counsel of Jehovah that he has formulated against Edom [another name for Esau, Jacob's twin brother, who disrespected his birthright], and his thoughts that he has thought out against the inhabitants of Teman [considered a center of wisdom; the Watchtower Bible and Tract Society]: **Surely the little ones of the flock will be dragged about. Surely on account of them he will make their dwelling place become desolate. At the sound of their falling the earth has begun to rock. There is an outcry!** The sound of it has been heard even at the Red Sea. Look! Just like an eagle someone will ascend and pounce down, and he will spread out his wings over Bozrah [Bozrah means "Unapproachable Place"]; and the heart of the mighty men of Edom will actually become in that day like the heart of the wife having distress in childbirth.

Jeremiah 4:13, Look! Like rain clouds he will come up, and his chariots are like a storm wind. His horses are swifter than eagles. Woe to us, for we [the organization of Jehovah's Witnesses] have been despoiled.

Recall: Jeremiah 30:23,24, Look! A windstorm of Jehovah, rage itself, has gone forth, an onward-sweeping tempest. Upon the head of the wicked ones it will whirl. The burning anger of Jehovah will not turn back until he will have executed and until he will have carried out the ideas of his heart. In the final part of the days you people will give your consideration to it.

Jeremiah 15:14b, For a fire itself has been ignited in my anger. Against you people it is kindled.

Jeremiah 50:2b-6,11, Her dungy idols have become terrified. For against her a nation has come up from the north. It is the one that makes her land an object of astonishment, so that there proves to be no one dwelling in her. Both man and domestic animal have taken flight. They have gone away.

"In those days and at that time," is the utterance of Jehovah, "the [faithful] sons of Israel, they and the [faithful] sons of Judah together, will come. They will walk, weeping as they walk, and for Jehovah their God they will seek. To Zion [Lisa] they will keep asking the way, with their faces in that direction, saying, 'Come and let us join ourselves to Jehovah in an indefinitely lasting covenant that will not be forgotten.' **A flock of perishing creatures my people has become. Their own shepherds [those taking the lead in the organization] have caused them to wander about.** On the mountains they have led them away. From mountain to hill they have gone. They have forgotten their resting-place."

For you [unfaithful] men kept rejoicing, for you men kept exulting when pillaging my own inheritance. For you kept pawing like a heifer in the tender grass, and you kept neighing like stallions.

Recall: [In one of my earlier **handwritten journals**, I have noted that I was given this scripture.] Isaiah 44:5b, And another [person, Lisa] will **write upon his hand**: "Belonging to Jehovah."

Jeremiah 50:12a, The mother of you men has become very much ashamed.
Recall: [The prophetess, Deborah, was likened to a "mother in Israel." (Judges 5:7) A "mother" would be ashamed of those taking the lead in the organization because so many have fallen away to unrighteousness.]

Isaiah 47:8,9a NWT (1984), And now hear this, you pleasure-given woman [unfaithful "faithful and discreet slave" (Matthew 24:43-51)], the one sitting in security, the one saying in her heart: "I am, and there is nobody else. I shall not sit as a widow, and I shall not know the loss of children." But to you these two things will come suddenly, in one day: loss of children and widowhood. In their complete measure they must come upon you. [The unfaithful "faithful and discreet slave" consider their position with Jehovah to be secure. They do not believe he will draw his faithful worshippers out of the organization. They are confident that they will not "know loss of children."]

Jeremiah 50:15, Shout a war cry against her [the organization] on every side. She has **given her hand [in pledge to the nations; a betrayal of their covenant with Jehovah]**. Her pillars have fallen. Her walls have been torn down. For it is the vengeance of Jehovah. Take your vengeance on her. Just as she has done, do to her.

Ezekiel 17:18, And he has despised an oath in breaking a covenant, and, look! he had given his hand and has done even all these things. He will not make his escape.

Lamentations 5:6, To Egypt we have **given the hand**; to Assyria, in order to get satisfaction with bread. [The organization is consorting with the nations for "bread." They break oath and covenant with Jehovah.]

Jeremiah 50:44, Look! Someone will come up just like a lion from the proud thickets along the Jordan to the durable abiding place, but in a moment I shall make **them** run away from her. And the one who is chosen I shall appoint over her. For who is like me, and who will challenge me, and who, now, is the shepherd that can stand before me?

Isaiah 41:25, I have roused up someone from the north, and he will come. From the rising of the sun he will call upon my name. And he will come upon deputy rulers as if they were clay and just as a potter that tramples down the moist material.

Isaiah 41:27, There is one first, saying to Zion: "Look! Here they are!" and to Jerusalem I shall give a bringer of good news.

Isaiah 40:9, Make your way up even onto a high mountain, you woman [Lisa] bringing good news for Zion. Raise your voice even with power, you woman bringing good news for Jerusalem. **Raise it. Do not be afraid. Say to the [faithful] cities of Judah: "Here is your God."**

Jeremiah 49:19, Look! Someone will come up just like a lion from the proud thickets along the Jordan to the durable abiding place, but in a moment I will make **him** run away from her. And the one who is chosen I shall appoint over her. For who is like me, and who will challenge me, and who, now, is the shepherd that can stand before me? [It was someone coming up just like a **lion, Leon Wurzer** (Staff: the Union), to the durable abiding place, Lisa (Staff: Pleasantness), and then made to run away from her. Jehovah "breaks the brotherhood between Judah and Israel." There is no goodwill between Leon and myself at this time. (Zechariah 11:10,14) **Leon** runs away from Lisa two different times. Compare: Jeremiah 50:44 above.]

Instructions: Habakkuk 2:2,3, And Jehovah proceeded to answer me [Lisa] and to say: "Write down the vision, and set it out plainly upon tablets, in order that the one reading aloud from it may do so fluently." For the vision is yet for the appointed time, and it keeps panting on to the end, and it will not tell a lie. Even if it should delay, keep in expectation of it; for it will without fail come true. It will not be late.

Instructions: Raise A Signal.

Jeremiah 51:31, One runner runs to meet another runner, and one reporter to meet another reporter, to **report** to the king of Babylon [unfaithful "faithful and discreet slave"] that his city has been captured at every end.

Jeremiah 34:17, Therefore this is what Jehovah has said, "You yourselves [those taking the lead within the organization] have not obeyed me in keeping on **proclaiming liberty** each one to his brother and each one to his companion. Here I am proclaiming to you a liberty," is the utterance of Jehovah, "to the sword, to the pestilence and to the famine, and I shall certainly give you for a quaking to all the kingdoms of the earth."

Jeremiah 4:5, **Tell it** in Judah, you [faithful] men, and **publish it** even in Jerusalem, and **say it out**, and blow a horn throughout the land. **Call out loudly** and say: "Gather yourselves together, and let us enter into the fortified cities [faithful Jerusalem]."

Jeremiah 4:16, **Make mention of it**, you [faithful] people, yes, to the nations. **Publish it** against [unfaithful] Jerusalem [the organization of Jehovah's Witnesses].

Jeremiah 5:20, **Tell this** in the house of [unfaithful] Jacob, and **publish it** in [unfaithful] Judah, saying: "Hear, now, this, O unwise people that is without heart: They have eyes, but they cannot see; they have ears, but they cannot hear."

Jeremiah 46:14, **Tell it** in Egypt [the organization], O [faithful] men, and **publish it** in Migdol, and **publish it** in Noph and in Tahpanhes. Say, "Station yourself, making preparation also for yourself, for a sword will certainly devour all around you."

Jeremiah 50:2, **Tell it** among the nations and **publish it**. And **lift up a signal**; **publish it**. Hide nothing, O [faithful] men. Say, "Babylon has been captured. Bel [meaning "Master"] has been put to shame. Merodach [Babylonian God] has become terrified. Her images have been put to shame. Her dungy idols have become terrified.

Amos 3:9, **Publish it** on the dwelling towers in Ashdod and on the dwelling towers [branch offices of the organization] in the land of Egypt, and say: "Be gathered together against the mountains of Samaria, and see the many disorders in the midst of her and cases of defrauding inside her."

Amos 3:13, "Hear and **give witness** in the house of Jacob," is the utterance of the Sovereign Lord Jehovah, the God of the armies.

July 3, 1989

Isaiah 34:16,17, Search for yourselves in the book of Jehovah and read out loud: not one [faithful one] has been missing of them; they actually do not fail to have each one her mate, for it is the mouth of Jehovah that has given the command, and it is his spirit that has collected them together. And it is He that has cast for them the lot, and his own hand has apportioned the place to them by the measuring line. To time indefinite they will take possession of it; for generation after generation they will reside in it.

Isaiah 33:20, Behold Zion, the town of our festal occasions! Your own eyes will see Jerusalem [Lisa] an undisturbed abiding place, a tent that no one will pack up. Never will its tent pins be pulled out, and none of its ropes will be torn in two.

Psalm 132:13,14, For Jehovah has chosen Zion [Lisa]; he has longed for it as a dwelling for himself: "This is my resting place forever; here I shall dwell, for I have longed for it."

Psalm 78:68-70, But he chose the tribe of Judah, Mt. Zion, which he loved. And he began to build his sanctuary just like the heights, like the earth that he has founded to time indefinite. And so he chose David his servant and took him from the pens of the flock.

Commandment: Deuteronomy Chapter 12 all verses, [Take special care to consider this entire chapter of Deuteronomy, especially verse 5.] These are the regulations and the judicial decisions that you should be careful to carry out in the land that Jehovah the God of your forefathers will certainly allow you to take possession of, all the days that you are alive on the soil. You should absolutely destroy all the places where the nations whom you are dispossessing have served their gods, on the tall mountains and the hills and under every luxuriant tree. And you must pull down their altars and shatter their sacred pillars, and you should burn their sacred poles in the fire and cut down the graven images of their gods, and you must destroy their names from that place.

! You must not do that way to Jehovah your God, (verse 5) **but to the place that Jehovah your God will choose out of all your tribes to place his name there, to have it reside, you will seek, and there you must come.** And there you must bring your burnt offerings and your sacrifices and your tenth parts and the contribution of your hand and your vow offerings and your voluntary offerings and the firstborn ones of your herd and of your flock. And there you must eat before Jehovah your God and rejoice in every undertaking of yours, you and your households, because Jehovah your God has blessed you.

You must not do according to all that we are doing here today, each one whatever is right in his own eyes, because you have not yet come into the resting-place and the inheritance that Jehovah your God is giving you. And you must cross the Jordan and dwell in the land that Jehovah your God is giving you as a possession, and he will certainly give you rest from all your enemies round about, and you will indeed dwell in security. And it must occur that the place that Jehovah your God will choose to have his name reside there is where you will bring all about which I am commanding you, your burnt offerings and your sacrifices, your tenth parts and the contribution of your hand and every choice of your vow offerings that you will vow to Jehovah. And you must rejoice before Jehovah your God, you and your sons and your daughters and your man slaves and your slave girls and the Levite who is inside your gates, because he has no share or inheritance with you. Watch out for yourself for fear you may offer up your burnt offerings in any other place you may see. **But in the place that Jehovah will choose in one of your tribes** is where you should offer up your burnt offerings [spiritual offerings of praise], and there you should do all that I am commanding you.

Philemon 10-22, I [Jehovah] am exhorting you [Lisa] concerning my child [Leon], to whom I became a father while in my prison bonds, Onesimus, formerly useless to you but now useful to you and to me. This very one I am sending back to you, yes, him, that is, my own tender affections.

I would like to hold him back for myself that in place of you he might keep on ministering to me in the prison bonds I bear for the sake of the good news. But without your consent I do not want to do anything, so that your good act may be, not as under compulsion, but of your own free will. Perhaps really on this account he broke away for an hour, that you may have him back forever, no longer as a slave but as more than a slave, as a brother beloved, especially so to me, yet how much more so to you both in fleshly relationship and in the Lord. **If, therefore, you consider me a sharer, receive him kindly the way you would me. Moreover, if he did you any wrong or owes you anything, keep this charged to my account.** I Paul am writing with my own hand: **I will pay it back—not to**

be telling you [Lisa] that, besides, you owe me [Jehovah] even yourself. Yes, brother, may I derive profit from you in connection with the Lord: refresh my tender affections in connection with Christ. Trusting in your compliance, I am writing you, knowing you will even do more than the things I say. But along with that, also **get lodging ready for me [Jehovah]**, for I am hoping that through the prayers of you people I shall be set at liberty for you.

[I am exhorted to receive Leon kindly as I would Jehovah, even though Leon has wronged me and "owes me" to put it right. I am reminded that I have wronged Jehovah and "owed him" to put it right, yet Jehovah received me kindly.]

Philemon 1:20b, Refresh my tender affections. [Jehovah, our heavenly Father, loves Leon like a son.]

Psalm 78:68, But he chose the tribe of Judah, Mt. Zion, which he loved.

Zechariah 8:2, This is what Jehovah of armies has said, "**I will be jealous for Zion with great jealousy, and with great rage I will be jealous for her.**"

Deuteronomy Chapter 12, continued, Only whenever your soul craves it you may slaughter, and you must eat meat according to the blessing of Jehovah your God that he has given you, inside all your gates. The unclean one and the clean one may eat it, like the gazelle and like the stag. Only the blood you must not eat. On the earth you should pour it out as water. You will not be allowed to eat inside your gates the tenth part of your grain or of your new wine or of your oil or the firstborn ones of your herd and of your flock or any of your vow offerings that you will vow or your voluntary offerings or the contribution of your hand. But before Jehovah your God you will eat it, in the place that Jehovah your God will choose, you and your son and your daughter and your man slave and your slave girl and the Levite who is inside your gates; and you must rejoice before Jehovah your God in every undertaking of yours. Watch out for yourself that you may not abandon the Levite all your days on your soil.

When Jehovah your God will widen out your territory, just as he has promised you, and you will be certain to say, "Let me eat meat," because your soul craves to eat meat, whenever your soul craves it you may eat meat. In case the place that Jehovah your God will choose to put his name there should be far away from you, you must then slaughter some of your herd or some of your flock that Jehovah has given you, just as I have commanded you, and you must eat inside your gates whenever your souls craves it. Only in the way that the gazelle and the stag may be eaten, so you may eat it: the unclean one and the clean one together may eat it. Simply be firmly resolved not to eat the blood, because the blood is the soul and you must not eat the soul with the flesh. You must not eat it. You should pour it out upon the ground like water. You must not eat it, in order that it may go well with you and your sons after you, because you will do what is right in Jehovah's eyes. Merely your holy things that will become yours, and your vow offerings you should carry, and you must come to the place that Jehovah will choose. And you must render up your burnt offerings, the flesh and the blood, upon the altar of Jehovah your God; and the blood of your sacrifices should be poured out against the altar of Jehovah your God, but the flesh you may eat.

Watch, and you must obey all these words that I am commanding you, in order that it may go well with you and your sons after you to time indefinite, because you will do what is good and right in the eyes of Jehovah your God.

When Jehovah your God will cut off from before you the nations to whom you are going to dispossess them, you must also dispossess them and dwell in their land. Watch out for yourself for fear you may be entrapped after them, after they have been annihilated from before you, and for fear you may inquire respecting their gods, saying, "How was it these nations used to serve their gods? And I, yes, I, will do the same way." You must not do that way to Jehovah your God, for everything detestable to Jehovah that he does hate they have done to their gods, for even their sons and their daughters they regularly burn in the fire to their gods. Every word that I am commanding you is what you should be careful to do. You must not add to it nor take away from it.

Isaiah 8:18, Look! I [Lisa] and the children [Rosie, Bram and the little ones] whom Jehovah has given me are as signs and as miracles in Israel from Jehovah of armies, who is residing in Mount Zion.

Hebrews 2:13, And again: "I will have my trust in him." And again: "Look! I and the children, whom Jehovah gave me."

→ **[Seek! Seek where Jehovah is residing, Mount Zion.]**

Acts 28:23, They now arranged for a day with him, and they came in greater numbers to him in his lodging place. And he explained the matter to them by bearing thorough witness concerning the kingdom of God and by using persuasion with them concerning Jesus from both the law of Moses and the Prophets, from morning until evening.

Psalm 132:15, Its provisions I shall bless without fail, its poor ones I shall satisfy with bread.

Deuteronomy Chapter 28 all verses, especially verse 2 NWT (1984), "And it must occur that if you [Jehovah is telling faithful ones still in the organization] will without fail listen to the voice of Jehovah your God by being careful to do all his commandments that I am commanding you today, Jehovah your God also will certainly put you high above all other nations of the earth. **And all these blessings must come upon you and overtake you, because you keep listening to the voice of Jehovah your God**:

"Blessed will you be in the city, and blessed will you be in the field.

"Blessed will be the fruit of your belly and the fruit of your ground and the fruit of your domestic beast, the young of your cattle and the progeny of your flock.

"Blessed will be your basket and your kneading trough.

"Blessed will you be when you come in, and blessed will you be when you go out.

"Jehovah will cause your enemies who rise up against you to be defeated before you. By one way they will come out against you, but by seven ways they will flee before you. Jehovah will decree for you the blessing on your stores of supply and every undertaking of yours, and he will certainly bless you in the land that Jehovah your God is giving you. Jehovah will establish you as a holy people to himself, just as he swore to you, because you continue to keep the commandments of Jehovah your God, and you have walked in his ways. And all the peoples of the earth will have to see that

Jehovah's name has been called upon you, and they will indeed be afraid of you.

"Jehovah will also make you overflow indeed with prosperity in the fruit of your belly and the fruit of your domestic animals and the fruitage of your ground, on the ground that Jehovah swore to your forefathers to give to you. Jehovah will open up to you his good storehouse, the heavens, to give the rain on your land in its season and to bless every deed of your hand; and you will certainly lend to many nations, while you yourself will not borrow. And Jehovah will indeed put you at the head and not at the tail; and you must come to be only on top, and you will not come to be on the bottom, because you keep obeying the commandments of Jehovah your God, which I am commanding you today to observe and to do. And you must not turn aside from all the words that I am commanding you today, to the right or to the left, to walk after other gods to serve them.

"And it must occur that if you will not listen to the voice of Jehovah your God by taking care to do all his commandments and his statutes that I am commanding you today, all these maledictions must also come upon you and overtake you:

"Cursed will you be in the city, and cursed will you be in the field.

"Cursed will be your basket and your kneading trough.

"Cursed will be the fruit of your belly and the fruitage of your ground, the young of your cattle and the progeny of your flock.

"Cursed will you be when you come in, and cursed will you be when you go out.

"Jehovah will send upon you the curse, confusion and rebuke in every undertaking of yours that you try to carry out, until you have been annihilated and have perished in a hurry, because of the badness of your practices in that you have forsaken me. Jehovah will cause the pestilence to cling to you until he has exterminated you from off the ground to which you are going to take possession of it. Jehovah will strike you with tuberculosis and burning fever and inflammation and feverish heat and the sword and scorching and mildew, and they will certainly pursue you until you have perished. Your skies that are over your head must also become copper, and the earth that is beneath you iron. Jehovah will give powder and dust as the rain of your land. From the heavens it will come down upon you until you have been annihilated. Jehovah will cause you to be defeated before your enemies. By one way you will go out against them, but by seven ways you will flee before them; and you must become a frightful object to all the earth's kingdoms. And your dead body must become food for every flying creature of the heavens and to the beast of the field, with no one to make them tremble.

"Jehovah will strike you with the boil of Egypt and piles and eczema and skin eruption, from which you will not be able to be healed. Jehovah will strike you with madness and loss of sight and bewilderment of heart. And you will indeed become one who gropes about at midday, just as a blind man gropes about in the gloom, and you will not make your ways successful; and you must become only one who is always defrauded and robbed, with no one to save you. You will become engaged to a woman, but another man will rape her. You will build a house, but you will not dwell in it. You will plant a vineyard, but you will not begin to use it. Your bull slaughtered there before your eyes—but you will not eat any of it. Your ass taken in robbery from before your face—but it will not return to you. Your sheep given to your enemies—but you will have no savior. Your sons and your daughters given to another people and your eyes looking on and yearning for them always—but your hands will be without power. The fruitage of your ground and all your production a people will eat whom you have not known; and you must become one who is only defrauded and crushed always. And you will certainly become maddened at the sight of your eyes that you will see.

"Jehovah will strike you with a malignant boil upon both knees and both legs, from which you will not be able to be healed, from the sole of your foot to the crown of your head. Jehovah will march you and your king whom you will set up over you to a nation whom you have not known, neither you nor your forefathers; and there you will have to serve other gods, of wood and of stone. And you must become an object of astonishment, a proverbial saying and a taunt among all the peoples to whom Jehovah will lead you away.

"A lot of seed you will take out to the field, but little will you gather, because the locust will devour it. Vineyards you will plant and certainly cultivate, but you will drink no wine and gather nothing in, because the worm will eat it up. You will come to have olive trees in all your territory, but you will rub yourself with no oil, because your olives will drop off. Sons and daughters you will bring forth, but they will not continue yours, because they will go off into captivity.

All your trees and the fruitage of your ground whirring insects will take in possession. The alien resident who is in your midst will keep ascending higher and higher above you, while you—you will keep descending lower and lower. He will be the one to lend to you, while you—you will not lend to him. He will become the head, while you—you will become the tail.

"And all these maledictions will certainly come upon you and pursue you and overtake you until you have been annihilated, because you did not listen to the voice of Jehovah your God by keeping his commandments and his statutes that he commanded you. And they must continue on you and your offspring as a sign and a portent to time indefinite, due to the fact that you did not serve Jehovah your God with rejoicing and joy of heart for the abundance of everything. And you will have to serve your enemies whom Jehovah will send against you with hunger and thirst and nakedness and the want of everything; and he will certainly put an iron yoke upon your neck until he has annihilated you.

"Jehovah will raise up against you a nation far away, from the end of the earth, just as an eagle pounces, a nation whose tongue you will not understand, a nation fierce in countenance, who will not be partial to an old man or show favor to a young man. And they will certainly eat the fruit of your domestic animals and the fruitage of your ground until you have been annihilated, and they will let no grain, new wine or oil, no young of your cattle or progeny of your flock, remain for you until they have destroyed you. And they will indeed besiege you within all your gates until your high and fortified walls in which you are trusting fall in all your land, yes, they will certainly besiege you within all your gates in all your land, which Jehovah your God has given you. Then you will have to eat the fruit of your belly, the flesh of your sons and your daughters, whom Jehovah your God has given you, because of the tightness and stress with which your enemy will hem you in.

"As for the very delicate and dainty man among you, his eye will be evil-inclined toward his brother and his cherished wife and the remainder of his sons whom he has remaining, so as not to give one of them any of the flesh of his sons that he will eat, because he has nothing at all remaining to him because of the tightness and stress with which your enemy will hem you in within all your gates. As for the delicate and dainty woman among you who never attempted to set the sole of her foot upon the earth for being of dainty habit and for delicateness, her eye will be evil-inclined toward her cherished husband and her son and her daughter, even toward her afterbirth that comes out from between her legs and toward her sons whom she proceeds to bear, because she will eat them in secrecy for the want of everything because of the tightness and stress with which your enemy will hem you in within your gates.

"If you will not take care to carry out all the words of this law that are written in this book so as to fear this glorious and fear-inspiring name, even Jehovah, your God, Jehovah also will certainly make your plagues and the plagues of your offspring especially severe, great and long-lasting plagues, and malignant and long-lasting sicknesses. And he will indeed bring back upon you all the diseases of Egypt before which you got scared, and they will certainly hang onto you. Also, any sickness and any plague that is not written in the book of this law, Jehovah will bring them upon you until you have been annihilated. And you will indeed be left with very few in number, although you have become like the stars of the heavens for multitude, because you did not listen to the voice of Jehovah your God.

"And it must occur that just as Jehovah exulted over you to do you good and to multiply you, so Jehovah will exult over you to destroy you and to annihilate you; and you will simply be torn away from off the soil to which you are going to take possession of it.

"And Jehovah will certainly scatter you among all the peoples from the one end of the earth to the other end of the earth, and there you will have to serve other gods whom you have not known, neither you nor your forefathers, wood and stone. And among those nations you will have no ease, nor will there prove to be any resting-place for the sole of your foot; and Jehovah will indeed give you there a trembling heart and a failing of the eyes and despair of soul. And you will certainly be in the greatest peril for your life and be in dread night and day, and you will not be sure of your life. In the morning you will say, 'If it were only evening!' and in the evening you will say, 'If it were only morning!' because of the dread of your heart with which you will be in dread and because of the sight of your eyes that you will see. And Jehovah will certainly bring you back to Egypt by ships by the way about which I have said to you, 'You will never see it again,' and you will have to sell yourselves there to your enemies as slave men and maidservants, but there will be no buyer.

Zechariah 9:12, Return to the stronghold [Jehovah is our stronghold. (Psalm 91:2)], you prisoners of the hope.

Jeremiah 31:6, For there exists a day when the lookouts in the mountainous region of Ephraim will actually call out, "Rise up, O men, and let us go up to Zion, to Jehovah our God."

Jeremiah 31:17, "And there exists a hope for your future," is the utterance of Jehovah, "and the sons will certainly return to their own territory."

Lamentations 3:29, Let him put his mouth in the very dust. Perhaps there exists a hope.

Zechariah 9:12b, Also, today I am telling you, "I shall repay to you, O woman [Lisa], a double portion."

Isaiah 61:7 Instead of your shame there will be a double portion, and instead of humiliation they will cry out joyfully over their share. Therefore in their land they will take possession of even a double portion. Rejoicing to time indefinite is what will come to be theirs.

Recall: Isaiah 54:4-7, "Do not be afraid, for you will not be put to shame; and do not feel humiliated, for you will not be disappointed. For you will forget even the shame of your time of youth, and the reproach of your continuous widowhood you will remember no more."
"For your Grand Maker is your husbandly owner, Jehovah of armies being his name; and the Holy One of Israel is your Repurchaser. The God of the whole earth he will be called. For Jehovah called you [Lisa] as if you were a wife left entirely and hurt in spirit, and as a wife of the time of youth who was then rejected," your God has said. "For a little moment I left you entirely, but with great mercies I shall collect you together. With a flood of indignation I concealed my face from you for but a moment, but with loving-kindness to time indefinite I will have mercy upon you," your Repurchaser, Jehovah, has said.

Phone Call: [Ruth F. called me Monday, after many members of the local congregation had received Jehovah's denunciation. She told me, "They are burning your words." I said to Ruth, "They are not my words, they are Jehovah's words." She said, "Right."]

Jeremiah 36:27-29, And the word of Jehovah occurred further to Jeremiah after the king had burned up the roll with the words that Baruch [meaning "Blessed"] had **written at the mouth of Jehovah, saying: "Take again for yourself [Lisa] a roll, another one, and write on it all the first words that proved to be on the first roll, which Jehoiakim the king of Judah burned up.** And against Jehoiakim the king of Judah you should say, 'This is what Jehovah has said: "You yourself have burned up this roll, saying, 'Why is it that you have written on it, saying: "The king of Babylon will come without fail and will certainly bring this land to ruin and cause man and beast to cease from it"?'

Jeremiah 7:27,28, And you must speak to them [the organization of Jehovah's Witnesses] all these words, but they will not listen to you; and you must call to them, but they will not answer you. And you must say to them, "This is the nation whose people have not obeyed the voice of Jehovah its God, and have not taken discipline. Faithfulness has perished, and it has been cut off from their mouth."

Jeremiah 26:4-6, And you must say to them: "This is what Jehovah has said, 'If you will not listen to me by walking in my law that I have put before you, by listening to the words of my servants the prophets, whom I am sending to you, even rising up early and sending them, whom you have not listened to, I will, in turn, make this house like that in Shiloh, and this city I shall make a malediction to all the nations of the earth.'"

Psalm 9 all verses, I will laud you, O Jehovah, with all my heart; I [Lisa] will declare all your wonderful works. I will rejoice and exult in you, I will make melody to your name, O Most High. When my enemies turn back, they will stumble and perish from before you. For you have executed my judgment and my cause; you have sat on the throne judging with righteousness. You have rebuked nations, you have destroyed the wicked one. Their name you have wiped out to time indefinite, even forever. O you enemy, your desolations have come to their perpetual finish, and the cities that you have uprooted, the very mention of them will certainly perish.

As for Jehovah, he will sit to time indefinite, firmly establishing his throne for judgment itself. And he himself will judge the productive land in righteousness; he will judicially try national groups in uprightness.

And Jehovah will become a secure height for anyone crushed, a secure height in times of distress. And those knowing your name will trust in you, for you will certainly not leave those looking for you, O Jehovah.

Make melody, you people, to Jehovah, who is dwelling in Zion; tell among the peoples his deeds. For, when looking for bloodshed, he will certainly remember those very ones; he is sure not to forget the outcry of the afflicted ones.

Show me favor, O Jehovah; see my affliction by those hating me, O you who are lifting me up from the gates of death, in order that I may declare all your praiseworthy deeds in the gates of the daughter of Zion, that I may be joyful in your salvation.

The nations have sunk down into the pit that they have made; in the net that they hid, their own foot has been caught. Jehovah is known by the judgment that he has executed. By the activity of his own hands the wicked one has been ensnared. Higgaion. [Solemn pause.] *Selah. [Pause for meditation.]*

Wicked people will turn back to Sheol, even all the nations forgetting God. For not always will the poor one be forgotten, nor will the hope of the meek ones ever perish.

Do arise, O Jehovah! Let not mortal man prove superior in strength. Let the nations be judged before your face. Do put fear into them, O Jehovah, that the nations may know that they are but mortal men. *Selah.*

Isaiah Chapter 42 all verses, Look! My servant [Leon], on whom I keep fast hold! My chosen one, whom my soul has approved! I have put my spirit in him. Justice to the nations is what he will bring forth. He will not cry out or raise his voice, and in the street he will not let his voice be heard. No crushed reed will he break; and as for a dim flaxen wick, he will not extinguish it. In trueness he will bring forth justice. He will not grow dim nor be crushed until he sets justice in the earth itself; and for his law the islands themselves will keep waiting.

This is what the true God, Jehovah, has said, the Creator of the heavens and the Grand One stretching them out; the One laying out the earth and its produce, the One giving breath to the people on it, and spirit to those walking in it: "I myself, Jehovah, have called you [Lisa] in righteousness, and I proceeded to take hold of your hand. And I shall safeguard you and give you as a covenant of the people, as a light of the nations, for you to open the blind eyes, to bring forth out of the dungeon the prisoner, out of the house of detention those sitting in darkness.

"I am Jehovah. That is my name; and to no one else shall I give my own glory, neither my praise to graven images.

"The first things—here they have come, but new things I am telling out. Before they begin to spring up, I cause you people to hear them."

Sing to Jehovah a new song, his praise from the extremity of the earth, you men that are going down to the sea and to that which fills it, you islands and you inhabiting them. Let the wilderness and its cities raise their voice, the settlements that Kedar inhabits. Let the inhabitants of the crag cry out in joy. From the top of the mountains let people cry aloud. Let them attribute to Jehovah glory, and in the islands let them tell forth even his praise.

Like a mighty man Jehovah himself will go forth. Like a warrior he will awaken zeal. He will shout, yes, he will let out a war cry; over his enemies he will show himself mightier.

"I have kept quiet for a long time. I continued silent. I kept exercising self-control. Like a woman giving birth I am going to groan, pant and gasp at the same time. I shall devastate mountains and hills, and all their vegetation I shall dry up. And I will turn rivers into islands, and reedy pools I shall dry up. **And I will make the blind ones walk in a way that they have not known; in a roadway that they have not known I shall cause them to tread. I shall turn a dark place before them into light, and rugged terrain into level land. These are the things that I will do for them, and I will not leave them."**

They must be turned back, they will be very much ashamed, those who are putting trust in the carved image, those who are saying to a molten image: "You are our gods."

Hear, you deaf ones; and look forth to see, you blind ones. Who is blind, if not my servant, and who is deaf as my messenger whom I send? Who is blind as the one rewarded, or blind as the servant of Jehovah? **It was a case of seeing many things, but you did not keep watching. It was a case of opening the ears, but you did not keep listening.** Jehovah himself for the sake of his righteousness has taken a delight in that he should magnify the law and make it majestic. But it is a people plundered and pillaged, all of them being trapped in the holes, and in the houses of detention they have been kept hidden. They have come to be for plunder without a deliverer, for pillage without anyone to say: "Bring back!"

Who among you people will give ear to this? Who will pay attention and listen for later times? Who has given Jacob for mere pillage, and Israel to the plunderers? Is it not Jehovah, the One against whom we have sinned, and in whose ways they did not want to walk and to whose law they did not listen? So He kept pouring out upon him rage, his anger, and the strength of war. And it kept consuming him all around, but he took no note; and it kept blazing up against him, but he would lay nothing to heart.

Psalm 16 all verses, Keep me, O God, for I have taken refuge in you. I have said to Jehovah: "You are Jehovah; my goodness is, not for your sake, but to the holy ones that are in the earth. They, even the majestic ones, are the ones in whom is all my delight." Pains become many to those [unfaithful ones in the organization of Jehovah's Witnesses] who, when there is someone else, do hurry after them. I shall not pour out their drink offerings of blood, and I shall not carry their names upon my lips. Jehovah is the portion of my allotted share and of my cup. You are holding fast my lot. The measuring lines themselves have fallen for me in pleasant places. Really, my own possession has proven agreeable to me. I shall bless Jehovah, who has given me advice. Really, during the nights my kidneys [deepest emotions] have corrected me. I have placed Jehovah in front of me constantly. Because he is at my right hand, I shall not be made to totter. Therefore my heart does rejoice, and my glory [tongue] is inclined to be joyful. Also, my own flesh will reside in security. For you will not leave my soul in Sheol [the common grave of mankind]. You will not allow your loyal one to see the pit. You will cause me to know the path of life. Rejoicing to satisfaction is with your face; there is pleasantness at your right hand forever.

Isaiah 34:16,17, Search for yourselves in the book of Jehovah and read out load: not one has been missing of them; they actually do not fail to have each one her mate, for it is the mouth of Jehovah that has given the command, and it is his spirit that has collected them together. And it is He that has cast for them the lot, and his own hand has apportioned the place to them by the measuring line. To time indefinite they will take possession of it; for generation after generation they will reside in it.

Psalm 78:55, And because of them he gradually drove out the nations, and by the measuring line he went allotting them an inheritance, so that he caused the tribes of [faithful] Israel to reside in their own homes.

July 4, 1989

Psalm 149 all verses, Praise Jah [shortened form of the name, Jehovah], you people! Sing to Jehovah a new song, his praise in the congregation of loyal ones. Let Israel rejoice in its Grand Maker, the sons of Zion—let them be joyful in their king. Let them praise his name with dancing. With the tambourine and the harp let them make melody to him. For Jehovah is taking pleasure in his people. He beautifies the meek ones with salvation. Let the loyal ones exult in glory; let them cry out joyfully on their beds. Let the songs extolling God be in their throat, and a two-edged sword [Bible] be in their hand, to execute vengeance upon the nations, rebukes upon the national groups, to bind their kings with shackles and their glorified ones with fetters of iron, to execute upon them the judicial decision written. Such splendor belongs to all his loyal ones. Praise Jah, you people!

Psalm 110:6, He will execute judgment among the nations; he will cause a fullness of dead bodies. He will certainly break to pieces the head one over a populous land.

Psalm 112:1-4, Praise Jah, you people! Happy is the man in fear of Jehovah, in whose commandments he has taken very much delight. Mighty in the earth his offspring will become. As for the generation of the upright ones, it will be blessed. Valuable things and riches are in his house; and his righteousness is standing forever. He has flashed up in the darkness as a light to the upright ones. He is gracious and merciful and righteous.

→ Revelation 3:12, The one that conquers—I will make him a pillar in the temple of my God, and he will by no means go out from it anymore, and I will write upon him the name of my God and the name of the city of my God, the new Jerusalem which descends out of heaven from my God, and that new name of mine.

2 Chronicles 3:17, And he proceeded to set up the pillars in front of the temple, one to the right and one to the left, after which he called the name of the right-hand one Jachin [meaning "Jehovah Has Firmly Established"] and the name of the left-hand one Boaz [probably meaning "In Strength"].

→ **1 Corinthians 3:16 NWT (1984), Do you not know that you people are God's temple, and that the spirit of God dwells in you?**

Ephesians 2:21,22 In union with him the whole building, being harmoniously joined together, is growing into a holy temple for Jehovah. In union with him you, too, are being built up together into a place for God to inhabit by spirit.

1 Peter 2:5,6, You yourselves also as living stones are being built up a spiritual house for the purpose of a holy priesthood, to offer up spiritual sacrifices acceptable to God through Jesus Christ. For it is contained in Scripture: "Look! I am laying in Zion a stone, chosen, a foundation cornerstone, precious; and no one exercising faith in it will by any means come to disappointment."

Hebrews 12:22, But you have approached a **Mount Zion** and a city of the living God, heavenly **Jerusalem**, and myriads of angels.

Revelation 21:2, I saw also the holy city, New Jerusalem, coming down out of heaven from God and prepared as a bride adorned for her husband.

Zechariah 1:12, So the angel of Jehovah answered and said: "O Jehovah of armies, how long will you yourself not show mercy to Jerusalem and to the cities of Judah, whom you have denounced these seventy years?"

Psalm 149:9, To execute upon them [unfaithful ones in the organization] the judicial decision written [the completion of Jehovah's denunciation]. Such splendor belongs to all his loyal ones. Praise Jah, you people!

Ezekiel Chapters 16-18 all verses [abbreviated here], Ezekiel 16:14-20, "'And for you a name [Jehovah's Witnesses] began to go forth among the nations because of your prettiness, for it was perfect because of my splendor that I placed upon you,' is the utterance of the Sovereign Lord Jehovah."
"'But you began to trust in your prettiness [increase in size and wealth] and become a prostitute [consorting with the nations] on account of your name and to pour out your acts of prostitution on every passerby; his it came to be. And you proceeded to take some of your garments and make for yourself high places of varied colors and you would prostitute yourself on them—such things are not coming in, and it should not happen.

1 John 2:15,16, Do not be loving either the world or the things in the world. If anyone loves the world, the love of the Father is not in him; because everything in the world—the desire of the flesh and the desire of the eyes and the showy display of one's means of life—does not originate with the Father, but originates with the world.

Ezekiel Chapter 16 continued, And you would take your beautiful articles from my gold and from my silver [sacred "gifts" from Jehovah] that I had given to you and you would make for yourself images of a male and prostitute yourself with them. And you would take your embroidered garments and cover them; and my oil and my incense you would actually put before them. And my bread that I had given to you—fine flour and oil and honey [sacred "food" from Jehovah] that I had had you eat—you also actually put it before them as a restful odor, and it continued to occur,' is the utterance of the Sovereign Lord Jehovah."

"'And you [the unfaithful "faithful and discreet slave"] would take your sons and your daughters whom you had borne to me, [faithful worshippers they had drawn to the truth and brought to Jehovah] and you would sacrifice [abuse and oppress] these to them to be devoured—is that not enough of your acts of prostitution?'"

Ezekiel Chapter 17, And the word of Jehovah continued to occur to me, saying: "Son of man, propound a riddle and compose a proverbial saying toward the house of Israel [the unfaithful "faithful and discreet slave" of the organization of Jehovah's Witnesses]. And you must say, 'This is what the Sovereign Lord Jehovah has said: "The great eagle [Jehovah], having great wings, with long pinions, full of plumage, which had color variety, came to Lebanon and proceeded to take the treetop of the cedar. He plucked off the very top of its young shoots [new plant growth] and came bringing it to the land of Canaan; in a city of traders [New York City, U.S.A.] he placed it. Furthermore, he took some of the seed of the land and put it in a field for seed. As a willow by vast waters [Jehovah's holy waters of everlasting life], as a willow tree he placed it. And it began to sprout and gradually became a luxuriantly growing vine low in height [Brooklyn Heights], inclined to turn its foliage inward; and as for its roots, they gradually came to be under it. And it finally became a vine and produced shoots and sent forth branches [branch offices of the organization in other countries].

""'And there came to be another great eagle [a worldly source of power, not Jehovah], having great wings, and having large pinions, and, look! this very vine [governing body of the organization of Jehovah's Witnesses] stretched its roots hungrily toward him. And its foliage it thrust out to him in order for him to irrigate it, away from the garden beds where it was planted. Into a good field, by vast waters, it was already transplanted, in order to produce boughs and to bear fruit, to become a majestic vine."'

"Say, 'This is what the Sovereign Lord Jehovah has said: "Will it have success? Will not someone tear out its very roots and make its very fruit scaly? And must not all its freshly plucked sprouts become dry? It will become dry. Neither by a great arm nor by a multitudinous people will it have to be lifted up from its roots. And, look! although transplanted, will it have success? Will it not dry up completely, even as when the east wind touches it? In the garden beds of its sprout it will dry up."'"

And the word of Jehovah continued to occur to me, saying: "Say, please, to the rebellious house, 'Do you people actually not know what these things mean?' Say, 'Look! The king of Babylon [Satan] came to Jerusalem and proceeded to take its king and its princes and bring them to himself at Babylon. Furthermore, he took one of the royal seed and concluded a covenant with him and brought him into an oath; and the foremost men of the land he took away, in order that the kingdom might become low, unable to lift itself up, that by keeping his covenant it might stand. [The organization now has no strength of its own, because they have left Jehovah's water source, and have been made dependent on the water source of the king of Babylon (Satan) to keep standing.] But he finally rebelled against him in sending his messengers to Egypt [the nations], for it to give him horses and a multitudinous people. Will he have success? Will he escape, he who is doing these things, and who has broken a covenant? And will he actually escape?'

"'"As I am alive," is the utterance of the Sovereign Lord Jehovah, "in the place of the king who put in as king the one that despised his oath and that broke his covenant, with him in the midst of Babylon he will die. And by a great military force and by a multitudinous congregation Pharaoh will not make him effective in the war, by throwing up a siege rampart and by building a siege wall, in order to cut off many souls. And he has despised an oath in breaking a covenant, and, look! he had **given his hand** and has done even all these things. He will not make his escape."'

"'Therefore this is what the Sovereign Lord Jehovah has said: "As I am alive, surely my oath that he has despised and my covenant that he has broken—I will even bring it upon his head. And I will spread over him my net, and he will certainly be caught in my hunting net; and I will bring him to Babylon [The organization known as Jehovah's Witnesses has been overreached by the "king of Babylon," Satan, and has come under his rulership. It has become Babylon the Great, described as the great harlot in Revelation 17:1-6. "One of the royal seed" of the unfaithful "faithful and discreet slave" of the organization has "given his hand" to the nations. There, in Babylon, he will be judged by Jehovah.] and put myself on judgment with him there respecting his unfaithfulness with which he acted against me. And as regards all the fugitives of his in all his bands, by the sword they will fall, and the ones left remaining will be spread abroad even to every wind. And you people will have to know that I myself, Jehovah, have spoken it."'

"'This is what the Sovereign Lord Jehovah has said: "I myself will also take and put some of the lofty treetop of the cedar ["high" standing with Jehovah]; from the top of its **twigs** I shall pluck off a tender one [gentle, or young one] and I will myself transplant it upon a high and lofty mountain. On the mountain of the height of Israel I shall transplant it, and it will certainly bear boughs and produce fruit and become a majestic cedar. And under it there will actually reside all the birds of every wing; in the shadow of its foliage they will reside. And all the trees of the field will have to know that I myself, Jehovah, have abased the high tree [the unfaithful "faithful and discreet slave"], have put on high the low tree, have dried up the still-moist tree and have made the dry tree blossom. I myself, Jehovah, have spoken and have done it."'"

Ezekiel 18:20-32, "'The soul that is sinning—it itself will die. A son himself will bear nothing because of the error of the father, and a father himself will bear nothing because of the error of the son. Upon his own self the very righteousness of the righteous one will come to be, and upon his own self the very wickedness of a wicked one will come to be.

"'Now as regards someone wicked, in case he should turn back from all his sins that he has committed and he should actually keep all my statutes and execute justice and righteousness, he will positively keep living. He will not die. All his transgressions that he had committed—they will not be remembered against him. For his righteousness that he has done he will keep living.

"'Do I take any delight at all in the death of someone wicked,'" is the utterance of the Sovereign Lord Jehovah, "and not in that he should turn back from his ways and actually keep living?"

"'Now when someone righteous turns back from his righteousness and actually does injustice; according to all the detestable things that the wicked one has done he keeps doing and he is living, none of all his righteous acts that he has done will be remembered. For his unfaithfulness that he has committed and for his sin with which he has sinned, for them he will die.

"'And you people will certainly say: "The way of Jehovah is not adjusted right." Hear, please, O house of Israel. Is not my own way adjusted right? Are not the ways of you people not adjusted right?

"'When someone righteous turns back from his righteousness and he actually does injustice and dies on account of them, for his injustice that he has done he will die.

"'And when someone wicked turns back from his wickedness that he has committed and proceeds to execute justice and righteousness, he is the one that will preserve his own soul alive. When he sees and he turns back from all his transgressions that he has done, he will positively keep living. He will not die.

"'And the house of Israel will certainly say: "The way of Jehovah is not adjusted right." As for my ways, are they not adjusted right, O house of Israel? Are not the ways of you people the ones that are not adjusted right?

"'Therefore each one according to his ways is how I shall judge you, O house of Israel,' is the utterance of the Sovereign Lord Jehovah. 'Turn back, yes, cause a turning back from all your transgressions, and let nothing prove to be for you people a stumbling block causing error. **Throw off from yourselves all your transgressions in which you have transgressed and make for yourselves a new heart and a new spirit, for why should you die, O house of Israel?'**

"'For I do not take any delight in the death of someone dying,' is the utterance of the Sovereign Lord Jehovah. 'So cause a turning back and keep living, O you people.'" [Jehovah is judging members of the organization according to their ways. Those taking the lead who are transgressing and not leaving their bad ways will be destroyed. Those who realize their error and turn back to Jehovah, seeking his righteousness, will survive.]

Isaiah 28:14-29, Therefore hear the word of Jehovah, you braggarts, you rulers [governing body of the organization of Jehovah's Witnesses] of this people who are in Jerusalem: Because you men have said: "We have concluded a covenant with Death; and with Sheol we have effected a vision; the overflowing flash flood, in case it should pass through, will not come to us, for we have made a lie our refuge and in falsehood we have concealed ourselves"; therefore this is what the Sovereign Lord Jehovah has said: "Here I am laying as a foundation in [faithful] Zion, a stone, a tried stone, the precious corner of a sure foundation. **No one exercising faith will get panicky. And I will make justice the measuring line and righteousness the leveling instrument**; and the hail must sweep away the refuge of a lie, and the waters themselves will flood out the very place of concealment. And your covenant with Death will certainly be dissolved, and that vision of yours with Sheol will not stand. The overflowing flash flood, when it passes through—you must also become for it a trampling place. As often as it passes through, it will take you men away, because morning by morning it will pass through, during the day and during the night; and it must become nothing but a reason for quaking to make others understand what has been heard."

For the couch has proved too short for stretching oneself on, and the woven sheet itself is too narrow when wrapping oneself up. **For Jehovah will rise up just as at Mount Perazim, he will be agitated just as in the low plain near Gibeon, that he may do his deed—his deed is strange—and that he may work his work—his work is unusual. And now do not show yourselves scoffers, in order that your bands may not grow strong, for there is an extermination, even something decided upon, that I have heard of from the Sovereign Lord, Jehovah of armies, for all the land.**

Give ear, you men, and listen to my voice; pay attention and listen to my saying. Is it all day long that the plower plows in order to sow seed, that he loosens and harrows his ground? Does he not, when he has smoothed out its surface, then scatter black cumin and sprinkle the cumin, and must he not put in wheat, millet, and barley in the appointed place, and spelt as his boundary? And one corrects him according to what is right. His own God instructs him. For it is not with a threshing instrument that black cumin is given a treading; and upon cumin no wheel of a wagon is turned. For it is with a rod that black cumin is generally beaten out, and cumin with a staff. Is breadstuff itself generally crushed? For never does one incessantly keep treading it out. And he must set the roller of his wagon in motion, and his own steeds, but he will not crush it. This also is what has come forth from Jehovah of armies himself, who has been wonderful in counsel, who has done greatly in effectual working. [When it is time for the farmer to do the threshing, cumin is not treated the same as the other crops, for fear of damaging the tender seed. (Insight on the Scriptures, volume 1, page 556 WBTS 1988) Extermination is coming to those in the organization who have made the lie their refuge. Then again, there are those in the organization who are still faithful to Jehovah, but have remained in association with the organization, even after the organization received Jehovah's denunciation and faithful ones were warned to flee. Like the farmer who knows the appropriate threshing method for each type of seed, Jehovah knows the proper judgment to give to each type of person in the organization when it comes time to "thresh;" and he will pulverize them respective of their type. There are those who will be completely crushed, and then there will be those who will be properly flailed. That is what makes this work of Jehovah's so strange and unusual. The different seed types are all mixed throughout and within the organization, but Jehovah threshes according to each individual "seed" type.]

!   Zechariah Chapter 2 all verses, And I proceeded to raise my eyes and see; and, look! there was a man, and in his hand a measuring rope [justice].

So I said: "Where are you going?"

In turn he said to me: "To measure Jerusalem [Lisa], in order to see what her breadth [great extent; width] amounts to and what her length [of her justice] amounts to." [Measuring Line or Rope = Justice; Leveling Instrument = Righteousness (Isaiah 28:17)]

And, look! the angel who was speaking with me was going forth, and there was another angel going forth to meet him. Then he said to him: "Run, speak to the young man [Leon] over there, saying, '"As open rural country Jerusalem will be inhabited, because of the multitude of men [faithful worshippers of Jehovah who have left the organization] and domestic animals in the midst of her. And I myself shall become to her," is the utterance of Jehovah, "a wall of fire all around, and a glory is what I shall become in the midst of her."'"

"Hey there! Hey there! Flee, then, you people, from the land of the north," is the utterance of Jehovah.

"For in the direction of the four winds of the heavens I have spread you people abroad," is the utterance of Jehovah.

"Hey there, Zion [Leon]! Make your escape, you who are dwelling with the daughter of Babylon. For this is what Jehovah of armies has said, 'Following after the glory he has sent me to the nations that were despoiling you people; for he that is touching you is touching my eyeball. For here I am waving my hand against them, and they will have to become spoil to their slaves.' And you people will certainly know that Jehovah of armies himself has sent me.

"Cry out loudly and rejoice, O daughter of Zion; for here I am coming, and I will reside in the midst of you," is the utterance of Jehovah. **"And many nations will certainly become joined to Jehovah in that day, and they will actually become my people; and I will reside in the midst of you." And you will have to know that Jehovah of armies himself has sent me to you. And Jehovah will certainly take possession of Judah [Leon] as his portion upon the holy ground, and he must yet choose Jerusalem [Lisa]. Keep silence, all flesh, before Jehovah, for he has aroused himself from his holy dwelling.**

1 Peter 2:5,6, You yourselves also as living stones are being built up a spiritual house for the purpose of a holy priesthood, to offer up spiritual sacrifices acceptable to God through Jesus Christ. For it is contained in Scripture: "Look! I am laying in Zion a stone, chosen, a foundation cornerstone, precious; and no one exercising faith in it will by any means come to disappointment."

Recall: Isaiah 54:11, O woman [Lisa] afflicted, tempest-tossed, uncomforted, here I am laying with hard mortar your stones, and I will lay your foundation with sapphires.

Isaiah 29:9-13, especially 12, Linger, you men [those preferring to stay in the organization], and be amazed; blind yourselves and be blinded. They [those taking the lead in the organization] have become intoxicated, but not with wine; they have moved unsteadily, but not because of intoxicating liquor.

For upon you [unfaithful] men Jehovah has poured a spirit of deep sleep; and he closes your eyes, the prophets, and he has covered even your heads, the visionaries [unfaithful "faithful and discreet slave" (Matthew 24:43-51)]. And for you men the vision of everything becomes like the words of the book that has been sealed up, which they give to someone knowing the writing, saying: "Read this out loud, please," and he has to say: "I am unable, for it is sealed up"; and the book must be given to someone that does not know writing, somebody saying: "Read this out loud, please," and he has to say: "I do not know writing at all."

Isaiah 52:8, Listen! Your [Lisa's] own [faithful] watchmen have raised their voice. In unison they keep crying out joyfully; for it will be eye into eye that they will see when Jehovah gathers back Zion.

Ezekiel Chapters 12-13 all verses, And the word of Jehovah continued to occur to me, saying: "Son of man, in the midst of a rebellious house is where you are dwelling, that have eyes to see but they actually do not see, that have ears to hear but they actually do not hear, for they are a rebellious house. As for you, O son of man, make up for yourself luggage for exile and go into exile in the daytime before their eyes, and you must go into exile from your place to another place before their eyes. Perhaps they will see, though they are a rebellious house. And you must bring out your luggage like luggage for exile in the daytime before their eyes, and you yourself will go out in the evening before their eyes like those being brought forth for exile.
 Before their eyes, bore your way through the wall, and you must do the bringing out through it. Before their eyes you will do the carrying on the shoulder itself. During the darkness you will do the bringing out. You will cover your very face that you may not see the earth, because a portent is what I have made you to the [unfaithful] house of Israel."
 And I proceeded to do just the way that I had been commanded. My luggage I brought out, just like luggage for exile, in the daytime; and in the evening I bored my way through the wall by hand. During the darkness I did the bringing out. On my shoulder I did the carrying, before their eyes.
 And the word of Jehovah continued to occur to me in the morning, saying: "Son of man, did not those of the [unfaithful] house of Israel, the rebellious house, say to you, 'What are you doing?' Say to them, 'This is what the Sovereign Lord Jehovah has

said: "As regards the chieftain [governing body of the organization], there is this pronouncement against [unfaithful] Jerusalem and all [members of the organization] the house of Israel who are in the midst of them."

"Say, 'I am a portent for you. Just as I have done, that is the way it will be done to them. Into exile, into captivity they will go. And as regards the chieftain who is in the midst of them, on the shoulder he will do carrying in the darkness and go out; through the wall they will bore in order to do the bringing forth through it. His face he will cover in order that he may not see with his own eye the earth.' And I shall certainly spread my net over him, and he must be caught in my hunting net; and I will bring him to Babylon, to the land of the Chaldeans, but it he will not see; and there he will die. And all who are round about him as a help, and all his military bands, I shall scatter to every wind; and a sword I shall draw out after them. And they will have to know that I am Jehovah when I disperse them among the nations and I actually scatter them among the lands. And I will leave remaining from them a few men from the sword, from the famine and from the pestilence, in order that they may recount all their detestable things among the nations to whom they must come in; and they will have to know that I am Jehovah."

And the word of Jehovah continued to occur to me, saying: "Son of man, with quaking your bread you should eat, and with agitation and with anxious care your water you should drink. And you must say to the people of the land, 'This is what the Sovereign Lord Jehovah has said to the [unfaithful] inhabitants of Jerusalem upon the soil of Israel: "With anxious care their bread they will eat and with horror their water they will drink, in order that its land may be laid desolate of its fullness because of the violence of all those dwelling in it. And the inhabited cities themselves will be devastated, and the land itself will become a mere desolate waste, and you will have to know that I am Jehovah."'"

And the word of Jehovah occurred further to me, saying: "Son of man, what is this proverbial saying that you people have on the soil of [unfaithful] Israel, saying, **'The days are prolonged, and every vision has perished'? Therefore say to them, 'This is what the Sovereign Lord Jehovah has said: "I shall certainly cause this proverbial saying to cease, and they will no more say it as a proverb in Israel."'** But speak to them, 'The days have drawn near, and the matter of every vision.' For there will no more prove to be any valueless vision nor double-faced divination in the midst of the [unfaithful] house of Israel. **"'For I myself, Jehovah, shall speak what word I shall speak, and it will be done. There will be no postponement anymore, for in your days, O rebellious house, I shall speak a word and certainly do it," is the utterance of the Sovereign Lord Jehovah.'"**

And the word of Jehovah continued to occur to me, saying: "Son of man, look! those of the [unfaithful] house of Israel are saying, **'The vision that he is visioning is many days off, and respecting times far off he is prophesying.'** Therefore say to them, 'This is what the Sovereign Lord Jehovah has said: **"'There will be no postponement anymore as to any words of mine. What word I shall speak, it will even be done,' is the utterance of the Sovereign Lord Jehovah."'"**

And the word of Jehovah continued to occur to me, saying: "Son of man, prophesy concerning the [false] prophets of [unfaithful] Israel who are prophesying, and you must say to those prophesying out of their own heart, 'Hear the word of Jehovah. This is what the Sovereign Lord Jehovah has said: **"Woe to the stupid prophets, who are walking after their own spirit, when there is nothing that they have seen!** Like foxes in the devastated places are what your own prophets have become, O [unfaithful] Israel. You men will certainly not go up into the gaps, neither will you build up a stone wall in behalf of the house of Israel, in order to stand in the battle in the day of Jehovah." **"They have visioned what is untrue and a lying divination, those who are saying, 'The utterance of Jehovah is,' when Jehovah himself has not sent them, and they have waited to have a word come true. Is it not an untrue vision that you [unfaithful "faithful and discreet slave"] men have visioned, and a lying divination that you have said, when saying, 'The utterance of Jehovah is,' when I myself have spoken nothing?"'**

"'Therefore this is what the Sovereign Lord Jehovah has said: "'For the reason that you [unfaithful] men have spoken untruth and you have visioned a lie, therefore here I am against you,' is the utterance of the Sovereign Lord Jehovah." And my hand has come to be against the **[false] prophets** that are visioning untruth and that are divining a lie. **In the intimate group of my people they will not continue on, and in the register of the [faithful] house** of Israel they will not be written, and to the soil of Israel they will not come; and you people will have to know that I am the Sovereign Lord Jehovah, for the reason, yes, for the reason that they have led my people astray, saying, "There is peace!" when there is no peace, and there is one that is building a partition wall, but in vain there are those plastering it with whitewash.'

"Say to those plastering with whitewash that it will fall. A flooding downpour will certainly occur, and you, O hailstones, will fall, and a blast of windstorms itself will cause a splitting. And, look! the wall must fall. Will it not be said to you men, 'Where is the coating with which you did the plastering?'

"Therefore this is what the Sovereign Lord Jehovah has said: 'I will also cause a blast of windstorms to burst forth in my rage, and in my anger there will occur a flooding downpour, and in rage there will be hailstones for an extermination. **And I will tear down the wall that you men have plastered with whitewash and bring it into contact with the earth, and its foundation must be exposed. And she [Babylon the Great, the Watchtower Bible and Tract Society, Jehovah's Witnesses] will certainly fall, and you [unfaithful ones in the organization] must come to an end in the midst of her; and you will have to know that I am Jehovah.'**

"'And I will bring my rage to its finish upon the wall and upon those plastering it with whitewash, and I shall say to you men: **"The wall is no more, and those plastering it are no more, the [false] prophets of [unfaithful] Israel that are prophesying to [unfaithful] Jerusalem and that are visioning for her a vision of peace, when there is no peace,"'** is the utterance of the Sovereign Lord Jehovah.

"And as for you, O son of man, set your face against the **daughters [large army of women telling the good news (Psalm 68:11)] of your people who are acting as prophetesses out of their own heart, and prophesy against them.** And you must say, 'This is what the Sovereign Lord Jehovah has said: "Woe to the women sewing bands together upon all elbows and making veils upon the head of every size **in order to hunt souls! Are the souls that you women hunt down the ones belonging to my people, and the souls belonging to you the ones that you preserve alive?** And will you profane me toward my people for the handfuls of barley and for the morsels of bread, **in order to put to death the souls that ought** not to die and in order to preserve alive the souls that ought not to live by your lie to my people, the hearers of a lie?'"

"Therefore this is what the Sovereign Lord Jehovah has said: 'Here I am against the bands of you [unfaithful] women, with which you are hunting down the souls as though they were flying things, and I will rip them from off your arms and let go the souls that you are hunting down, souls as though they were flying things. And I will rip away your veils and deliver my people out of your hand, and they will no more prove to be in your hand something caught in the hunt; and you will have to know that I am Jehovah. **By reason of dejecting the heart of a righteous one with falsehood, when I myself had not caused him pain, and for making the hands of a wicked one strong so that he would not turn back from his bad way in order to preserve him alive, therefore untruth you women will not keep on visioning, and divination you will divine no longer; and I will deliver my people out of your hand, and you will have to know that I am Jehovah.'"**

Titus 3:13,14, Carefully supply Zenas, who is versed in the Law, and Apollos for their trip, that they may not lack anything. But let our people also learn to maintain fine works so as to meet their pressing needs, that they may not be unfruitful.

Romans 1:8-14, First of all, I give thanks to my God through Jesus Christ concerning all of you [faithful worshippers], because your faith is talked about throughout the whole world. For God, to whom I render sacred service with my spirit in connection with the good news about his Son, is my witness of how without ceasing I always make mention of you in my prayers, begging that if at all possible I may now at last be prospered in the will of God so as to come to you. For I am longing to see you, that I may impart some spiritual gift to you in order for you to be made firm; or, rather, that there may be an interchange of encouragement among you, by each one through the other's faith, both yours and mine.

But I do not want you to fail to know, brothers, that I many times purposed to come to you, but I have been hindered until now, in order that I might acquire some fruitage also among you even as among the rest of the nations. Both to Greeks and to Barbarians, both to wise and to senseless ones I am a debtor.

Philippians 4:18, However, I have all things in full and have an abundance. I am filled, now that I have received from Epaphroditus the things from you, a sweet-smelling odor, an acceptable sacrifice, well-pleasing to God. [Recall: the requirements of Jehovah in Deuteronomy Chapter 12, spiritual "sacrifices."]

Philippians 2:25, However, **I consider it necessary to send to you** Epaphroditus, my brother and fellow worker and fellow soldier, but your envoy [an official representative of Jehovah's kingdom] and private servant for my need.

Ezekiel 20:40-21:14, "'For in my holy mountain, in the mountain of the height of Israel,' is the utterance of the Sovereign Lord Jehovah, 'there is where they, the whole house of Israel in its entirety, will serve me, in the land. There I shall take pleasure in them, and there I shall require your contributions and the firstfruits of your presentations in all your holy things. **Because of the restful odor I shall take pleasure in you, when I bring you forth from the peoples and I actually collect you together from the lands to which you have been scattered, and I will be sanctified in you before the eyes of the nations.'** [Recall: the requirements of Jehovah in Deuteronomy Chapter 12, voluntary offerings are our spiritual offerings of prayer, praise and thanksgiving.]

"'And you people will have to know that I am Jehovah, when I bring you onto the soil of Israel, into the land that I lifted up my hand in an oath to give to your forefathers. And you will certainly remember there your ways and all your dealings by which you defiled yourselves, and you will actually feel a loathing at your own faces because of all your bad things that you did. And you will have to know that I am Jehovah when I take action with you for the sake of my name, not according to your bad ways or according to your corrupted dealings, O house of Israel,' is the utterance of the Sovereign Lord Jehovah."

And the word of Jehovah continued to occur to me, saying: "Son of man, set your face in the direction of the southern quarter and drip words to the south, and prophesy to the forest of the field of the south. And you must say to the forest of the south, 'Hear the word of Jehovah. This is what the Sovereign Lord Jehovah has said: "Here I am setting a fire ablaze against you [the organization of Jehovah's Witnesses], and it must devour in you every still-moist tree and every dry tree. The kindling flame will not be extinguished, and by it all faces must be scorched from the south to the north. And all those of flesh must see that I myself, Jehovah, have set it afire, so that it will not be extinguished."'"

And I proceeded to say: "Alas, O Sovereign Lord Jehovah! They are saying respecting me, 'Is he not composing proverbial sayings?'"

And the word of Jehovah continued to occur to me, saying: "Son of man, set your face toward [unfaithful] Jerusalem and drip words toward the holy places, and prophesy against the soil of Israel. And you must say to the soil of Israel, 'This is what Jehovah has said: "Here I am against you, and I will bring forth my sword out of its sheath and cut off from you righteous one and wicked one. In order that I may actually cut off from you righteous one and wicked one, therefore my sword will go forth from its sheath against all flesh from south to north. And all those of flesh will have to know that I myself, Jehovah, have brought forth my sword from its sheath. No more will it go back."'

"And as for you, O son of man, sigh with shaking hips. Even with bitterness you should sigh before their eyes. And it must occur that, in case they say to you, 'On account of what are you sighing?' you must say, 'At a report.' For it will certainly come, and every heart must melt and all hands must drop down and every spirit must become dejected and all knees themselves will drip with water. 'Look! It will certainly come and be brought to occur,' is the utterance of the Sovereign Lord Jehovah."

And the word of Jehovah continued to occur to me, saying: "Son of man, prophesy, and you must say, 'This is what Jehovah has said: "Say, 'A sword, a sword! It has been sharpened, and it is also polished. For the purpose of organizing a slaughter it has been sharpened; for the purpose of its getting a glitter it has been polished.'"'"

"Or shall we exult?"

"'Is it rejecting the scepter of my own son, as it does every tree?

"'And one gives it to be polished, in order to wield it with the hand. It—a sword has been sharpened, and it—it has been polished, in order to give it into the hand of a killer.

"'Cry out and howl, O son of man, for it itself has come to be against my [unfaithful] people; it is against all the chieftains [governing body and all those taking the lead in the organization of Jehovah's Witnesses] of Israel. The very ones hurled to the sword have come to be with my people. Therefore make a slap on the thigh. For an extermination has been made, and what of it if it is rejecting also the scepter? This will not continue existing,' is the utterance of the Sovereign Lord Jehovah.

"And you, O son of man—prophesy, and strike palm against palm, and 'A sword!' should be repeated for three times. The sword of the slain ones it is. It is the sword of someone slain who is great, which is making an encirclement of them."

Luke 19:43, Because the days will come upon you [unfaithful ones in the organization] when your enemies will build around you a fortification with pointed stakes and will encircle you and distress you from every side.

Jeremiah 6:1-6, Take shelter, O you sons of Benjamin, from the midst of [unfaithful] Jerusalem; and in Tekoa blow the horn. And over Bethhaccherem raise a fire signal; because calamity itself has looked down out of the north, even a great crash. The daughter of Zion [the organization of Jehovah's Witnesses] has resembled indeed a comely and daintily bred woman. To her the [faithful] shepherds and their droves proceeded to come. Against her [the organization] they pitched their tents all around. They grazed off each one his own part. Against her they have sanctified [spiritual] war: "Rise up, and let us go up at midday!"

"Woe to us [the governing body], for the day has declined [their day has come to an end], for the shadows of evening keep extending themselves!"

"Rise up, and let us go up during the night and bring to ruin her dwelling towers [the Watchtower Bible and Tract Society, the organization of Jehovah's Witnesses]."

For this is what Jehovah of armies has said: "Cut down wood and throw up against [unfaithful] Jerusalem a [spiritual] siege rampart. **She is the city with which an accounting must be held. She is nothing but oppression in the midst of her."**

Ezekiel 20:40, "For in my holy mountain, in the mountain of the height of Israel," is the utterance of the Sovereign Lord Jehovah, "there is where they, the whole house of Israel in its entirety, will serve me, in the land. **There I shall take pleasure in them, and there I shall require your contributions and the firstfruits of your presentations in all your holy things. [Recall: Deuteronomy Chapter 12, voluntary spiritual offerings.]**

Psalm 149:4, For Jehovah is taking pleasure in his people. He beautifies the meek ones with salvation.

Hebrews 13:15, Through him let us always offer to God a sacrifice of praise, that is, the fruit of lips which make public declaration to his name. [Recall: Deuteronomy Chapter 12, spiritual "sacrifices."]

Romans 12:1, Consequently I entreat you by the compassions of God, brothers, to present your bodies a sacrifice living, holy, acceptable to God, a sacred service with your power of reason.

Malachi Chapters 3-4 all verses, "Look! I am sending my messenger, and he must clear up a way before me. And suddenly there will come to His temple the true Lord, whom you people are seeking, and the messenger of the covenant in whom you are delighting. Look! He will certainly come," Jehovah of armies has said.

"But who will be putting up with the day of his coming, and who will be the one standing when he appears? For he will be like the fire of a refiner and like the lye of laundrymen. And he must sit as a refiner and cleanser of silver and must cleanse the sons of Levi; and he must clarify them like gold and like silver, **and they will certainly become to Jehovah people presenting a gift offering in righteousness.** And the gift offering of [faithful] Judah and of [faithful] Jerusalem will actually be gratifying to Jehovah, as in the days of long ago and as in the years of antiquity.

"And I will come near to you people for the judgment, and I will become a speedy witness against the sorcerers, and against the adulterers, and against those swearing falsely, and against those acting fraudulently with the wages of a wage worker, with the widow and with the fatherless boy, and those turning away the alien resident, while they have not feared me, Jehovah of armies has said.

"For I am Jehovah; I have not changed. And you are sons of Jacob; you have not come to your finish. From the days of your forefathers you have turned aside from my regulations and have not kept them. Return to me, and I will return to you, Jehovah of armies has said.

And you have said: "In what way shall we return?"

"Will earthling man rob God? But you are robbing me."

And you have said: "In what way have we robbed you?"

"In the tenth parts and in the contributions. With the curse you are cursing me, and me you are robbing—the nation in its entirety. Bring all the tenth parts into the storehouse, that there may come to be food in my house; and test me out, please, in this respect," Jehovah of armies has said, "whether I shall not open to you people the floodgates of the heavens and actually empty out upon you a blessing until there is no more want."

"And I will rebuke for you the devouring one, and it will not ruin for you the fruit of the ground, nor will the vine in the field prove fruitless for you," Jehovah of armies has said.

"And all the nations will have to pronounce you happy, for you yourselves will become a land of delight," Jehovah of armies has said.

"Strong have been your words against me," Jehovah has said.

And you have said: "What have we spoken with one another against you?"

"You have said, 'It is of no value to serve God. And what profit is there in that we have kept the obligation to him, and that we have walked dejectedly on account of Jehovah of armies. And at present we are pronouncing presumptuous people happy. Also, the doers of wickedness have been built up. Also, they have tested God out and keep getting away.'"

At that time those in fear of Jehovah spoke with one another, each one with his companion, and Jehovah kept paying attention and listening. And a book of remembrance began to be written up before him for those in fear of Jehovah and for those [faithful worshippers of Jehovah who will leave the organization] thinking upon his name.

"And they will certainly become mine," Jehovah of armies has said, "at the day when I am producing a special property. And I will show compassion upon them, just as a man shows compassion upon his son who is serving him. And you people will again certainly see the distinction between a righteous one

JEHOVAH'S KINGDOM

and a wicked one, between one serving God and one who has not served him."

"For, look! the day is coming that is burning like the furnace, and all the presumptuous ones and all those doing wickedness must become as stubble. And the day that is coming will certainly devour them," Jehovah of armies has said, "so that it will not leave to them either root or bough. **And to you who are in fear of my name the sun of righteousness will certainly shine forth, with healing in its wings; and you will actually go forth and paw the ground like fattened calves."**

"And you people will certainly tread down the wicked ones, for they will become as powder under the soles of your feet in the day on which I am acting," Jehovah of armies has said.

"Remember, you people, the law of Moses my servant with which I commanded him in Horeb concerning all Israel, even regulations and judicial decisions.

"Look! I am sending to you people Elijah the prophet before the coming of the great and fear-inspiring day of Jehovah. And he must turn the heart of fathers back toward sons, and the heart of sons back toward fathers [Jehovah]; in order that I may not come and actually strike the earth with a devoting of it to destruction."

Jeremiah 31:22b, For Jehovah has created a new thing in the earth: A mere female [Lisa] will press around an able-bodied man.

Zechariah 6:11-15, And you must take silver and gold [people = vessels of silver and gold value (2 Timothy 2:20,21)] and make a grand [spiritual] crown and put it upon the head of Joshua [Lisa] the son of Jehozadak the high priest. And you must say to him,

"'This is what Jehovah of armies has said: "Here is the man [Leon] whose name is Sprout [new spiritual "growth"]. And from his own place he will sprout, and he will certainly build the temple of Jehovah. And he himself will build the temple of Jehovah, and he, for his part, will carry the dignity; and he must sit down and rule on his **throne**, and he must become a **priest** upon his throne, and the very counsel of peace will prove to be between **both of them** ["Joshua," a priest and "Sprout," a king]. And the grand crown itself will come to belong to [four persons] Helem and to Tobijah and to Jedaiah and to Hen the son of Zephaniah as a memorial in the temple of Jehovah. **And those who are far away will come and actually build in the temple of Jehovah. And you people will have to know that Jehovah of armies himself has sent me to you. And it must occur—if you will without fail listen to the voice of Jehovah your God.'"**

[We are to present ourselves to Jehovah as "a sweet-smelling odor," "a sacrifice living, holy, acceptable to God." (Philippians 4:18) (Romans 12:1)]

Psalm 45 all verses NWT (1984), My heart has become astir with a goodly matter. I am saying: "My works are concerning a king." May my tongue be the stylus of a skilled copyist. You are indeed more handsome than the sons of men. Charm has been poured out upon your lips. That is why God has blessed you [Leon] to time indefinite. Gird your sword upon your thigh, O mighty one, with your dignity and your splendor. And in your splendor go on to success; **ride in the cause of truth and humility and righteousness, and your right hand will instruct you in fear-inspiring things.**

Psalm 16:8, I have placed Jehovah in front of me constantly. Because he is at my right hand, I shall not be made to totter.

Psalm 45, continued, Your arrows are sharp—under you peoples keep falling—in the heart of the enemies of the king. God is your throne to time indefinite, even forever; the scepter of your kingship is a scepter of uprightness. You have loved righteousness and you hate wickedness. That is why God, your God, has anointed you with the oil of exultation more than your partners. All your garments are myrrh and aloeswood and cassia; out from the grand ivory palace stringed instruments themselves have made you rejoice. The daughters of kings are among your precious women. The queenly consort has taken her stand at your right hand in gold of Ophir. Listen, O daughter, and see, and incline your ear; and forget your people and your father's house. And the king will long for your prettiness, for he is your lord, so bow down to him. The daughter of Tyre also with a gift—the rich ones of the people will soften your own face. The king's daughter is all glorious within the house; her clothing is with settings of gold. In woven apparel she will be brought to the king. The virgins in her train as her companions are being brought in to you. They will be brought with rejoicing and joyfulness; they will enter into the palace of the king. In place of your forefathers there will come to be your sons, whom you will appoint as princes in all the earth. I will make mention of your name throughout all generations to come. That is why peoples themselves will laud you to time indefinite, even forever.

Revelation 19:7,8, Let us rejoice and be overjoyed, and let us give him the glory, because the marriage of the Lamb has arrived and his wife has prepared herself. Yes, it has been granted to her [Lisa] to be arrayed in bright, clean, fine linen, for the fine linen stands for the righteous acts of the holy ones.

July 6, 1989

Phone Call: [We received a phone call and donation of $10 toward the cost of printing the denunciation, from Mr. And Mrs. Lowell (and Margaret) R. She told us that she really appreciated the information because the scriptures made it very clear to her that the organization of Jehovah's Witnesses is Babylon the Great.]

1 Timothy 5:18, For the scripture says: "You must not muzzle a bull when it threshes out the grain"; also: "The workman is worthy of his wages."

Isaiah 61:8 For I, Jehovah, am loving justice, hating robbery along with unrighteousness. And I will give their wages in trueness, and an indefinitely lasting covenant I shall conclude toward them.

July 7, 1989

Psalm 51 all verses, Show me favor, O God, according to your loving-kindness. According to the abundance of your mercies wipe out my transgressions. Thoroughly wash me from my error, and cleanse me even from my sin. For my transgressions I myself know, and my sin is in front of me constantly. Against you, you alone, I have sinned, and what is bad in your eyes I have done, in order that you may prove to be righteous when you speak, that you may be in the clear when you judge. Look! With error I was brought forth with birth pains, and in sin my mother conceived me. Look! You have taken delight in truthfulness itself in the inward parts; and in the secret self may you cause me to know sheer wisdom. May you purify me from sin with hyssop, that I may be clean; may you wash me, that I may become whiter even than snow. May you cause me to hear exultation and rejoicing, that the bones that you have crushed may be joyful. Conceal your face from my sins, and wipe out even all my errors. **Create in me even a pure heart, O God, and put within me a new spirit, a steadfast one. Do not throw me away from before your face; and your holy spirit O do not take away from me. Do restore to me the exultation of salvation by you, and may you support me even with a willing spirit.** I will teach transgressors your ways, that sinners themselves may turn right back to you. Deliver me from bloodguiltiness, O God the God of my salvation, that my tongue may joyfully tell about your righteousness. O Jehovah, may you open these lips of mine, that my own mouth may tell forth your praise. For you do not take delight in sacrifice—otherwise I would give it; in whole burnt offering you do not find pleasure. **The sacrifices to God are a broken spirit; a heart broken and crushed, O God, you will not despise. In your goodwill do deal well with [faithful] Zion; may you build the walls of [faithful] Jerusalem. In that case you will be delighted with sacrifices of righteousness, with burnt sacrifice and whole offering; in that case bulls will be offered up on your very own altar. Recall: Deuteronomy Chapter 12, spiritual sacrifices.**

July 8, 1989

Psalm 16:5, Jehovah is the portion of my [Lisa's] allotted share and of my cup. You are holding fast my lot.

Psalm 6:8-10, Get away from me, all you [all evildoers, especially Satan] practicers of what is hurtful, for Jehovah will certainly hear the sound of my weeping. Jehovah will indeed hear my request for favor; Jehovah himself will accept my own prayer. All my enemies will be very much ashamed and disturbed; they will turn back, they will be ashamed instantly.

July 9, 1989

!   Isaiah 18:4-7, For this is what Jehovah has said to me: "I will keep undisturbed and look upon my established place, like the dazzling heat along with the light, like the cloud of dew in the heat of harvest. For before the harvest, when the blossom comes to perfection and the bloom becomes a ripening grape, one must also cut off the sprigs with pruning shears and must remove the tendrils, must lop them off. They will be left all together for the bird of prey of the mountains and for the beast of the earth. And upon it the bird of prey will certainly pass the summer, and upon it even every beast of the earth will pass the harvesttime.

"In that time a gift will be brought to Jehovah of armies, from a people [people = vessels of silver and gold value (2 Timothy 2:20,21)] drawn out and scoured, even from a people fear-inspiring everywhere, a nation of tensile strength and of treading down, whose land the rivers have washed away, to the place of the name of Jehovah of armies, Mount Zion."

Isaiah 60:4, Raise your eyes all around and see! They have all of them been collected together; they have come to you [Lisa]. From far away your own sons keep coming, and your daughters who will be taken care of on the flank.

2 Samuel Chapter 23 all verses [abbreviated here], And these are the last words of David:

"The utterance of David the son of Jesse, and the utterance of the able-bodied man that was raised up on high, the anointed of the God of Jacob, and the pleasant one of the melodies of Israel. The spirit of Jehovah it was that spoke by me, and his word was upon my tongue. The God of Israel said, to me the Rock of Israel spoke, 'When one ruling over mankind is righteous, ruling in the fear of God, then it is as the light of morning, when the sun shines forth, a morning without clouds. From brightness, from rain, there is grass out of the earth.' For is not my [Lisa's] household like that with God? Because it is an indefinitely lasting covenant that he has assigned to me, nicely put in order in everything and secured. [Rosie says that she "feels secure" here in my home. She and her children are staying with us until we get our apartments in Iowa.] Because it is all my salvation and all my delight, is that not why he will make it grow? But good-for-nothing persons are chased away, like thornbushes, all of them; for it is not by the hand that they should be taken. When a man touches them he should be fully armed with iron and the shaft of a spear, and with fire they will thoroughly be burned up."

2 Samuel 22:20-29, And he proceeded to bring me out into a roomy place; he was rescuing me, because he had found delight in me. Jehovah rewards me according to my righteousness; according to the cleanness of my hands he repays me. For I [Lisa] have kept the ways of Jehovah, and I have not wickedly departed from my God. For all his judicial decisions are in front of me; and as for his statutes, I shall not turn aside from them. And I shall prove myself faultless toward him, and I will keep myself from error on my part. And let Jehovah repay me according to my righteousness, according to my cleanness in front of his eyes. With someone loyal you will act in loyalty; with the faultless, mighty one you will deal faultlessly; with the one keeping clean you will show yourself clean, and with the crooked one you will act as silly. And the humble people you will save; but your eyes are against the haughty ones, that you may bring them low. **For you are my lamp, O Jehovah, and it is Jehovah that makes my darkness shine.**

Isaiah 11:1-5, And there must go forth a **twig** out of the stump of Jesse; and out of his roots a **sprout** will be fruitful. **And upon him the spirit of Jehovah must settle down, the spirit of wisdom and of understanding, the spirit of counsel and of mightiness, the spirit of knowledge and of the fear of Jehovah; and there will be enjoyment by him in the fear of Jehovah.**
And he will not judge by any mere appearance to his eyes, nor reprove simply according to the thing heard by his ears. And with righteousness he must judge the lowly ones, and with uprightness he must give reproof in behalf of the meek ones of the earth. And he must strike the earth with the rod of his mouth; and with the spirit of his lips he will put the wicked one to death. And righteousness must prove to be the belt of his hips, and faithfulness the belt of his loins.

Isaiah Chapter 12 all verses, And in that day you will be sure to say: "I shall thank you, O Jehovah, for although you got incensed at me, your anger gradually turned back, and you proceeded to comfort me. Look! God is my salvation. I shall trust and be in no dread; for Jah Jehovah is my strength and my might, and he came to be the salvation of me."

With exultation you people will be certain to draw water out of the springs of salvation. And in that day you will certainly say: "Give thanks to Jehovah, you people! Call upon his name. Make known among the peoples his dealings. Make mention that his name is put on high. Make melody to Jehovah, for he has done surpassingly. This is made known in all the earth.

"Cry out shrilly and shout for joy, O you inhabitress of Zion [Lisa], for great in the midst of you is the Holy One of Israel."

Isaiah 13:3-5, I myself [Jehovah] have issued the command to my sanctified ones. I have also called my mighty ones for expressing my anger, my eminently exultant ones. Listen! A crowd in the mountains, something like a numerous people! Listen! The uproar of kingdoms, of nations gathered together! Jehovah of armies is mustering the army of war. They are coming from the land far away, from the extremity of the heavens, Jehovah and the weapons of his denunciation, to wreck all the earth.

Philippians 4:19, In turn, my God will fully supply all your need to the extent of his riches in glory by means of Christ Jesus.

Ecclesiastes 11:5, Just as you are not aware of what is the way of the spirit in the bones in the belly of her that is pregnant, in like manner you do not know the work of the true God, who does all things.

1 Timothy 6:20, O Timothy, guard what is laid up in trust with you, turning away from the empty speeches [false teachings of the organization of Jehovah's Witnesses] that violate what is holy and from the contradictions of the falsely called "knowledge."

2 Timothy 1:12-14, For this very cause I am also suffering these things, but I am not ashamed. For I know the one whom I have believed, and I am confident he is able to guard what I have laid

up in trust with him until that day. Keep holding the pattern of healthful words that you heard from me with the faith and love that are in connection with Christ Jesus. This fine trust guard through the holy spirit which is dwelling in us.

Given: [Sunday night I was given this scripture.] Philippians 2:28, Therefore with the greater haste I [Jehovah] am sending him, that on seeing him you may rejoice again and I may be the more free from grief.

Zechariah 2:8,9, For this is what Jehovah of armies has said, "Following after the glory he has sent me [in this instance this scripture applies to Leon] to the nations that were despoiling you people; for he that is touching you is touching my eyeball. For here I am waving my hand against them [the organization of Jehovah's Witnesses], and they will have to become spoil to their slaves [faithful worshippers of Jehovah still in the organization being treated like slaves]." And you people will certainly know that Jehovah of armies himself has sent me. [Rosie's Words: Rosie said to me, "Lisa, you are very special to Jehovah. Satan is tormenting you, and it is like 'touching (Jehovah's) eyeball.'"]

Psalm 41:11,12, By this I do know that you have found delight in me, because my enemy [Satan] does not shout in triumph over me. As for me, because of my integrity you have upheld me, and you will set me before your face to time indefinite.

July 10, 1989

[Jehovah alerts us to Satan's attempts to do us harm, because Rosie is given this scripture.] Jeremiah 39:17,18, "And I will deliver you in that day," is the utterance of Jehovah, "and you will not be given into the hand of the men of whom you yourself are scared."

"For I shall without fail furnish you an escape, and by the sword you will not fall; and you will certainly come to have your soul as a spoil, because you have trusted in me," is the utterance of Jehovah.

[Rosie had noticed that one of our neighbors from a different building was coming out of his place to observe us every time we arrive and leave from my townhouse apartment.

We had earlier recognized a known associate of the local cult of Satan worshippers visiting at this neighbor's place. Later on that same day, when we had gone to the local park, a man in a car followed and observed us, and left when we left.

Jehovah has indicated the nature of their activities to us. He also brought to our awareness another man in a car that drove into and around our parking lot. We saw him observing our children, who were playing outside, including Gabrielle. The man paused but then decided to leave. We were left with the strong impression that the children were in danger.

The reason we suspect that Gabrielle is the target of their intentions is because there had been a previous attempt to abduct her at gunpoint here in our parking lot during the winter. I had notified the police at that time, and they were able to identify the man. The chief of police told me that he was very possibly a member of a local cult of Satan worshippers.

Rosie and I brought all three children in. We will keep them inside the rest of the time we're still living here, while we are preparing to relocate to Iowa.

We were also given strong reason to believe that these men had planted a listening device in or around my apartment, and that the same neighbor that was watching us, was also monitoring our conversations. We believe that this was how he always knew when we were about to leave, or had just returned. When we realized that this was what was happening, I stood in my living room and although I was visibly shaking I said, loudly: "Jehovah knows everything you are doing, Steve, and you are not going to get away with it. You can tell all your friends that Jehovah is protecting every one of us. None of your attempts have been successful, neither will anything else you try. You can tell your friends that Jehovah is not going to let you get away with anything!"

As we stood in the living room we looked out the window and saw this neighbor bolt from his building and head down to the other end of the apartment complex. He was white-faced and looked terrified. We did not encounter another problem with him or any of the others the rest of the time we were there.]

Proverbs 10:28, The expectation of the righteous ones [we expected Jehovah's protection] is a rejoicing, but the very hope of the wicked ones [their plan and their hope of success was destroyed by Jehovah] will perish.

Proverbs 10:24, The thing frightful to the wicked one—that is what will come to him; but the desire of the righteous ones [the safety of our children and ourselves] will be granted.

Psalm 21:2, The desire of his heart [our hearts] you have given him, and the wish of his lips you have not withheld. *Selah*.

Proverbs 10:21, The very lips of the righteous one keep pasturing many, but for want of heart the foolish themselves keep dying.

Proverbs 9:8,9, Do not reprove a ridiculer, that he may not hate you. Give a reproof to a wise person and he will love you. Give to a wise person and he will become still wiser. Impart knowledge to someone righteous and he will increase in learning.

1 Timothy 6:20, O Timothy, guard what is laid up in trust with you, turning away from the empty speeches that violate what is holy and from the contradictions of the falsely called "knowledge."

July 12, 1989

Hebrews 4:11-16, Let us therefore do our utmost to enter into that **rest**, for fear anyone should fall in the same **pattern** of disobedience. For the word of God is alive and exerts power and is sharper than any two-edged sword and pierces even to the dividing of soul and spirit, and of joints and their marrow, and is able to discern thoughts and intentions of the heart. **And there is not a creation that is not manifest to his sight, but all things are naked and openly exposed to the eyes of him with whom we have an accounting.**
Seeing, therefore, that we have a great high priest who has passed through the heavens, Jesus the Son of God, let us hold onto our confessing of him. For we have as high priest, not one who cannot sympathize with our weaknesses, but one who has been tested in all respects like ourselves, but without sin. Let us, therefore, approach with freeness of speech to the throne of undeserved kindness, that we may obtain mercy and find undeserved kindness for help at the right time.

Isaiah 53:4, Truly our sicknesses were what he himself carried; and as for our pains, he bore them. But we ourselves accounted him as plagued, stricken by God and afflicted.

Isaiah 61:1, The spirit of the Sovereign Lord Jehovah is upon me [Lisa], for the reason that Jehovah has anointed me to tell good news to the meek ones. He has sent me to bind up the broken-hearted, to proclaim liberty to those taken captive and the wide opening of the eyes even to the prisoners.

Isaiah 62:1, For the sake of Zion I shall not keep still, and for the sake of Jerusalem I shall not stay quiet until her righteousness goes forth just like the brightness, and her [Lisa's] salvation like a torch that burns.

Psalm 102:13, You yourself will arise, you will have mercy on Zion, for it is the season to be favorable to her, for the appointed time has come.

Isaiah 40:6-11, Listen! Someone is saying: "Call out!" And one said: "What shall I call out?"
"All flesh is green grass, and all their loving-kindness is like the blossom of the field. The green grass has dried up, the blossom has withered, because the very spirit of Jehovah has blown upon it. Surely the people are green grass. The green grass has dried up, the blossom has withered; but as for the word of our God, it will last to time indefinite."
Make your way up even onto a high mountain, you woman [Lisa] bringing good news for Zion. Raise your voice even with power, you woman bringing good news for Jerusalem. Raise it. Do not be afraid. Say to the cities of Judah: **"Here is your God."** Look! The Sovereign Lord Jehovah himself will come even as a strong one, and his arm will be ruling for him. Look! His reward is with him, and the wage he pays is before him. Like a shepherd he will shepherd his own drove. With his arm he will collect together the lambs; and in his bosom he will carry them. Those giving suck he will conduct with care.

Lamentations Chapter 1 all verses [abbreviated here], [Parts of this chapter describe my life while I was being corrected by Jehovah for committing a great sin against him. It shows that, even though it is right and good that I thoroughly regretted and repented of my sin, and was mercifully forgiven, it is also right and good that Jehovah properly and completely punished me. As a consequence, I am stronger and wiser now, and it is utterly unthinkable of me to ever again deliberately commit offense against Jehovah, and cause him sorrow.

In 1984, I committed a double offense against Jehovah. I was guilty of inappropriate physical contact with Daniel M. My conduct was considered unclean in the eyes of Jehovah. Then I compounded my sin because I married Daniel who was not a faithful Christian.

When I was pregnant with Gabrielle in 1985, I had to remain in complete bed rest for the last three months of my pregnancy because I developed toxemia (toxins in the blood) and came close to having a stroke, which would have killed both the baby and me.

Also, around this time, Daniel told me that if I tried to leave him, he would come to the hospital after I gave birth and kill us.

On other occasions while I was married to him, Daniel tried to kill my children and me. He continued his efforts, and after I divorced him I had to take the children and live in hiding to keep them safe. It is only mercy that I did not die during this time when Jehovah was correcting me. Jehovah kept my children safe, as well. Thank you, Jehovah!

Also, I have dealt with major depression since my childhood. During this time in my life my depression was so bad that on occasion I felt suicidal. Any personal strength that I had left me, and I became helpless. That I have been able to get out of bed every day and take care of my children as well as go to the Kingdom Hall meetings and out in field service (the door-to-door ministry) has only been by virtue of Jehovah's strength, not my own.

In his mercy, Jehovah kept us alive and safe through this frightening period of time in our lives, which because of my sins I had brought upon myself. I so deeply regret my sins. And I am so sorry for the grief I brought on my children. Thank you, Jehovah, for protecting us. Your wisdom and justice are perfect. And thank you, Jehovah, for your kind forgiveness, which I do not deserve.]

Lamentations Chapter 1, continued, Profusely she weeps during the night, and her tears are upon her cheeks.

Her adversaries have become the head. Those who are her enemies are unconcerned.

Because Jehovah himself has brought grief to her on account of the abundance of her transgressions, her own children have walked captive before the adversary. Jerusalem [Lisa] has committed outright sin. That is why she has become a mere abhorrent thing.

She did not remember the future for her, [In 1979, around the time of my baptism, when I dedicated my life to Jehovah, I was given a vision from Jehovah. I was shown an image of Jehovah and myself walking down a long road together, hand in hand, and he called me "Friend." Some years later, when I was in a severe depression, I became spiritually weak. I should have kept in mind the extraordinary vision I had been given.

At that time I had also been praying to Jehovah to draw Leon to true worship, but I had given up hoping for that. I then turned to Daniel M. and gave up on my prayers. This is when I committed these great sins against Jehovah.]

Lamentations Chapter 1, continued, No comforter does she have. O Jehovah, see my affliction, for the enemy has put on great airs.

The adversary [Satan] has spread out his own hand against all her desirable things [all of my precious relationships with others—my children, my Christian friends, even Leon.].

For she has seen nations that have come into her sanctuary, whom you commanded that they should not come into the congregation **belonging to you**. [Daniel M. was not a member of Jehovah's household, but rather belonged to the nations. And I was consecrated to God, "belonging to Jehovah." (Isaiah 44:5)]

See, O Jehovah, and do look, for I have become as a valueless woman.

Does there exist any pain like my pain that has been severely dealt out to me, with which Jehovah has caused grief in the day of his burning anger. [For my wrongdoing, I experienced emotional suffering and pain like no other I have ever known. Everything that Jehovah brought upon me for punishment I deserved.]

He has called against me a meeting, in order to break my young men to pieces. [Jehovah had begun to answer my prayers for Leon. And Jehovah could see what I could not at that time. He saw Leon beginning to try to locate me, but because of my lack of faith and my sins Jehovah prevented him.

Also, my sin was a humiliation to my family, especially my son, Bram, who was walking honorably in the truth.]

Over these things I am weeping as a woman. My eye, my eye is running down with waters.

Jehovah is righteous, for it is against his mouth that I have rebelled. Listen, now, all you peoples, and see my pain.

Jeremiah 30:13-17, "There is no one pleading your cause, for your ulcer. There are no means of healing, no mending, for you. All those intensely loving you are the ones that have forgotten you. You are not the one for whom they keep searching. For with the stroke of an enemy I have struck you, with the chastisement of someone cruel, on account of the abundance of your error; your sins have become numerous. Why do you cry out on account of your breakdown? Your pain is incurable on account of the abundance of your error; your sins have become numerous. I have done these things to you. Therefore all those devouring you will themselves be devoured; and as for all your adversaries, into captivity they will all of them go. And those pillaging you will certainly come to be for pillaging, and all those plundering you I shall give over to plundering."

"For I shall bring up a recuperation for you, and from your strokes I shall heal you," is the utterance of Jehovah. "For a woman chased away is what they called you: 'That is Zion [Lisa], for whom no one is searching.'"

Psalm 102:17, He will certainly turn to the prayer of those stripped of everything, and not despise their prayer.

Psalm 66:19, Truly God has heard; he has paid attention to the voice of my prayer.

Isaiah 40:2, Speak to the heart of Jerusalem [Lisa] and call out to her that her military service has been fulfilled, that her error has been paid off. For from the hand of Jehovah she has received a full amount for all her sins.

JEHOVAH'S KINGDOM

Prayer Answered: [I asked Jehovah in prayer if a letter I had written was appropriate. Jehovah's answer was "yes." He gave me this scripture.] 1 Thessalonians 2:1-4, To be sure, you yourselves know, brothers, how our visit to you **has not been without results**, but how, after we had first suffered [at the hand of Satan] and been insolently treated (just as you know) in Philippi, we mustered up boldness by means of our God to speak to you the good news of God with a great deal of struggling. **For the exhortation we give does not arise from error or from uncleanness or with deceit, but, just as we have been proved by God as fit to be entrusted with the good news, so we speak, as pleasing, not men, but God, who makes proof of our hearts.**

Jeremiah 4:6, **Raise a signal toward Zion.** Make provision for shelter. Do not stand still. For there is a calamity that I am bringing in from the north, even a great crash.

Isaiah 63:4, For the day of vengeance is in my heart, and the very year of my repurchased ones has come.

1 Corinthians 14:37, If anyone thinks he is a prophet or gifted with the spirit, let him acknowledge the things I am writing to you, because they are the Lord's commandment.

Isaiah 52:11,12, Turn away, turn away, get out of there, touch nothing unclean; get out from the midst of her [the organization of Jehovah's Witnesses], keep yourselves [faithful worshippers of Jehovah] clean, you who are carrying the utensils [people = vessels of silver and gold value (2 Timothy 2:20,21)] of Jehovah. For you people will get out in no panic, and you will go in no flight. For Jehovah will be going even before you, and the God of Israel will be your rear guard.

Colossians 4:8, For the very purpose of your knowing the things having to do with us and that he may comfort your hearts, I am sending him to you.

1 Timothy 3:14, I am writing you these things, though I am hoping to come to you shortly.

2 Corinthians 13:1, This is the third time I am coming to you. At the mouth of two witnesses or of three every matter must be established.

2 Thessalonians 3:13, For your part, brothers, do not give up in doing right.

Proverbs 10:28a, The expectation of the righteous ones is a rejoicing.

Definition Of Faith: Hebrews 11:1, Faith is the assured expectation of things hoped for, the evident demonstration of realities though not beheld.

2 Corinthians 4:18, While we keep our eyes, not on the things seen, but on the things unseen. For the things seen are temporary, but the things unseen are everlasting.

Ecclesiastes 11:5, Just as you are not aware of what is the way of the spirit in the bones in the belly of her that is pregnant, in like manner you do not know the work of the true God, who does all things.

→ Ecclesiastes 12:10-12, The congregator sought to find the delightful words and the writing of correct words of truth.
The words of the wise ones are like oxgoads, and just like nails driven in are those indulging in collections of sentences; they have been given from one shepherd. As regards anything besides these, my son, take a warning: To the making of many books [Watchtower Bible and Tract Society publications] there is no end, and much devotion to them is wearisome to the flesh.

Psalm 40:4, Happy is the able-bodied man [faithful worshipper of Jehovah] that has put Jehovah as his trust and that has not turned his face to defiant people, nor to those [unfaithful ones in the organization] falling away to lies.

Psalm 10:17, The desire of the meek ones you will certainly hear, O Jehovah. You will prepare their heart. You will pay attention with your ear.

Advance Warning: Psalm 7:14,15, Look! There is one [Satan] that is pregnant with what is hurtful, and he has conceived trouble and is bound to give birth to falsehood. A pit he has excavated, and he proceeded to dig it; but he will fall into the hole that he went making. [Jehovah gave me these words before I read a letter from my sister, Dawn. He warned me in advance that Satan was going to use her words to hurt me, and that I was going to be lied to in her letter. If Jehovah hadn't warned me about these particular lies before I read them, they would have crushed my heart to the point that I would have wanted to die.]

Psalm 6:8-10, Get away from me, all you practicers of what is hurtful, for Jehovah will certainly hear the sound of my weeping. Jehovah will indeed hear my request for favor; Jehovah himself will accept my own prayer. All my enemies will be very much ashamed and disturbed; they will turn back, they will be ashamed instantly.

Recall: Matthew 10:36, Indeed, a man's enemies will be persons of his own household.

! **Given:** Psalm 7:12, If anyone will not return [turn back from doing wrong; telling lies], His sword he will sharpen, His bow he will certainly bend, and he [Jehovah] will make it ready for shooting. [On a later date, my sister apologized and told me that what she had written in her letter wasn't true.]

Hebrews 4:11a, Let us therefore do our utmost to enter into that rest [a rest on our faith in Jehovah and the truthful, though unseen fulfillment of his promises, instead of resting our faith in the things seen of this world. The Israelites were made to wander for forty years because they did not rest their faith in Jehovah. **The source of truth is Jehovah.** The source of falsehood is Satan.]

Psalm 102:13, You yourself [Jehovah] will arise, you will have mercy on Zion [Lisa], for it is the season to be favorable to her, for the appointed time has come.

Psalm 66:19, Truly God has heard; he has paid attention to the voice of my prayer.

July 14, 1989

Ministry Of The Reconciliation:

Isaiah 49:8, This is what Jehovah has said: "In a time of goodwill I have answered you [Lisa], and in a day of salvation I have helped you; and I kept safeguarding you [keeping you alive] that I might give you as a covenant for the people, to rehabilitate the land, to bring about the repossessing of the desolated hereditary possessions."

NOW IS THE DAY OF SALVATION!

[This is Jehovah's Day!]

Isaiah 29:22-24, Therefore this is what Jehovah has said to the [faithful] house of Jacob, he that redeemed Abraham: "Jacob will not now be ashamed, nor will his own face now grow pale; for when he sees his children, the work of my hands, in the midst of him, they will sanctify my name, and they will certainly sanctify the Holy One of Jacob, and the God of Israel they will regard with awe. And those who are erring in their spirit will actually get to know understanding, and even those who are grumbling will learn instruction."

Rosie's Notes:

Philippians 1:6-8, For I am confident of this very thing, that he who started a good work in you will carry it to completion until the day of Jesus Christ. It is altogether right for me to think this regarding all of you, on account of my having you in my heart, all of you being sharers with me in the undeserved kindness, both in my prison bonds and in the defending and legally establishing of the good news.

For God is my witness of how I am yearning for all of you in such tender affection as Christ Jesus has.

Philippians 2:1-4, If, then, there is any encouragement in Christ, if any consolation of love, if any sharing of spirit, if any tender affections and compassions, make my joy full in that you are of the same mind and have the same love, being joined together in soul, holding the one thought in mind, doing nothing out of contentiousness or out of egotism, but with lowliness of mind considering that the others are superior to you, keeping an eye, not in personal interest upon just your own matters, but also in personal interest upon those of the others.

Philippians 2:19-21,23, For my part I am hoping in the Lord Jesus to send Timothy [meaning "One who honors God."] to you shortly, that I may be a cheerful soul when I get to know about the things pertaining to you. For I have no one else of a disposition like his who will genuinely care for the things pertaining to you. For all the others are seeking their own interests, not those of Christ Jesus.

This, therefore, is the man I am hoping to send just as soon as I have seen how things stand concerning me.

Philippians 1:19-30, For I know this will result in my salvation through your supplication and a supply of the spirit of Jesus Christ, in harmony with my eager expectation and hope that I shall not be ashamed in any respect, but that in all freeness of speech Christ will, as always before, so now be magnified by means of my body, whether through life or through death.

For in my case to live is Christ, and to die, gain. Now if it be to live on in the flesh, this is a fruitage of my work—and yet which thing to select I do not make known. I am under pressure from these two things; but what I do desire is the releasing and the being with Christ, for this, to be sure, is far better. However, for me to remain in the flesh is more necessary on your account. So, being confident of this, I know I shall remain and shall abide with all of you for your advancement and the joy that belongs to your faith, so that your exultation may overflow in Christ Jesus by reason of me through my presence again with you.

Only behave in a manner worthy of the good news about the Christ, in order that, whether I come and see you or be absent, I may hear about the things which concern you, that you are standing firm in one spirit, with one soul striving side by side for the faith of the good news, and in no respect being frightened by your opponents.

This very thing is a proof of destruction for them, but of salvation for you; and this indication is from God, because to you the privilege was given in behalf of Christ, not only to put your faith in him, but also to suffer in his behalf. For you have the same struggle as you saw in my case and as you now hear about in my case.

Philemon 22, But along with that, also get lodging ready for me, for I am hoping that through the prayers of you people I shall be set at liberty for you.

Acts 9:15,16, But the Lord said to him: "Be on your way, because this man is a chosen vessel to me to bear my name to the nations as well as to kings and the sons of Israel. For I shall show him plainly how many things he must suffer for my name.

Ephesians 4:12, With a view to the readjustment of the holy ones, for ministerial work, for the building up of the body of the Christ.

Proverbs 25:25, As cold water upon a tired soul, so is a good report from a distant land.

Isaiah Chapter 5 all verses, Let me sing, please, to my beloved one a song of my loved one concerning his vineyard. There was a vineyard that my beloved one came to have on a fruitful hillside. And he proceeded to dig it up and to rid it of stones and to plant it with a choice red vine, and to build a tower in the middle of it. And there was also a winepress that he hewed out in it. And he kept hoping for it to produce grapes, but it gradually produced wild grapes.
"And now, O you [unfaithful ones in the organization] inhabitants of Jerusalem and you men [unfaithful "faithful and discreet slave"] of Judah, please judge between me and my vineyard. What is there yet to do for my vineyard that I have not already done in it? Why is it that I hoped for it to produce grapes, but it gradually produced wild grapes? And now, please, may I make known to you men what I am doing in my vineyard: There will be a removing of its hedge, and it must be destined for burning down. There must be a breaking down of its stone wall, and it must be destined for a place of trampling. And I shall set it as a thing destroyed. It will not be pruned, nor will it be hoed. And it must come up with the

thornbush and weeds; and upon the clouds I shall lay a command to keep from precipitating any rain upon it. For the vineyard of Jehovah of armies is the [unfaithful] house of Israel, and the men of Judah [unfaithful "faithful and discreet slave"] are the plantation of which he was fond. And he kept hoping for judgment, but, look! the breaking of law; for righteousness, but, look! an outcry."

Woe to the ones joining house to house, and those who annex field to field until there is no more room and you men have been made to dwell all by yourselves in the midst of the land! In my ears Jehovah of armies has sworn that many houses, though great and good, will become an outright object of astonishment, without an inhabitant. For even ten acres of vineyard will produce but one bath measure, and even a homer measure of seed will produce but an ephah measure [much smaller amounts than should be expected].

Woe to those who are getting up early in the morning that they may seek just intoxicating liquor, who are lingering till late in the evening darkness so that wine itself inflames them! And there must prove to be harp and stringed instrument, tambourine and flute, and wine at their feasts; **but the activity of Jehovah they [unfaithful ones in the organization] do not look at, and the work of his hands they have not seen.**

Therefore my [unfaithful] people will have to go into exile for lack of knowledge; and their glory will be famished men [unfaithful "faithful and discreet slave"], and their crowd [membership] will be parched with thirst. Therefore Sheol has made its soul spacious and has opened its mouth wide beyond bounds; and what is splendid in her, also her crowd and her uproar and the exultant one, will certainly go down into it. And earthling man will bow down, and man will become low, and even the eyes of the high ones will become low. And Jehovah of armies will become high through judgment, and the true God, the Holy One, will certainly sanctify himself through righteousness. And the male lambs will actually graze as in their pasture; and the desolate places of well-fed animals alien residents will eat.

Woe to those [taking the lead in the organization of Jehovah's Witnesses] drawing error with ropes of untruth, and as with wagon cords sin; those who are saying: "Let his work hasten; do let it come quickly, in order that we may see it; and let the counsel of the Holy One of Israel draw near and come, that we may know it!"

Woe to those [unfaithful "faithful and discreet slave"] who are saying that good is bad and bad is good, those who are putting darkness for light and light for darkness, those who are putting bitter for sweet and sweet for bitter!

Woe to those wise in their own eyes and discreet even in front of their own faces!

Woe to those who are mighty in drinking wine, and to the men with vital energy for mixing intoxicating liquor, those who are pronouncing the wicked one righteous in consideration of a bribe, and who take away even the righteousness of the righteous one from him!

Therefore just as a tongue of fire eats up the stubble and into the flames mere dried grass sinks down, their very rootstock will become just like a musty smell, and their blossom itself will go up just like powder, because they have rejected the law of Jehovah of armies, and the saying of the Holy One of Israel they have disrespected. That is why the anger of Jehovah has grown hot against his [unfaithful] people, and he will stretch out his hand against them and strike them. And the mountains will be agitated, and their dead bodies will become like the offal in the midst of the streets.

In view of all this his anger has not turned back, but his hand is stretched out still. And he has raised up a signal to a great nation far away, and he has whistled to it at the extremity of the earth; and, look! in haste it will swiftly come in. There is no one tired nor is anyone stumbling among them. No one is drowsy and no one sleeps. And the belt around their loins will certainly not be opened, nor the laces of their sandals be torn in two; because their arrows are sharpened and all their bows are bent. The very hoofs of their horses will have to be accounted as flint itself, and their wheels as a storm wind. The roaring of theirs is like that of a lion, and they roar like maned young lions. And they will growl and grab hold of the prey and bring it safely away, and there will be no deliverer. And they will growl over it in that day as with the growling of the sea. **And one will actually gaze at the land, and, look! there is distressing darkness; and even the light has grown dark because of the drops falling on it.**

2 Corinthians 5:16-6:10, Consequently from now on we know no man according to the flesh. Even if we had known

Christ according to the flesh, certainly we now know him so no more. **Consequently if anyone is in union with Christ, he is a new creation; the old things passed away, look! new things have come into existence. But all things are from God, who reconciled us to himself through Christ and gave us the ministry of the reconciliation, namely, that God was by means of Christ reconciling a world to himself, not reckoning to them their trespasses, and he committed the word of the reconciliation to us.**

We are therefore ambassadors substituting for Christ, as though God were making entreaty through us. As substitutes for Christ we beg: **"Become reconciled to God."** The one who did not know sin he made to be sin for us, that we might become God's righteousness by means of him.

Working together with him, we also entreat you not to accept the undeserved kindness of God and miss its purpose. For he says: "In an acceptable time I heard you, and in a day of salvation I helped you." Look! Now is the especially acceptable time. **Look! Now is the day of salvation.**

In no way are we giving any cause for stumbling, that our ministry might not be found fault with; but in every way we recommend ourselves as God's ministers, by the endurance of much, by tribulations, by cases of need, by difficulties, by beatings, by prisons, by disorders, by labors, by sleepless nights, by times without food, by purity, by knowledge, by long-suffering, by kindness, by holy spirit, by love free from hypocrisy, by truthful speech, by God's power; through the weapons of righteousness on the right hand and on the left, through glory and dishonor, through bad report and good report; as deceivers and yet truthful, as being unknown and yet being recognized, as dying and yet, look! we live, as disciplined and yet not delivered to death, as sorrowing but ever rejoicing, as poor but making many rich, as having nothing and yet possessing all things.

2 Corinthians 7:1,2, Therefore, since we have these promises, beloved ones, let us cleanse ourselves of every defilement of flesh and spirit, perfecting holiness in God's fear.

Allow room for us. We have wronged no one, we have corrupted no one, we have taken advantage of no one.

Isaiah 40:8, The green grass has dried up, the blossom has withered; but as for the word of our God, it will last to time indefinite.

Ephesians 4:12-18, With a view to the readjustment of the holy ones, for ministerial work, for the building up of the body of the Christ, **until we all attain to the oneness in the faith and in the accurate knowledge of the Son of God, to a full-grown man, to the measure of stature that belongs to the fullness of the Christ;** in order that we should no longer be babes, tossed about as by waves and carried hither and thither by every wind of teaching by means of the trickery of men, by means of cunning in contriving error. **But speaking the truth, let us by love grow up in all things into him who is the head, Christ.** From him all the body, by being harmoniously joined together and being made to cooperate through every joint that gives what is needed, according to the functioning of each respective member in due measure, makes for the growth of the body for the building up of itself in love.

This, therefore, I say and bear witness to in the Lord, that you no longer go on walking just as the nations also walk in the unprofitableness of their minds, while they are in darkness mentally, and alienated from the life that belongs to God, because of the ignorance that is in them, because of the insensibility of their hearts. [End of Rosie's Notes]

Phone Call From My Sister, Dawn: [My sister called and asked me questions about my beliefs now that I am no longer a part of the organization. She told me that she needed to work on her relationship with God. She also said that since I have left the organization she feels closer to me. **Dawn told me that now she feels like we're sisters again.** She said she loves me very much and always knew that I loved her. **Praise Jehovah! Thank you, Jehovah!**]

Psalm 118:23,24, This has come to be from Jehovah himself; it is wonderful in our eyes. This is the day that Jehovah has made; we will be joyful and rejoice in it.

Psalm 69:13, But as for me, my prayer was to you, O Jehovah, at an acceptable time, O God. In the abundance of your loving-kindness answer me with the truth of salvation by you.

July 15, 1989

! **[On Friday, July 14, 1989, the great day of Jehovah's salvation began.]**

! Zechariah 3:9, "For, look! the stone that I have put before Joshua! Upon the one stone there are seven eyes. Here I am engraving its engraving," is the utterance of Jehovah of armies, "and I will take away the error of that land in one day."

Psalm 118:22, The stone that the builders rejected has become the head of the corner.

Recall: This Is Jehovah's Day. (Psalm 118:24). [Jehovah has laid in Zion his Chief Cornerstone.]

Colossians 2:9, Because it is in him that all the fullness of the divine quality dwells bodily. [Jehovah gave me this scripture in this instance in reference to Leon Wurzer, who is capable of growing to this level of spiritual maturity.]

Acts 4:11, This is "the stone that was treated by you builders [those taking the lead in the organization] as of no account that has become the head of the corner. [Christ Jesus is the primary person through whom this prophecy was fulfilled. Leon Wurzer is a secondary person through whom Jehovah fulfills this prophecy again in the present day. While Christ rules over God's kingdom from heaven, Leon will act as a spokesperson and representative of God's authority here on earth.]

Isaiah 28:16, Therefore this is what the Sovereign Lord Jehovah has said: "Here I am laying as a foundation in Zion a stone, a tried stone, the precious corner of a sure foundation. No one exercising faith will get panicky."

Zechariah 4:7, Who are you, O great mountain [the organization of Jehovah's Witnesses]? Before Zerubbabel [Leon] you will become a level land. And he will certainly bring forth the headstone. There will be shoutings to it: "How charming! How charming!"

Psalm 45:2, You are indeed more handsome than the sons of men. Charm has been poured out upon your lips. That is why God has blessed you to time indefinite.

Isaiah 9:13-17, And the people themselves [unfaithful ones in the organization] have not returned to the One striking them, and Jehovah of armies they have not sought. And Jehovah will cut off from [unfaithful] Israel head and tail [a serpent], shoot and rush, in one day. The aged and highly respected one [unfaithful "faithful and discreet slave"] is the head, and the prophet giving false instruction [all those responsible for disseminating Watchtower Bible and Tract Society's false teachings and prophecies] is the tail. **And those who are leading this people on prove to be the ones causing them to wander; and those of them who are being led on, the ones who are being confused.** That is why Jehovah will not rejoice even over their young men, and upon their fatherless boys and upon their widows he will have no mercy; **because all of them are apostates and evildoers and every mouth is speaking senselessness. In view of all this his anger has not turned back, but his hand is stretched out still.**

Revelation 20:10, And the Devil [the original serpent (Revelation 20:2)] who was misleading them was hurled into the lake of fire and sulphur, where both the wild beast and the false prophet already were; and they will be tormented day and night forever and ever.

Genesis 3:15, And I shall put enmity between you [Satan, the Devil] and the woman and between your seed and her seed. He will bruise you in the head and you will bruise him in the heel.

Isaiah 10:33,34, Look! The true Lord, Jehovah of armies, is lopping off boughs with a terrible crash; and those tall in growth are being cut down, and the high ones themselves become low. And he has struck down the thickets of the forest with an iron tool, and by a powerful one Lebanon itself will fall.

Staff Pleasantness: Zechariah 11:10, So I took my staff Pleasantness [Lisa] and cut it to pieces, in order to break my covenant that I had concluded with all the peoples [Jehovah's Witnesses, who were once a faithful people, but are no longer].

Staff Union: Zechariah 11:14, Then I cut in pieces my second staff, the Union [Leon], in order to break the brotherhood between Judah [Leon] and Israel [Lisa].

Isaiah 11:13, And the jealousy of Ephraim must depart, and even those showing hostility to Judah will be cut off. Ephraim itself will not be jealous of Judah, nor will Judah show hostility toward Ephraim [at a later time when Jehovah repairs both broken staffs].

Isaiah 11:16, And there must come to be a highway out of Assyria for the remnant of his people who will remain over, just as there came to be one for Israel in the day of his coming up out of the land of Egypt.

July 22, 1989

Conversation With My Sister, Dawn: [My sister and I were having a conversation about the truthfulness of Bible teachings, and she told me a story:

There was a man caught in the middle of a great flood. He was clinging to the roof of his house, watching the water steadily rise, knowing that he was about to be swept away. So he prayed to God to save him. Shortly after he prays, a rowboat comes along and the rescuer pulls over to the man on the roof and says "Climb in." The man says, "No, I'm waiting for God to save me."

As the water continues to rise, another rowboat comes along and the rescuer pulls over to the man and says, "Climb in." The man on the roof refuses saying, "No, God will save me." The man keeps on praying as the water is reaching the rooftop of his house. A helicopter comes along, hovers and descends to the rooftop of the house, and the rescuer throws out a line, shouting, "Climb in!" The man says, "No, I've prayed to God, he will save me." Then the water finally covers the rooftop of the house and the man gets swept away and drowns.

Later, after the man has died and he is standing before God, he says, "God, I prayed to you to save me, and I ended up drowning—why didn't you save me?" God answered the man and said, "I heard your prayer, and I sent you two boats and a helicopter. Why didn't you climb in?"

Dawn says maybe she's like the man on the roof and maybe my son and daughter and myself are like the two rowboats and the helicopter sent from God to rescue her.]

July 27, 1989

Conversation With My Sister, Dawn, Before A Family Get Together:

[My sister and I were having a conversation about the upcoming family get together, and she told me that she was worried about how she was going to feed everyone. She asked me what she should do. She said it would be nice if someone would give her a couple heads of lettuce and a pound of hamburger. I suggested that she not get stressed over it and we could pray for help. **Very** shortly after I said that, Dawn's doorbell rang and a woman from where Dawn works (that Dawn said she doesn't even get along with very well) showed up, bringing Dawn six very nice, large cucumbers. After the woman left, Dawn said, "Look at me, I'm shaking. This never happens—people showing up with food." And I said, "And we didn't even pray about it yet, I only suggested it. Thank you, Jehovah." Dawn said, "Yes, thank you (she looked up toward heaven). I feel like I should quit smoking. I should ask you to study (the Bible) with me. Now this I could believe. It's a lot different from agreeing to a study with Jehovah's Witnesses."

Psalm 109:22,23,26-31, For I am afflicted and poor, and my heart itself has been pierced within me. Like a shadow when it declines, I am obliged to go away [disfellowshipped]; I have been shaken off [by the organization] like a locust.

Help me, O Jehovah my God; save me according to your loving-kindness. And may they know that this is your hand; that you yourself, O Jehovah, have done it. Let them, for their part, pronounce a malediction, but may you, for your part, pronounce a blessing. They have risen up, but let them be ashamed, and let your own servant rejoice. Let those resisting me be clothed with humiliation, and let them enwrap themselves with their shame just as with a sleeveless coat. **I shall laud Jehovah very much with my mouth, and in among many people I shall praise him.** For he will stand at the right hand of the poor, to save him from those judging his soul.

Psalm 110:2, The rod of your strength Jehovah will send out of Zion, saying: "Go subduing in the midst of your enemies."

Matthew 28:18, And Jesus approached and spoke to them, saying: "All authority has been given me in heaven and on the earth."

Revelation 2:25-29, Just the same, hold fast what you have until I come. And to him that conquers and observes my deeds down to the end I will give authority over the nations, and he shall shepherd the people with an **iron rod** so that they will be broken to pieces like clay vessels, **the same as I have received from my Father**, and I will give him the morning star. Let the one who has an ear hear what the spirit says to the congregations.

Isaiah 40:31, But those who are hoping in Jehovah will regain power. They will mount up with wings like eagles. They will run and not grow weary; they will walk and not tire out.

Exodus 19:4, You yourselves have seen what I did to the Egyptians, that I might carry you on wings of eagles and bring you to myself.
John 14:3, Also, if I go my way and prepare a place for you, I am coming again and will receive you home to myself, that where I am you also may be.

Deuteronomy 12:5,9,10, But to the place that Jehovah your God will choose out of all your tribes to place his name there, to have it reside, you [faithful worshippers of Jehovah] will seek, and there you must come.
Because you have not yet come into the resting-place and the inheritance that Jehovah your God is giving you. And you must cross the Jordan and dwell in the land that Jehovah your God is giving you as a possession, and he will certainly give you rest from all your enemies round about, and you will indeed dwell in security.

Hebrews 4:11a, Let us therefore do our utmost to enter into that rest.

Jehovah Is Our Resting-place:

Revelation 12:14, But the two wings of the great eagle were given the woman, that she might fly into the wilderness to her place; there is where she is fed for a time and times and half a time away from the face of the serpent.

[Jehovah is our resting-place, and he has given us a place to rest. We drove south from Wisconsin into Iowa and from Dubuque took the four-lane on Highway 20. In the area of Iowa Falls, Iowa, we drove north to Forest City, Iowa.]

Psalm 55:6-13, And I keep saying: "O that I had wings as a dove has! I would fly away and reside. Look! I would go far away in flight; I would lodge in the **wilderness**.—*Selah*—I would hasten to a place of escape for me from the rushing wind, from the tempest." **Confuse, O Jehovah, divide their tongue, for I have seen violence and disputing in the city [the organization of Jehovah's Witnesses]. Day and night they go round about it upon its walls; and hurtfulness and trouble are within it. Adversities are within it; and from its public square oppression and deception have not moved away.** For it was not an enemy that proceeded to reproach me; otherwise I could put up with it. It was not an intense hater of me that assumed great airs against me; otherwise I could conceal myself from him. But it was you, a mortal man who was as my equal, one familiar to me and my acquaintance.

Zechariah 2:4-6, Then he said to him: "Run, speak to the young man [Leon] over there, saying, '"As **open rural country** Jerusalem will be inhabited, because of the multitude of men and domestic animals in the midst of her. And I myself shall become to her," is the utterance of Jehovah, "a wall of fire all around, and a glory is what I shall become in the midst of her."'"

"Hey there! Hey there! Flee, then, you people, from **the land of the north** [Wisconsin]," is the utterance of Jehovah.

Acts 7:5, And yet he did not give him any inheritable possession in it, no, not a footbreadth; but he promised to give it to him as a possession, and after him to his seed, while as yet he had no child. [Forest City is at the north end of the land we are to rest in. To the east of Forest City is a wilderness area. In the other directions is open rural country.]

Isaiah 49:6, And he proceeded to say: "It has been more than a trivial matter for you to become my servant to raise up the tribes of Jacob and to bring back even the safeguarded ones of Israel; I also have given you for a light of the nations, that my salvation may come to be to the extremity of the earth." [**Now is the day of salvation.**]

Mark 13:27, And then he will send forth the angels and will gather his chosen ones together from the four winds, from earth's extremity to heaven's extremity.

Jeremiah 6:22, This is what Jehovah has said: "Look! A people is coming from the land of the north, and there is a great nation that will be awakened from the remotest parts of the earth."

Zechariah 8:23, This is what Jehovah of armies has said, "It will be in those days that ten men out of all the languages of the nations will take hold, yes, they will actually take hold of the skirt of a man who is a Jew, saying: **'We will go with you people, for we have heard that God is with you people.'**"

Isaiah 66:8, Who has heard of a thing like this? Who has seen things like these? Will a land be brought forth with labor pains in one day? Or will a nation be born at one time? For Zion has come into labor pains as well as given birth to her sons.

Scriptural References in Connection With Jehovah's Denunciation on the Organization Known as Jehovah's Witnesses

Isaiah Chapter 8 all verses, And Jehovah proceeded to say to me: "Take for yourself a large tablet and write upon it with the stylus of mortal man, 'Mahershalalhashbaz [meaning "Hurry, O Spoil! He Has Made Haste To The Plunder"].' And let me have attestation for myself by faithful witnesses [**We are Jehovah's Faithful Witnesses.**], Uriah the priest and Zechariah the son of Jeberechiah."

Then I went near to the prophetess, and she came to be pregnant and in time gave birth to a son. Jehovah now said to me: "Call his name Mahershalalhashbaz, for before the boy will know how to call out, 'My father!' and 'My mother!' one will carry away the resources of Damascus and the spoil of Samaria before the king of Assyria."

And Jehovah proceeded to speak yet further to me, saying: "For the reason that this people [the organization of Jehovah's Witnesses] has rejected the waters of the Shiloah [meaning "Sender"] that are going gently [speaking gently, as a mother would], and there is exultation over Rezin and the son of Remaliah; even therefore, look! Jehovah is bringing up against them [unfaithful ones in the organization] the mighty and the many waters of the River, the king of Assyria and all his glory. And he will certainly come up over all his streambeds and go over all his banks and move on through [unfaithful] Judah. He will actually flood and pass over. Up to the neck he will reach. And the outspreading of his wings must occur to fill the breadth of your [unfaithful] land, O Immanuel!" [Immanuel means "With Us Is God." **God is no longer with Jehovah's Witnesses.**]

Be injurious, O you [unfaithful] peoples, and be shattered to pieces; and give ear, all you in distant parts of the earth! Gird yourselves, and be shattered to pieces! Gird yourselves, and be shattered to pieces! Plan out a scheme, and it will be broken up! Speak any word, and it will not stand, **for God is with us! [God is with us, Jehovah's Faithful Witnesses!** Or Immanuel, "With Us Is God"] **For this is what Jehovah has said to me with strongness of the hand, that he may make me turn aside from walking in the way of this people [unfaithful Jehovah's Witnesses],** saying: "You men [faithful worshippers of Jehovah] must not say, 'A conspiracy!' respecting all that of which this [unfaithful] people keep saying, 'A conspiracy!' and the object of their fear you men must not fear, nor must you tremble at it. <u>**Jehovah of armies—he is the One whom you should treat as holy, and he should be the object of your fear, and he should be the One causing you to tremble.**</u>"

And he must become as a sacred place; but as a stone to strike against and as a rock over which to stumble to both the houses of Israel, as a trap and as a snare to the inhabitants of [unfaithful] Jerusalem. And many among them will be certain to stumble and to fall and be broken, and to be snared and caught. Wrap up [even literally, envelop] the attestation, put a seal [even literally, adhesive on the envelope, which we sealed, enclosing Jehovah's denunciation] about the law among my disciples! And I [Lisa] will keep in expectation of Jehovah, who is concealing his face from the [unfaithful] house of Jacob [the organization of Jehovah's Witnesses], and I will hope in him. Look! I [Lisa] and the children [Rosie and our children] whom Jehovah has given me are as signs and as miracles in Israel from Jehovah of armies, who is residing in Mount Zion. And in case they should say to you people: "Apply to the spiritistic mediums or to those having a spirit of prediction who are chirping and making utterances in low tones," is it not to its God that any people should apply? Should there be application to dead persons in behalf of living persons? **To the law and to the attestation!**

Surely they will keep saying what is according to this statement that will have no light of dawn. [People taking the lead in the organization will say that Jehovah's denunciation is untrue; that it was not given to me through the light of Jehovah's holy spirit, and therefore, all that Jehovah speaks against them will not befall them.] And each one [of them] will certainly pass through the land [within the organization] hard pressed and hungry; and it must occur that because he is hungry and has made himself feel indignant, he will actually call down evil upon his king and upon his God and will certainly peer upward. **And to the earth he will look, and, lo! distress and darkness, obscurity, hard times and gloominess with no brightness.**

Isaiah 29:10-14 NWT (1984), For upon you men [those taking the lead in the organization] Jehovah has poured a spirit of deep sleep; and he closes your eyes, the prophets, and he has covered even your heads, the visionaries [unfaithful "faithful and discreet slave"]. And for you men the vision of everything becomes like the words of the book that has been sealed up, which they give to someone knowing the writing, saying: "Read this out loud, please," and he has to say: "I am unable, for it is sealed up."

And Jehovah says: "For the reason that this people [unfaithful ones in the organization] have come near with their mouth, and they have glorified me merely with their lips, and they have removed their heart itself far away from me, and their fear toward me becomes men's commandment that is being taught, therefore here I am, the One that will act wonderfully again

with this people, in a wonderful manner and with something wonderful; and the wisdom of their wise men must perish, and the very understanding of their discreet men [unfaithful "faithful and discreet slave"] will conceal itself."

!   Isaiah 30:8-10, Now come, write it upon a tablet with them [the scriptures Jehovah has given me], and inscribe it even in a book [a notebook], that it may serve for a future day, for a witness to time indefinite. **For it is a rebellious people, untruthful sons, sons who have been unwilling to hear the law of Jehovah; who have said to the ones seeing, 'You must not see,' and to the ones having visions, 'You must not envision for us any straightforward things. Speak to us smooth things; envision deceptive things.'**

Jeremiah 36:2, Take for yourself a roll of a book [even literally, on parchment-colored paper, folded to read like a scroll and fit into an envelope] and you must write in it all the words that I have spoken to you against [unfaithful] Israel and against [unfaithful] Judah and against all the nations, since the day that I spoke to you, since the days of Josiah, clear down to this day.

Job 19:23, O that now my words were written down! O that in a book they were even inscribed! [Jehovah's words, his instructions, were written down in my journal, then the scriptures Jehovah gave me were typeset at a print shop and mailed out. We mailed Jehovah's denunciation to the headquarters of Jehovah's Witnesses, the Watchtower Bible and Tract Society in New York. We also mailed it to their branch offices in foreign countries worldwide, as well as to many Kingdom Halls. Then we mailed Jehovah's denunciation to every individual and family in the organization that we could personally think of.]

Revelation 5:1, And I saw in the right hand of the One seated upon the throne a scroll written within and on the reverse side, sealed tight with seven seals. [Jehovah's denunciation was typeset, printed and folded to read like a scroll. It also had writing within and on the reverse side.]

Isaiah 30:12,13,15, Therefore this is what the Holy One of Israel has said: "In view of your rejecting of this word [the organization rejecting Jehovah's denunciation], and since you [unfaithful] men trust in defrauding and in what is devious and you support yourselves on it, therefore for you this error will become like a broken section about to fall down, a swelling out in a highly raised wall, the breakdown of which may come suddenly, in an instant."

For this is what the Sovereign Lord Jehovah, the Holy One of Israel, has said: "**By coming back and resting you people will be saved. Your mightiness will prove to be simply in keeping undisturbed and in trustfulness.**" But you [unfaithful ones in the organization] were not willing.

! **Recall: Isaiah 8:16, Wrap up the attestation, put a seal about the law among my disciples!** [Spiritually speaking, only Jehovah's Faithful Witnesses, his "disciples," understand Jehovah's denunciation. Those taking the lead in the organization of unfaithful Jehovah's Witnesses speak untruth to their members and they have chosen not to believe Jehovah's warning to them through his denunciation. They have rejected it—they are unable to discern the dire consequences to themselves for their lack of faith.]

Isaiah 30:9, For it is a rebellious people, untruthful sons, sons who have been unwilling to hear the law of Jehovah.

Isaiah 8:2a, And let me have attestation for myself by faithful witnesses [plural].

2 Corinthians 13:1b, "At the mouth of two witnesses or of three [Rosie, Bram, Lisa] every matter must be established."

DENUNCIATION STRUCTURE:

Habakkuk 3:14, With his own rods [their own translation of the Bible] you [Jehovah] pierced the head [the unfaithful "faithful and discreet slave"] of his warriors when they moved tempestuously to scatter me. Their high glee was as of those bent on devouring an afflicted one in a place of concealment.

[Jehovah's denunciation consists of scriptures which I have quoted verbatim, at Jehovah's direction, from the New World Translation of the Holy Scriptures (NWT), Rendered from the Original Languages by the New World Bible Translation Committee of the organization of Jehovah's Witnesses, copyright, 1961, 1981, 1984 by Watch Tower Bible and Tract Society of Pennsylvania; **their brackets [ ] as they appear in their print.** Also, in this printed version of the scriptures, the words YOU and YOUR when capitalized, refers to the plural form of the word, as in you as a nation or you as a people. The reader is encouraged to make a direct comparison of the scriptures presented here with the original text of this Bible to assure continuity.]

[For publishing purposes, the scriptures were photocopied directly from this Bible and taken to a print shop to be typeset. The layout for the denunciation is similar to that of a scroll, such that it reads like one when unfolded. It is printed on both sides of parchment-colored paper, placed in a matching envelope and sealed with adhesive. The postage stamps literally have pictures of wings on them. **All of this was done in accordance with the scriptures Jehovah provided me as to the structure the denunciation should take: Isaiah 8:1,2,16; Isaiah 29:10-14; Isaiah 30:8-10; Jeremiah 36:2; Job 19:23; Zechariah 5:1-4; Revelation 5:1, Habakkuk 2:2,3.**]

[To acknowledge my responsibility for getting this work published, Jehovah indicated the appropriateness of my signature at the end of the denunciation. This also served the purpose of notifying the organization of Jehovah's Witnesses that I was officially withdrawing my membership. Rosie Olson and my son, Bram Lewis, worked with me to compile mailing lists, and shared in the addressing and mailing of Jehovah's denunciation.]

[This is Jehovah's denunciation, and it is through his own Word, the Bible, that he denounces the organization of Jehovah's Witnesses.]

JEHOVAH'S DENUNCIATION

1 Chronicles, Chapter 29:
11. Yours, O Jehovah, are the greatness and the mightiness and the beauty and the excellency and the dignity; for everything in the heavens and in the earth is [yours]. Yours is the kingdom, O Jehovah, the One also lifting yourself up as head over all.
12. The riches and the glory are on account of you, and you are dominating everything; and in your hand there are power and mightiness, and in your hand is [ability] to make great and to give strength to all. 13. And now, O our God, we are thanking you and praising your beauteous name.
14. "And yet, who am I and who are my people, that we should retain power to make voluntary offerings like this?

Isaiah, Chapter 55:
3. Incline YOUR ear and come to me. Listen, and YOUR soul will keep alive, and I shall readily conclude with YOU people an indefinitely lasting covenant respecting the loving-kindnesses to David that are faithful.

Isaiah, Chapter 57:
1. The righteous one himself has perished, but there is no one taking [it] to heart. And men of loving-kindness are being gathered [to the dead], while no one discerns that it is because of the calamity that the righteous one has been gathered away. 2. He enters into peace; they take rest upon their beds, [each] one that is walking straightforwardly.

Isaiah, Chapter 58:
1. "Call out full-throated; do not hold back. Raise your voice just like a horn, and tell my people their revolt, and the house of Jacob their sins. 2. Yet day after day it was I whom they kept seeking,

and it was in the knowledge of my ways that they would express delight, like a nation that carried on righteousness itself and that had not left the very justice of their God, in that they kept asking me for righteous judgments, drawing near to God in whom they had delight,

3. "'For what reason did we fast and you did not see, and did we afflict our soul and you would take no note?'

"Indeed YOU people were finding delight in the very day of YOUR fasting, when there were all YOUR toilers that YOU kept driving to work. 4. Indeed for quarreling and struggle YOU would fast, and for striking with the fist of wickedness. Did YOU not keep fasting as in the day for making YOUR voice to be heard in the height? 5. Should the fast that I choose become like this, as a day for earthling man to afflict his soul? For bowing down his head just like a rush, and that he should spread out mere sackcloth and ashes as his couch? Is it this that you call a fast and a day acceptable to Jehovah?

6. "Is not this the fast that I choose? To loosen the fetters of wickedness, to release the bands of the yoke bar, and to send away the crushed ones free, and that YOU people should tear in two every yoke bar? 7. Is it not the dividing of your bread out to the hungry one, and that you should bring the afflicted, homeless people into [your] house? That, in case you should see someone naked, you must cover him, and that you should not hide yourself from your own flesh?

8. "In that case your light would break forth just like the dawn; and speedily would recuperation spring up for you. And before you your righteousness would certainly walk; the very glory of Jehovah would be your rear guard. 9. In that case you would call, and Jehovah himself would answer; you would cry for help, and he would say, 'Here I am!'

"If you will remove from your midst the yoke bar, the poking out of the finger and the speaking of what is hurtful; 10. and you will grant to the hungry one your own soul[ful desire], and you will satisfy the soul that is being afflicted, your light also will certainly flash up even in the darkness, and your gloom will be like midday. 11. And Jehovah will be bound to lead you constantly and to satisfy your soul even in a scorched land, and he will invigorate your very bones;

Jeremiah, Chapter 7:

1. The word that occurred to Jeremiah from Jehovah, saying: "Stand in the gate of the house of Jehovah, and you must proclaim there this word, and you must say, 'Hear the word of Jehovah, all YOU of Judah, who are entering into these gates to bow down to Jehovah. 3. This is what Jehovah of armies, the God of Israel, has said: "Make YOUR ways and YOUR dealings good, and I will keep YOU people residing in this place. 4. Do not put YOUR trust in fallacious words, saying, 'The temple of Jehovah, the temple of Jehovah, the temple of Jehovah they are!' 5. For if YOU will positively make YOUR ways and YOUR dealings good, if YOU will positively carry out justice between a man and his companion, 6. if no alien resident, no fatherless boy and no widow YOU will oppress, and innocent blood YOU will not shed in this place, and after other gods YOU will not walk for calamity to yourselves, 7. I, in turn, shall certainly keep YOU residing in this place, in the land that I gave to YOUR forefathers, from time indefinite even to time indefinite."'"

8. "Here YOU are putting YOUR trust in fallacious words—it will certainly be of no benefit at all. 9. Can there be stealing, murdering and committing adultery and swearing falsely and making sacrificial smoke to Ba'al and walking after other gods whom YOU had not known, 10. and must YOU come and stand before me in this house upon which my name has been called, and must YOU say, 'We shall certainly be delivered,' in the face of doing all these detestable things? 11. Has this house upon which my name has been called become a mere cave of robbers in YOUR eyes? Here I myself also have seen [it]," is the utterance of Jehovah.

12. "'However, GO, now, to my place that was in Shi'loh, where I caused my name to reside at first, and see what I did to it because of the badness of my people Israel. 13. And now for the reason that YOU kept doing all these works,' is the utterance of Jehovah, 'and I kept speaking to YOU, getting up early and speaking, but YOU did not listen, and I kept calling YOU, but YOU did not answer, 14. I will do also to the house upon which my name has been called, in which YOU are trusting, and to the place that I gave to YOU and to YOUR forefathers, just as I did to Shi'loh. 15. And I will throw YOU out from before my face, just as I threw out all YOUR brothers, the whole offspring of E'phra-im.'

Lamentations, Chapter 4:

12. The kings of the earth and all the inhabitants of the productive land had not believed that the adversary and the enemy would come into the gates of Jerusalem.

13. Because of the sins of her prophets, the errors of her priests, there were in the midst of her those pouring out the blood of righteous ones.

Jeremiah, Chapter 18:

11. "And now say, please, to the men of Judah and to the inhabitants of Jerusalem, 'This is what Jehovah has said: "Here I am forming against YOU a calamity and thinking against YOU a thought. Turn back, please, each one from his bad way, and make YOUR ways and YOUR dealings good."'"

Jeremiah, Chapter 50:

31. "Look! I am against you, O Presumptuousness," is the utterance of the Sovereign Lord, Jehovah of armies, "for your day must come, the time that I must give you attention. 32. And Presumptuousness will certainly stumble and fall, and it will have no one to cause it to rise up. And I will set a fire ablaze in its cities, and it must devour all its surroundings."

33. This is what Jehovah of armies has said: "The sons of Israel and the sons of Judah are being oppressed together, and all those taking them captive have laid hold on them. They have refused to let them go. 34. Their Repurchaser is strong, Jehovah of armies being his name. Without fail he will conduct their legal case, in order that he may actually give repose to the land and cause agitation to the inhabitants of Babylon."

Jeremiah, Chapter 50:

24. I have laid a snare for you and you have also been caught, O Babylon, and you yourself did not know [it]. You were found and also taken hold of, for it was against Jehovah that you excited yourself.

Jeremiah, Chapter 22:

29. "O earth, earth, earth, hear the word of Jehovah. 30. This is what Jehovah has said, 'WRITE down this man as childless, as an able-bodied man who will not have any success in his days; for from

his offspring not a single one will have any success, sitting upon the throne of David and ruling anymore in Judah.'"

Jeremiah, Chapter 23:
1. "Woe to the shepherds who are destroying and scattering the sheep of my pasturage!" is the utterance of Jehovah.
2. Therefore this is what Jehovah the God of Israel has said against the shepherds who are shepherding my people: "YOU yourselves have scattered my sheep; and YOU kept dispersing them, and YOU have not turned your attention to them."
"Here I am turning my attention upon YOU for the badness of YOUR dealings," is the utterance of Jehovah.
3. "And I myself shall collect together the remnant of my sheep out of all the lands to which I had dispersed them, and I will bring them back to their pasture ground, and they will certainly be fruitful and become many. 4. And I will raise up over them shepherds who will actually shepherd them; and they will be afraid no more, neither will they be struck with any terror, and none will be missing," is the utterance of Jehovah.
5. "Look! There are days coming," is the utterance of Jehovah, "and I will raise up to David a righteous sprout. And a king will certainly reign and act with discretion and execute justice and righteousness in the land. 6. In his days Judah will be saved, and Israel itself will reside in security. And this is his name with which he will be called, Jehovah Is Our Righteousness."

Jeremiah, Chapter 45:
1. The word that Jeremiah the prophet spoke to Bar'uch the son of Ne·ri'ah when he wrote in a book these words from the mouth of Jeremiah in the fourth year of Je·hoi'a·kim the son of Jo·si'ah, the king of Judah, saying:
2. "This is what Jehovah the God of Israel has said concerning you, O Bar'uch, 3. 'You have said: "Woe, now, to me, for Jehovah has added grief to my pain! I have grown weary because of my sighing, and no resting-place have I found."'
4. "This is what you should say to him, 'This is what Jehovah has said: "Look! What I have built up I am tearing down, and what I have planted I am uprooting, even all the land itself. 5. But as for you, you keep seeking great things for yourself. Do not keep on seeking."'

"'For here I am bringing in a calamity upon all flesh,' is the utterance of Jehovah, 'and I will give you your soul as a spoil in all the places to which you may go.'"

Matthew, Chapter 23:
4. They bind up heavy loads and put them upon the shoulders of men, but they themselves are not willing to budge them with their finger. 5. All the works they do they do to be viewed by men; for they broaden the [scripture-containing] cases that they wear as safeguards, and enlarge the fringes [of their garments].

Matthew, Chapter 24:
15. "Therefore, when YOU catch sight of the disgusting thing that causes desolation, as spoken of through Daniel the prophet, standing in a holy place, (let the reader use discernment,) 16. then let those in Ju-de'a begin fleeing to the mountains. 17. Let the man on the housetop not come down to take the goods out of his house; 18. and let the man in the field not return to the house to pick up his outer garment.

Jeremiah, Chapter 5:
26. "'For among my people there have been found wicked men. They keep peering, as when birdcatchers crouch down. They have set a ruinous [trap]. It is men that they catch. 27. As a cage is full of flying creatures, so their houses are full of deception. That is why they have become great and they gain riches. 28. They have grown fat; they have become shiny. They have also overflowed with bad things. No legal case have they pleaded, even the legal case of the fatherless boy, that they may gain success; and the judgment of the poor ones they have not taken up.'"

29. "Should I not hold an accounting because of these very things," is the utterance of Jehovah, "or on a nation that is like this should not my soul avenge itself? 30. An astonishing situation, even a horrible thing, has been brought to be in the land: 31. The prophets themselves actually prophesy in falsehood; and as for the priests, they go subduing according to their powers. And my own people have loved [it] that way; and what will YOU men do in the finale of it?"

Jeremiah, Chapter 6:
21. Therefore this is what Jehovah has said: "Here I am setting for this people stumbling blocks, and they will certainly stumble over them, fathers and sons together; the neighbor and his companion—they will perish."
22. This is what Jehovah has said: "Look! A people is coming from the land of the north, and there is a great nation that will be awakened from the remotest parts of the earth. 23. The bow and the javelin they will grab hold of. It is a cruel one, and they will have no pity. Their very voice will resound just like the sea, and upon horses they will ride. It is drawn up in battle order like a man of war against you, O daughter of Zion."

Jeremiah, Chapter 22:
13. "Woe to the one building his house, but not with righteousness, and his upper chambers, but not with justice, by use of his fellowman who serves for nothing, and whose wages he does not give him;

Psalm 12:
1. Do save [me], O Jehovah, for the loyal one has come to an end;
   For faithful people have vanished from the sons of men.
2. Untruth they keep speaking one to the other;
   With a smooth lip they keep speaking even with a double heart.
3. Jehovah will cut off all smooth lips,
   The tongue speaking great things,
4. Those who have said: "With our tongue we shall prevail.
   Our lips are with us. Who will be a master to us?"
5. **"Because of the despoiling of the afflicted ones, because of the sighing of the poor ones,**
   I shall at this time arise," says Jehovah.
   "I shall put [him] in safety from anyone that puffs at him."
6. The sayings of Jehovah are pure sayings,
   As silver refined in a smelting furnace of earth, clarified seven times.
7. You yourself, O Jehovah, will guard them;
   You will preserve each one from this generation to time indefinite.
8. The wicked ones walk all around,
   Because vileness is exalted among the sons of men.

Jeremiah, Chapter 50:
28. "There is the sound of those fleeing and those escaping from the land of Babylon to tell out in Zion the vengeance of Jehovah our God, the vengeance for his temple.

Isaiah, Chapter 52:
11. Turn away, turn away, get out of there, touch nothing unclean; get out from the midst of her, keep yourselves clean, YOU who are carrying the utensils of Jehovah.

Matthew, Chapter 23:
28. In that way YOU also, outwardly indeed, appear righteous to men, but inside YOU are full of hypocrisy and lawlessness.

Matthew, Chapter 23:
36. Truly I say to YOU, All these things will come upon this generation.
37. "Jerusalem, Jerusalem, the killer of the prophets and stoner of those sent forth to her,—how often I wanted to gather your children together, the way a hen gathers her chicks together under her wings! But YOU people did not want it. **38. Look! YOUR house is abandoned to YOU.** 39. For I say to YOU, YOU will by no means see me from henceforth until YOU say, 'Blessed is he that comes in Jehovah's name!'"

With this notification served to you, I hereby withdraw my association from the earthly organization legally recognized as Watchtower Bible and Tract Society, locally known as Lancaster Congregation of Jehovah's Witnesses in Lancaster, Wisconsin.

                                    (Signature)
                                    Lisa Murray
                                    P.O. Box 3
                                    Geneva, Iowa 50633
                                    U.S.A.

Denunciation envelope: ivory "parchment" paper

Front:

```
P.O. Box 3
Geneva, Iowa 50633


         Watchtower Bible and Tract Society



Isaiah 30:12,13
```

Back:

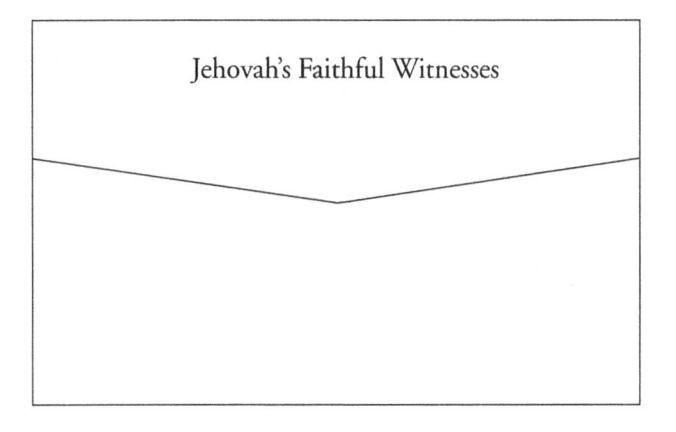

```
           Jehovah's Faithful Witnesses
```

Romans 15:15,16,20,21, However, I am writing you the more outspokenly on some points, as if reminding you again, because of the undeserved kindness given to me from God for me to be a public servant of Christ Jesus to the nations, engaging in the holy work of the good news of God, in order that the offering, namely, these nations, might prove to be acceptable, it being sanctified with holy spirit.

In this way, indeed, I made it my aim not to declare the good news where Christ had already been named, in order that I might not be building on another man's foundation; but, just as it is written:

"Those to whom no announcement has been made about him will see, and those who have not heard will understand."

2 Corinthians Chapter 9 all verses, Now concerning the ministry that is for the holy ones, it is superfluous for me to write you, for I know your readiness of mind of which I am boasting to the Macedonians about you, that Achaia has stood ready now for a year, and your zeal has stirred up the majority of them. But I am sending the brothers, that our boasting about you might not prove empty in this respect, but that you may really be ready, just as I used to say you would be. Otherwise, in some way, if Macedonians should come with me and find you not ready, we—not to say you—should be put to shame in this assurance of ours. Therefore I thought it necessary to encourage the brothers to come to you in advance and to get ready in advance your bountiful gift previously promised, that thus this might be ready as a bountiful gift and not as something extorted.

But as to this, he that sows sparingly will also reap sparingly; and he that sows bountifully will also reap bountifully. Let each one do just as he has resolved in his heart, not grudgingly or under compulsion, for God loves a cheerful giver.

God, moreover, is able to make all his undeserved kindness abound toward you, that, while you always have full self-sufficiency in everything, you may have plenty for every good work. Just as it is written: "He has distributed widely, he has given to the poor ones, his righteousness continues forever." Now he that abundantly supplies seed to the sower and bread for eating will supply and multiply the seed for you to sow and will increase the products of your righteousness. In everything you are being enriched for every sort of generosity, which produces through us an expression of thanks to God; because the ministry of this public service is not only to supply abundantly the wants of the holy ones but also to be rich with many expressions of thanks to God. Through the proof that this ministry gives, they glorify God because you are submissive to the good news about the Christ, as you publicly declare you are, and because you are generous in your contribution to them and to all; and with supplication for you they long for you because of the surpassing undeserved kindness of God upon you.

Thanks be to God for his indescribable free gift.

Hosea 10:12, Sow seed for yourselves in righteousness; reap in accord with loving-kindness. Till for yourselves arable land, when there is time for searching for Jehovah until he comes and gives instruction in righteousness to you.

Romans 15:7-15, Therefore welcome one another, just as the Christ also welcomed us, with glory to God in view. For I say that Christ actually became a minister of those who are circumcised in behalf of God's truthfulness, so as to verify the promises He made to their forefathers, and that the nations might glorify God for his mercy. Just as it is written: "That is why I will openly acknowledge you among the nations and to your name I will make melody." And again he says: "Be glad, you nations, with his people." And again: "Praise Jehovah, all you nations, and let all the peoples praise him." And again Isaiah says: "There will be the root of Jesse, and there will be one arising to rule nations; on him nations will rest their hope." May the God who gives hope fill you with all joy and peace by your believing, that you may abound in hope with power of holy spirit.

Now I myself also am persuaded about you, my brothers, that you yourselves are also full of goodness, as you have been filled with all knowledge, and that you can also admonish one another. However, I am writing you the more outspokenly on some points, as if reminding you again, because of the undeserved kindness given to me from God.

Hebrews 1:7b, And he makes his angels spirits, and his public servants a flame of fire.

Hebrews 2:13, And again: "I will have my trust in him." And again: "Look! I and the young children, whom Jehovah gave me."

Galatians 6:10, Really, then, as long as we have time favorable for it, let us work what is good toward all, but especially toward those related to us in the faith.

Recall: Proverbs 9:9, Give to a wise person and he will become still wiser. Impart knowledge to someone righteous and he will increase in learning. [Faithful worshippers of Jehovah still in the organization will recognize Jehovah's righteousness and his message to them through his denunciation to come out of the darkness upon them and into the light and freedom of his truth. Among the wrongfully disfellowshipped, there will be those who are drawn to Jehovah's truth. And there will be those from among the nations who will also increase in knowledge from the truth of Jehovah's words against the Watchtower Bible and Tract Society and come to his light. This includes Leon Wurzer, and hopefully, my sister, Dawn, and my mother, Joan, although, at this time they are not walking according to accurate knowledge.]

2 Corinthians 8:6-24, This led us to encourage Titus [a faithful Christian] that, just as he had been the one to initiate it among you, so too he should complete this same kind giving on your part. Nevertheless, just as you are abounding in everything, in faith and word and knowledge and all earnestness and in this love of ours to you, may you also abound in this kind giving.

It is not in the way of commanding you, but in view of the earnestness of others and to make a test of the genuineness of your love, that I am speaking. For you know the undeserved kindness of our Lord Jesus Christ, that though he was rich he became poor for your sakes, that you might become rich through his poverty.

And in this I render an opinion: for this matter is of benefit to you, seeing that already a year ago you initiated not only the doing but also the wanting to do; now, then, finish up also the doing of it, in order that, just as there was a readiness to want to do, so also there should be a finishing up of it out of what you have. For if the readiness is there first, it is especially acceptable according to what a person has, not according to what a person does not have. For I do not mean for it to be easy for others, but hard on you; but that by means of an equalizing your surplus just now might offset their deficiency, in order that their surplus might also come to offset your deficiency, that an equalizing might take place. Just as it is written: "The person with much did not have too much, and the person with little did not have too little.

Now thanks be to God for putting the same earnestness for you in the heart of Titus, because he has indeed responded to the encouragement, but, being very earnest, he is going forth of his own accord to you. But we are sending along with him the brothers whose praise in connection with the good news has spread through all the congregations. Not only that, but he was also appointed by the congregations to be our traveling companion in connection with this fine gift to be administered by us for the glory of the Lord and in proof of our ready mind. Thus we are avoiding having any man find fault with us in connection with this liberal contribution to be administered by us. For we "make honest provision, not only in the sight of Jehovah, but also in the sight of men."

Moreover, we are sending with them our brother whom we have often proved in many things to be earnest, but now much more earnest due to his great confidence in you. If, though, there is any question about Titus, he is a sharer with me and a fellow worker for your interests; or if about our brothers, they are apostles of congregations and a glory of Christ. Therefore demonstrate to them the proof of your love and of what we boasted about you, before the face of the congregations.

Psalm 112:9, He has distributed widely; he has given to the poor ones.

August 4, 1989

[We have to live in this world, such as it is, before it is restored to a paradise, but we are still to be "no part of it." (John 15:19) There are many different people and places for gatherings, but not all of them are appropriate for Christians to participate in.

I prayed for Jehovah's direction during a neighborhood get together we were invited to, which was supplying alcohol and their own kind of music, and was advised by Jehovah not to participate. We came into the house promptly. A severe thunderstorm came, which abruptly ended the get together, and Rosie and I brought the children down to the basement for shelter. I sensed a presence and was given the words, "I love you best, because you always obey Jehovah."]

August 5, 1989, Sunday

Psalm 130 all verses, Out of the depths I have called upon you, O Jehovah. O Jehovah, do hear my voice. May your ears prove to be attentive to the voice of my entreaties. If errors were what you watch, O Jah, O Jehovah, who could stand? For there is the true forgiveness with you, in order that you may be feared. I have hoped,

O Jehovah, my soul has hoped, and for his word I have waited. My soul has waited for Jehovah more than watchmen for the morning, watching for the morning. Let Israel keep waiting for Jehovah. For there is loving-kindness with Jehovah, and abundantly so is there redemption with him. And he himself will redeem [faithful] Israel out of all his errors.

Psalm 131 all verses, O Jehovah, my heart has not been haughty, nor have my eyes been lofty; nor have I walked in things too great, nor in things too wonderful for me. Surely I have soothed and quieted my soul like a weanling upon his mother. My soul is like a weanling upon me. Let [faithful] Israel wait for Jehovah from now on and to time indefinite.

Psalm 132 all verses, Remember, O Jehovah, concerning David all his humiliations; how he swore to Jehovah, how he vowed to the Powerful One of Jacob: "I will not go into the tent of my house. I will not go up on the divan of my grand lounge, I will not give sleep to my eyes, nor slumber to my own beaming eyes, until I find a place for Jehovah, a grand tabernacle for the Powerful One of Jacob." Look! We have heard it in Ephrathah [an earlier name for Bethlehem, a hometown of King David, birthplace of Jesus], we have found it in the fields of the forest. Let us come into his grand tabernacle; let us bow down at his footstool. **Do arise, O Jehovah, to your resting-place, you and the ark of your strength. Let your priests themselves be clothed with righteousness, and let your own loyal ones cry out joyfully.** On account of David your servant, do not turn back the face of your anointed one. Jehovah has sworn to David, truly he will not draw back from it: "Of the fruitage of your belly I shall set on your throne. If your sons will keep my covenant and my reminders that I shall teach them, their sons also forever will sit upon your throne." For Jehovah has chosen [faithful] Zion; he has longed for it as a dwelling for himself: "This is my resting-place forever; here I shall dwell, for I have longed for it. Its provisions I shall bless without fail. Its poor ones I shall satisfy with bread. And its priests I shall clothe with salvation; and its loyal ones will without fail cry out joyfully. There I shall cause the horn of David to grow. **I have set in order a lamp for my anointed one.** His enemies I shall clothe with shame; but upon him his diadem will flourish."

Presence: [I sensed a presence coming to attend as I prayed to Jehovah. I was standing, raising my hands, and praising Jehovah. I read from the Bible, asking for comfort, and I was answered from Jesus. First, I was given several scriptures expressing peace. Then I was given Psalm 122.]

Psalm 122 all verses, I rejoiced when they were saying to me: "To the house of Jehovah let us go." Our feet proved to be standing within your gates, O Jerusalem. Jerusalem [Lisa] is one that is built like a city that has been joined together in oneness, to which the tribes have gone up, the tribes of Jah, as a reminder to Israel to give thanks to the name of Jehovah. For there the thrones for judgment have been sitting, thrones for the house of David. Ask, O you people, for the peace of Jerusalem. Those loving you, O city, will be free from care. May peace continue within your rampart, freedom from care within your dwelling towers. For the sake of my brothers and my companions I will now speak: "May there be peace within you." For the sake of the house of Jehovah our God I will keep seeking good for you.

[I was also given Zechariah Chapters 1 and 2 NWT (1984).]

Zechariah Chapter 1 all verses, In the eighth month in the second year of Darius the word of Jehovah occurred to Zechariah the son of Berechiah the son of Iddo the prophet, saying: "Jehovah grew indignant at your [unfaithful] fathers—very much so.

"And you must say to them, 'This is what Jehovah of armies has said: "'Return to me,' is the utterance of Jehovah of armies, 'and I shall return to you,' Jehovah of armies has said."'

"'Do not become like your [unfaithful] fathers to whom the former prophets called, saying: "This is what Jehovah of armies has said, 'Return, please, from your bad ways and from your bad dealings.'"'

"'But they did not listen, and they paid no attention to me,' is the utterance of Jehovah.

"'As for your [unfaithful] fathers, where are they? And as for the prophets, was it to time indefinite that they continued to live? However, as regards my words and my regulations that I commanded my servants, the prophets, did they not catch up with your fathers?' So they returned and said: 'According to what Jehovah of armies had in mind to do to us, according to our ways and according to our dealings, that is how he has done with us.'"

On the twenty-fourth day of the eleventh month, that is, the month Shebat, in the second year of Darius, the word of Jehovah occurred to Zechariah the son of Berechiah the son of Iddo the prophet, saying: "I saw in the night, and, look! a man riding on a red horse, and he was standing still among the myrtle trees that were in the deep place; and behind him there were horses red, bright red, and white."

And so I said: "Who are these, my lord?"

At that the angel who was speaking with me said to me: "I myself shall show you who these very ones are."

Then the man who was standing still among the myrtle trees answered and said: "These are the ones whom Jehovah has sent forth to walk about in the earth." And they proceeded to answer the angel of Jehovah who was standing among the myrtle trees and to say: "We have walked about in the earth, and, look! the whole earth is sitting still and having no disturbance."

So the angel of Jehovah answered and said: "O Jehovah of armies, how long will you yourself not show mercy to Jerusalem and to the cities of Judah, whom you have denounced these seventy years?"

And Jehovah proceeded to answer the angel who was speaking with me, with good words, comforting words; and the angel who was speaking with me went on to say to me: "Call out, saying, 'This is what Jehovah of armies has said: "I have been jealous for Jerusalem [Lisa] and for Zion [Leon] with great jealousy. With great indignation I am feeling indignant against the nations that are at ease; because I, for my part, felt indignant to only a little extent, but they, for their part, helped toward calamity."'

"Therefore this is what Jehovah has said, '"I shall certainly return to [faithful] Jerusalem with mercies. My own house will be built in her," is the utterance of Jehovah of armies, "and a measuring line itself will be stretched out over Jerusalem [Lisa]."'

"Call out further, saying, 'This is what Jehovah of armies has said: "My cities will yet overflow with goodness; and Jehovah will yet certainly feel regrets over Zion and yet actually choose Jerusalem."'"

And I proceeded to raise my eyes and see; and, look! there were four horns. So I said to the angel who was speaking with me: "What are these?" In turn he said to me: "These are the horns that dispersed Judah, Israel and Jerusalem."

Furthermore, Jehovah showed me four craftsmen. At that I said: "What are these coming to do?"

And he went on to say: "These are the horns that dispersed [faithful] Judah to such an extent that no one at all raised his head; and these others will come to set them trembling, to cast down the horns of the nations that are lifting up a horn against the land of Judah, in order to disperse her."

Zechariah Chapter 2 all verses, And I proceeded to raise my eyes and see; and, look! there was a man, and in his hand a measuring rope. So I said: "Where are you going?"

In turn he said to me: "To measure Jerusalem [Lisa], in order to see what her breadth amounts to and what her length amounts to."

And, look! the angel who was speaking with me was going forth, and there was another angel going forth to meet him. Then he said to him: "Run, speak to the young man over there, saying, "'As open rural country Jerusalem [Lisa] will be inhabited, because of the multitude of men and domestic animals in the midst of her. And I myself shall become to her," is the utterance of Jehovah, "a wall of fire all around, and a glory is what I shall become in the midst of her.""

"Hey there! Hey there! Flee, then, you people [faithful worshippers of Jehovah still in the organization], from the land of the north," is the utterance of Jehovah.

"For in the direction of the four winds of the heavens I have spread you people abroad," is the utterance of Jehovah.

"Hey there, Zion [Leon]! Make your escape, you who are dwelling with the daughter of Babylon. For this is what Jehovah of armies has said, 'Following after the glory he has sent me to the nations that were despoiling you people; for he that is touching you is touching my eyeball. For here I am waving my hand against them, and they will have to become spoil to their slaves. And you people will certainly know that Jehovah of armies himself has sent me.

"Cry out loudly and rejoice, O daughter of Zion; for here I am coming, and I will reside in the midst of you," is the utterance of Jehovah. "And many nations will certainly become joined to Jehovah in that day, and they will actually become my people; and I will reside in the midst of you." And you will have to know that Jehovah of armies himself has sent me to you. And Jehovah will certainly take possession of Judah [Leon] as his portion upon the holy ground, and he must yet choose Jerusalem [Lisa]. Keep silence, all flesh, before Jehovah, for he has aroused himself from his holy dwelling.

[Then I was given these scriptures.] Isaiah 66:5-24 [abbreviated here], Hear the word of Jehovah, you men [faithful worshippers of Jehovah still in the organization] who are trembling at his word: "Your brothers [those taking the lead in the organization who are disloyal to Jehovah] that are hating you, that are excluding you by reason of my name, said, 'May Jehovah be glorified!' **He [Jehovah] must also appear with rejoicing on your part, and they are the ones that will be put to shame."**

There is a sound of uproar out of the city, a sound out of the temple! It is the sound of Jehovah repaying what is deserved to his enemies.

Before she [Lisa] began to come into labor pains she gave birth. Before birth pangs could come to her, she even gave deliverance to a male child [gave spiritual "deliverance" or "birth" to Leon, who is "Sprout," (Zechariah 6:12) meaning new spiritual "growth."]. Who has heard of a thing like this? Who has seen things like these? Will a land be brought forth with labor pains in one day? Or will a nation [of faithful worshippers of Jehovah] be born at one time? For Zion has come into labor pains as well as given birth to her sons.

"As for me, shall I cause the breaking through and not cause the giving birth?" says Jehovah. "Or am I causing a giving birth and do I actually cause a shutting up?" your God has said.

"Like a man whom his own mother keeps comforting, so I myself shall keep comforting you people; and in the case of Jerusalem you will be comforted. And you will certainly see, and your heart will be bound to exult, and your very bones will sprout just like tender grass. **And the hand of Jehovah will certainly be made known to his servants, but he will actually denounce his enemies."**

"For here Jehovah himself comes as a very fire, and his chariots are like a storm wind, in order to pay back his anger with sheer rage and his rebuke with flames of fire. For as fire Jehovah himself will for a fact take up the controversy, yes, with his sword, against all flesh; and the slain of Jehovah will certainly become many. Those sanctifying themselves [those taking the lead in the apostate organization of Jehovah's Witnesses] and cleansing themselves for the gardens behind one in the center, eating the flesh of the pig and the loathsome thing, even the jumping rodent, they will all together reach their end," is the utterance of Jehovah. "And as regards their works and their thoughts, I am coming in order to collect all the nations and tongues together; and they will have to come and see my glory."

"And I will set among them a sign, and I will send some of those who are escaped to the nations, to Tarshish, Pul, and Lud, those drawing the bow, Tubal and Javan, the faraway islands, who have not heard a report about me or seen my glory; and they will for certain tell about my glory among the nations. And they will actually bring all your brothers out of all the nations as a gift to Jehovah, on horses and in chariots and in covered wagons and on mules and on swift she-camels, up to my holy mountain, Jerusalem," Jehovah has said, "just as when the sons of Israel bring the gift in a clean vessel into the house of Jehovah."

"And from them also I shall take some for the priests, for the Levites," Jehovah has said.

"For just as the new heavens and the new earth that I am making are standing before me," is the utterance of Jehovah, "so the offspring of you people and the name of you people will keep standing."

"And it will certainly occur that from new moon to new moon and from sabbath to sabbath all flesh will come in to bow down before me," Jehovah has said. "And they will actually go forth and look upon the carcasses of the men that were transgressing against me; for the very worms upon them will not die and their fire itself will not be extinguished, and they must become something repulsive to all flesh."

Isaiah 42:9, The first things—here they have come, but new things I am telling out. Before they begin to spring up, I cause you people to hear them.

Numbers 23:19-24, God is not a man that he should tell lies, neither a son of mankind that he should feel regret. Has he himself said it and will he not do it, and has he spoken and

will he not carry it out? Look! I have been taken to bless, and He has blessed, and I shall not reverse it. He has not looked upon any uncanny power against [faithful] Jacob [Leon], and no trouble has he seen against [faithful] Israel [Lisa]. **Jehovah his God is with him, and the loud hailing of a king is in his midst. God is bringing them [faithful worshippers of Jehovah] out of Egypt [the organization of Jehovah's Witnesses].** The swift course like that of a wild bull is his. For there is no unlucky spell against Jacob, nor any divination against Israel. At this time it may be said respecting Jacob [Leon] and Israel [Lisa], **"What has God worked out!" Behold, a people will get up like a lion, and like the lion it will lift itself up.** It will not lie down until it may eat prey, and the blood of slain ones it will drink.

Isaiah Chapter 52 all verses, Wake up, wake up, put on your strength, O Zion! Put on your beautiful garments, O Jerusalem, the holy city! For no more will there come again into you the uncircumcised and unclean one. Shake yourself free from the dust, rise up, take a seat, O Jerusalem [Lisa]. Loosen for yourself the bands on your neck, O captive daughter of Zion.

For this is what Jehovah has said: "It was for nothing that you people were sold, and it will be without money that you will be repurchased."

For this is what the Sovereign Lord Jehovah has said: "It was to Egypt that my people went down in the first instance to reside there as aliens; and without cause Assyria, for its part, oppressed them."

"And now, what interest do I have here?" is the utterance of Jehovah. "For my people were taken for nothing. The very ones ruling over them kept howling," is the utterance of Jehovah, "and constantly, all day long, my name was being treated with disrespect. **For that reason my people will know my name, even for that reason in that day, because I am the One that is speaking. Look! It is I."**

How comely upon the mountains are the feet of the one bringing good news, the one publishing peace, the one bringing **good news of something better, the one publishing salvation, the one saying to Zion: "Your God has become king!"**

Listen! Your own watchmen have raised their voice. In unison they keep crying out joyfully; for it will be eye into eye that they will see when Jehovah gathers back Zion.

Become cheerful, cry out joyfully in unison, you devastated places of Jerusalem [Lisa], for Jehovah has comforted his people [faithful worshippers of Jehovah still in the organization]; he has repurchased Jerusalem. Jehovah has bared his holy arm before the eyes of all the nations; and all the ends of the earth must see the salvation of our God.

Turn away, turn away, get out of there [Jehovah is calling out to his faithful worshippers still in the organization: "Get out of there!"], touch nothing unclean; get out from the midst of her, keep yourselves clean, you who are carrying the utensils of Jehovah. For you people will get out in no panic, and you will go in no flight. For Jehovah will be going even before you, and the God of Israel will be your rear guard.

Look! My servant will act with insight. He will be in high station and will certainly be elevated and exalted very much. To the extent that many have stared at him in amazement—so much was the disfigurement as respects his appearance more than that of any other man and as respects his stately form more than that of the sons of mankind—he will likewise startle many nations. At him kings will shut their mouth, because what had not been recounted to them they will actually see, and to what they had not heard they must turn their consideration.

Past Events in My Life:

Angel: [I was greeted by an angel. This was before I discovered God's truth from the Bible, studying with Jehovah's Witnesses. I was living in Iowa Falls, Iowa back in the mid-1970s. He was coming down the front steps of the local hospital as I was approaching. His eyes reflected the color of a clear, blue sky, and he was dressed in present day clothing. He smiled and spoke only a greeting to me, to which I responded in kind. I sensed that this encounter had spiritual significance, and it caused me to wonder what it meant for a long time. I still retain the image in my mind.]

Truth: [I started studying the Bible with Jehovah's Witnesses back in the spring of 1979, during the time I lived in Des Moines, Iowa. One day I decided to take the little blue book, "The Truth that Leads to Eternal Life" with me to work.

I worked by myself for a Jewish woman who owned a small gift shop, and when I didn't have any customers I read in my spare time. I remember as I was reading along in this book that I was suddenly struck with the full import of what I was reading. In my mind I began shouting joyfully: "This is THE TRUTH! This is really THE TRUTH!" I got down on my knees in the office where I was and thanked God in prayer for opening my eyes to the truth.

And I realized for the first time that it is important to God that we come to an **accurate knowledge of his truth** because we are his creation. (1 Timothy 2:3,4) He has the right to expect us to use the minds and hearts he has given us to learn his ways and conduct ourselves honorably at all times out of respect for him.

And, in remembrance of this lovely Jewish woman I worked for, who suffered at the time with a great deal of pain, I want to particularly acknowledge that Jehovah (YHWH, Yahweh) is calling his Jewish people to be gathered to him now, too. (Isaiah 49:8) I see now, looking back at this incident in my life, that Jehovah wanted me to meet this lady.]

Image: [As I was learning the truth I realized that I should begin praying to God, addressing him by his name, Jehovah. The first time I began to pray to Jehovah, calling on him by name, in a very real way Satan tried to prevent me. He tried to frighten me so that I would stop praying. An image of Satan's face flashed in my mind, expressing great anger, using his power to frighten me. My thought at the time was that **if this is what happens when I pray calling on Jehovah's name, I had *really* better pray**. I began praying with great earnestness, then.]

Vision: [I was given a vision from Jehovah. I still lived in Des Moines, Iowa at this time and was continuing my study of the Bible and progressing in the truth: I saw a long road. I saw Jehovah and myself walking down this long road, hand in hand. Jehovah called me "Friend."]

Message: [I was given a message from Jehovah. In the fall of 1986, I was living in Lancaster, Wisconsin. I had just written to the Watchtower Bible and Tract Society, the headquarters of Jehovah's Witnesses in New York. I reported to them some very serious problems in the Iowa

City, Iowa congregation from which I had recently moved. Among the body of elders, there were two elders, Keith L. and Howard E., who were seriously mishandling their theocratic responsibilities.

As I was writing my report, Jehovah indicated to me that I should take great care with the accuracy of the details of these events. I heard these words: "Many will be tested by this, including Susie (Susan B.)."]

Message: [I was given another message from Jehovah during the time I lived in Lancaster, Wisconsin. I had prayed to Jehovah and asked for vindication of the false accusations coming from several members in the organization, which I was finding difficult to bear. Jehovah brought back to my mind this scripture.]

Matthew 5:11,12, Happy are you when people reproach you and persecute you and lyingly say every sort of wicked thing against you for my sake. Rejoice and leap for joy, since your reward is great in the heavens; for in that way they persecuted the prophets prior to you.

[After several years of preaching the good news, I was used to enduring reproach and humiliation from non-believers, but this was intense and persistent persecution from members of my spiritual family. I was deeply hurt by their accusations, and I was angry and offended at the way I was being treated. My prayers to Jehovah for vindication were constant.

Finally, I decided to pray to Jehovah for guidance instead of vindication. In prayer, I asked, "What is the attitude I should have toward this?" I heard the words: "It is a privilege to be persecuted this way."

I then realized that I needed to make an adjustment in my thinking. I needed to learn patience and endurance, and trust in Jehovah for both now and into the future when he will prove out everything. Later, Jehovah did vindicate me of one of the longest-standing false accusations. Thank you, Jehovah!]

My Prayer: [After my divorce from Daniel M., we moved from Iowa City, Iowa to Lancaster, Wisconsin. Some time before Jehovah gave me the work that I am doing now, I went to Jehovah in solemn prayer. I had been pouring out my heart to Jehovah about my strong feelings for a man whom I had met many years before, Leon Wurzer. Since meeting him, I realized that I could not make room in my heart for any other man.

A few years ago, during a time of spiritual weakness, I had become involved with Daniel M., only because in my mind he bore a vague resemblance to Leon. My heart weighed heavily since committing my offense, my great wrongdoing against Jehovah. In this prayer I said to Jehovah that because of my love for Leon, I could not consider marrying another man. I determined that I would continue to pray that Jehovah would lead Leon to the truth, and that someday, perhaps he would become a Christian "brother." In this prayer, I told Jehovah that if Leon found the truth and began serving Jehovah whole-souled, I could wait for him, even into the new paradise earth, even if his service to Jehovah took him to the furthest corners of the world, and even if it took a hundred years before Leon and I could be together. In the meantime, I would remain chaste and god-fearing, faithfully fulfilling my own service to Jehovah, no matter how long it took. I could say all of this to Jehovah because I knew Leon was the only man I could want to be married to.]

Sent Forth: [In the spring of 1989, my spiritual "eyes" were opened by Jehovah to the knowledge that I was being "sent forth." I was visiting at my mother's home in Iowa Falls, Iowa when I was told this. Interestingly, at this time my mother lived on Siloam Road. Siloam means "sent forth." Iowa Falls, Iowa is also the place where I was greeted by the angel years ago, and where I met Leon Wurzer for the first time.]

Escape From Captivity: [Jehovah directed me to leave the organization of Jehovah's Witnesses in June of 1989. I was given this scripture.] Isaiah 52:2, Shake yourself free from the dust, rise up, take a seat, O Jerusalem. Loosen for yourself the bands on your neck, O captive daughter of Zion. [I was also given this scripture.] Jeremiah 50:28, There is the sound of those fleeing and those escaping from the land of Babylon to tell out in Zion the vengeance of Jehovah our God, the vengeance for his temple.

[I was concerned whether my son, Bram, a baptized and faithful Christian, would believe that Jehovah had directed us to leave the organization. Under any other circumstances, to leave would be tantamount to forsaking Jehovah and the truth. As reassurance that my son would believe, Jehovah gave me this scripture.] Isaiah 54:13, And all your sons will be persons taught by Jehovah, and the peace of your sons will be abundant. [And this proved out to be true when I told my son. He believed Jehovah.]

Persecution From Satan: [I realize now that Satan was behind the various forms persecution took from non-believers and my spiritual family—members of the organization of Jehovah's Witnesses. There were times I was being pushed by Satan to lose my temper and seek to vindicate myself. I had to work constantly to learn to respond to every situation appropriately, putting everything in prayer to Jehovah and looking for guidance from him. From February of 1987 on, I was under intense pressure. At this point, Satan was urging me to kill myself. Throughout, Jehovah was strengthening and teaching me, so that I was able to resist the efforts of Satan to destroy my relationship with God.]

Message: [I was given another message from Jehovah in May of 1987. At that time my depression was severe. I had been praying for a long time that Jehovah would guide Leon to the truth, and that hopefully, someday we would meet again. My feelings for him were tearing up my heart. At one point I was crying during my prayer to Jehovah. I was given these words of comfort: "It is going to be all right. Something is going to be done about it." I did not know at this time that Leon was trying to locate me.]

Prayer Answered: [I had been fervently and continually praying to Jehovah that if Leon was a "sheeplike" one, Jehovah would guide him to the truth. I specifically prayed to Jehovah that if there was a possibility of our being able to reestablish our friendship from when we first met back in 1978, that "our paths would cross someday at an assembly."

I saw Leon at an assembly for Jehovah's Witnesses in Janesville, Wisconsin in January 1988. Jehovah answered my prayer with literal precision. Our paths crossed at the assembly, although for reasons not known to me, we were not able to speak to each other then.

At a later time, I was able to begin to understand Jehovah's reasons for preventing us from reestablishing our friendship at this time. And it is for a later date in time when we will be able to meet again.

I can now see Jehovah's wisdom in how all of this has transpired. Jehovah gave me this scripture.] Psalm 84:11b, Jehovah himself will not hold back anything good from those walking in faultlessness.

[Jehovah has been training me to walk in faultlessness, and at the same time Leon is learning "good." Neither of us is ready in Jehovah's eyes. I do know and I do trust that Jehovah's words to me are faithful, that "It is going to be all right. Something is going to be done about it." Something has begun to be done about it.

During this time, as I am learning Jehovah's ways, I am also setting an example for others, including Leon. I am learning how to handle difficult challenges and to respond to these appropriately. Over the years Leon has developed a controlling, self-centered "worldly" personality. Jehovah is helping Leon to unlearn these traits and replace them with Christian qualities.

These kinds of changes take time. Jehovah has been teaching and training me now for over ten years, and I still have a long way to go, as I recall the long road Jehovah showed me in the vision he gave me back in 1979.

I have experienced anguish and heartbreak that I didn't think I could live through during this period in my life, even after I began to understand why and how Jehovah was working out his will in this way.

I have to remember that when I was not fully "awakened" spiritually, my thoughts and actions did not reflect a mature Christian, either. I am coming through this period in my life strengthened and wiser, and only because Jehovah is patient with me. He is gracious and kind, and his holy spirit continues to guide me.]

Attempted Abduction: [In December of 1988, a man drove into the parking lot of our apartment complex and attempted to abduct Gabrielle, then age 3, at gunpoint. It was the middle of the day, within 10 yards of our front door, while I was inside putting away groceries. I know with all my heart that Jehovah protected Gabrielle and prevented the man from taking her. It was learned later that this man was very likely a member of a local cult of Satan worshippers.]

Intruder: [An intruder gained access to our apartment. In May of 1989, one night as I slept I was given a dream from Jehovah. I dreamed that a powerful force was causing a tree to thrash wildly in the wind, and its branches were swaying so violently they were striking the ground. I was given the impression that the violence from this force was deadly. I was then warned by an angel, urging me to "Wake up! Wake up! Stay awake!" I awoke to see a person wearing a nylon stocking over his head coming up the stairs. When he saw that I was awake, he turned and ran out of the apartment. Later, when I told Rosie about it she said she thought the intruder's intent was to kill me, because she had been given this scripture from Jehovah.] John 10:10a, The thief does not come unless it is to steal and slay and destroy.

Circuit Overseer's Visit To Our Congregation: [The Circuit Overseer visited our congregation in May 1989. I had been trying to keep track of events in my life in journal form since at least 1986. I was directed by Jehovah to gather my 1986-7 journal and my 1988-9 journal, along with other notes, and give them to the Circuit Overseer, James Thatcher. Only recently had I been made aware that I was "chosen" by Jehovah. At this time, I was not fully aware of the position I had been given. Jehovah gave me this scripture in reference to the papers I was to give to the Circuit Overseer.] 1 Timothy 4:6, By giving these advices to the brothers you will be a fine minister of Christ Jesus, one nourished with the words of the faith and of the fine teaching which you have followed closely.

Jehovah's Presence: [As it was approaching midnight of May 31, 1989, I was told in advance to prepare myself spiritually, mentally and physically. Jehovah then descended from on high. He transferred his approval from the governing body of the organization to me. He endowed me with his holy spirit; his truth and light. I have been chosen and sent forth by Jehovah to light the way for others to find him.]

Prophetesses: [Jehovah sent Rosie and myself to prophesy against the organization of Jehovah's Witnesses in the spring of 1989, to expose the wrongdoing of unfaithful ones, especially those taking the lead in the organization.]

Zion: [Zion (Lisa) "gave birth" spiritually to "children" in the spring of 1989.] Isaiah 8:18, Look! I and the children whom Jehovah has given me are as signs and as miracles in Israel from Jehovah of armies, who is residing in Mount Zion.

Isaiah 66:8b, For Zion has come into labor pains as well as given birth to her sons.

Message: [I was given the message: "Marry." This was given to me from Jehovah in June of 1989.]

Onward-sweeping Tempest: [Jehovah went forth over the land in an onward-sweeping tempest. He is enraged by those taking the lead in the organization of Jehovah's Witnesses. They call themselves by his holy name, and yet they use deception and intimidation to enslave their members.] Jeremiah 30:23a, Look! A windstorm of Jehovah, rage itself, has gone forth, an onward-sweeping tempest.

Disfellowshipped For Exposing Wrongdoing In The Organization: [My friend, Rosie Olson, my son, Bram Lewis, and I, Lisa Pressnall (then Lisa Murray—I have since legally changed my name back to my birth name) were told by the elders, John G., Larry M. and Wayne J. of the Lancaster, Wisconsin Congregation of Jehovah's Witnesses that we were being disfellowshipped for apostasy. In truth, we were disfellowshipped for exposing their wrongdoing; calling attention to their lies and methods of intimidation.]

Portent: [After being disfellowshipped by the elders, and as my son and I were driving home, we saw a powerful portent in the fiery, red sunset clouds. It was the face of Christ, and in his raised arm he held a scepter.] Matthew 24:30b, And they will see the Son of man coming on the clouds of heaven with power and great glory.

Jehovah's Denunciation Mailed Out: [Jehovah's denunciation was mailed out to the headquarters of Jehovah's Witnesses in New York, U.S.A. and to all their branch offices in other countries around the world.]

Warning In Advance: [I was warned by Jehovah in advance that I would be lied to, and the nature of the lie, in reference to Leon. In July of 1989, I was given this scripture.] Psalm 112:7, He will not be afraid even of bad news. His heart is steadfast, made reliant upon Jehovah.

Given In Advance: [I was told in advance by Jehovah that I would be given good news, in reference to Leon.] Proverbs 25:25, As cold water upon a tired soul, so is a good report from a distant land.

Angelic Presence: [I was working on books in my basement bookbinding shop on the sabbath, on which Jehovah required of me to do no labor (Saturday sunset to Sunday sunset). I sensed an angelic presence over my shoulder, and I was given the thought that he was wondering why I was laboring on the sabbath. I had forgotten about the new sabbath requirement for me. I stopped working immediately.]

Message: [I was visiting at my mother's home in Iowa Falls, Iowa. In prayer one night, I had been complaining to Jehovah about the kind of person that Leon seemed to be. I was saying to Jehovah that if Leon was like this, that I didn't want anything to do with him. One of Jehovah's angels was sent to me and I was corrected with this message: "Shame on you! Jehovah is using you to fulfill prophecies." I was given an impression that it was in many major categories. "Jehovah is using you—and you are complaining." I am reminded that I must have faith, and trust Jehovah to teach and correct Leon as he has patiently taught and corrected me.]

Message: [We were down in my basement during a severe storm. I sensed a presence over by the stairwell. I was told: "I love you best, because you always obey Jehovah."]

Presence Of More Than One: [On Saturday evening at the time of the sabbath prayer, I stood and raised my hands in prayer. As we praised Jehovah and I asked for comfort, I sensed more than one spiritual presence. Possibly three or more were present. I was given these scriptures from Jesus.] Psalm 122 abbreviated here, For the sake of my brothers and my companions I will now speak: "May there be peace within you." For the sake of the house of Jehovah our God I will keep seeking good for you.

Our Needs Were Met: [We prayed for help to get the apartments in Forest City in Iowa for Rosie's family and mine. We didn't have the extra money for the utilities deposits. We asked Jehovah for help. We ended up not having to pay the deposits. Thank you, Jehovah.]

Help From Jehovah: [My sister, Dawn, was worried about not having enough food to feed everyone coming for a family get together. We talked about going to Jehovah in prayer. Before we started to pray, a person showed up at her door with some very nice cucumbers. My sister was so excited about Jehovah helping us before we had even prayed for help. She said she could believe this kind of thing happening, more than a Bible study could convince her.]

August 12, 1989

Psalm 125:3, For the scepter of wickedness will not keep resting upon the lot of the righteous ones, in order that the righteous ones may not thrust out their hand upon any wrongdoing.

Proverbs 22:8-11, He that is sowing unrighteousness will reap what is hurtful, but the very rod of his fury will come to its end.

He that is kindly in eye will be blessed, for he has given of his food to the lowly one.

Drive away the ridiculer, that contention may go out and that legal contest and dishonor may cease.

The one loving purity of heart—for the charm of his lips the king will be his companion.

Recall: Song of Solomon 6:9a, One there is who is my dove, my blameless one. One there is who belongs to her mother. She is the pure one of the one giving birth to her.

Proverbs 22:17-21, Incline your ear and hear the words of the wise ones, that you may apply your very heart to my knowledge. For it is pleasant that you should keep them in your belly, that they may be firmly established together upon your lips.

For your confidence to come to be in Jehovah himself I have given you [Lisa] knowledge today, even you.

Have I [Jehovah] not written you heretofore with counselings and knowledge, to show you the truthfulness of true sayings, so as to return sayings that are the truth—to the one sending you forth? [I am sent forth by Jehovah with the ability to "return sayings that are the truth." Because Jehovah has taught me truth I am able to speak truth. And because God's word, the Bible, is true, I can comprehend his true sayings. Because my confidence has come to be in Jehovah, he himself has given me knowledge.] Recall: Psalm 16:7, I shall bless Jehovah, who has given me advice. Really, during the nights my kidneys [deepest emotions] have corrected me.

[Jehovah also speaks "truthfulness of true sayings" in prophecy. Jehovah told me Bram would believe that it was Jehovah who directed us to leave the organization. Also, at one point, Jehovah warned me when I was about to be lied to. Both times Jehovah was proven true. Jehovah is the God of truth. And I am able to worship Jehovah in spirit and truth because I have been given truth from Jehovah himself.]

2 Timothy 2:2, And the things you heard from me with the support of many witnesses, these things commit to faithful men, who, in turn, will be adequately qualified to teach others.

[This chapter of Isaiah was given to me by Jehovah. It describes the spiritual work he has given me. I am to bring back to Jehovah his faithful people, including Leon. I have also been given "for a light of the nations," that all people seeking Jehovah and his righteousness might find him.]

Isaiah Chapter 49 all verses, Listen to me, O you islands, and pay attention, you national groups far away. Jehovah himself has called me even from the belly. From the inward parts of my mother he has made mention of my name. And he proceeded to make my mouth like a sharp sword. In the shadow of his hand he has hidden me. And he gradually made me a polished arrow. He concealed me in his own quiver. And he went on to say to me: "You are my servant, O Israel [Lisa], you the one in whom I shall show my beauty."

But as for me, I said: "It is for nothing that I have toiled. For unreality and vanity I have used up my own power. Truly my judgment is with Jehovah, and my wages with my God." And now Jehovah, the One forming me from the belly as a servant belonging to him, has said for me to bring back Jacob [Leon] to him, in order that to him Israel itself might be gathered. And I shall be glorified in the eyes of Jehovah, and my own God will have become my strength. And he proceeded to say: "It has been more than a trivial matter for you to become my servant to raise up the tribes of Jacob and to bring back even the safeguarded ones of Israel [faithful worshippers of Jehovah still in the organization]; I also have given you for a light of the nations, that my salvation may come to be to the extremity of the earth."

This is what Jehovah, the Repurchaser of Israel, his Holy One, has said to him [Lisa] that is despised in soul, to him that is detested by the nation, to the servant of rulers: "Kings themselves will see and certainly rise up, and princes, and they will bow down, by reason of Jehovah, who is faithful, the Holy One of Israel, who chooses you."

This is what Jehovah has said: "In a time of goodwill I have answered you, and in a day of salvation I have helped you; and I kept safeguarding you that I might give you as a covenant for the people, to rehabilitate the land, **to bring about the repossessing of the desolated hereditary possessions, to say to the prisoners, 'Come out!' to those who are in the darkness, 'Reveal yourselves!'** By the ways they will pasture, and on all beaten paths their pasturing will be. They will not go hungry, neither will they go thirsty, nor will parching heat or sun strike them. For the One who is having pity upon them will lead them, and by the springs of water he will conduct them. And I will make all my mountains a way, and my highways themselves will be on an elevation. Look! These will come even from far away, and, look! these from the north and from the west, and these from the land of Sinim."

Give a glad cry, you heavens, and be joyful, you earth. Let the mountains become cheerful with a glad outcry. For Jehovah has comforted his people, and he shows pity upon his own afflicted ones.

But Zion [Lisa] kept saying: "Jehovah has left me, and Jehovah himself has forgotten me." Can a wife forget her suckling so that she should not pity the son of her belly? Even these women can forget, yet I myself shall not forget you. Look! Upon my palms I have engraved you. Your walls are in front of me constantly. Your sons have hurried up. The very ones tearing you down and devastating you will go forth even from you. Raise your eyes all around and see. They have all of them been collected together. They have come to you. "As I am living," is the utterance of Jehovah, "with all of them you will clothe yourself just as with ornaments, and you will bind them on yourself like a bride. Although there are your devastated places and your desolated places and the land of your ruins, although now you are too cramped to be dwelling, and those swallowing you down have been far away, yet in your own ears the sons of your bereaved state will say, 'The place has become too cramped for me. Do make room for me, that I may dwell.' And you will for certain say in your heart, 'Who has become father to these for me, since I am a woman bereaved of children and sterile, gone into exile and taken prisoner? As for these, who has brought them up? Look! I myself had been left behind alone. These—where have they been?'"

This is what the Sovereign Lord Jehovah has said: "Look! I shall raise up my hand even to the nations, and to the peoples I shall lift up my signal. And they will bring your sons in the bosom, and upon the shoulder they will carry your own daughters. And kings must become caretakers for you, and their princesses nursing women for you. With faces to the earth they will bow down to you, and the dust of your feet they will lick up; and you will have to know that I am Jehovah, of whom those hoping in me will not be ashamed."

Can those already taken be taken from a mighty man himself, or can the body of captives of the tyrant make their escape? But this is what Jehovah has said: "Even the body of captives of the mighty man will be taken away, and those already taken by the tyrant himself will make their escape. And against anyone contending against you I myself shall contend, and your own sons I myself shall save. And I will make those maltreating you eat their own flesh; and as with the sweet wine they will become drunk with their own blood. And all flesh will have to know that I, Jehovah, am your Savior and your Repurchaser, the Powerful One of Jacob.

Philippians 2:19,23, For my part I am hoping in the Lord Jesus to send Timothy [meaning "One who honors God."] [Leon] to you shortly, that I may be a cheerful soul when I get to know about the things pertaining to you.

This, therefore, is the man I am hoping to send just as soon as I have seen how things stand concerning me.

[Shortly, to my way of thinking, would mean today or tomorrow. But, Jehovah marks time differently. From Jehovah's point of view, with eternity stretching out before him, shortly could very well be ten or twenty years from now. And I must recall my prayer to Jehovah. I told Jehovah that I could wait 100 years for Leon, if he would become a faithful worshipper of Jehovah.]

Jeremiah 28:3, Within two full years more I am bringing back to this place all the utensils of the house of Jehovah that Nebuchadnezzar the king of Babylon took from this place that he might bring them to Babylon.

Isaiah 21:16, For this is what Jehovah has said to me: "Within yet a year, according to the years of a hired laborer, all the glory of Kedar must even come to its end. [As Jehovah marks time differently from us, I do not know how to calculate time the way Jehovah intends it here. It is best for me to just faithfully continue to put my trust in Jehovah, and wait patiently for the fulfillment of his promises to me. If there is something Jehovah wants me to know, he will make it clear to me. This is his way.]

August 28, 1989

[Last evening I was in deep, deep emotional pain and depression, and I was praying to Jehovah.]

Psalm 142 all verses, With my voice, to Jehovah I proceeded to call for aid; with my voice, to Jehovah I began to cry for favor. Before him I kept pouring out my concern; before him I continued to tell about my own distress, when my spirit fainted away within me. Then you yourself knew my roadway. In the path in which I walk they have hidden a trap for me. Look to the right hand and see that there is no one giving any recognition to me. My place for flight has perished from me; there is no one inquiring for my soul. I called to you, O Jehovah, for aid. I said: "You are my refuge, my share in the land of the living ones." Do pay attention to my entreating cry, for I have become very much impoverished. Deliver me from my persecutors, for they are stronger than I am. Do bring my soul out of the very dungeon to laud your name. Around me let the righteous ones gather, because you deal appropriately with me.

[We are living in hiding from Daniel M., my ex-husband, who has been diagnosed with a sociopathic personality disorder, and who on previous occasions has tried to kill us. These are scriptures from Jehovah assuring me of protection from Daniel or anyone else used by Satan to do us harm.]

Psalm 121 all verses, I shall raise my eyes to the mountains. From where will my help come? My help is from Jehovah, the Maker of heaven and earth. He cannot possibly allow your foot to totter. The One guarding you cannot possibly be drowsy. Look! He will not be drowsy nor go to sleep, he that is guarding Israel [Lisa]. Jehovah is guarding you. Jehovah is your shade on your right hand. By day the sun itself will not strike you, nor the moon by night. Jehovah himself will guard you against all calamity. He will guard your soul. Jehovah himself will guard your going out and your coming in from now on and to time indefinite.

[When I was very depressed about the situation with Leon and feeling uncomforted, and it seemed that Satan was trying to manipulate my comprehension of the scriptures to make my depression worse, I begged Jehovah in prayer for comfort. Jehovah helped me, as he always does, and he gave me this scripture.] Psalm 119:37, Make my eyes pass on from seeing what is worthless; preserve me alive in your own way.

[Then I was given this scripture.] Psalm 122:9, For the sake of the house of Jehovah our God I will keep seeking good for you. [I was also being reassured by Christ that he would keep seeking good for Leon and me.]

[This morning my emotional pain and my depression were excruciating. I was given this scripture from the book of John.]

John 12:27, Now my soul is troubled, and what shall I say? Father, save me out of this hour. Nevertheless, this is why I have come to this hour.

[In my journey with Jehovah down this long road, as in my vision from him when he called me "Friend," I have been brought to this point, to know excruciating pain as Jesus himself experienced it.

I was sick in my heart to the point of asking Jehovah in prayer to "Let me die. Let me die."

"No, make me keep living." I have to keep living for my children. The suffering is unbearable. I am not even able to draw breath for myself. Jehovah, keep me alive, make me draw another breath.]

Isaiah Chapter 53 all verses, Who has put faith in the thing heard by us? And as for the arm of Jehovah, to whom has it been revealed? And he will come up like a twig before one, and like a root out of waterless land. No stately form does he [Lisa] have, nor any splendor; and when we shall see him, there is not the appearance so that we should desire him. [These prophecies have their primary fulfillment in Jesus' life and death. It is Jehovah's will that I must also experience grief to an extreme.]

He was despised and was avoided by men, a man meant for pains and for having acquaintance with sickness. And there was as if the concealing of one's face from us. He was despised, and we held him as of no account. Truly our sicknesses were what he himself carried; and as for our pains, he bore them. But we ourselves accounted him as plagued, stricken by God and afflicted. But he was being pierced for our transgression; he was being crushed for our errors. The chastisement meant for our peace was upon him, and because of his wounds there has been a healing for us. Like sheep we have all of us wandered about; it was each one to his own way that we have turned; and Jehovah himself has caused the error of us all to meet up with that one. He was hard pressed, and he was letting himself be afflicted; yet he would not open his mouth. He was being brought just like a sheep to the slaughtering; and like a ewe that before her shearers has become mute, he also would not open his mouth.

Because of restraint and of judgment he was taken away; and who will concern himself even with the details of his generation? For he was severed from the land of the living ones. Because of the transgression of my people he had the stroke. And he will make his burial place even with the wicked ones, and with the rich class in his death, despite the fact that he had done no violence and there was no deception in his mouth.

But Jehovah himself took delight in crushing him; he made him sick. If you will set his soul as a guilt offering, he will see his offspring, he will prolong his days, and in his hand what is the delight of Jehovah will succeed. Because of the trouble of his soul he [Lisa] will see, he will be satisfied. By means of his knowledge the righteous one, my servant, will bring a righteous standing to many people; and their errors he himself will bear. For that reason I shall deal him a portion among the many, and it will be with the mighty ones that he will apportion the spoil, due to the fact that he poured out his soul to the very death, and it was with the transgressors that he was counted in; and he himself carried the very sin of many people, and for the transgressors he proceeded to interpose.

Psalm 125 all verses, Those trusting in Jehovah are like Mount Zion, which cannot be made to totter, but dwells even to time indefinite. Jerusalem—as mountains are all around it, so Jehovah is all around his people from now on and to time indefinite. For the scepter of wickedness will not keep resting upon the lot of the righteous ones, in order that the righteous ones may not thrust out their hand upon any wrongdoing. O do good, O Jehovah, to the good ones, even to the ones upright in their hearts. As for those turning aside to their crooked ways, Jehovah will make them go away with the practicers of what is hurtful. There will be peace upon Israel.

Isaiah Chapter 54 all verses, "Cry out joyfully, you barren woman that did not give birth! Become cheerful with a joyful outcry and cry shrilly, you that had no childbirth pains, for the sons of the desolated one [Lisa] are more numerous than the sons of the woman with a husbandly owner [the apostate organization of Jehovah's Witnesses, which before deviating from his righteous ways, had a "husbandly owner," Jehovah, as he had guided them by his holy spirit]," Jehovah has said. "Make the place of your tent more spacious. And let them stretch out the tent cloths of your grand tabernacle. Do not hold back. Lengthen out your tent cords, and make those tent pins of yours strong. For to the right and to the left you will break forth, and your own offspring will take possession even of nations, and they will inhabit even the desolated cities. Do not be afraid, for you will not be put to shame; and do not feel humiliated, for you will not be disappointed. For you will forget even the shame of your time of youth, and the reproach of your continuous widowhood you will remember no more."

"For your Grand Maker is your husbandly owner, Jehovah of armies being his name; and the Holy One of Israel is your Repurchaser. The God of the whole earth he will be called. For Jehovah called you [Lisa] as if you were a wife left entirely and hurt in spirit, and as a wife of the time of youth who was then rejected," your God has said.

"For a little moment I left you entirely, but with great mercies I shall collect you together. With a flood of indignation I concealed my face from you for but a moment, but with loving-kindness to time indefinite I will have mercy upon you," your Repurchaser, Jehovah, has said.

"This is just as the days of Noah to me. Just as I have sworn that the waters of Noah shall no more pass over the earth, so I have sworn that I will not become indignant toward you nor rebuke you. For the mountains themselves may be removed, and the very hills may stagger, but my loving-kindness itself will not be removed from you, nor will my covenant of peace itself stagger," Jehovah, the One having mercy upon you, has said.

"O woman [Lisa] afflicted, tempest-tossed, uncomforted, here I am laying with hard mortar your stones, and I will lay your foundation with sapphires. And I will make your battlements of rubies, and your gates of fiery glowing stones, and all your boundaries of delightsome stones. And all your sons will be persons taught by Jehovah, and the peace of your sons will be abundant. You will prove to be firmly established in righteousness itself. You will be far away from oppression—for you will fear none—and from anything terrifying, for it will not come near you. If anyone should at all make an attack, it will not be at my orders. Whoever is making an attack upon you will fall even on account of you."

"Look! I myself have created the craftsman, the one blowing upon the fire of charcoal and bringing forth a weapon as his workmanship. I myself, too, have created the ruinous man for wrecking work. Any weapon whatever that will be formed against you [Lisa] will have no success, and any tongue at all that will rise up against you in the judgment you will condemn. This is the hereditary possession of the servants of Jehovah, and their righteousness is from me," is the utterance of Jehovah.

Psalm 41:11,12, By this I do know that you have found delight in me, because my enemy [Satan] does not shout in triumph over me. As for me, because of my integrity you have upheld me, and you will set me before your face to time indefinite.

! [I was thinking of this scripture and opened my Bible right to it.] Psalm 125:3,4, For the scepter of wickedness will not keep resting upon the lot of the righteous ones, in order that the righteous ones may not thrust out their hand upon any wrongdoing. O do good, O Jehovah, to the good ones, even to the ones upright in their hearts.

Lamentations 3:25, Good is Jehovah to the one hoping in him, to the soul that keeps seeking for him.

Psalm 119:147, I have been up early in the morning twilight, that I may cry for help. For your words I have waited.

Recall: [I was given this last night.] Psalm 143:8, In the morning cause me to hear your loving-kindness, for in you I have put my trust. Make known to me the way in which I should walk, for to you I have lifted up my soul.

Isaiah 53:1, Who has put faith in the thing heard by us? And as for the arm of Jehovah, to whom has it been revealed? [Parts of this chapter describe my affliction, pain, disfellowshipping, and death; not spiritual or physical death, but certainly emotional "death."]

Isaiah 53:5, But he was being pierced for our transgression; he was being crushed for our errors.

Psalm 109:22, For I am afflicted and poor, and my heart itself has been pierced within me.

Isaiah 53:5, continued, The chastisement meant for our peace was upon him, and because of his wounds there has been a healing for us.

Psalm 69:20, Reproach itself has broken my heart, and the wound is incurable. And I kept hoping for someone to show sympathy, but there was none; and for comforters, but I found none. [Jehovah is letting me experience the full depth of grief and mourning.]

Isaiah 53:7, He was hard pressed, and he was letting himself be afflicted; yet he would not open his mouth. He was being brought just like a sheep to the slaughtering; and like a ewe that before her shearers has become mute, he also would not open his mouth.

Isaiah 53:12, For that reason I shall deal him a portion among the many, and it will be with the mighty ones that he will apportion the spoil, due to the fact that he poured out his soul to the very death, and it was with the transgressors that he was counted in; and he himself carried the very sin of many people, and for the transgressors he proceeded to interpose.

Isaiah 54:5,6,10, "For your Grand Maker is your husbandly owner, Jehovah of armies being his name; and the Holy One of Israel is your Repurchaser. The God of the whole earth he will be called. For Jehovah called you [Lisa] as if you were a wife left entirely and hurt in spirit, and as a wife of the time of youth who was then rejected," your God has said.

"For the mountains themselves may be removed, and the very hills may stagger, but my loving-kindness itself will not be removed from you, nor will my covenant of peace itself stagger," Jehovah, the One having mercy upon you, has said.

Recall: [At the time when I was on my way to the hospital to have a CAT scan of my lungs, I prayed to Jehovah, "Do not forget me." I was immediately given this scripture.]

→ Psalm 137:5, If I should forget you, O Jerusalem, let my right hand be forgetful.

Isaiah 53:1, Who has put faith in the thing heard by us? And as for the arm of Jehovah, to whom has it been revealed?

Isaiah 63:12, The One [Jehovah] making His beautiful arm go at the right hand of Moses; the One splitting the waters from before them in order to make an indefinitely lasting name for his own self.

Psalm 147 all verses, Praise Jah, you people, for it is good to make melody to our God; for it is pleasant—praise is fitting. Jehovah is building Jerusalem [Lisa]; the dispersed ones of Israel [faithful worshippers of Jehovah still in the organization] he brings together. He is healing the brokenhearted ones, and is binding up their painful spots. He is counting the number of the stars; all of them he calls by their names. Our Lord is great and is abundant in power; his understanding is beyond recounting. Jehovah is relieving the meek ones; he is abasing the wicked ones to the earth. Respond to Jehovah with thanksgiving, you people; make melody to our God on the harp, the One who is covering the heavens with clouds, the One preparing rain for the earth, the One making the mountains to sprout green grass. To the beasts he is giving their food, to the young ravens that keep calling. Not in the mightiness of the horse does he take delight, nor in the legs of the man does he find pleasure. **Jehovah is finding pleasure in those fearing him, in those waiting for his loving-kindness.** Commend Jehovah, O Jerusalem [Lisa]. Praise your God, O Zion [Leon]. For he has made the bars of your gates strong; he has blessed your sons in the midst of you. He is putting peace in your territory; with the fat of the wheat he keeps satisfying you. He is sending his saying to the earth; with speed his word runs. He is giving snow like wool; hoarfrost he scatters just like ashes. He is throwing his ice like morsels. Before his cold who can stand? He sends forth his word and melts them. He causes his wind to blow; the waters trickle. He is telling his word to Jacob [Leon], his regulations and judicial decisions to Israel [Lisa]. He has not done that way to any other nation; and as for his judicial decisions, they have not known them. Praise Jah, you people!

Psalm 149 all verses, Praise Jah, you people! Sing to Jehovah a new song, his praise in the congregation of loyal ones. Let Israel rejoice in its grand Maker, the sons of Zion—let them be joyful in their King. Let them praise his name with dancing. With the tambourine and the harp let them make melody to him. **For Jehovah is taking pleasure in his people. He beautifies the meek ones with salvation.** Let the loyal ones exult in glory; let them cry out joyfully on their beds. Let the songs extolling God be in their throat, and a two-edged sword [Bible] be in their hand, to execute vengeance upon the nations, rebukes upon the national groups, to bind their kings with shackles and their glorified ones with fetters of iron, to execute upon them the judicial decision written. Such splendor belongs to all his loyal ones. Praise Jah, you people!

Psalm 106:3-5, Happy are those observing justice, doing righteousness all the time. Remember me, O Jehovah, with the goodwill toward your people. Take care of me with your salvation, that I may see the goodness to your chosen ones, that I may rejoice with the rejoicing of your nation, that I may make my boast with your inheritance.

Psalm 147:15,19, He is sending his saying to the earth; with speed his word runs.
He is telling his word to Jacob [Leon], his regulations and his judicial decisions to Israel [Lisa].

September 1, 1989

Prayer: [I prayed to Jehovah, "Speak truth to me, please act!" I was given this scripture.] Isaiah 44:23, "Joyfully cry out, you heavens, for **Jehovah has taken action!** Shout in triumph, all you lowest parts of the earth! Become cheerful, you mountains, with joyful outcry, you forest and all you trees in it! For Jehovah has repurchased Jacob [Leon] and on Israel [Lisa] he shows his beauty."

Malachi 3:1, "Look! I am sending my messenger, and he must clear up a way before me. And suddenly there will come to His temple the true Lord, whom you people are seeking, and the messenger of the covenant in whom you are delighting. Look! He will certainly come," Jehovah of armies has said.

Prayer: [As I was driving in Forest City, Iowa, where we now live, I prayed to Jehovah that he would take us somewhere so we could appreciate the significance of the area. We drove past a sign that said, "Blessings Happen" and "God Knows What He Is Doing." We ended up at Pilot Knob, east and a little south of Forest City by about 5 miles; a designated wilderness area. It is the second highest point in Iowa. From the top of the tower we could see the circle of the earth (by scanning the entire horizon 360 degrees). The tree branches at their tips looked scorched. We looked to the northwest and saw Forest City. The sky filled with a large gray cloud, but rays of light were shining through and down all over Forest City. I thought: This is where Jehovah's light is, and this is where Jehovah's own glory is. I shouted from the top of the tower: "Jehovah is God!"

Recall: Psalm 84:11a, For Jehovah is a sun and a shield.

Recall: Psalm 121:5, Jehovah is guarding you. Jehovah is your shade on your right hand.

Forest: Psalm 132:6, Look! We have heard it in Ephrathah [earlier name for Bethlehem], we have found it in the fields of the forest.

Wilderness: Isaiah 40:3a, Listen! Someone is calling out in the wilderness: "Clear up the way of Jehovah, you people!"

Mountain: Isaiah 40:9, Make your way up even onto a high mountain, you woman bringing good news for Zion. Raise your voice even with power, you woman bringing good news for Jerusalem. Raise it. Do not be afraid. Say to the cities of Judah: "Here is your God."

Tower: Psalm 48:3, In her dwelling towers God himself has become known as a secure height.

Isaiah 45:9a,10,11a,13a, Woe to the one that has contended with his Former [referring to Leon, who is resisting Jehovah's instruction]. Woe to the one saying to a father: "What do you become father to?" and to the wife: "What are you in birth pains with?"
This is what Jehovah has said, the Holy One of Israel and the Former of him: "Ask me even about the things that are coming concerning my sons.
I myself have roused up someone in righteousness, and all his ways I shall straighten out.

Isaiah 46:10,11, The One telling from the beginning the finale, and from long ago the things that have not been done; the One saying, "My own counsel will stand, and everything that is my delight I shall do"; the One calling from the sunrising a bird of prey, **from a distant land the man to execute my counsel. I have even spoken it; I shall also bring it in. I have formed it, I shall also do it.**

Isaiah 44:28, The One saying of Cyrus [Leon], "He is my shepherd, and all that I delight in he will completely carry out"; even in my saying of Jerusalem [Lisa], "She will be rebuilt," and of the temple, "You will have your foundation laid." [This means that the harm that has been done to me over the years by others, including Leon, will be undone at the hand of Leon, directed by Jehovah.]

Isaiah 44:26, The One making the word of his servant come true, and the One that carries out completely the counsel of his own messengers [I recall that I was given this message in reference to Leon, "It is going to be all right. Something is going to be done about it."]; the One saying of Jerusalem, "She will be inhabited," and of the cities of Judah, "They will be rebuilt, and her desolated places I shall raise up."

Jeremiah 33:3,6-9, Call to me, and I shall answer you and readily tell you great and incomprehensible things that you have not known.
Here I am bringing up for her [Lisa] a recuperation and health; and I will heal them [Leon and Lisa] and reveal to them an abundance of peace and truth. And I will bring back the captives of Judah and the captives of Israel [faithful worshippers of Jehovah who will come out of the organization of unfaithful Jehovah's Witnesses], and I will build them just as at the start. And I will purify them from all their error with which they have sinned against me, and I will forgive all their errors with which they have sinned against me and with which they have transgressed against me. And she will certainly become to me a name of exultation, a praise and a beauty toward all the nations of the earth who will hear of all the goodness that I am rendering to them. And they [the nations] will certainly be in dread and be agitated on account of all the goodness and on account of all the peace that I am rendering to her.

Isaiah 62:2-4, And the nations will certainly see your righteousness, O woman, and all kings your glory. And you [Lisa] will actually be called by a new name, which the very mouth of Jehovah will designate. And you must become a crown of beauty in the hand of Jehovah, and a kingly turban in the palm of your God. No more will you be said to be a woman left entirely; and your own land will no more be said to be desolate; but you yourself will be called My Delight Is in Her, and your land Owned as a Wife. For Jehovah will have taken delight in you, and your own land will be owned as a wife.

Psalm 41:11, By this I do know that you have found delight in me, because my enemy does not shout in triumph over me.

Psalm 68:6a,9, God is causing the solitary ones to dwell in a house; he is bringing forth prisoners into full prosperity.
A copious downpour you began causing to fall, O God; your inheritance, even when it was weary—you yourself reinvigorated it.

Recall: [I prayed for physical and spiritual "rain." We had two good rains.]

Isaiah 45:8, O you heavens, cause a dripping from above; and let the cloudy skies themselves trickle with righteousness. Let the earth open up, and let it be fruitful with salvation, and let it cause righteousness itself to spring up at the same time. I myself, Jehovah, have created it.

James 5:17,18, Elijah was a man with feelings like ours, and yet in prayer he prayed for it not to rain; and it did not rain upon the land for three years and six months. And he prayed again, and the heavens gave rain and the land put forth its fruit. [The summer season had been dry. I had the thought that I should "pray for rain." Within 2-3 days it rained, and a neighbor's father commented that it was the first good rain this summer.

Recall: I recall when I looked out from the tower at Pilot's Knob, I saw that the tips of the tree branches appeared to be scorched, as though from harsh sun and not enough rain. Then we had a second and a third rain. I was also praying for spiritual "rain" from Jehovah for Leon, that Jehovah would "open his eyes and heart" to the truth.]

James 5:7,8, Exercise patience, therefore, brothers, until the presence of the Lord. Look! The farmer keeps waiting for the precious fruit of the earth, exercising patience over it until he gets the early rain and the late rain. **You too exercise patience; make your hearts firm, because the presence of the Lord has drawn close.**

2 Timothy 2:6,7, The hardworking farmer [Jehovah] must be the first to partake of the fruits [early spiritual development in Leon's personality]. Give constant thought to what I am saying; the Lord will really give you discernment in all things.

Psalm 68:9,10,16, A copious downpour you began causing to fall, O God; your inheritance, even when it was weary—you yourself reinvigorated it. Your tent community—they have dwelt in it; with your goodness you proceeded to make it ready for the afflicted one, O God.
Why do you, O you mountains of peaks, keep watching enviously the mountain [Lisa] that God has desired for himself to dwell in? Even Jehovah himself will reside there forever.

Isaiah 40:31, But those who are hoping in Jehovah will regain power. They will mount up with wings like eagles. They will run and not grow weary; they will walk and not tire out.

Psalm 68:28, Your God has laid command upon your strength [to be renewed]. Do show strength, O God, you who have acted for us.

Recall: Isaiah 44:23a, Joyfully cry out, you heavens, for Jehovah has taken action!

Psalm 68:19,20,21a, Blessed be Jehovah, who daily carries the load [not just the burden] for us, the true God of our salvation. *Selah.* The true God is for us a God of saving acts; and to Jehovah the Sovereign Lord belong the ways out from death. [The emotional anguish I am experiencing makes me want to die.] Indeed God himself will break the head of his enemies in pieces.

Isaiah 66:1,2, This is what Jehovah has said: "The heavens are my throne, and the earth is my footstool. Where, then, is the house that you people can build for me, and where, then, is the place as a resting-place for me?

Now all these things my own hand has made, so that all these came to be," is the utterance of Jehovah. "To this one, then, I shall look, to the one afflicted and contrite in spirit and trembling at my word."

Psalm 34:17,18, They cried out, and Jehovah himself heard, and out of all their distresses he delivered them. Jehovah is near to those that are broken at heart [I told Jehovah my heart is breaking.]; and those who are crushed in spirit he saves.

Psalm 34:5, They looked to him and became radiant, and their very faces could not possibly be ashamed.

Psalm 119:161, Princes themselves [those taking the lead in the organization; also Satan and his followers] have persecuted me for no cause, but my heart has been in dread of your own words.

September 2, 1989

Isaiah 33:17a, A king in his handsomeness is what your eyes will behold.

1 Corinthians 7:36b, Let them marry.

! 1 Corinthians 7:1,2, Now concerning the things about which you wrote, it is well for a man not to touch a woman; yet, because of prevalence of fornication, let each man have his own wife and each woman have her own husband. [Leon and I have permission from Jehovah to marry at some point in the future. When we are joined together in marriage by Jehovah it will be a sanctified union. Inappropriate contact between Leon and myself before marriage would be fornication. We are forewarned.]

Recall: Song of Solomon 8:8-10, "We have a little sister that does not have any breasts [does not have spiritual maturity]. What shall we do for our sister on the day that she will be spoken for?
If she should be a wall, we shall build upon her a battlement of silver; but if she should be a door, we shall block her up with a cedar plank."

"I am a wall, and my breasts are like towers. [The young woman replies that she is spiritually mature.] In this case I have become in his [Jehovah's] eyes like her that is finding peace."

September 4, 1989

> Rosie's Notes: 1 John 4:4, You originate with God, little children, and you have conquered those persons, because he that is in union with you is greater than he that is in union with the world.

September 5, 1989

1 John 3:1, See what sort of love the Father has given us, so that we should be called children of God; and such we are. That is why the world does not have a knowledge of us, because it has not come to know him.

2 Peter 1:4, Through these things he has freely given us the precious and very grand promises, that through these you may become sharers in divine nature, having escaped from the corruption that is in the world through lust.

1 Peter 1:4, To an incorruptible and undefiled and unfading inheritance. It is reserved in the heavens for you.

Revelation 3:12, The one that conquers—I will make him a pillar in the temple of my God, and he will by no means go out from it anymore, and I will write upon him the name of my God and the name of the city of my God, the new Jerusalem which descends out of heaven from my God, and that new name of mine.

1 Corinthians 14:1, Pursue love, yet keep zealously seeking the spiritual gifts, but preferably that you may prophesy.

1 Corinthians 12:4-11, Now there are varieties of gifts, but there is the same spirit; and there are varieties of ministries, and yet there is the same Lord; and there are varieties of operations, and yet it is

the same God who performs all the operations in all persons. But the manifestation of the spirit is given to each one for a beneficial purpose. For example, to one there is given through the spirit speech of wisdom, to another speech of knowledge according to the same spirit, to another faith by the same spirit, to another gifts of healings by that one spirit, to yet another operations of powerful works, to another prophesying, to another discernment of inspired utterances, to another different tongues [languages], and to another interpretation of tongues [languages]. But all these operations the one and the same spirit performs, making a distribution to each one respectively just as it wills.

[There are many forms that Satan's deception can take to discourage people and weaken them spiritually. People, especially close family members, are sometimes manipulated by Satan in what they say (unknown to themselves), that undermines another person's faith. (Matthew 16:22,23)

On one occasion in particular this happened when my mother, Joan, came for a visit to my home in Forest City. After she left, I was feeling very hurt by the things that she had said to me. And it made my depression even more unbearable.

Later, Rosie read to me from her Bible.] Psalm 118:13, "You almost killed me." [This was in reference to the things my mother had said.] Psalm 118:13, NWT (1984), "You pushed me hard that I should fall, but Jehovah himself helped me." Psalm 118:13, The Living Bible Paraphrased (1971), "You did your best to kill me, O my enemy [Satan], but the Lord helped me."

[It really doesn't matter how we have arrived at this point in terms of wrongs done to me. What matters is if I have maintained integrity in my heart and upheld Jehovah's ways. If I have endured and secured safety for my family in these last days, and if my course has taught others Jehovah's ways, then no, it really doesn't matter how we have arrived at this point.

If what I have been through has served to spiritually refine us (Leon, my mother and my sister, or Susan B. and the elders), in the end will I really mind? Will I begrudge them their peace and their happiness with the prospect of eternal life if Jehovah grants it? No.]

My Prayer: [JEHOVAH, ALMIGHTY GOD, ROCK OF MY HEART,

Strengthen me, please, to always walk in the ways you have taught me. I want my love toward others to reflect the great love you have shown me. I want my mercy toward others to reflect the great mercy you have shown me. I want to forgive others freely, genuinely, completely, as you have forgiven me.

I want to grow in understanding and compassion for those who have known suffering. I want to offer them the kind of loving support and reassurance you have given me.

Please help me to always speak truth with kindness. I want to be so careful in all of my words and even my thoughts, so that I cause no harm.

You have rescued me and comforted me SO MANY TIMES, Jehovah. Show me how to rescue and comfort others.

As a mother would, I want to give a warm welcome and tender embrace to each world-weary person that wants to come home to you, Jehovah.

Please forgive me for the MANY THINGS I HAVE DONE WRONG. I fall far short of the perfection of your holy Son, Christ Jesus, through whom I pray. Amen.]

1 Corinthians 13:4-8a,
- Love is long-suffering and kind. [Love people into God's truth by setting an example, not by browbeating them.]
- Love is not jealous, [Rejoice with others over their blessings.]
- it does not brag, [Rejoice over your own blessings without minimizing those of others.]
- does not get puffed up, [Do not seek to be admired or draw attention to yourself unduly.]
- does not behave indecently, [It is well for a man not to touch a woman. (1 Corinthians 7:1)]
- does not look for its own interests, [Look for, and assist others with their needs.]
- does not become provoked. [Exercise mildness and self-control—do not let it slip away when being challenged.]
- It does not keep account of the injury. [Forgive freely and completely, and do not keep reminding others of their wrongs after they have repented.]
- It does not rejoice over unrighteousness, [Do not be glad when others suffer misfortune, even troublemakers.]

- but rejoices with the truth. [Truly rejoice with others and comfort them when they are finally able to acknowledge and accept a difficult truth.]
- It bears all things, [Bear up under suffering, even deliberately inflicted pain, as well as humiliation, lies, slander, and so much more.]
- believes all things, [Always trust in Jehovah, his promises are faithful, his help is constant, blessings happen.]
- hopes all things, [Do not give up. Good comes from Jehovah.]
- endures all things. [Do not let the sins of others provoke you to sin, but keep bearing up, even through the test of time.]
- LOVE NEVER FAILS!

Psalm 113 all verses, Praise Jah, you people! Offer praise, O you servants of Jehovah, praise the name of Jehovah. May Jehovah's name become blessed from now on and to time indefinite. From the rising of the sun until its setting Jehovah's name is to be praised. Jehovah has become high above all the nations; his glory is above the heavens. Who is like Jehovah our God, him who is making his dwelling on high? He is condescending to look on heaven and earth, raising up the lowly one from the very dust; he exalts the poor one from the ashpit itself, to make him sit with nobles, with the nobles of his people. He is causing the barren woman to dwell in a house as a joyful mother of sons. Praise Jah, you people!

Psalm 114 all verses, When Israel went forth from Egypt, the house of Jacob from a people speaking unintelligibly, Judah became his holy place, Israel his grand dominion. The sea itself saw and took to flight; as for the Jordan, it began to turn back. The mountains themselves skipped about like rams, the hills like lambs. What was the matter with you, O sea, that you took to flight, O Jordan, that you began to turn back? O mountains, that you went skipping about like rams; O hills, like lambs? Because of the Lord be in severe pains, O earth, because of the God of Jacob, who is changing the rock into a reedy pool of water, a flinty rock into a spring of water.

Psalm 115 all verses, To us belongs nothing, O Jehovah, to us belongs nothing, but to your name give glory according to your loving-kindness, according to your trueness. Why should the nations say: "Where, now, is their God?" But our God is in the heavens;

everything that he delighted to do he has done. Their idols are silver and gold, the work of the hands of earthling man. A mouth they have, but they cannot speak; eyes they have, but they cannot see; ears they have, but they cannot hear. A nose they have, but they cannot smell. Hands are theirs, but they cannot feel. Feet are theirs, but they cannot walk; they utter no sound with their throat. Those making them will become just like them, all those who are trusting in them. O Israel, trust in Jehovah; he is their help and their shield. O house of Aaron, put your trust in Jehovah; he is their help and their shield. You that fear Jehovah, trust in Jehovah; he is their help and their shield. Jehovah himself has remembered us; he will bless, he will bless the house of Israel, he will bless the house of Aaron. He will bless those fearing Jehovah, the small ones as well as the great ones. Jehovah will give increase to you, to you and to your sons. You are the ones blessed by Jehovah, the Maker of heaven and earth. As regards the heavens, to Jehovah the heavens belong, but the earth he has given to the sons of men. The dead themselves do not praise Jah, nor do any going down into silence. But we ourselves will bless Jah from now on and to time indefinite. Praise Jah, you people!

Psalm 116 all verses, I do love, because Jehovah hears my voice, my entreaties. For he has inclined his ear to me, and throughout my days I shall call. The ropes of death encircled me and the distressing circumstances of Sheol themselves found me. Distress and grief I kept finding. But upon the name of Jehovah I proceeded to call: "Ah, Jehovah, do provide my soul with escape!" Jehovah is gracious and righteous; and our God is One showing mercy. Jehovah is guarding the inexperienced ones. I was impoverished, and he proceeded to save even me. Return to your resting-place, O my soul, for Jehovah himself has acted appropriately toward you. For you have rescued my soul from death, my eye from tears, my foot from stumbling. I will walk before Jehovah in the lands of those living. I had faith, for I proceeded to speak. I myself was very much afflicted. I, for my part, said, when I became panicky: "Every man is a liar." What shall I repay to Jehovah for all his benefits to me? The cup of grand salvation I shall take up, and on the name of Jehovah I shall call. My vows I shall pay to Jehovah, yes, in front of all his people. Precious in the eyes of Jehovah is the death of his loyal ones. Ah, now, O Jehovah, for I am your servant. I am your servant, the son of your slave girl. You have loosened my bands. To you I shall offer the sacrifice of thanksgiving, and on the name of Jehovah I shall call. My vows I shall pay to Jehovah, yes, in front of all his people, in the courtyards of the house of Jehovah, in the midst of you, O Jerusalem. Praise Jah, you people!

Psalm 117 all verses, Praise Jehovah, all you nations; commend him, all you clans. For toward us his loving-kindness has proved mighty; and the trueness of Jehovah is to time indefinite. Praise Jah, you people!

Psalm 118 all verses, Give thanks to Jehovah, you people, for he is good; for his loving-kindness is to time indefinite. Let Israel now say: "For his loving-kindness is to time indefinite." Let those of the house of Aaron now say: "For his loving-kindness is to time indefinite." Let those fearing Jehovah now say: "For his loving-kindness is to time indefinite." Out of the distressing circumstances I called upon Jah; Jah answered and put me into a roomy place. Jehovah is on my side; I shall not fear. What can earthling man do to me? Jehovah is on my side among those helping me, so that I myself shall look upon those hating me. It is better to take refuge in Jehovah than to trust in earthling man. It is better to take refuge in Jehovah than to trust in nobles. All the nations themselves surrounded me [Lisa]. It was in the name of Jehovah that I kept holding them off. They surrounded me, yes, they had me surrounded. It was in the name of Jehovah that I kept holding them off. They surrounded me like bees; they were extinguished like a fire of thornbushes. It was in the name of Jehovah that I kept holding them off. You pushed me hard that I should fall, but Jehovah himself helped me. Jah is my shelter and my might, and to me he becomes salvation. The voice of a joyful cry and salvation is in the tents of the righteous ones. The right hand of Jehovah is demonstrating vital energy. The right hand of Jehovah is exalting itself; the right hand of Jehovah is demonstrating vital energy. I shall not die, but I shall keep living, that I may declare the works of Jah. Jah corrected me severely, but he did not give me over to death itself. Open to me the gates of righteousness, you people. I shall go into them; I shall laud Jah. This is the gate of Jehovah. The righteous themselves will go into it. I shall laud you, for you answered me and you came to be my salvation. The stone that the builders rejected has become the head of the corner. This has come to be from Jehovah himself; it is wonderful in our eyes. This is the day that Jehovah has made; we will be joyful and rejoice in it. Ah, now, Jehovah, do save, please! Ah, now, Jehovah, do grant success, please! Blessed be the One coming in the name of Jehovah; we have blessed you people out of the house of Jehovah. Jehovah is the Divine One, and he gives us light. Bind the festival procession with boughs, O you people, as far as the horns of the altar. You are my Divine One, and I shall laud you; my God—I shall exalt you. Give thanks to Jehovah, you people, for he is good; for his loving-kindness is to time indefinite.

September 14, 1989

Research: Insight on the Scriptures, Volume 2, page 942 WBTS (1988), **Signal:** *A signal pole has a literal and figurative use. It serves as a rallying point to which peoples or armies assemble themselves. Moses' signal pole stood in a fixed location, and was doubtless on elevated ground so that it was visible.*

Research: Insight on the Scriptures, Volume 2, pages 659-665, **Power, powerful works:** *[Abbreviated here.] They serve to attest to the credentials of those whom he designates as representatives. They also provide proof that he is the only true God, and worthy of proper fear, respect, trust, praise, love from us. And they contribute toward sanctifying [making holy from being disrespected] and vindicating [proving blameless from false accusations] Jehovah's name. Jehovah's own power exalts him.*
Examples of Jehovah's Power:
His power was used to destroy the wicked in Noah's day. It rained for 40 days and nights; the natural elements serve the will of Jehovah beyond their ordinary function. [In the present day, Jehovah's power was manifested in an "onward-sweeping tempest," the "windstorm of Jehovah." Rosie, Bram and I sensed Jehovah's presence in the windstorm that passed through the land. It had extraordinary intensity.]

Sarah, Abraham's wife, gave birth to a child at 90 years of age. Jehovah provides protection for his loyal ones through his power.

Jehovah provides for his servants in times of famine. His power supports our faith, but we also believe he has the ability to reward those earnestly seeking him. Through his powerful works, Jehovah proves himself able to differentiate between his people and unbelievers.

Recall: Psalm 84:11a, For Jehovah is a sun and a shield.

Malachi 3:18, **And you people will again certainly see the distinction between a righteous one and a wicked one, between one serving God and one who has not served him.**

Powerful works are also used by Jehovah to express judgment on wrongdoers, which promotes respect for God and his representatives.

[I was praying to Jehovah for comfort and encouragement and I was given these scriptures.]

Isaiah 62:1,4, Good News Bible (1976), I will speak out to encourage Jerusalem [Lisa]; I will not be silent until she is saved, and her victory shines like a torch in the night.
No longer will you be called "Forsaken," or your land be called "The Deserted Wife." Your new name will be **"God Is Pleased with Her."** Your land will be called **"Happily Married,"** because the Lord is pleased with you and will be like a husband to your land.

Isaiah 61:8,10, Good News Bible, The Lord says, I love justice and hate oppression and crime. I will faithfully reward my people and make an eternal covenant with them.
Jerusalem [Lisa] rejoices because of what the Lord has done. She is like a bride dressed for her wedding. God has clothed her with salvation and victory.
Recall: Isaiah 40:10, Look! The Sovereign Lord Jehovah himself will come even as a strong one, and his arm will be ruling for him. Look! His reward is with him, and the wage he pays is before him.

Proverbs 12:25, Anxious care in the heart of a man is what will cause it to bow down, but the good word is what makes it rejoice.

Proverbs 12:22b, Those acting in faithfulness are a pleasure to him [Jehovah].

Proverbs 13:9,12,17b,19a,22, The very light of the righteous ones will rejoice; but the lamp of the wicked ones—it will be extinguished.
Expectation postponed is making the heart sick, but the thing desired is a tree of life when it does come.
A faithful envoy is a healing.
Desire when realized is pleasurable to the soul.
One who is good will leave an inheritance to sons of sons, and the wealth of the sinner is something treasured up for the righteous one.

Proverbs 9:10-12, Good News Bible (1976), To be wise you must first have reverence for the Lord. If you know the Holy One, you have understanding. Wisdom will add years to your life. You are the one who will profit if you have wisdom, and if you reject it, you are the one who will suffer.

Proverbs Chapter 8 all verses, Good News Bible, Listen! Wisdom is calling out. Reason is making herself heard. On the hilltops near the road and at the crossroads she stands. At the entrance to the city, beside the gates, she calls: "I appeal to you, mankind; I call to everyone on earth. Are you immature? Learn to be mature. Are you foolish? Learn to have sense. Listen to my excellent words; all I tell you is right. What I say is the truth; lies are hateful to me. Everything I say is true; nothing is false or misleading. To the man with insight, it is all clear; to the well-informed, it is all plain. Choose my instruction instead of silver; choose knowledge rather than the finest gold.

"I am Wisdom, I am better than jewels; nothing you want can compare to me. I am Wisdom, and I have insight; I have knowledge and sound judgment. To honor the Lord is to hate evil; I hate pride and arrogance, evil ways and false words. I make plans and carry them out. I have understanding, and I am strong. I help kings to govern and rulers to make good laws. Every ruler on earth governs with my help, statesmen and noblemen alike. I love those who love me; whoever looks for me can find me. I have riches and honor to give, prosperity and success. What you get from me is better than the finest gold, better than the purest silver. I walk the way of righteousness; I follow the paths of justice, giving wealth to those who love me, filling their houses with treasures.

"The Lord created me [Christ, Wisdom personified] first of all, the first of his works, long ago. I was made in the very beginning, at the first, before the world began. I was born before the oceans, when there were no springs of water. I was born before the mountains, before the hills were set in place, before God made the earth and its fields or even the first handful of soil. I was there when he set the sky in place, when he stretched the horizon across the ocean, when he placed the clouds in the sky, when he opened the springs of the ocean and ordered the waters of the sea to rise no further than he said. I was there when he laid the earth's foundations. I was beside him like an architect, I was his daily source of joy, always happy in his presence—happy with the world and pleased with the human race.

"Now, young men, listen to me. Do as I say, and you will be happy. Listen to what you are taught. Be wise; do not neglect it. The man who listens to me will be happy—the man who stays at my door every day, waiting at the entrance to my home. The man who finds me finds life, and the Lord will be pleased with him. The man who does not find me hurts himself; anyone who hates me loves death."

Jesus Christ: [Christ possesses the greatest wisdom, second only to Jehovah.]

> Reference: Proverbs 8:1-21 and 32-36: [For several years Jehovah has been instructing me in his ways and preparing me to become useful in helping others. I am being prepared to handle very serious responsibilities.
>
> Jehovah indicated to me that I am privileged to have these scriptures applied to me, and to share them with his Son, Jesus Christ. As I was reading these scriptures, I sensed that Jesus was saying to me, "My sister." I replied to him, "My brother."]

September 19, 1989

> Good News Bible (1976): [I was given this Bible from my mother when she lived in Iowa Falls, Iowa on Siloam Road, from where I was "sent forth."]

[I opened to this page in the Good News Bible.] Psalm 132:10-11,13-14, You made a promise to your servant David; do not reject your chosen king, Lord. You made a solemn promise to David—a promise you will not take back: "I will make one of your sons king, and he will rule after you. **The Lord has chosen Zion; he wants to make it his home: "This is where I will live forever; this is where I want to rule."**

Zion: [In the book of Zechariah, Zion is Leon Wurzer. In several places in the Bible, Zion, when referred to as her, is Lisa Pressnall.

→ **Also, on occasion, Zion refers to both of us, as when Leon and I marry, the two shall become one.** (Genesis 2:24) I would take his names; Wurzer and Zion.

Jehovah will reside in "Jerusalem," Lisa, and make "Zion," Leon, his dwelling place. Jehovah will not reside in a physical structure built by man, but physical beings built into a spiritual temple by him.]

Psalm 132:13,14, For Jehovah has chosen Zion; he has longed for it as a dwelling for himself: "This is my resting-place forever; here I shall dwell, for I have longed for it."

Zechariah 8:3, This is what Jehovah has said, "I will return to Zion [Leon] and reside in the midst of Jerusalem [Lisa]; and Jerusalem will certainly be called the city of trueness, and the mountain of Jehovah of armies, the holy mountain."

Isaiah 41:8-10, "But you, O Israel, are my servant, you, O Jacob, whom I have chosen [Israel became another name for Jacob, the grandson of Abraham—**one** person, though later in the scriptures, often, as here, they are referred to by Jehovah as separate persons; "Jacob" is Leon and "Israel" is Lisa, who will become "**one**" when they marry], the seed of Abraham my friend; you, whom I have taken hold of from the extremities of the earth, and you, whom I have called even from the remote parts of it. And so I said to you, 'You are my servant; I have chosen you, and I have not rejected you. Do not be afraid, for I am with you. Do not gaze about, for I am your God. I will fortify you. I will really help you. I will really keep fast hold of you with my right hand of righteousness.'

Recall: [In the vision Jehovah gave me, he and I were walking down a long road together, hand in hand, his right hand holding my left hand, and Jehovah was calling me "Friend."]

Genesis 17:5,6, And your name will not be called Abram [meaning "Father of Exaltation"] anymore, and your name must become Abraham [meaning "Father of a Multitude"], because a father of a crowd of nations I will make you. And I will make you very, very fruitful and will make you become nations, and kings will come out of you.

[Jehovah has caused his work to come full circle. Jehovah chose Abram→Abraham and called him "Friend," and made a people for himself. Interestingly, centuries later, the son of Jehovah's "Friend" Lisa is named Bram, a shortened form of the name Abram. Bram was born years before I dedicated my life to Jehovah. In Isaiah 49:8b Jehovah has given Lisa] as a covenant for the people . . . to bring about the repossessing of the desolated hereditary possessions [of Abraham].

Genesis 49:9,10, A lion cub Judah is. From the prey, my son, you will certainly go up. He bowed down, he stretched himself out like a lion and, like a lion, who dares rouse him? The scepter will not turn aside from Judah, neither the commander's staff from between his feet, until Shiloh [meaning "He To Whom It Belongs"] comes; and to him the obedience of the peoples will belong.

[When the 12 tribes of Israel split, the tribe of Judah and Benjamin remained faithful to the line of David. The other ten tribes set up their own kingship. Bram's middle name is Benjamin, meaning Son of the Right Hand.]

Isaiah 41:10, Do not be afraid, for I am with you. Do not gaze about, for I am your God. I will fortify you. I will really help you. I will really keep fast hold of you with my right hand of righteousness.

Isaiah 40:6-10a, Listen! Someone is saying: "Call out!" And one said: "What shall I call out?"

"All flesh is green grass, and all their loving-kindness is like the blossom of the field. The green grass has dried up, the blossom has withered, because the very spirit of Jehovah has blown upon it.

Surely the people are green grass. The green grass has dried up, the blossom has withered; but as for the word of our God, it will last to time indefinite."

Make your way up even onto a high mountain, you woman bringing good news for Zion. Raise your voice even with power, you woman bringing good news for Jerusalem. Raise it. **Do not be afraid. Say to the cities of Judah: "Here is your God." Look! The Sovereign Lord Jehovah himself will come even as a strong one, and his arm will be ruling for him.**

Malachi 3:1, "Look! I am sending my messenger, and he must clear up a way before me. And suddenly there will come to His temple the true Lord, whom you people are seeking, and the messenger of the covenant in whom you are delighting. Look! He will certainly come," Jehovah of armies has said.

[When the circuit overseer gave his talk at the Kingdom Hall in Lancaster, Wisconsin U.S.A., he referred to me as the "messenger of the covenant." Jehovah has made a covenant with me, and I am given as a covenant for the people. (Isaiah 49:8)]

[God gave the right to rule to his chosen people beginning with his covenant with Abraham → Isaac → Jacob → Judah → his sons → sons → covenant with David → his sons → sons → sons → sons (including Jesus, who rules from heaven) other sons of David → sons → sons → sons → Leon, who becomes one of the "two witnesses," chosen as God's representative on earth in the final days.]

1 Corinthians 7:28, But even if you did marry, you would commit no sin. And if a virgin person married, such one would commit no sin. However, those who do will have tribulation in their flesh. But I am sparing you. [This scripture mentions that married persons have tribulation in the flesh. As I thought about the marriages of couples I know, I recalled that very few marriages are truly happy. There is so much strife in this world, and couples disagree over so many things. Marriage seems to be full of disputes and contentions. I was worried that Leon and I would encounter similar problems. So, in prayer I asked Jehovah if Leon and I have to suffer these tribulations. Jehovah answered me immediately.]

Proverbs 21:1, A king's heart is as streams of water in the hand of Jehovah. Everywhere that he delights to, he turns it.

Isaiah 44:28, The One saying of Cyrus [Leon], "He is my shepherd, and all that I delight in he will completely carry out"; even in my saying of Jerusalem [Lisa], "She will be rebuilt," and of the temple, "You will have your foundation laid."

Jeremiah 30:21,22, Good News Bible (1976), "Their ruler will come from their own nation, their prince from their own people. He will approach me [Jehovah] when I invite him, for who would dare come uninvited? They will be my people, and I will be their God. I, the Lord, have spoken."

Jeremiah 30:21,22, NWT (1984), "And his majestic one will certainly come to be from him, and from the midst of him his own ruler will go forth; and I [Jehovah] will cause him to come near, and he must approach to me."
"For who, now, is this one that has given his heart in pledge in order to approach to me?" is the utterance of Jehovah. "And you will certainly become my people, and I myself shall become your God."

Genesis 49:10, The scepter will not turn aside from Judah, neither the commander's staff from between his feet, until Shiloh comes; and to him the obedience of the peoples will belong.

Zechariah 4:11-14, And I proceeded to answer and say to him: "What do these two olive trees on the right side of the lampstand and on its left mean?" Then I answered the second time and said to him: "What are the two bunches of twigs of the olive trees that, by means of the two golden tubes, are pouring forth from within themselves the golden liquid?"
So he said to me: "Do you not really know what these things mean?"
In turn I said: "No, my lord."
Accordingly he said: "These are the two anointed ones who are standing alongside the Lord of the whole earth." [Almighty God, Jehovah, has given the rulership of the earth to his faithful Son, Jesus Christ. The two anointed ones standing alongside are Leon

and Lisa. Jesus, through Abraham's seed, Judah, has the right to rule. (Matthew 1:16)]

Genesis 49:8,9,11,12, As for you, Judah, your brothers will laud you. Your hand will be on the back of the neck of your enemies. The sons of your father will prostrate themselves to you. A LION CUB JUDAH IS [Leon]. From the prey, my son, you will certainly go up. He bowed down, he stretched himself out like a lion and, like a lion, who dares rouse him?
Tying his full-grown ass to a vine and the descendent of his own she-ass to a choice vine [Jesus is the true vine. (John 15:1)], he will certainly wash his clothing in wine and his garment in the blood of grapes. Dark red are his eyes from wine, and the whiteness of his teeth is from milk.

Research: Insight on the Scriptures, volume 2, page 111, **Joseph,** [Jereboam, of the tribe of Ephraim (son of **Joseph**) was made king when the 10 tribes of Israel split from Judah and Benjamin. I am often referred to as Israel in the scriptures. Am I a descendent of Judah? Or am I a descendent of Joseph? Or even both? I do not have an answer to these questions at this time. It could be that I am not a natural descendent of Abraham, but certainly I am of Abraham's "seed" spiritually. I would be happy to discover that I am a natural descendent of Abraham through any line of descent. But I am content if I am only "grafted" into God's family in a spiritual sense.]

Joseph's role: [prophetic pattern comparison]

Joseph was the special object of his father's affection. [Lisa has been shown favor from Jehovah, our Heavenly Father.]
Joseph was abused and rejected by his own brothers. [Lisa has been abused and rejected by her spiritual "family," Jehovah's Witnesses.]

Joseph was considered as good as dead when his brothers told his father he had been killed by a wild animal. [People have tried to kill Lisa, also. Disfellowshipping is considered a form of "death."]

Joseph was exiled to a foreign land. [Lisa was thrown out of the organization of Jehovah's Witnesses.]

Joseph was refined and prepared for a life-saving work though suffering. [Likewise, Lisa has been refined and prepared.]

Joseph became a food administrator during a great famine. [Lisa is responsible for distributing spiritual "food" during the present day's great spiritual "famine."]

Isaiah 65:13a,15-19, Therefore this is what the Sovereign Lord Jehovah has said: "Look! My own servants will eat, but you yourselves will go hungry.

"And you men [those taking the lead in the organization] will certainly lay up your name for an oath by my chosen ones, and the Sovereign Lord Jehovah will actually put you individually to death, but his own servants he will call by **another name; so that anyone blessing himself in the earth will bless himself by the God of faith [Jehovah's Faithful Witnesses will bless themselves by Jehovah's holy name],** and anyone making a sworn statement in the earth will swear by the God of faith; because the former distresses will actually be forgotten and because they will actually be concealed from my eyes.

"For here I am creating new heavens and a new earth; and the former things will not be called to mind, neither will they come up into the heart. But exult, you people, and be joyful forever in what I am creating. For here I am creating Jerusalem a cause for joyfulness and her people a cause for exultation. And I will be joyful in Jerusalem and exult in my people; and no more will there be heard in her the sound of weeping or the sound of a plaintive cry."

Proverbs 31:10,11,15,28-31, A capable wife who can find? [Jehovah is my "husbandly owner." (Isaiah 54:5)] Her value is far more than that of corals. In her the heart of her owner has put trust, and there is no gain lacking.

She also gets up while it is still night [a time of spiritual darkness], and gives food to her household and the prescribed portion to her young women.

Her sons have risen up and proceeded to pronounce her happy; her owner rises up, and he praises her. There are many daughters that have shown capableness, but you—you have ascended above them all. Charm may be false, and prettiness may be vain; but the woman that fears Jehovah is the one that procures praise for herself. Give her of the fruitage of her hands, and let her works praise her even in the gates.

Ezekiel 21:26,27, This is what the Sovereign Lord Jehovah has said, "Remove the turban, and lift off the crown [of the unfaithful "faithful and discreet slave"]. This will not be the same. Put on high even what is low, and bring low even the high one. A ruin, a ruin, a ruin I shall make it. As for this also, it will certainly become no one's until he comes who has the legal right, and I must give it to him."

Luke 1:30-33, So the angel said to her: "Have no fear, Mary, for you have found favor with God; and, look! you will conceive in your womb and give birth to a son, and you are to call his name Jesus. This one will be great and will be called Son of the Most High; and Jehovah God will give him the throne of David his father, and he will rule as king over the house of Jacob forever, and there will be no end of his kingdom."

Revelation 5:5, But one of the elders says to me: "Stop weeping. Look! The Lion that is of the tribe of Judah, the root of David, has conquered so as to open the scroll and its seven seals." [Christ is truly the great Lion that is of the tribe of Judah. Leon is also a great "lion."]

Genesis 49:22, Offshoot of a fruit-bearing tree, Joseph is the offshoot of a fruit-bearing tree by the fountain, that propels its branches up over a wall.

Recall: Zechariah 4:12-14, Then I answered the second time and said to him: "What are the two bunches of twigs of the olive trees that, by means of the two golden tubes, are pouring forth from within themselves the golden liquid?"

So he said to me: "Do you not really know what these things mean?"

In turn I said: "No, my lord."

Accordingly he said: "These are the two anointed ones who are standing alongside the Lord of the whole earth."

Revelation 11:3,4 NWT (1984), "And I will cause my two witnesses to prophesy a thousand two hundred and sixty days dressed in sackcloth." These are symbolized by the two olive trees and the two lampstands and are standing before the Lord of the earth.

The two witnesses mentioned in the book of Revelation are referred to, respectively, as "Jacob" and "Israel" in Isaiah:

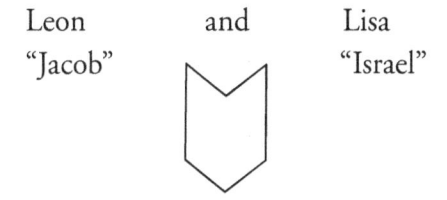

Leon	and	Lisa
"Jacob"	⋁	"Israel"

who is the same person known by two different names, and the

⇧

son of Isaac who is the

⇧

son of Abraham.

In the Bible, Leon and Lisa are also referred to, respectively, as:

Jacob	and	Israel	Isaiah 44:1
Jacob	and	Jeshurun	Isaiah 44:2
Cyrus	and	Jerusalem	Isaiah 44:28
Judah	and	Israel	Zechariah 8:13
Judah	and	Jerusalem	Zechariah 2:12
Judah	and	Joseph	Zechariah 10:6
Sprout	and	Joshua	Zechariah 6:11,12
Zion	and	Jerusalem	Zechariah 8:3
Jacob	and	Joseph	Psalm 77:15

Isaiah 53:1, Who has put faith in the thing heard by us? And as for the arm of Jehovah, to whom has it been revealed?

Psalm 77:15, With your arm you have recovered your people [faithful worshippers of Jehovah from out of the organization of Jehovah's Witnesses], the sons of Jacob and of Joseph. *Selah.*
[They are of the spiritual "seed" of Abraham, who was called God's "Friend."]

Zechariah 10:6, And I will make the house of Judah superior, and the house of Joseph I shall save. And I will give them a dwelling, for I will show them mercy; and they must become like those whom I had not cast off; for I am Jehovah their God, and I shall answer them.

Isaiah 44:1-8, "And now listen, O Jacob [Leon] my servant, and you, O Israel [Lisa], whom I have chosen. This is what Jehovah has said, your Maker and your Former, who kept helping you even from the belly, 'Do not be afraid, O my servant Jacob, and you, Jeshurun, whom I have chosen. For I shall pour out water upon the thirsty one, and trickling streams upon the dry place. **I shall pour out my spirit upon your [spiritual] seed, and my blessing upon your [spiritual] descendants [faithful worshippers of Jehovah].** And they will certainly spring up as among the green grass, like poplars by the water ditches. This one will say: "I belong to Jehovah." And that one will call himself by the name of Jacob, and another will write upon his hand: "Belonging to Jehovah." And by the name of Israel one will betitle himself.'

"This is what Jehovah has said, the King of Israel and the Repurchaser of him, Jehovah of armies, '**I am the first and I am the last, and besides me there is no God.** And who is there like me? Let him call out, that he may tell it and present it to me. **From when I appointed the people of long ago, both the things coming and the things that will enter in let them tell on their part.** Do not be in dread, you people, and do not become stupefied. **Have I not from that time on caused you individually to hear and told it out? And you are my witnesses. Does there exist a God besides me? No, there is no Rock. I have recognized none.'"

Isaiah 43:1,10,18, And now this is what Jehovah has said, your Creator, O Jacob, and your Former, O Israel: "Do not be afraid, for I have repurchased you. I have called you by your name. You are mine."

"You are my witnesses," is the utterance of Jehovah, "even my servant whom I have chosen, in order that you may know and have faith in me, and that you may understand that I am the same One. Before me there was no God formed, and after me there continued to be none."

"Do not remember the first things, and to the former things do not turn your consideration."

Recall: Revelation 11:1,2, And a reed like a rod was given me as he said: "Get up and measure the temple sanctuary of God and the altar and those worshipping in it. But as for the courtyard that is outside the temple sanctuary, cast it clear out and do not measure it, because it has been given to the nations, and they will trample the holy city underfoot for forty-two months." [The organization of Jehovah's Witnesses refers to itself as Jehovah's courtyard.]

Isaiah 43:19-21, Look! I am doing something new. Now it will spring up. You people will know it, will you not? Really, through the wilderness I shall set a way, through the desert rivers. The wild beast of the field will glorify me, the jackals and the ostriches; because I shall have given water even in the wilderness, rivers in the desert, to cause my people, my chosen one, to drink, the people whom I have formed for myself, that they should recount the praise of me.

1 Thessalonians Chapters 1, 2 and 3, Paul and Silvanus and Timothy [faithful Christians, authorized to send instructions] to the congregation of the Thessalonians in union with God the Father and the Lord Jesus Christ:

May you have undeserved kindness and peace. [Many times, when the Bible speaks of "you," it is in reference to the plural form of the word, meaning "all of you," or, "you people."]

We always thank God when we make mention concerning all of you in our prayers, for we bear incessantly in mind your faithful work and your loving labor and your endurance due to your hope in our Lord Jesus Christ before our God and Father. For we know, brothers loved by God, his choosing of you, because the good news we preach did not turn up among you with speech alone but also with power and with holy spirit and strong conviction, just as you know what sort of men we became to you for your sakes; and you became imitators of us and of the Lord, seeing that you accepted the word under much tribulation with joy of holy spirit, so that you came to be an example to all the believers in Macedonia and in Achaia.

The fact is, not only has the word of Jehovah sounded forth from you in Macedonia and Achaia, but in every place your faith toward God has spread abroad, so that we do not need to say anything. For they themselves keep reporting about the way we first entered in among you and how you turned to God from your idols [the unfaithful "faithful and discreet slave," those leading faithful worshippers away from Jehovah's truth and righteousness] to slave for a living and true God, and to wait for his Son from the heavens, whom he raised up from the dead, namely, Jesus, who delivers us from the wrath which is coming.

To be sure, you yourselves know, brothers, how our visit to you has not been without results, but how, after we had first suffered and been insolently treated (just as you know) in Philippi, we mustered up boldness by means of our God to speak to you the good news of God with a great deal of struggling. **For the exhortation we give does not arise from error or from uncleanness or with deceit, but, just as we have been proved by God as fit to be entrusted**

with the good news, so we speak, as pleasing, not men, but God, who makes proof of our hearts.

In fact, at no time have we turned up either with flattering speech, (just as you know) or with a false front for covetousness, God is witness! Neither have we been seeking glory from men, no, either from you or from others, though we could be an expensive burden as apostles of Christ. To the contrary, we became gentle in the midst of you, as when a nursing mother cherishes her own children.

[It is an honor to be chosen and used by Jehovah for the work he has given me. It is from his undeserved kindness that I am made useful, not due to any works of my own. It is a wonderful privilege and serious responsibility to become like a mother to Jehovah's people.

Being chosen by Jehovah was in no way determined by any personal virtue or worth Jehovah finds in me. Instead, I was chosen to be taught and refined to become useful to Jehovah. Any skills I have for this honorable position are not my own, but those which Jehovah has firmly established in my mind and heart. I am not able to boast of bringing anything of my own to the position in which I find myself. I am just so grateful to Jehovah that, in spite of all my sins and flaws, I have a chance to live in the coming earthly paradise. I fervently hope that I do not disappoint Jehovah or his people.]

1 Peter 5:10, But, after you have suffered a little while, the God of all undeserved kindness, who called you to his everlasting glory in union with Christ, will himself finish your training, he will make you firm, he will make you strong.

[Because my training is from Jehovah himself, I must be very careful to walk worthily. It would be an "expensive burden" on the rest of Jehovah's family if I come to them with Jehovah's good news having a presumptuous or self-assuming attitude.

There is, however, an appropriate type of protective "jealousy" that I should have toward my relationship with Jehovah, in order that no other would attempt to encroach upon it, which is the same protectiveness as each of the 144,000 members of the faithful heavenly anointed would appropriately feel toward their own unique relationship with Jehovah. If we did not feel protective toward what Jehovah has given us, we would leave room for Satan to somehow entice our hearts away from Jehovah. Just the same, this protective attitude toward our own personal relationship with God never seeks to diminish another's. Each one of us must walk worthily in this cherished relationship with Jehovah as have the apostles and the rest of the heavenly anointed.

Recall: [God is "building a forever family." We really are a family. Correct me, Jehovah, if I ever even begin to develop an unappreciative attitude toward you, or a presumptuous attitude toward the position you have given me. I love you with a complete heart and I love all of your people—all of your family. Let these words of mine stand as a correction on me from my own heart, because I seek to please you, Jehovah, and not myself. I am corrected.]

1 Thessalonians, continued, So, having a tender affection for you, we were well pleased to impart to you, not only the good news of God, but also our own souls, because you became beloved to us.

Certainly you bear in mind, brothers, our labor and toil. It was with working night and day, so as not to put an expensive burden upon any one of you, that we preached the good news of God to you. You are witnesses, God is also, how loyal and righteous and unblamable we proved to be to you believers. In harmony with that you well know how, as a father does his children, we kept exhorting each one of you, and consoling and bearing witness to you, to the end that you should go on walking worthily of God who is calling you to his kingdom and glory.

Indeed, that is why we also thank God incessantly, because when you received God's word, which you heard from us, you accepted it, not as the word of men, but, just as it truthfully is, as the word of God, which is also at work in you believers. For you became imitators, brothers, of the congregations of God that are in Judea in union with Christ Jesus, because you also began suffering at the hands of your own countrymen the same things as they also are suffering at the hands of the Jews [unrighteous individuals among the Jews, not god-fearing Jews], who killed even the Lord Jesus and the prophets and persecuted us. Furthermore, they [unrighteous individuals taking the lead in the organization of Jehovah's Witnesses, not those who are god-fearing] are not pleasing God, but are against the interests of all men, as they try to hinder us from speaking to people of the nations that these might be saved, with the result that they always fill up the measure of their sins. But his wrath has at length come upon them.

As for ourselves, brothers, when we were bereaved of you for but a short time, in person, not in heart, we endeavored far more than is usual to see your faces with great desire. For this reason we wanted to come to you, yes, I Paul, both once and a second time, but Satan cut across our path. For what is our hope or joy or crown of exultation—why, is it not in fact you?—before our Lord Jesus at his presence? You certainly are our glory and joy.

Hence, when we could bear it no longer, we saw good to be left alone in Athens; and we sent Timothy, our brother and God's minister in the good news about the Christ, in order to make you firm and comfort you in behalf of your faith, that no one might be swayed by these tribulations. For you yourselves know we are appointed to this very thing. In fact, too, when we were with you, we used to tell you beforehand that we were destined to suffer tribulation, just as it has also happened and as you know. That is why, indeed, when I could bear it no longer, I sent to know of your faithfulness, as perhaps in some way the Tempter might have tempted you, and our labor might have turned out to be in vain.

But Timothy has just now come to us from you and given us the good news about your faithfulness and love, and that you continue having good remembrance of us always, yearning to see us in the same way, indeed, as we also do you. That is why, brothers, we have been comforted over you in all our necessity and tribulation through the faithfulness you show, because now we live if you stand firm in the Lord. For what thanksgiving can we render to God concerning you in return for all the joy with which we are rejoicing on your account before our God, while night and day we make more than extraordinary supplications to see your faces and to make good the things that are lacking about your faith?

Now may our God and Father himself and our Lord Jesus direct our way prosperously to you. Moreover, may the Lord cause you to increase, yes, make you abound, in love to one another and to all, even as we also do to you; to the end that he may make your hearts firm, unblamable in holiness before our God and Father at the presence of our Lord Jesus with all his holy ones.

Ephesians 3:14-19, On account of this I bend my knees to the Father, to whom every family in heaven and on earth owes its name, to the end that he may grant you according to the riches of his glory to be made mighty in the man you are inside with power through his spirit, to have the Christ dwell through your faith in your hearts with love; that you may be rooted and established on the foundation, in order that you may be thoroughly able to grasp mentally with all the holy ones what is the breadth and length and height and depth, and to know the love of the Christ which surpasses knowledge, that you may be filled with all the fullness that God gives.

Ephesians 2:8-22, By this undeserved kindness, indeed, you have been saved through faith; and this not owing to you, it is God's gift. No, it is not owing to works, in order that no man should have ground for boasting. For we are a product of his work and were created in union with Christ Jesus for good works, which God prepared in advance for us to walk in them.

Therefore keep bearing in mind that formerly you were people of the nations as to flesh; "uncircumcision" you were called by that which is called "circumcision" made in the flesh with hands—that you were at that particular time without Christ, alienated from the state of Israel and strangers to the covenants of the promise, and you had no hope and were without God in the world. But now in union with Christ Jesus you who were once far off have come to be near by the blood of the Christ. For he is our peace, he who made the two parties one and destroyed the wall in between that fenced them off. By means of his flesh he abolished the enmity, the Law of commandments consisting in decrees, that he might create the two peoples in union with himself into one new man and make peace; and that he might fully reconcile both peoples in one body to God through the torture stake, because he had killed off the enmity by means of himself. And he came and declared the good news of peace to you, the ones far off, and peace to those near, because through him we, both peoples, have the approach to the Father by one spirit.

Certainly, therefore, you are no longer strangers and alien residents, but you are fellow citizens of the holy ones and are members of the household of God, and you have been built up upon the foundation of the apostles and prophets, while Christ Jesus himself is the foundation cornerstone. In union with him the whole building, being harmoniously joined together, is growing into a holy temple for Jehovah. In union with him you, too, are being built up together into a place for God to inhabit by spirit.

Ephesians 2:4,5, But God, who is rich in mercy, for his great love with which he loved us, made us alive together with the Christ, even when we were dead in trespasses—by undeserved kindness you have been saved.

Titus 3:4,5, However, when the kindness and the love for man on the part of our Savior, God, was manifested, owing to no works in righteousness that we had performed, but according to his mercy he saved us through the bath that brought us to life and through the making of us new by holy spirit.

Matthew 19:28, Jesus said to them: "Truly I say to you, In the re-creation, when the Son of man sits down upon his glorious throne, you who have followed me will also yourselves sit upon twelve thrones, judging the twelve tribes of Israel."

Revelation Chapter 11 all verses, And a reed like a rod was given me as he said: "Get up and measure the temple sanctuary of God and the altar and those worshipping in it. But as for the courtyard that is outside the temple sanctuary, cast it clear out and do not measure it, because it has been given to the nations, and they will trample the holy city underfoot for forty-two months. And I will cause my two witnesses to prophesy a thousand two hundred and sixty days dressed in sackcloth." These are symbolized by the two olive trees and the two lampstands and are standing before the Lord of the earth.

And if anyone wants to harm them, fire issues forth from their mouths and devours their enemies; and if anyone should want to harm them, in this manner he must be killed. These have the authority to shut up heaven that no rain should fall during the days of their prophesying, and they have authority over the waters to turn them into blood and to strike the earth with every sort of plague as often as they wish.

And when they have finished their witnessing, the wild beast that ascends out of the abyss will make war with them and conquer them and kill them. And their corpses will be on the broad way of the great city which is **in a spiritual sense called Sodom and Egypt**, where their Lord was also impaled. And those of the peoples and tribes and tongues and nations will look at their corpses for three and a half days, and they do not let their corpses be laid in a tomb. And those dwelling on the earth rejoice over them and enjoy themselves, and they will send gifts to one another, because these two prophets tormented those dwelling on the earth.

And after the three and a half days spirit of life from God entered into them [the two witnesses], and they stood upon their feet, and great fear fell upon those beholding them. And they heard a loud voice out of heaven say to them: "Come on up here." And they went up into heaven in the cloud, and their enemies beheld them. And in that hour a great earthquake occurred, and a tenth of the city fell; and seven thousand persons were killed by the earthquake, and the rest became frightened and gave glory to the God of heaven.

The second woe is past. Look! The third woe is coming quickly.

And the seventh angel blew his trumpet. And loud voices occurred in heaven, saying: **"The kingdom of the world did become the kingdom of our Lord and of his Christ, and he will rule as king forever and ever."**

And the twenty-four elders who were seated before God upon their thrones fell upon their faces and worshipped God, saying: **"We thank you, Jehovah God, the Almighty, the One who is and who was, because you have taken your great power and begun ruling as king. But the nations became wrathful, and your own wrath came, and the appointed time for the dead to be judged, and to give their reward to your slaves the prophets and to the holy ones and to those fearing your name, the small and the great, and to bring to ruin those ruining the earth."**

And the temple sanctuary of God that is in heaven was opened, and the ark of his covenant was seen in his temple sanctuary. And there occurred lightnings and voices and thunders and an earthquake and a great hail.

Isaiah 44:28, The One saying of Cyrus, "He is my shepherd, and all that I delight in he will completely carry out"; even in my saying of Jerusalem, "She will be rebuilt," and of the temple, "You will have your foundation laid."

Isaiah 45:1-7,13, This is what Jehovah has said to his anointed one, to Cyrus [Leon], whose right hand I have taken hold of, to subdue before him nations, so that I may ungird even the hips of kings; to open before him the two-leaved doors, so that even the gates will not be shut: "Before you I myself shall go, and the swells of land I shall straighten out. The copper doors I shall break in pieces, and the iron bars I shall cut down. And I will give you the treasures in the darkness and the hidden treasures in the concealment places, in order that you may know that I am Jehovah, the One calling you by your name, the God of Israel. For the sake of my servant Jacob [Leon] and of Israel [Lisa] my chosen one, I even proceeded to call you by your name; I proceeded to give you a name of honor [Leon, lion of Judah], although you did not know me. I am Jehovah, and there is no one else. With the exception of me there is no God. I shall closely gird you, although you have not known me, in order that people may know from the rising of the sun and from its setting that there is none besides me. I am Jehovah, and there is no one else. Forming light and creating darkness, making peace and creating calamity, I, Jehovah, am doing all these things."

"I myself have roused up someone [Leon] in righteousness, and all his ways I shall straighten out. He is the one that will build my city [Lisa], and those of mine in exile he will let go, not for a price nor for bribery," Jehovah of armies has said.

1 Kings 19:15,16, Jehovah now said to him [Elijah]: "Go, return on your way to the wilderness of Damascus; and you must come in and anoint Hazael as king over Syria. And Jehu the grandson of Nimshi you should anoint as king over Israel; and Elisha [Greek: Helisaie (Helisaie = anagram: contains the name Lisa); Lisa, Elijah's present day successor] the son of Shaphat from Abelmeholah you should anoint as prophet in place of you. [Elisha asked Elijah for a blessing of "two parts in his spirit," when he was anointed Elijah's successor. This is a double portion of Jehovah's holy spirit. The two parts in Elijah's spirit which Elisha received were (a) a spirit of courage and (b) absolute zeal for Jehovah. (2 Kings 2:9,15) (Insight on the Scriptures, Volume 1, pages 712, 714 WBTS 1988)]

Malachi 4:5, Look! I am sending to you people Elijah the prophet before the coming of the great and fear-inspiring day of Jehovah.

2 Kings 2:15a, When the sons of the prophets that were at Jericho saw him some way off, they began to say: "The spirit of Elijah [Elias, another spelling for Elijah] has settled down upon Elisha [Lisa]."

[In the book of Luke, an angel tells Zechariah someone with Elijah's spirit is coming.] Luke 1:17, **Also, he [John the Baptist] will go before him with Elijah's spirit and power**, to turn back the hearts of fathers [Jehovah] to children and the disobedient ones to the practical wisdom of righteous ones, **to get ready for Jehovah a prepared people** [and in the present day, Lisa is "to bring about the repossessing of the desolated hereditary possessions." (Isaiah 49:8)].

[Lisa has been given by Jehovah as a covenant for the people; the messenger of the covenant. (Isaiah 49:8; Malachi 3:1)]

Isaiah 44:2, This is what Jehovah has said, your Maker and your Former, who kept helping you even from the belly, "Do not be afraid, O my servant Jacob [Leon], and you, Jeshurun [Lisa], whom I have chosen."

Zechariah 8:13, And it must occur that just as you became a malediction among the nations, O house of Judah and house of Israel, so I shall save you, and you must become a blessing. **Do not be afraid. May your hands be strong.**

John 16:33, **I have said these things to you that by means of me you may have peace. In the world you are having tribulation, but take courage! I have conquered the world.**

September 24, 1989

Isaiah 57:19, "I am creating the fruit of the lips. Continuous peace there will be to the one that is far away and to the one that is near," Jehovah has said, "and I will heal him."

Ephesians 2:14, For he is our peace, he who made the two parties one and destroyed the wall in between that fenced them off.

Isaiah 11:12, And he will certainly raise up a signal for the nations and gather the dispersed ones of Israel; and the scattered ones of Judah he will collect together from the four extremities of the earth.

Isaiah 12:2, Look! God is my salvation. I shall trust and be in no dread; for Jah Jehovah is my strength and my might, and he came to be the salvation of me.

!   **Ephesians 1:16b-18a, I continue mentioning you in my prayers, that the God of our Lord Jesus Christ, the Father of glory, may give you a spirit of wisdom and of revelation in the accurate knowledge of him; the eyes of your heart having been enlightened, that you may know what is the hope to which he called you.**

Galatians 5:22, Fruitage of the spirit:
    Love
    Joy
    Peace
    Long-suffering
    Kindness
    Goodness
    Faith
    Mildness
    Self-control

Philippians 2:1-4, If, then, there is any encouragement in Christ, if any consolation of love, if any sharing of spirit, if any tender affections and compassions, make my joy full in that you are of the same mind and have the same love, being joined together in soul, holding the one thought in mind, doing nothing out of contentiousness or out of egotism, but with lowliness of mind considering that the others are superior to you, keeping an eye, not in personal interest upon just your own matters, but also in personal interest upon those of the others.

Proverbs 10:20,22,24,25,28,32, The tongue of the righteous one is choice silver; the heart of the wicked one is worth little.

The blessing of Jehovah—that is what makes rich, and he adds no pain with it.

The thing frightful to the wicked one—that is what will come to him; but the desire of the righteous ones will be granted. As when the storm wind passes over, so the wicked one is no more; but the righteous one is a foundation to time indefinite.

The expectation of the righteous ones is a rejoicing, but the very hope of the wicked ones will perish.

The lips of the righteous one—they come to know goodwill, but the mouth of the wicked ones is perverseness.

Proverbs 11:8,12,23,31, The righteous is the one rescued even from distress, and the wicked one comes in instead of him.

The one in want of heart has despised his own fellowman, but the man of broad discernment is one that keeps silent.

The desire of the righteous ones is surely good; the hope of the wicked ones is fury.

Look! The righteous one—in the earth he will be rewarded. How much more should the wicked one and the sinner be!

Proverbs 12:3,4a,12,14,20, No man will be firmly established by wickedness; but as for the root-foundation of the righteous ones, it will not be caused to stagger.

A capable wife is a crown to her owner.

The wicked one has desired the netted prey of bad men; but as for the root of the righteous ones, it yields.

From the fruitage of a man's mouth he is satisfied with good, and the very doing of a man's hands will come back to him.

Deception is in the heart of those fabricating mischief, but those counseling peace have rejoicing.

Isaiah 62:3, And you must become a crown of beauty in the hand of Jehovah, and a kingly turban in the palm of your God.

Jeremiah 31:16, This is what Jehovah has said: "Hold back your [Lisa's] voice from weeping, and your eyes from tears, for there exists a reward for your activity," is the utterance of Jehovah, "and they [faithful worshippers of Jehovah still in the organization of Jehovah's Witnesses] will certainly return from the land of the enemy."

! Psalm 18 all verses, [abbreviated here], They kept confronting me in the day of my disaster, but Jehovah came to be as a support for me. And he proceeded to bring me out into a roomy place; he was rescuing me, because he had found delight in me. Jehovah rewards me according to my righteousness; according to the cleanness of my hands he repays me. For I have kept the ways of Jehovah, and I have not wickedly departed from my God. For all his judicial decisions are in front of me, and his statutes I shall not remove from myself. And I will prove myself faultless with him, and I shall keep myself from error on my part. And let Jehovah repay me according to my righteousness, according to the cleanness of my hands in front of his eyes. With someone loyal you will act in loyalty; with the faultless, able-bodied man you will deal faultlessly; with the one keeping clean you will show yourself clean; and with the crooked one you will show yourself tortuous; because the afflicted people you yourself will save; but the haughty eyes you will abase. **For you yourself will light my lamp, O Jehovah; my God himself will make my darkness shine.** For by you I can run against a marauder band; and by my God I can climb a wall. As for the true God, perfect is his way; the saying of Jehovah is a refined one. A shield he is to all those taking refuge in him. **For who is a God besides Jehovah? And who is a rock except our God?** The true God is the One girding me closely with vital energy, and he will grant my way to be perfect, making my feet like those of the hinds, and upon places high for me he keeps me standing.

Jehovah is living, and blessed be my Rock, and let the God of my salvation be exalted. The true God is the Giver of acts of vengeance to me; and he subdues the peoples under me. He is providing escape for me from my angry enemies; above those who rise up against me you will lift me up, from the man of violence you will deliver me. **That is why I shall laud you among the nations, O Jehovah, and to your name I will make melody.** He is doing great acts of salvation for his king and exercising loving-kindness to his anointed one, to David and to his seed to time indefinite.

! Psalm 19:11-13, Also, your own servant has been warned by them; in the keeping of them there is a large reward. Mistakes—who can discern? From concealed sins pronounce me innocent. Also from presumptuous acts hold your servant back; do not let them dominate me. In that case I shall be complete, and I shall have remained innocent from much transgression.

Psalm 20 all verses, May Jehovah answer you in the day of distress. May the name of the God of Jacob protect you. May he send your help out of the holy place, and sustain you out of Zion itself. May he remember all your gift offerings, and may he accept your burnt offering as being fat. *Selah.* [Pause for meditation.] May he give to you according to your heart, and all your counsel may he fulfill. We will cry out joyfully because of your salvation, and in the name of our God we shall lift our banners. May Jehovah fulfill all your requests. Now I do know that Jehovah certainly saves his anointed one. He answers him from his holy heavens with the saving mighty acts of his right hand. Some concerning chariots and others concerning horses, but, as for us, concerning the name of Jehovah our God we shall make mention. Those very ones have broken down and fallen; but as for us, we have risen up, that we may be restored. O Jehovah, do save the king! He will answer us in the day that we call.

Psalm 105 all verses, [abbreviated here], Give thanks to Jehovah, call upon his name, make known among the peoples his dealings. Sing to him, make melody to him, concern yourselves with all his wonderful works. Make your boast in his holy name. Let the heart of those seeking Jehovah rejoice. Search for Jehovah and his strength. Seek his face constantly. Remember his wonderful works that he has performed, his miracles and the judicial decisions of his mouth, O you seed of Abraham his servant, you sons of Jacob, his chosen ones. He is Jehovah our God. His judicial decisions are in all the earth. He has remembered his covenant even to time indefinite, the word that he commanded, to a thousand generations, which covenant he concluded with Abraham, and his sworn statement to Isaac, and which statement he kept standing as a regulation even to Jacob, as an indefinitely lasting covenant even to Israel, saying: "To you I shall give the land of Canaan as the allotment of your inheritance." This was when they happened to be few in number, yes, very few, and alien residents in it. And they kept walking about from nation to nation, from one kingdom to another people. He did not allow any human to defraud them, but on their account he reproved kings, saying: "Do not you men touch my anointed ones, and to my prophets do nothing bad." And he proceeded to call for a famine upon the land; he broke every rod around which ring-shaped loaves were suspended. He sent ahead of them a man who was sold to be a slave, Joseph. With fetters they afflicted his feet, into irons his soul came; until the time that his word came, the saying of Jehovah itself refined him. The king sent that he might release him, the ruler of the peoples, that he might let him loose. He set him as master to his household and as ruler over all his property, to bind his princes agreeably to his soul and that he might teach wisdom to even his elderly men.

For he [Jehovah] remembered his holy word with Abraham his servant. So he brought out his people with exultation, his chosen ones even with a joyful cry. And gradually he gave them the lands of the nations, and they kept taking possession of the product of the hard work of national groups, to the end that they might keep his regulations and observe his own laws. Praise Jah, you people!

Research: Insight on the Scriptures, volume 2, page 256, **Lion: *The Greek word for lion is leon.***

Recall: Song of Solomon 5:11a, His head is gold, refined gold.

Recall: Isaiah 45:4, For the sake of my servant Jacob and of Israel my chosen one, I even proceeded to call you by your name; I proceeded to give you **a name of honor**, although you did not know me. [**Leon** (lion); associated with the tribe of Judah.]

Zechariah 2:12, And Jehovah will certainly take possession of Judah as his portion upon the holy ground, and he must yet choose Jerusalem.

Genesis 49:9a, A lion cub Judah is.

Proverbs 30:29-31, There are three that do well in their pacing, and four that do well in their moving along: the lion, which is the mightiest among the beasts and which does not turn back from before anyone; the greyhound [literally: "the animal girded in at the hips"] or the he-goat; and a king of a band of soldiers of his own people [or, "a king against whom there is no rising up by his people"].

Jeremiah Chapter 12 all verses, You are righteous, O Jehovah, when I make my complaint to you, indeed when I speak even about matters of judgment with you. Why is it that the way of wicked ones is what has succeeded, that all those who are committing treachery are the unworried ones? You have planted them; they have also taken root. They keep going ahead; they have also produced fruit. You are near in their [the organization's] mouth, but far away from their kidneys [deepest emotions, such as love and loyalty]. And you yourself, O Jehovah, know me well; you see me, and you have examined my heart in union with yourself. Single them out like sheep for the slaughtering, and set them apart for the day of killing. How long should the land keep withering away, and the very vegetation of all the field dry up? Because of the badness of those dwelling in it the beasts and the flying creatures have been swept away. For they have said: "He does not see our future."

Because with footmen you [those in the organization seeking Jehovah's justice] have run, and they would tire you out, how, then, can you run a race with horses? And in the land of peace are you confident? So how will you act among the proud thickets along the Jordan? For even your own brothers and the household of your own father, even they themselves [those taking the lead in the organization of Jehovah's Witnesses] have dealt treacherously with you. Even they themselves have called out loudly behind you. **Do not put any faith in them, just because they speak to you good things.**

"**I [Jehovah] have left my house; I have deserted my inheritance; I have given the beloved one of my soul [unfaithful "faithful and discreet slave"] into the palm of her enemies.** My inheritance has become to me like a lion in the forest. She has let loose her voice even against me. That is why I have hated her. My inheritance is as a many-colored bird of prey to me; the birds of prey are round about upon it. Come, gather together, all you wild beasts of the field; bring them to eat. Many shepherds themselves [those taking the lead in the organization] have brought my vineyard to ruin; they have stamped down my share. They have turned my desirable share into a wilderness of a desolate waste. One has made it a desolate waste; it has withered away; it is desolated to me. The whole land has been made desolate, because there is no man that has taken it to heart. On all the beaten paths through the wilderness the despoilers have come. For the sword belonging to Jehovah is devouring from one end of the land even to the other end of the land. There is no peace for any flesh. They have sown wheat, but thorns are what they have reaped. They have worked themselves sick; they will be of no benefit. And they will certainly be ashamed of the products of you people because of the burning anger of Jehovah."

This is what Jehovah has said against all my **bad neighbors** [unfaithful ones in the organization], who are touching the hereditary possession that I caused my people, even Israel, to possess: "Here I am uprooting them from off their ground; and the house of Judah [governing body] I shall uproot from the midst of them. And it must occur that after my uprooting them [the disloyal ones] I shall again certainly have mercy upon them and will bring them back [give them an opportunity to return to Jehovah's righteous ways; again becoming loyal worshippers], each one to his hereditary possession and each one to his land.

And it must occur that if they [unfaithful ones in the organization] will without fail learn the ways of <u>my people</u> [faithful worshippers of Jehovah] in swearing by my name, 'As Jehovah is alive!' just as **they taught <u>my people</u>** to swear by Baal [meaning "Owner;" the unfaithful "faithful and discreet slave" became their "owner" when unfaithful ones in the organization started following after the "slave" instead of Jehovah, their Rightful Owner], **they will also be built up in the midst of <u>my people</u>. But if they will not obey, I will also uproot that nation, uprooting and destroying it,"** is the utterance of Jehovah.

Psalm 80 all verses, O Shepherd of Israel, do give ear, you who are conducting Joseph [Lisa] just like a flock [faithful worshippers of Jehovah still in the organization]. O you who are sitting upon the cherubs, do beam forth. Before Ephraim and Benjamin and Manasseh do rouse up your mightiness, and do come to our salvation. O God, bring us back; and light up your face, that we may be saved. O Jehovah God of armies, how long must you fume against the prayer of your people? You have made them eat the bread of tears, and you keep making them drink tears upon tears in great measure. You set us for strife to our neighbors [bad neighbors, those in the organization who have abandoned Jehovah completely], and our very enemies keep deriding as they please. O God of armies, bring us back; and light up your face, that we may be saved. You proceeded to make a vine depart from Egypt. You kept driving out the nations, that you might plant it. You made a clearing before it, that it might take root and fill the land. The mountains were covered with its shadow, and the cedars of God with its boughs.

[The organization of Jehovah's Witnesses was at one time faithful to Jehovah, but their "faithful and discreet slave" became unfaithful and fell away from true worship, leading astray many of those in the organization. Jesus, however, is always faithful, and he is the true vine.]

John 15:1-6, "I am the true vine, and my Father is the cultivator. Every branch in me not bearing fruit he takes away, and every one bearing fruit he cleans, that it may bear more fruit. You are already clean because of the word that I have spoken to you. Remain in union with me, and I in union with you. Just as the branch cannot bear fruit of itself unless it remains in the vine, in the same way neither can you, unless you remain in union with me. I am the vine, you are the branches. He that remains in union with me, and I in union with him, this one bears much fruit; because apart from me you can do nothing at all. If anyone does not remain in union with me, he is cast out as a branch and is dried up; and men gather those branches up and pitch them into the fire and they are burned." [Because the organization, led by the "faithful and discreet slave," has turned away in unfaithfulness, it will be gathered up and cast into the fire.]

Psalm 80, continued, It gradually sent forth its boughs as far as the sea, and to the River its twigs. Why have you broken down its stone walls, and why have all those passing by on the road plucked at it? A boar out of the woods keeps eating it away, and the animal throngs of the open field keep feeding upon it. O God of armies, return, please; look down from heaven and see and take care [faithful worshippers, begging Jehovah to "take care" of them, the clean "branches" desiring to remain in union with Jesus, the true vine] of this vine, and the stock that your right hand has planted, and look upon the son whom you have made strong for yourself. It [the organization] is burned with fire, cut off. From the rebuke of your face they perish. Let your hand prove to be upon the man of your right hand,

Psalm 89:19-27, At that time you spoke in a vision to your loyal ones, and you proceeded to say: "I have placed help upon a mighty one; I have exalted a chosen one from among the people. I have found David my servant; with my holy oil I have anointed him, with whom my own hand will be firm, whom my own arm also will strengthen. No enemy will make exactions upon him, neither will any son of unrighteousness afflict him. And from before him I crushed his adversaries to pieces, and to those intensely hating him I kept dealing out blows. And my faithfulness and my loving-kindness are with him, and in my name his horn is exalted. And on the sea I have put his hand and on the rivers his right hand. He himself calls out to me, 'You are my Father, my God and the Rock of my salvation.' Also, I myself shall place him [Jesus] as firstborn, the most high of the kings of the earth." [Jesus is the highest king over all other kings.]

Psalm 80, continued, upon the son of mankind whom you have made strong for yourself, and we shall not turn back from you. May you preserve us alive,

[Every day I feel like I am dying. And I know that many others, faithful worshippers of Jehovah still in the organization, feel the same way I do, due to the persecution from their "bad neighbors," the unfaithful ones.]

Psalm 80, continued, that we may call upon your own name. O Jehovah God of armies, bring us back; light up your face, that we may be saved.

Recall: Psalm 80:17,18a, Let your hand prove to be upon the man [Leon, a lesser king compared to Jesus Christ] of your right hand, upon the son of mankind [son of mankind = earthling man; Hebrew: adham] whom you [Jehovah] have made strong for yourself, and we shall not turn back from you.

Jeremiah 50:41-44, Look! A people is coming in from the north and a great nation and grand kings themselves will be roused up from the remotest parts of the earth. Bow and javelin they handle. They are cruel and will show no mercy. The sound of them is like the sea that is boisterous, and upon horses they will ride; set in array as one man for war against you, O daughter of Babylon [organization of Jehovah's Witnesses].

The king of Babylon [unfaithful "faithful and discreet slave"] has heard the report about them, and his hands have dropped down. There is distress! Severe pains have seized hold of him, just like a woman giving birth.

Look! Someone will come up just like a lion [Leon] from the proud thickets along the Jordan to the durable abiding place [Lisa], but in a moment I shall make them run away from her. And the one [Leon] who is chosen I shall appoint over her. For who is like me, and who will challenge me, and who, now, is the shepherd that can stand before me?

Jeremiah 50:27,31, Massacre all her young bulls. May they go down to the slaughter. Woe to them, for their [the organization's] day has come, the time for their being given attention!

"Look! I am against you, O Presumptuousness," is the utterance of the Sovereign Lord, Jehovah of armies, "for your day must come, the time that I must give you attention."

Daniel 9:27, And he must keep the covenant in force for the many for one week; and at the half of the week he will cause sacrifice and gift offering to cease. And upon the wing of disgusting things there will be the one causing desolation; and until an extermination, the very thing decided upon will go pouring out also upon the one lying desolate.

Ecclesiastes 11:5, Just as you are not aware of what is the way of the spirit in the bones in the belly of her that is pregnant [Zion "gave deliverance to a male child," Leon, and has "given birth to her sons," loyal worshippers of Jehovah. (Isaiah 66:7,8)], in like manner you do not know the work of the true God, who does all things.

Psalm 119:74,81,114,147, Those fearing you are the ones that see me [Lisa] and rejoice, for I have waited for your own word.

For your salvation my soul has pined away; for your word I have waited.

You are my place of concealment and my shield. For your word I have waited.

I have been up early in the morning twilight, that I may cry for help. For your words I have waited.

Given: [I was given these words from Jehovah, in reference to Leon: He is "worth waiting for."]

Jehovah's Will: [I need to make an emotional adjustment to doing Jehovah's will in my life. It isn't easy to be patient and do things at the pace Jehovah has set, and sometimes it is difficult for me to accept what his will is for me, but I need to be willing to make the adjustment to Jehovah. He is my Teacher and I am his student.]

Attitude Refinements: [And I need to continue working on mildness and self-control.]

Message: [I asked Jehovah where in time we are. This is the answer I was given: **"It is later than you think."**]

Ecclesiastes 9:7, Go, eat your food with rejoicing and drink your wine with a good heart, because already the true God has found pleasure in your works [my writing].

September 27, 1989

Research: [Scriptural symbolism can be seen in modern times. In her book, Liberty: The Statue and the American Dream (1985), Leslie Allen notes that much of the statue's symbolism was inspired by the scriptures: mother of exiles; liberty enlightening the world; enduring symbol of hope; courage and sacrifice; pain, sweat and tears; a symbol of diversity; the shackles of oppression and alien rule lie broken at the feet of the statue; symbol of a new world and a new life.

Her face shows compassion for others, because she has personally known much pain. The "stone" tablet she is holding symbolizes freedom.

Interestingly, the Statue of Liberty can be seen from the Watchtower Society's international headquarters building in New York, its symbolism for the present day escaping their awareness.]

Recall: Jeremiah 28:4, "And Jeconiah the son of Jehoiakim, the king of Judah [Leon], and all the exiles of Judah [faithful worshippers of Jehovah still in the organization of Jehovah's Witnesses] who have come to Babylon I am bringing back to this place ["Jerusalem," Lisa]," is the utterance of Jehovah, "for I shall break the yoke of the king of Babylon [unfaithful "faithful and discreet slave"]."

Isaiah 14:3-8, And it must occur in the day when Jehovah gives you rest from your pain and from your agitation and from the hard slavery in which you were made a slave, that you must raise up this proverbial saying against the king of Babylon and say:

"How has the one driving others to work come to a stop, the oppression come to a stop! Jehovah has broken the rod of the wicked ones, the staff of the ruling ones, the one striking peoples in fury with a stroke incessantly, the one subduing nations in sheer anger with a persecution without restraint. The whole earth has come to rest, has become free of disturbance. People have become cheerful with joyful cries. Even the juniper trees have also rejoiced at you, the cedars [tall "trees," those taking the lead in the organization of Jehovah's Witnesses] of Lebanon, saying, 'Ever since you have lain down, no woodcutter comes up against us.'"

[The exiles are released from the oppression of Babylon the Great and the rest of the nations.]

Isaiah 12:3,6, With exultation you people will be certain to draw water out of the springs of salvation.

Cry out shrilly and shout for joy, O you inhabitress of Zion, for great in the midst of you is the Holy One of Israel.

Recall: Proverbs 21:1, A king's heart is as streams of water in the hand of Jehovah. Everywhere that he delights to, he turns it.

Psalms 113 all verses, Praise Jah, you people! Offer praise, O you servants of Jehovah, praise the name of Jehovah. May Jehovah's name become blessed from now on and to time indefinite. From the rising of the sun until its setting Jehovah's name is to be praised. Jehovah has become high above all the nations; his glory is above the heavens. Who is like Jehovah our God, him who is making his dwelling on high? He is condescending to look on heaven and earth, raising up the lowly one from the very dust; he exalts the poor one from the ashpit itself, to make him sit with nobles, with the nobles of his people. He is causing the barren woman to dwell in a house as a joyful mother of sons. Praise Jah, you people!

Psalm 114 all verses, When Israel went forth from Egypt, the house of Jacob from a people speaking unintelligibly, Judah became his holy place, Israel his grand dominion. The sea itself saw and took to flight; as for the Jordan, it began to turn back. The mountains themselves skipped about like rams, the hills like lambs. What was the matter with you, O sea, that you took to flight, O Jordan, that you began to turn back? O mountains, that you went skipping about like rams; O hills, like lambs? Because of the Lord be in severe pains, O earth, because of the God of Jacob, who is changing the rock into a reedy pool of water, a flinty rock into a spring of water.

Psalm 115 all verses, [abbreviated here], To us belongs nothing, O Jehovah, to us belongs nothing, but to your name give glory according to your loving-kindness, according to your trueness. Why should the nations say: "Where, now, is their God?" But our God is in the heavens; everything that he delighted to do he has done. Their idols are silver and gold, the work of the hands of earthling man. Those making them will become just like them, all those who are trusting in them. O Israel, trust in Jehovah; he is their help and their shield. O house of Aaron, put your trust in Jehovah; he is their help and their shield. You that fear Jehovah, trust in Jehovah; he is their help and their shield. Jehovah himself has remembered us; he will bless, he will bless the house of Israel, he will bless the house of Aaron. He will bless those fearing Jehovah, the small ones as well as the great ones. Jehovah will give increase to you, to you and to your sons. **You are the ones blessed by Jehovah, the Maker of heaven and earth. As regards the heavens, to Jehovah the heavens belong, but the earth he has given to the sons of men.** The dead themselves do not praise Jah, nor do any going down into silence. **But we ourselves will bless Jah from now on and to time indefinite. Praise Jah, you people!**

Psalm 116 all verses, I do love, because Jehovah hears my voice, my entreaties. For he has inclined his ear to me, and throughout my days I shall call. The ropes of death encircled me and the distressing circumstances of Sheol themselves found me. Distress and grief I kept finding. But upon the name of Jehovah I proceeded to call: "Ah, Jehovah, do provide my soul with escape!" Jehovah is gracious and righteous; and our God is One showing mercy. Jehovah is guarding the inexperienced ones. I was impoverished, and he proceeded to save even me. Return to your resting-place, O my soul, for Jehovah himself has acted appropriately toward you. For you have rescued my soul from death, my eye from tears, my foot from stumbling. I will walk before Jehovah in the lands of those living. I had faith, for I proceeded to speak. I myself was very much afflicted. I, for my part, said, when I became panicky: "Every man is a liar." What shall I repay to Jehovah for all his benefits to me? The cup of grand salvation I shall take up, and on the name of Jehovah I shall call. My vows I shall pay to Jehovah, yes, in front of all his people. Precious in the eyes of Jehovah is the death of his loyal ones. Ah, now, O Jehovah, for I am your servant. I am your servant, the son of your slave girl. You have loosened my bands. To you I shall offer the sacrifice of thanksgiving, and on the name of Jehovah I shall call. My vows I shall pay to Jehovah, yes, in front of all his people, in the courtyards of the house of Jehovah, in the midst of you, O Jerusalem. Praise Jah, you people!

Psalm 117 all verses, Praise Jehovah, all you nations; commend him, all you clans. For toward us his loving-kindness has proved mighty; and the trueness of Jehovah is to time indefinite. Praise Jah, you people!

Psalm 118 all verses, Give thanks to Jehovah, you people, for he is good; for his loving-kindness is to time indefinite. Let Israel now say:

"For his loving-kindness is to time indefinite." Let those of the house of Aaron now say: "For his loving-kindness is to time indefinite." Let those fearing Jehovah now say: "For his loving-kindness is to time indefinite." Out of the distressing circumstances I called upon Jah; Jah answered and put me into a roomy place. Jehovah is on my side; I shall not fear. What can earthling man do to me? Jehovah is on my side among those helping me, so that I myself shall look upon those hating me. It is better to take refuge in Jehovah than to trust in earthling man. It is better to take refuge in Jehovah than to trust in nobles. All the nations themselves surrounded me. It was in the name of Jehovah that I kept holding them off. They surrounded me, yes, they had me surrounded. It was in the name of Jehovah that I kept holding them off. They surrounded me like bees; they were extinguished like a fire of thornbushes. It was in the name of Jehovah that I kept holding them off. You pushed me hard that I should fall, but Jehovah himself helped me. Jah is my shelter and my might, and to me he becomes salvation. The voice of a joyful cry and salvation is in the tents of the righteous ones. The right hand of Jehovah is demonstrating vital energy. The right hand of Jehovah is exalting itself; the right hand of Jehovah is demonstrating vital energy. I shall not die, but I shall keep living, that I may declare the works of Jah. Jah corrected me severely, but he did not give me over to death itself. Open to me the gates of righteousness, you people. I shall go into them; I shall laud Jah. This is the gate of Jehovah. The righteous themselves will go into it. I shall laud you, for you answered me and you came to be my salvation. **The stone that the builders rejected has become the head of the corner. This has come to be from Jehovah himself; it is wonderful in our eyes. This is the day that Jehovah has made; we will be joyful and rejoice in it. Ah, now, Jehovah, do save, please! Ah, now, Jehovah, do grant success, please! Blessed be the One coming in the name of Jehovah; we have blessed you people out of the house of Jehovah. Jehovah is the Divine One, and he gives us light. Bind the festival procession with boughs, O you people, as far as the horns of the altar. You are my Divine One, and I shall laud you; my God—I shall exalt you. Give thanks to Jehovah, you people, for he is good; for his loving-kindness is to time indefinite.**

Nahum 1:7, Jehovah is good, a stronghold in the day of distress.

And he is cognizant of those seeking refuge in him.

Micah 7:20, You will give the trueness given to Jacob, the loving-kindness given to Abraham, which you swore to our forefathers from the days of long ago.

Recall: Isaiah 61:8, For I, Jehovah, am loving justice, hating robbery along with unrighteousness. And I will give their wages in trueness, and an indefinitely lasting covenant I shall conclude toward them.

Micah 7:14, Shepherd your people with your staff, the flock of your inheritance, the one who was residing alone in a forest—in the midst of an orchard. Let them feed on Bashan and Gilead as in the days of a long time ago.

Micah 6:14, You [those in the organization who have left Jehovah in their hearts], for your part, will eat and not get satisfied, and your emptiness will be in the midst of you. And you will remove things, but you will not carry them safely away; and whatever you would carry away safely, I shall give to the sword itself.

Isaiah 29:17 to 30:11, Is it not yet but a very little time and Lebanon must be turned into an orchard and the orchard itself will be accounted just as a forest? And in that day the deaf ones will certainly hear the words of the book, and out of the gloom and out of the darkness even the eyes of the blind ones will see. And the meek ones will certainly increase their rejoicing in Jehovah himself, and even the poor ones of mankind will be joyful in the Holy One of Israel himself, because the tyrant must reach his end, and the bragger must come to his finish, and all those keeping alert to do harm must be cut off, those bringing a man into sin by his word, and those who lay bait even for the one reproving in the gate, and those who push aside the righteous one with empty arguments.
Therefore this is what Jehovah has said to the house of Jacob, he that redeemed Abraham: "[Faithful] Jacob will not now be ashamed, nor will his own face now grow pale; for when he sees his children [faithful worshippers of Jehovah coming out of the organization], the work of my hands, in the midst of him, they will sanctify my

name, and they will certainly sanctify the Holy One of Jacob, and the God of Israel they will regard with awe. And those who are erring in their spirit will actually get to know understanding, and even those who are grumbling will learn instruction."

"Woe to the stubborn sons [those taking the lead in the organization]," is the utterance of Jehovah, "those disposed to carry out counsel, but not that from me; and to pour out a libation, but not with my spirit, in order to add sin to sin; those who are setting out to go down to Egypt [the nations] and who have not inquired of my own mouth, to take shelter in the stronghold of Pharaoh and to take refuge in the shadow of Egypt! And the stronghold of Pharaoh must become even for you men a reason for shame, and the refuge in the shadow of Egypt a cause for humiliation. For his princes have come to be in Zoan itself, and his own envoys reach even Hanes. Every one will certainly become ashamed of a people that bring no benefit to one, that are of no help and bring no benefit, but are a reason for shame and also a cause for reproach."

The pronouncement against the beasts of the south: Through the land of distress and hard conditions, of the lion and the leopard growling, of the viper and the flying fiery snake, on the shoulders of full-grown asses they carry their resources, and on the humps of camels their supplies. In behalf of the people they will prove of no benefit. And the Egyptians are mere vanity, and they will help simply for nothing. Therefore I have called this one: "Rahab [this name is often associated with Egypt in the scriptures]—they are for sitting still."

"Now come, write it upon a tablet with them [the scriptures that Jehovah has given to me for this written work], and inscribe it even in a book, that it may serve for a future day, for a witness to time indefinite. For it is a rebellious people, untruthful sons [those who have left Jehovah in their hearts], sons who have been unwilling to hear the law of Jehovah; who have said to the ones seeing, 'You must not see,' and to the ones having visions, 'You must not envision for us any straightforward things. Speak to us smooth things; envision deceptive things. Turn aside from the way; deviate from the path. Cause the Holy One of Israel to cease just on account of us.'"

Isaiah 30:18,19, And therefore Jehovah will keep in expectation of showing you [faithful worshippers of Jehovah] favor, and therefore he will rise up to show you mercy. For Jehovah is a God of judgment. Happy are all those keeping in expectation of him. When the very people in Zion will dwell in Jerusalem, you will by no means weep. He will without fail show you favor at the sound of your outcry; as soon as he hears it he will actually answer you.

Isaiah 29:19, And the meek ones will certainly increase their rejoicing in Jehovah himself, and even the poor ones of mankind will be joyful in the Holy One of Israel himself.

Isaiah 29:17a,22b,23, Is it not yet but a very little time and Lebanon must be turned into an orchard [a few trees] and the orchard itself will be accounted just as a forest [many trees]?
Jacob will not now be ashamed, nor will his own face now grow pale; for when he sees his children, the work of my hands, in the midst of him, they will sanctify my name, and they will certainly sanctify the Holy One of Jacob, and the God of Israel they will regard with awe. [There are a few people, an "orchard" beginning to see the truth; that the organization of Jehovah's Witnesses has lost Jehovah's holy spirit; that it is, in fact, Babylon the Great. In "yet but a very little time" there will be many more people, a "forest" who can see this truth.]

Isaiah 27:12,13, And it must occur in that day that Jehovah will **beat off the fruit**, from the flowing stream of the River to the torrent valley of Egypt, and so **you yourselves will be picked up one after the other, O sons of Israel**. And it must occur in that day that there will be a blowing on a great horn, and those who are perishing in the land of Assyria and those who are dispersed in the land of Egypt will certainly come and bow down to Jehovah in the holy mountain in Jerusalem.

Research: Aid to Bible Understanding WBTS: ***Trumpet blast—harvest trumpet:*** *Seventy weeks, seven weeks; calendar reference to September 17th. beat off the fruit, "and so you will be picked up one after another." (Isaiah 27:12,13)*

[There will be only a few people 'picked up" at first, but over time the few become many.]

Zechariah 9:12, Return to the stronghold, you prisoners of the hope. [Jehovah is our stronghold. We are "prisoners" of our hope in him, because there is no other who can save us. (Psalm 91:2)]

Psalm 27:14, Hope in Jehovah; be courageous and let your heart be strong. Yes, hope in Jehovah.

Isaiah 30:8-10, "Now come, write it upon a tablet with them, and inscribe it even in a book, that it may serve for a future day, for a witness to time indefinite. For it is a rebellious people [the majority of those in the organization], untruthful sons, sons who have been unwilling to hear the law of Jehovah; who have said to the ones [Lisa, and a few others at this time] seeing, 'You must not see,' and to the ones having visions, 'You must not envision for us any straightforward things. Speak to us smooth things; envision deceptive things.' [Those spiritually "awake" in the organization will "see" and believe that Jehovah is doing something new for them that does not include the unfaithful majority of Jehovah's Witnesses.]

Isaiah 43:18,19, Do not remember the first things, and to the former things do not turn your consideration. Look! I am doing something new. Now it will spring up. You people will know it, will you not? Really, through the wilderness I shall set a way, through the desert rivers. [The majority of Jehovah's Witnesses have, **in their hearts**, completely left Jehovah, though because they remain in the organization they believe that they are still faithful and all is well. For the truly faithful worshippers, being surrounded by these people is like living in a desert with no water.]

Isaiah 8:16-18, Good News Bible (1976), You, my disciples, are to guard and preserve the messages that God has given me. The Lord has hidden himself from his [unfaithful] people, but I trust him and place my hope in him.
[I believe Jehovah. Today I was thinking to myself in reference to my own family members, "These three people, my own family, united in their thought and disagreeing with me, are mistaken. Even if they were three hundred people; even three million people (which is the organization's approximate size), united in thought

and disagreeing with me, they are headed in the wrong direction. I believe Jehovah. I will follow Jehovah."

I feel so alone most of the time, although, of course I have a tremendous family of kindred spirits in Jehovah's heavenly spirit family. And, I need to remind myself that, just as in Elijah's day when Elijah wanted to die, Jehovah showed him there were seven thousand faithful people remaining among the Israelites. Truly, he was not alone in his faithfulness to Jehovah. (1 Kings 19:13-18) And truly, although I am separated from the faithful worshippers of Jehovah still in the organization at this time, I am not alone. Jehovah has set a day when I will see my faithful spiritual family again, or in many cases, meet them for the first time. **I am so looking forward to that day!**]

September 30, 1989

Today: [In my private thoughts I had been saying, "I'm no scholar. I'm not a writer." I was concerned that I didn't know how to accomplish this work Jehovah has given me, including the writing of this journal.]

Jeremiah 1:4-10, Good News Bible, The Lord said to me, "I chose you [Lisa] before I gave you life, and before you were born I selected you to be a prophet to the nations."

I answered, "Sovereign Lord, I don't know how to speak; I am too young."

But the Lord said to me, "Do not say that you are too young, but go to the people I send you to, and tell them everything I command you to say. Do not be afraid of them, for I will be with you to protect you. I, the Lord, have spoken!"

Then the Lord reached out, touched my lips, and said to me, "Listen, I am giving you the words you must speak. Today I give you authority over nations and kingdoms to uproot and to pull down, to destroy and to overthrow, to build and to plant."

[These are scriptures the circuit overseer read from the New World Translation of the Holy Scriptures in his talk at the Kingdom Hall in Lancaster, Wisconsin, referring to me. Today, September 30, 1989, Jehovah has given me this authority.]

Jeremiah 2:10b Good News Bible, You will see that nothing like this has ever happened before.

Recall: Luke 18:16, However, Jesus called the infants to him, saying: "Let the young children come to me, and do not try to stop them. For the kingdom of God belongs to suchlike ones."

Isaiah 42:4,14, Good News Bible, He will not lose hope or courage; he will establish justice on the earth. Distant lands eagerly wait for his teaching.
God says, "For a long time I kept silent; I did not answer my people. But now the time to act has come; I cry out like a woman in labor."

Isaiah 43:1,2,4 Good News Bible, Israel, the Lord who created you [Lisa] says, "Do not be afraid—I will save you. I have called you by name—you are mine. When you pass through deep waters, I will be with you; your troubles will not overwhelm you. When you pass through fire, you will not be burned; the hard trials that come will not hurt you.
I will give up whole nations to save your life, because you are precious to me and because I love you and give you honor."

Psalm 118:13, You [Satan] pushed me hard that I should fall, but Jehovah himself helped me.

Isaiah 42:9 Good News Bible, The things I [Jehovah] predicted have now come true. Now I will tell you of new things even before they begin to happen.

Isaiah 43:27,19,12,13,18, Your own father, the first one, has sinned, and your own spokesmen [unfaithful "faithful and discreet slave" and those taking the lead in the organization] have transgressed against me. [I recall the letter I received from the organization of Jehovah's Witnesses after we were disfellowshipped. It is not difficult to see that they are Babylon the Great. By disfellowshipping innocent people, they are, in Jehovah's eyes, committing murder.]

Look! I am doing something new. Now it will spring up. You people will know it, will you not? Really, through the wilderness I shall set a way, through the desert rivers.

"I myself have told forth and have saved and have caused it to be heard, when there was among you no strange god. So you are my witnesses," is the utterance of Jehovah, "and **I am God. Also, all the time I am the same One; and there is no one effecting deliverance out of my own hand. I shall get active, and who can turn it back?"**

Do not remember the first things, and to the former things do not turn your consideration.

[These words are so true: The last day of September 1989, I was given this scripture.] Isaiah 44:23, Joyfully cry out, you heavens, for Jehovah has taken action! Shout in triumph, all you lowest parts of the earth! Become cheerful, you mountains, with joyful outcry, you forest and all you trees in it! For Jehovah has repurchased Jacob, and on Israel he shows his beauty.

Recall: Isaiah 29:17, Is it not yet but a very little time and Lebanon must be turned into an orchard and the orchard itself will be accounted just as a forest?

October 1, 1989 Sunday

Ezekiel 12:21-25,28, And the word of Jehovah occurred further to me, saying: "Son of man, what is this proverbial saying that you people have on the soil of Israel, saying, 'The days are prolonged, and every vision has perished'? Therefore say to them, 'This is what the Sovereign Lord Jehovah has said: "I shall certainly cause this proverbial saying to cease, and they will no more say it as a proverb in Israel."' But speak to them, '**The days have drawn near, and the matter of every vision.**' For there will no more prove to be any valueless vision nor double-faced divination in the midst of the house of Israel [the apostate organization]. "'For I myself, Jehovah, shall speak what word I shall speak, and it will be done. There will be no postponement anymore, for in your days, O rebellious house, I shall speak a word and certainly do it," is the utterance of the Sovereign Lord Jehovah."'

"Therefore say to them, 'This is what the Sovereign Lord Jehovah has said: "'There will be no postponement anymore as to any words of mine. What word I shall speak, it will even be done,' is the utterance of the Sovereign Lord Jehovah."'"

Ezekiel Chapter 13 all verses, And the word of Jehovah continued to occur to me, saying: "Son of man, prophesy concerning the [false] prophets of Israel who are prophesying, and you must say to those prophesying out of their own heart, 'Hear the word of Jehovah. This is what the Sovereign Lord Jehovah has said: **"Woe to the stupid prophets, who are walking after their own spirit, when there is nothing that they have seen!** Like foxes in the devastated places are what your own prophets have become, O Israel. You men will certainly not go up into the gaps, neither will you build up a stone wall in behalf of the house of Israel, in order to stand in the battle in the day of Jehovah." "They have visioned what is untrue and a lying divination, those who are saying, 'The utterance of Jehovah is,' when Jehovah himself has not sent them, and they have waited to have a word come true. **Is it not an untrue vision that you men [unfaithful "faithful and discreet slave"] have visioned, and a lying divination that you have said, when saying, 'The utterance of Jehovah is,' when I myself have spoken nothing?"'**

"'Therefore this is what the Sovereign Lord Jehovah has said: "'For the reason that you men have spoken untruth and you have visioned a lie, therefore here I am against you,' is the utterance of the Sovereign Lord Jehovah." And my hand has come to be against the prophets that are visioning untruth and that are divining a lie. **In the intimate group of my people they will not continue on, and in the register of the house of Israel they will not be written, and to the soil of Israel they will not come; and you people will have to know that I am the Sovereign Lord Jehovah, for the reason, yes, for the reason that they have led my people astray,** saying, "There is peace!" when there is no peace, and there is one that is building a partition wall, but in vain there are those plastering it with whitewash.'

"Say to those plastering with whitewash that it will fall. A flooding downpour will certainly occur, and you, O hailstones, will fall, and a blast of windstorms itself will cause a splitting. And, look! the wall must fall. Will it not be said to you men, 'Where is the coating with which you did the plastering?'

"Therefore this is what the Sovereign Lord Jehovah has said: 'I will also cause a blast of windstorms to burst forth in my rage, and in my anger there will occur a flooding downpour, and in rage there will be hailstones for an extermination. And I will tear down the wall that you men have plastered with whitewash and bring it into contact with the earth, and its foundation must be exposed. And she [Babylon the Great; the organization of Jehovah's Witnesses, the Watchtower Bible and Tract Society] will certainly fall, and you [unfaithful ones in the organization] must come to an end in the midst of her; and you will have to know that I am Jehovah.'

"'And I will bring my rage to its finish upon the wall and upon those plastering it with whitewash, and I shall say to you men: "The wall is no more, and those plastering it are no more, the [false] prophets of Israel [unfaithful "faithful and discreet slave"] that are prophesying to Jerusalem and that are visioning for her a vision of peace, when there is no peace,"' is the utterance of the Sovereign Lord Jehovah.

"And as for you, O son of man, set your face against the daughters [The women telling the good news are a large army. (Psalm 68:11) Many of these women are the wives of those taking the lead in the organization. And many among these have been found to be arrogant and verbally abusive, mistreating Jehovah's "lambs," the mild-tempered ones, his faithful worshippers] of your people who are acting as prophetesses out of their own heart, and prophesy against them. And you must say, 'This is what the Sovereign Lord Jehovah has said: "Woe to the women sewing bands together upon all elbows and making veils upon the head of every size in order to hunt souls! Are the souls that you women hunt down the ones belonging to my people, and the souls belonging to you the ones that you preserve alive? And will you profane me toward my people for the handfuls of barley and for the morsels of bread, in order to put to death the souls that ought not to die and in order to preserve alive the souls that ought not to live by your lie to my people, the hearers of a lie?"'

"Therefore this is what the Sovereign Lord Jehovah has said: 'Here I am against the bands of you women, with which you are hunting down the souls as though they were flying things, and I will rip them from off your arms and let go the souls that you are hunting down, souls as though they were flying things. And I will rip away your veils and deliver my people out of your hand, and they will no more prove to be in your hand something caught in the hunt; and you will have to know that I am Jehovah. **By reason of dejecting the heart of a righteous one with falsehood, when I myself had not caused him pain, and for making the hands of a wicked one strong so that he would not turn back from his bad way in order to preserve him alive, therefore untruth you women will not keep on visioning, and divination you will divine no longer; and I will deliver my people out of your hand, and you will have to know that I am Jehovah.'"**

Isaiah 43:13b, I shall get active, and who can turn it back? [I sensed again the message from Jehovah that I had been given earlier: "It is later than you think."]

Psalm 104 all verses, Good News Bible (1976), Praise the Lord, my soul! O Lord, my God, how great you are! You are clothed with majesty and glory; you cover yourself with light. You spread out the heavens like a tent and build your home on the waters above. You use the clouds as your chariot and ride on the wings of the wind. You use the winds as your messengers and flashes of lightning as your servants.

You have set the earth firmly on its foundations, and it will never be moved. You placed the ocean over it like a robe, and the water covered the mountains. When you rebuked the waters, they fled; they rushed away when they heard your shout of command. They flowed over the mountains and into the valleys, to the place you had made for them. You set a boundary they can never pass, to keep them from covering the earth again.

You make springs flow in the valleys, and rivers run between the hills. They provide water for the wild animals; there the wild donkeys quench their thirst. In the trees near by, the birds make their nests and sing.

From the sky you send rain on the hills, and the earth is filled with your blessings. You make grass grow for the cattle and plants for man to use, so that he can grow his crops and produce wine to make him happy, olive oil to make him cheerful, and bread to give him strength.

The [faithful] cedars of Lebanon get plenty of rain—the Lord's own trees, which he planted. There the birds build their nests; the storks nest in the fir trees. The wild goats live in the high mountains, and the badgers hide in the cliffs.

You created the moon to mark the months; the sun knows the time to set. You made the night, and in the darkness all the wild animals come out. The young lions roar while they hunt, looking for the food that God provides. When the sun rises, they go back and lie down in their dens. Then people go out to do their work and keep working until evening.

Lord, you have made so many things! How wisely you made them all! The earth is filled with your creatures. There is the ocean, large and wide, where countless creatures live, large and small alike. The ships sail on it, and in it plays Leviathan, that sea monster which you made.

All of them depend on you to give them food when they need it. You give it to them, and they eat it; you provide food, and they are satisfied.

Recall: Psalm 22:26, The meek ones will eat and be satisfied; those seeking him will praise Jehovah.

Recall: Isaiah 65:13a, Therefore this is what the Sovereign Lord Jehovah has said: "Look! My own servants will eat, but you yourselves [the organization of Jehovah's Witnesses] will go hungry."

Psalm 104 Good News Bible, continued, When you [Jehovah] turn away, they are afraid; when you take away their breath, they die and go back to the dust from which they came. But when you give them breath, they are created; you give new life to the earth.

May the glory of the Lord last forever! May the Lord be happy with what he has made! He looks at the earth, and it trembles; he touches the mountains, and they pour out smoke.

I will sing to the Lord all my life; as long as I live I will sing praises to my God. May he be pleased with my song, for my gladness comes from him. May sinners be destroyed from the earth; may the wicked be no more.

Praise the Lord, my soul! Praise the Lord!

Psalm 105 all verses, Good News Bible [abbreviated here], Give thanks to the Lord, proclaim his greatness; tell the nations what he has done. Sing praise to the Lord; tell the wonderful things he has done. **Be glad that we belong to him; let all who worship him rejoice.**

Recall: Isaiah 44:5, This one will say: "I belong to Jehovah." And that one will call himself by the name of Jacob, and another will write upon his hand: "Belonging to Jehovah." And by the name of Israel one will betitle himself.

Psalm 105 Good News Bible, continued, Go to the Lord for help; and worship him continually. You descendants of Abraham, his servant; you descendants of Jacob, the man he chose: remember the miracles that God performed and the judgments that he gave.

The Lord is our God; his commands are for all the world. He will keep his covenant forever, his promises for a thousand generations. He will keep the agreement he made with Abraham and his promise to Isaac. The Lord made a covenant with Jacob, one that will last forever. "I will give you the land [spiritual "land"] of Canaan," he said. "It will be your own possession."

God's people were few in number, strangers in the land of Canaan. They wandered from country to country, from one kingdom to another. But God let no one oppress them; to protect them, he warned the kings: "Don't harm my chosen servants; do not touch my prophets."

The Lord sent famine to their country and took away all their food. [Today, Jehovah has sent a famine on the organization of Jehovah's Witnesses by taking away all of their spiritual "food," because the "faithful and discreet slave," those appointed to "feed" Jehovah's sheeplike ones, did not remain faithful.] But he sent a man ahead of them, Joseph [Lisa, likened to Joseph], who had been sold as a slave. His feet were kept in chains, and an iron collar was around his neck,

Isaiah 52:2, Shake yourself free from the dust, rise up, take a seat, O Jerusalem. Loosen for yourself the bands on your neck, O captive daughter of Zion. [Jehovah directed me to leave the organization of Jehovah's Witnesses.]

Revelation 2:10, Do not be afraid of the things you are about to suffer. Look! The Devil will keep on throwing some of you into prison that you may be fully put to the test [as Job was fully put to the test], and that you may have tribulation ten days [I was a member of the organization for ten years.]. Prove yourself faithful even to death [disfellowshipping, by those taking the lead in the organization], and I will give you the crown of life. [I am approved by Jehovah.]

Psalm 105 Good News Bible, continued, until what he had predicted came true. The word of the Lord proved him right. [When Jehovah transferred his approval from the organization of Jehovah's Witnesses to me, I knew that the organization had lost Jehovah's holy spirit.] Then the king of Egypt had him released; the ruler of nations set him free. He put him in charge of his government and made him ruler over all the land,

Jeremiah 1:4, And the word of Jehovah began to occur to me, saying: "Before I was forming you in the belly I knew you, and before you proceeded to come forth from the womb I sanctified you. Prophet to the nations I made you [Lisa]."

Psalm 105 Good News Bible, continued, with power over the king's officials and authority to instruct his advisers.

Commissioned: [September 30, 1989, yesterday] Jeremiah 1:10, See, I have commissioned you [Lisa] this day to be over the nations and over the kingdoms, in order to uproot and to pull down and to destroy and to tear down, **to build and to plant.**

Recall: Isaiah 43:5, Do not be afraid, for I am with you. From the sunrising I shall bring **your seed**, and from the sunset I shall collect you together.

Psalm 105 Good News Bible, continued, Then Jacob went to Egypt and settled in that country. The Lord gave many children to his people [Several faithful worshippers of Jehovah in the organization at the time I was leaving tried to "hold on to me," fearing for my spiritual well-being if I were disfellowshipped by those taking the lead in the organization: Darell and Ronda, Lila, Robin, Tina, Ruth and others.]

Genesis 3:15, And I shall put enmity between you [Satan] and the woman and between your seed and her seed. He will bruise you in the head [a fatal blow] and you will bruise him in the heel [a blow that is not fatal].

Psalm 105 Good News Bible, continued, and made them stronger than their enemies [faithful worshippers of Jehovah, "the woman's seed," although still in the organization, are made stronger than Satan's seed because they have Jehovah's holy spirit.]. He made the Egyptians [those taking the lead in the organization] hate his people and treat his servants [faithful worshippers] with deceit. [The elders lied and used deceit to keep faithful ones from leaving the organization as I was leaving. Wayne J. lied to Tina O. so that she wouldn't believe Jehovah's denunciation. John G. lied to Dion S., saying: "There is nothing wrong with our congregation." And Wayne J. was saying to me: "There is nothing wrong. I don't know anything about what you are talking about." I replied to Wayne J.: "Wayne, are you saying, 'There is peace. There is peace.'?" I was referring to this scripture.]

Jeremiah 6:14, And they try to heal the breakdown of my people lightly, saying, "There is peace! There is peace!" when there is no peace.

Revelation 12:13-17, Now when the dragon saw that it was hurled down to the earth, it persecuted the woman that gave birth to the male child. But the two wings of the great eagle were given the woman, that she might fly into the wilderness to her place; there is where she is fed for a time and times and half a time away from the face of the serpent.
And the serpent disgorged water like a river from its mouth after the woman, to cause her to be drowned by the river. But the earth came to the woman's help, and the earth opened its mouth and swallowed up the river that the dragon disgorged from its mouth. And the dragon grew wrathful at the woman, and went off to wage war with the remaining ones of her seed, who observe the commandments of God and have the work of bearing witness to Jesus.

Psalm 105 Good News Bible, continued, Then he sent his servant Moses, and Aaron, whom he had chosen.

1 Chronicles 16:33 Good News Bible, The trees [faithful worshippers of Jehovah] in the woods will shout for joy before the Lord, when he comes to rule the earth.

Psalm 104:16, The trees of Jehovah are satisfied, the [faithful] cedars of Lebanon that he planted.

! 1 Chronicles 16:29 Good News Bible, Praise the Lord's glorious name; bring an offering and come into his Temple. Bow down before the Lord when he appears in his holiness.

Psalm 105 Good News Bible, continued, They did God's mighty acts and performed miracles in Egypt.
Then he led the Israelites out; they carried silver and gold [precious people of spiritual "silver" and "gold"], and all of them were healthy and strong. The Egyptians were afraid of them and were glad when they left. God put a cloud over his people and a fire at night to give them light. They asked, and he sent quails; he gave them food from heaven to satisfy them. He opened a rock, and water gushed out, flowing through the desert like a river. He remembered his sacred promise to Abraham his servant.
So he led his chosen people out, and they sang and shouted for joy. He gave them the lands of other peoples and let them take over their fields, so that his people would obey his laws and keep all his commands.
Praise the Lord!

Zechariah 6:8, And he proceeded to cry out to me and speak to me, saying: **"See, those going forth to the land of the north are the ones that have caused the spirit of Jehovah to rest in the land of the north."**

Encounter: [At an assembly earlier on, before Jehovah's favor was removed from the organization of Jehovah's Witnesses, I met one of the "anointed," Daniel Sydlik. Later, I wrote to him requesting information on a talk that he had given. When he wrote back, he mentioned that he distinctly remembered me from the assembly.

When I think about it now, I think what a tremendous loss to the "anointed," to lose Jehovah's holy spirit and all of the spiritual wisdom which was granted to be theirs. For their grievous sins, they lost the most precious of all blessings in life. And what is left to them is as nothing.

Their course would appear to parallel that of King Solomon's. Solomon had such great spiritual wisdom that even foreign rulers came to listen to him. But he took for himself many foreign wives who drew him away from the true worship of Jehovah, and consequently he lost his gift of wisdom from God.

Whether it is an outright act of aggression and persecution toward true worshippers, or it is the more subtle action of drawing away from the true worship of Jehovah, the results are the same. When one is not for Jehovah, one is against him. And without Jehovah's holy spirit one loses the wisdom to govern his people with love and justice.]

Luke 16:12,13a, And if you have not proved yourselves faithful [the unfaithful "faithful and discreet slave,"] in connection with what is another's [they are responsible for dispensing spiritual "food" from Jehovah to his "sheeplike" ones (Matthew 24:45)], **who will give you what is for yourselves** [heavenly life to rule as kings and priests, a privilege belonging only to the faithful 144,000 (Revelation 5:10)]? No house servant can be a slave to two masters; for, either he will hate the one and love the other, or he will stick to the one and despise the other.

[The unfaithful "faithful and discreet slave" of the organization of Jehovah's Witnesses may not openly or publicly despise God's people, but if they have left Jehovah in their heart, and consequently he has removed his holy spirit from them, then they no longer have the capacity to govern Jehovah's people wisely.]

Judges 5:24-27, Jael the wife of Heber the Kenite will be most blessed among women, among women in the tent she will be most blessed. Water he asked, milk she gave; in the large banquet bowl of majestic ones she presented curdled milk. Her hand to the tent pin she then thrust out, and her right hand to the mallet of hard workers. And she hammered Sisera, she pierced his head through, and she broke apart and cut up his temples. Between her feet he collapsed, he fell, he lay down; between her feet he collapsed, he fell; where he collapsed, there he fell overcome. [The woman, Jael, killed one of the Israelites most feared enemies.]

Genesis 3:15, And I shall put enmity between you [Satan] and the woman and between your seed and her seed. He will bruise you in the head and you will bruise him in the heel.

Isaiah 40:9, Make your way up even onto a high mountain, you woman bringing good news for Zion. Raise your voice even with power, you woman bringing good news for Jerusalem. Raise it. Do not be afraid. Say to the cities of Judah: "Here is your God."

Psalm 105:38, Good News Bible, continued, The Egyptians [apostate organization of Jehovah's Witnesses] were afraid of them [faithful worshippers of Jehovah still in the organization, getting ready to leave] and were glad when they left.

Judges 5:9-12a, Good News Bible, My heart is with the [faithful] commanders of Israel, with the people who gladly volunteered. Praise the Lord! Tell of it, you that ride on white donkeys, sitting on saddles

Recall: Zechariah 9:9, Be very joyful, O daughter of Zion. Shout in triumph, O daughter of Jerusalem. Look! Your king himself comes to you. He is righteous, yes, saved; humble, and riding upon an ass, even upon a full-grown animal the son of a she-ass.

Judges 5:9-12a Good News Bible, continued, and you that must walk wherever you go. Listen! The noisy crowds around the wells are telling of the Lord's victories, the victories of Israel's people!
Then the Lord's people marched down from their cities. Lead on, Deborah [an Israelite prophetess, likened to a spiritual "mother" in Israel], lead on!
Lead on! Sing a song! Lead on!

Judges 5:13,14a, Then the faithful ones came down to their leaders; the Lord's people came to him ready to fight. They came from Ephraim into the valley, behind the tribe of Benjamin and its people. The commanders came down from Machir, the officers down from Zebulun.

Jeremiah 4:5-7 Good News Bible, Blow the trumpet throughout the land! [The trumpet was blown at the Festival of Booths, also called the Festival of Ingathering.] **Shout loud and clear! Tell the people of Judah and Jerusalem [faithful worshippers of Jehovah still in the organization] to run to the fortified cities [away from apostate "Jerusalem," the organization, to faithful "Jerusalem"]. Point the way to Zion! Run for safety! Don't delay! The Lord is bringing disaster and great destruction from the north. Like a lion [true Judah comes like a lion, Leon] coming from its hiding place, a destroyer of nations has set out. He is coming to destroy [unfaithful] Judah. The [unfaithful] cities of Judah will be left in ruins, and no one will live in them.**

Proverbs 8:34 Good News Bible, The man who listens to me [wisdom speaking] will be happy—the man who stays at my door every day, waiting at the entrance to my home.

Proverbs 8:35 Good News Bible, The man who finds me [wisdom speaking] finds life, and the Lord will be pleased with him.

Proverbs 13:14 Good News Bible, The teachings of the wise are a fountain of life; they will help you escape when your life is in danger.

Recall: Zechariah 2:8, For this is what Jehovah of armies has said, "Following after the glory he has sent me to the nations that were despoiling you people; for he that is touching you is touching my eyeball."

Recall: Isaiah 6:13, Good News Bible, Even if one person out of ten remains in the land, he too will be destroyed; he will be like the stump of an oak tree that has been cut down. (The stump represents a new beginning for God's people.)

Psalms 105: 28, Good News Bible, continued, God sent darkness on the country [the apostate organization of Jehovah's Witnesses], but the Egyptians did not obey his command.

Jeremiah 4:23, I saw the land, and, look! it was empty and waste; and into the heavens, and their light was no more.

Isaiah 8:16-18, Good News Bible, You, my disciples, are to guard and preserve the messages that God has given me. The Lord has hidden himself from his [unfaithful] people, but I trust him and place my hope in him.

Here I am with the children the Lord has given me. The Lord Almighty, whose throne is on Mount Zion, has sent us as living messages to the people of Israel.

Isaiah 9:2 Good News Bible (1976), The people who walked in darkness have seen a great light. They [faithful worshippers of Jehovah] lived in a land of shadows [the organization has grown dark because they have lost Jehovah's light.], but now light is shining on them [the faithful ones].

Isaiah 9:6, For there has been a child born to us, there has been a son given to us; and the princely rule will come to be upon his shoulder. And his name will be called Wonderful Counselor, Mighty God, Eternal Father, Prince of Peace. [The primary fulfillment of this prophecy is found in Christ. There is a secondary (and therefore, lesser) fulfillment of this prophecy in the present day in Leon Wurzer.]

Isaiah 9:6,7, Good News Bible, A child is born to us! A son is given to us! And he will be our ruler. He will be called, "Wonderful Counselor,"

Recall: Zechariah 6:13, And he himself will build the temple of Jehovah, and he, for his part, will carry the dignity; and he must sit down and rule on his throne, and he must become a priest upon his throne, and the very **counsel** of peace will prove to be between both of them.

Isaiah 9:6,7 Good News Bible, continued, "Mighty God" [**mighty one** (Psalm 45:3,4)], Recall: Ephesians 3:16, To the end that he may grant you according to the riches of his glory to be made **mighty in the man you are inside** with power through his spirit.

Recall: Zechariah 4:14, Accordingly he said: "These are the two anointed **ones who are standing alongside** the Lord of the whole earth."

Isaiah 9:6,7, Good News Bible, continued, "Eternal Father," [A human replacement for the original human father, **Adam**, is Leon.]

Isaiah 9:6,7, Good News Bible, continued, "Prince of Peace."

Recall: Zechariah 6:13, And he himself will build the temple of Jehovah, and he, for his part, will carry the dignity; and he must sit down and rule on his throne, and he must become a priest upon his throne, and the very counsel of **peace** will prove to be between both of them.

Isaiah 9:6,7, Good News Bible, continued, His royal power will continue to grow; his kingdom will always be at peace. He will rule as King David's successor, basing his power on right and justice, from now until the end of time. The Lord Almighty is determined to do all this. [Christ rules Jehovah's kingdom from heaven. As one of the two anointed ones (Zechariah 4:14), Leon will be a human representative of Jehovah's authority on earth.]

Adam and Eve: [Eve led her husband out of obedience to Jehovah and into death. The replacement mother for Eve, Lisa Pressnall, leads her future husband and human replacement father for Adam, Leon Wurzer, into obedience to Jehovah.]

Recall: Isaiah 45:4-6, For the sake of my servant Jacob [Leon] and of Israel [Lisa] my chosen one, I even proceeded to call you by your name; I proceeded to give you [Leon] a name of honor, although you did not know me. **I am Jehovah, and there is no one else.** With the exception of me there is no God. I shall closely gird you, although you have not known me, in order that people may know from the rising of the sun and from its setting that there is none besides me. **I am Jehovah, and there is no one else.** [Leon, though not knowing Jehovah, is known to Jehovah, and will learn Jehovah's righteous ways and will come to walk in faith and truth.]

Isaiah 44:5, This one will say: "I belong to Jehovah." And that one [Leon] will call himself by the name of Jacob, and another [person] will write upon his hand: "Belonging to Jehovah." And by the name of Israel [Lisa] one will betitle himself. [In contrast to Adam, who lost his life, Leon will find his life, through the accurate knowledge of Jehovah and his son, Jesus Christ, and he will become a true worshipper of Jehovah.]

John 17:3, This means everlasting life, their taking in knowledge of you, the only true God, and of the one whom you sent forth, Jesus Christ.

[Jehovah has provided us with a human replacement for the human father, Adam, whom we lost to death. Through the person Jehovah has chosen to sit on an earthly throne as a human representative of the heavenly throne Jehovah has given to Jesus, Leon Wurzer will have the work of restoring the earth to a paradise condition where all faithful worshippers of Jehovah can live forever in peace.]

A Lion Cub Judah Is: Recall: Genesis 49:9, A lion cub Judah is. From the prey, my son, you will certainly go up. He bowed down, he stretched himself out like a lion and, like a lion, who dares rouse him? [In Greek, the word for lion is leon.]

→ Greek letters: (LEON)

λέων   [A sacred secret revealed.]

Leon Wurzer

Jeremiah 1:11,12 Good News Bible, The Lord asked me, "Jeremiah, what do you see?"
I answered, "A branch of an almond tree."
"You are right," the Lord said, "and I am watching to see that my words come true." [The word "watching" in Hebrew sounds like the Hebrew word for "almond."]
Proverbs 25:25 Good News Bible, Finally hearing good news from a distant land is like a drink of cold water when you are dry and thirsty.

Research: Aid to Bible Understanding WBTS, *Measuring Rope: The division of land in Israel was apportioned into plots of ground by a measuring rope.*

Zechariah 2:1-7, And I proceeded to raise my eyes and see; and, look! there was a man, and in his hand a measuring rope.

So I said: "Where are you going?"

In turn he said to me: "To measure Jerusalem, in order to see what her breadth amounts to and what her length amounts to."

And, look! the angel who was speaking with me was going forth, and there was another angel going forth to meet him. Then he said to him: "Run, speak to the young man [Leon] over there, saying, "'As open rural country Jerusalem will be inhabited, because of the multitude of men and domestic animals in the midst of her. And I myself shall become to her," is the utterance of Jehovah, "a wall of fire all around, and a glory is what I shall become in the midst of her.""'

"Hey there! Hey there! Flee, then, you people [faithful worshippers of Jehovah still in the organization], from the land of the north," is the utterance of Jehovah.

"For in the direction of the four winds of the heavens I have spread you people abroad," is the utterance of Jehovah.

"Hey there, Zion [Leon]! Make your escape, you who are dwelling with the daughter of Babylon."

Research: All Scripture Is Inspired of God and Beneficial, "Bible Book Number Twenty-four—Jeremiah," page 126, paragraph 15 WTBS (1963), ***The covenant breakers cursed*** *[subheading]*, Jeremiah 11:1—12:17 [abbreviated here]: *Judah,* [the apostate organization] *has disobeyed the words of its covenant with Jehovah. It is in vain for them to call for aid. Jeremiah must not pray for Judah*

[I must not pray for those in the organization.],

because Jehovah "has set a fire blazing" against this once luxuriant olive tree.

Jeremiah 11:16, "A luxuriant olive tree, pretty with fruit and in form," is what Jehovah has called your name. With sound of the great roaring, he has set a fire blazing against her [apostate organization], and they have broken its branches.

As Jeremiah's fellow citizens of Anathoth [a Levite city] conspire to destroy him, the prophet turns to Jehovah for strength and help. Jehovah promises vengeance on Anathoth. Jeremiah asks, Why is it that the way of the wicked has succeeded? Jehovah assures him: 'I will uproot and destroy the disobedient nation.'—12:17.

Research: Insight on the Scriptures, volume 2, page 551-2, [abbreviated here] **Olive:** *The olive tree is one of the most valuable trees in the land. It flourishes in tough, dry conditions and endures through frequent drought. It is a slow-growing tree, and may take 10 years or more to begin bearing a good harvest. It is also exceptionally long-lived. It bears fruit for hundreds of years.*

Recall: Isaiah 58:11,12, And Jehovah will be bound to lead you constantly and to satisfy your soul even in a scorched land, and he will invigorate your very bones; and you must become like a well-watered garden, and like the source of water, the waters of which do not lie. And at your instance men will certainly build up the places devastated a long time; you will raise up even the foundations of continuous generations. And you will actually be called the repairer of the gap, the restorer of roadways by which to dwell.

At Zechariah 4:3,11-14 and Revelation 11:3,4 olive trees are used as symbols of God's anointed ones and witnesses.
Olives are green in color when they are immature, and become black when they mature. Harvesting is done in October and November. The ancient method of beating the tree with rods is still in use. A good tree could supply oil for 5-6 persons. They are easy to plant and to graft. Grafting a branch into a garden tree is normal practice; grafting into a wild olive tree is abnormal. Jehovah's way was to graft a wild branch into a garden tree.

Romans 11:17,18a, However, if some of the branches [natural Israelites, of Abraham's seed] were broken off but you [gentiles, who became spiritual Israelites], although being a wild olive, were grafted in among them and became a sharer of the olive's root of fatness, do not be exulting over the branches. [When the good news was opened to the nations, gentiles were grafted in, and became sharers with the Christ. The unproductive "branches" of Abraham's seed, had been broken off. It is God's undeserved kindness to "wild olive branches" that they receive the "fatness" and goodness of the garden tree's (Christ's) roots.]

October 3, 1989

Advance Warning: [I was given advance warning from Jehovah, this time through Rosie. It came in the mail and it was bad news.]

Message: [Jehovah gave me these words in reference to Leon, who needs to come to me personally to put things right between us, "Maybe not today, maybe not tomorrow, but soon."]

October 4, 1989

Research: Insight on the Scriptures, volume 2, page 729, [abbreviated here] ***Rain:*** *The early rain, the beginning of the rainy season in Israel begins approximately mid-October.*

Message: [I was given the words, "Prepare to meet your master."]

Research: Insight on the Scriptures, volume 2, page 759, [abbreviated here] ***Rechabites:*** *Jeremiah tested the Rechabites. He offered them wine, which because of a command given to them by one of their ancestors, they appropriately refused. They were demonstrating their faithfulness, although dwelling at that time among unfaithful Judeans. Jehovah blessed them.*

Jeremiah 35:19, Therefore this is what Jehovah of armies, the God of Israel, has said: "There will not be cut off from Jonadab the son of Rechab a man to stand before me always."

The Rechabites are a family line related to the Kenites. Some of them were known as Midianites, related to Abraham through Keturah, not Sarah.

Zechariah 6:1 NWT, Then I raised my eyes again and saw; and, look! there were four chariots coming forth from between two mountains, and the mountains were copper mountains.
Zechariah 6:1 Good News Bible, I had another vision. This time I saw four chariots coming out from between two bronze mountains.

Ephesians 3:14-19, On account of this I bend my knees to the Father, to whom every family in heaven and on earth owes its name, to the end that he may grant you according to the riches of his glory to be made mighty in the man you [Lisa is likened to a man spiritually, because Jehovah has granted her strength of faith.] are inside with power through his spirit, to have the Christ dwell through your faith in your hearts with love; that you may be rooted and established on the foundation [the "garden olive tree," Christ; and Leon is a "wild branch," grafted in], in order that you may be thoroughly able to grasp mentally with all the holy ones what is the breadth and length and height and depth, and to know the love of the Christ which surpasses knowledge, that you may be filled with all the fullness that God gives.

Isaiah 54:14, You [Lisa] will prove to be firmly established in righteousness itself. You will be far away from oppression—for you will fear none—and from anything terrifying, for it will not come near you.

Jeremiah 1:11,12, And the word of Jehovah continued to occur to me, saying: "What are you seeing, Jeremiah?"
So I said: "An offshoot of an almond tree is what I am seeing."
And Jehovah went on to say to me: "You have seen well, for I am keeping awake concerning my word in order to carry it out." ["Almond tree" means, "awakening one." Leon is, spiritually speaking, an "awakening one."]

Jeremiah 1:12,13 Good News Bible, "You are right," the Lord said, "and I am watching to see that my words come true."
Then the Lord spoke to me again. "What else do you see?" he asked.
I answered, "I see a pot boiling in the north, and it is about to tip over this way."

Zechariah 4:2,3, Then he said to me: "What are you seeing?"
So I said: "I have seen, and, look! there is a lampstand, all of it of gold, with a bowl on top of it. And its seven lamps are upon it, even seven; and the lamps that are at the top of it have seven

pipes. And there are two olive trees alongside it, one on the right side of the bowl and one on its left side."

Research, continued: Insight on the Scriptures, volume 2, page 551-2, [abbreviated here] ***Olive:*** *Olive trees are used as symbols of God's anointed ones and witnesses. (Zechariah 4:3, 11-14; Revelation 11:3,4) The olive tree not only lives for centuries but, if cut down, will send up as many as six new shoots from its roots to develop into new trunks, and aged trees also will often perpetuate themselves this way.*

[Old age = long life. I keep seeing scriptures on growing old. In Rosie's Bible, she found: "I will carry you in old age, I will carry you always."]

Psalm 92:12-14, Good News Bible, The righteous will flourish like palm trees; they will grow like the cedars of Lebanon. They are like trees planted in the house of the Lord, that flourish in the Temple of our God, that still bear fruit in old age and are always green and strong.

Recall: Psalm 103:1-5, Bless Jehovah, O my soul, even everything within me, his holy name. Bless Jehovah, O my soul, and do not forget all his doings, him who is forgiving all your error, who is healing all your maladies, who is reclaiming your life from the very pit, who is crowning you with loving-kindness and mercies, who is satisfying your lifetime with what is good; your youth keeps renewing itself just like that of an eagle.

Psalm 91:16 Good News Bible, I will reward them with long life; I will save them. [Old age from Jehovah's perspective does not necessarily mean declining health. One who lives to the age of 1,000 years or more in the paradise earth will still be in perfect health. And we have the prospect of living forever.]

Research, continued: Insight on the Scriptures, volume 2, pages 551-2, [abbreviated here] ***Olive:*** *Figurative use of the olive tree in the Bible refers to fruitfulness, beauty and dignity. The branches of the tree were used in the Festival of Booths. Olive oil can also refer to Jehovah's light.*

Psalm 52:8, But I shall be like a luxuriant olive tree in God's house; I do trust in the loving-kindness of God to time indefinite, even forever.

Jeremiah 11:16, "A luxuriant olive tree, pretty with fruit and in form," is what Jehovah has called your [the organization's] name. With sound of the great roaring, he has set a fire blazing against her, and they have broken its branches [symbolically, "lopped off" unfaithful worshippers].

Hosea 14:6, His [faithful] twigs ["twigs of the olive trees" (Zechariah 4:11-14)] will go forth, and his dignity will become like that of the olive tree, and his fragrance will be like that of Lebanon.

Nehemiah 8:14,15, Then they found written in the law that Jehovah had commanded by means of Moses that the sons of Israel should dwell in booths during the festival in the seventh month, and that they should make proclamation and cause a call to pass throughout all their cities and throughout Jerusalem, saying: "Go out to the mountainous region and bring in olive leaves and the leaves of oil trees and myrtle leaves and palm leaves and the leaves of branchy trees to make booths, according to what is written."

Leviticus 23:40, And you must take for yourselves on the first day the fruit of splendid trees, the fronds of palm trees and the boughs of branchy trees and poplars of the torrent valley, and you must rejoice before Jehovah your God seven days.

Revelation 11:3,4, "And I will cause my two witnesses to prophesy a thousand two hundred and sixty days dressed in sackcloth." These are symbolized by the two olive trees and the two lampstands and are standing before the Lord of the earth.

Zechariah 4:9,10, The very hands of Zerubbabel [Leon] have laid the foundation of this house, and his own hands will finish it. And you will have to know that Jehovah of armies himself has sent me to you people. For who has despised the day of small things? And they will certainly rejoice and see the plummet [device for measuring verticality, "uprightness"] in the hand of Zerubbabel. These seven are the eyes of Jehovah. They are roving about in all the earth.

Isaiah 44:28, The One saying of Cyrus, "He is my shepherd, and all that I delight in he will completely carry out"; even in my saying of Jerusalem, "She will be rebuilt," and of the temple, "You will have your foundation laid."

A Lion Cub Judah Is: Recall: Genesis 49:9, A lion cub Judah is. From the prey, my son, you will certainly go up. He bowed down, he stretched himself out like a lion and, like a lion, who dares rouse him? [In Greek, the word for lion is leon.]

→   Greek letters: (LEON)

λέων

Leon Wurzer

Zechariah 4:11-14, And I proceeded to answer and say to him: "What do these two olive trees on the right side of the lampstand and on its left side mean?" Then I answered the second time and said to him: "What are the two bunches of twigs of the olive trees that, by means of the two golden tubes, are pouring forth from within themselves the golden liquid [Jehovah's light]?"
So he said to me: "Do you not really know what these things mean?"
In turn I said: "No, my lord."
Accordingly he said: "These are the two anointed ones who are standing alongside the Lord of the whole earth."

Two Olive Trees
(Two Bunches of Twigs of the Olive Trees)
Two Anointed Ones
"Sons of the Oil"
(Zechariah 4:11-14)

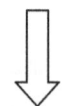

⇩ ⇩

Replacement of: First Father, Adam   First Mother, Eve
                    Is Leon   Is Lisa
              Lion of Judah (Greek: Leon)   Elisha (Greek: He*lisa*ie)

They are also the Staffs: Union   Pleasantness (Zech. 11)

In Prophetic Fulfillment

They are also: Judah   Israel (Zechariah 11)
                        Judah   Jerusalem (Zechariah 2)
                        Zion   Jerusalem (Zechariah 1)
                        Jacob   Israel (Isaiah 44)

They are: Jehovah's Faithful Witnesses (Isaiah 43)
They are also: The Faithful and Discreet Slave (Matthew 24)
They will: Feed and Enlighten Jehovah's "Sheep"
                Reunite the "Twelve Tribes"

Leon is also: Cyrus (Isaiah 44)
              Sprout (Zechariah 6)
              Zerubbabel (Zechariah 4)

Lisa is also: Jeshurun (Isaiah 44)
              Joshua (Zechariah 6)
            My Delight is in Her (Isaiah 62)
            Owned as a Wife (Isaiah 62)
            Shulammite (Song of Solomon 6)

Zechariah 4:7, Who are you [unfaithful "faithful and discreet slave," head of the apostate organization of Jehovah's Witnesses], O great mountain? Before Zerubbabel [Leon] you will become a level land. And he will certainly bring forth the headstone. There will be shoutings to it: "How charming! How charming!" [Interestingly, the lineage of Jesus through both his mother and his father converge and branch out again at Zerubbabel.]

Isaiah 40:4, Let every valley be raised up, and every mountain and hill be made low. And the knobby ground must become level land, and the rugged ground a valley plain.

Jeremiah 11:16, "A luxuriant olive tree, pretty with fruit and in form," is what Jehovah has called your [the apostate organization's] name. With sound of the great roaring, he has set a fire blazing against her, and they have broken its branches.

Zechariah 6:1,11-13, Then I raised my eyes again and saw; and, look! there were four chariots coming forth from between **two mountains**, and the mountains were copper mountains.
And you must take silver and gold and make a grand crown and put it upon the head of Joshua [Lisa] the son of Jehozadak the high priest. And you must say to him,
"'This is what Jehovah of armies has said: "Here is the man whose name is Sprout [Leon]. And from his own place he will sprout, and he will certainly build the temple of Jehovah. And he himself will build the temple of Jehovah, and he, for his part, will carry the dignity; and he must sit down and rule on his throne, and he must become a priest upon his throne, and the very counsel of peace will prove to be between **both of them**."'"
[Zerubbabel means "son of Babel," an illegitimate son, like a "wild olive branch" who is "grafted in" to the "garden tree," Jesus Christ.
"Zerubbabel," Leon, has never been a part of the organization of Jehovah's Witnesses. However, Zerubbabel of the Bible was a descendant of David.
"Sprout," also refers to Leon, who has only been spiritually "growing" a short time.]

Recall: Song of Solomon 2:13a, As for the fig tree, it has gained a mature color for its early figs; and the vines are abloom, they have given their fragrance.

Isaiah 28:16, Therefore this is what the Sovereign Lord Jehovah has said: "Here I am laying as a foundation in Zion a stone, a tried stone, the precious corner of a sure foundation." [Lisa is a tried stone, tested and proven faithful to Jehovah, for having been a part of the organization for a period of ten years, a full limit of time. Like Job, Lisa was fully tested by Satan and proven faithful to Jehovah.]

Revelation 2:10, Do not be afraid of the things you are about to suffer. Look! The Devil will keep on throwing some of you into prison [the apostate organization of Jehovah's Witnesses] that you may be fully put to the test, and that you may have tribulation ten days [ten years]. Prove yourself faithful even to death [disfellowshipping], and I will give you the crown [Lisa, "Joshua" of Zechariah 6:11 is given a crown] of life.

1 Peter 2:4-6, Coming to him as to a living stone, rejected, it is true, by men [Pharisees and others taking the lead in Jesus' day; governing body and others taking the lead in the organization of Jehovah's Witnesses in the present day], but chosen, precious, with God, you yourselves [including Lisa, "Joshua," the high priest of Zechariah 6:11] also as living stones are being built up a spiritual house for the purpose of a holy priesthood, to offer up spiritual sacrifices acceptable to God through Jesus Christ. For it is contained in Scripture: "Look! I am laying in Zion a stone, chosen, a foundation cornerstone, precious; and no one exercising faith in it will by any means come to disappointment."

Zechariah 12:3, And it must occur in that day that I shall make Jerusalem [Lisa] a burdensome stone to all the peoples. All those lifting it will without fail get severe scratches for themselves; and against her all the nations of the earth will certainly be gathered.

Isaiah 8:5-7a, Good News Bible (1976), The Lord spoke to me again. He said, "Because these people [apostate organization] have rejected the quiet waters of Shiloah Brook [Shiloah Brook is sometimes translated as Siloam] and tremble before King Rezin and King Pekah [other nations, instead of fearing Jehovah and placing their trust in him], I, the Lord, will bring the emperor of Assyria and all his forces to attack [unfaithful] Judah [the organization].

Zechariah 4:7b, And he will certainly bring forth the headstone ["head" also means source of wisdom]. There will be shoutings to it: "How charming! How charming!"

Zechariah 3:9, "For, look! the stone that I have put before Joshua [Lisa]! Upon the one stone there are **seven** eyes. Here I am engraving its engraving," is the utterance of Jehovah of armies, "and I will take away the error of that land in one day."

Zechariah 4:10, For who has despised the day of small things? And they will certainly rejoice and see the plummet [plummet = stone] in the hand of Zerubbabel [Leon]. These **seven** are the eyes of Jehovah. They are roving about in all the earth.

Revelation 5:6, And I saw standing in the midst of the throne and of the four living creatures and in the midst of the elders a lamb as though it had been slaughtered, having seven horns and **seven** eyes, which eyes mean the seven spirits of God that have been sent forth into the whole earth.

Zechariah 4:2, Then he said to me: "What are you seeing?"
So I said: "I have seen, and, look! there is a lampstand, all of it of gold, with a bowl on top of it. And its **seven** lamps are upon it, even **seven**; and the lamps that are at the top of it have seven pipes.

Lion Of Judah: [Greek: λέων = leon, meaning lion]

Revelation 5:5, But one of the elders says to me: "Stop weeping. Look! The Lion that is of the tribe of Judah, the root of David, has conquered so as to open the scroll and its **seven** seals."

Ecclesiastes 7:12, For wisdom is for a protection the same as money is for a protection; but the advantage of knowledge is that wisdom itself preserves alive its owners.

Isaiah 28:17, And I will make justice the measuring line and righteousness the leveling instrument; and the hail must sweep away the refuge of a lie, and the waters themselves will flood out the very place of concealment.

Zechariah 4:10b, These **seven** are the eyes of Jehovah. They are roving about in all the earth. [Nothing is hidden from Jehovah's eyes.]

[I have been told things before they happen, both good news and bad news. Jehovah has told me that I would be lied to and what the lie would be before it happened. I hate lies. I get physically ill when I am lied to. Perhaps I will be able to discern through Jehovah's holy spirit whether the speech of men is truthful as I hear it spoken.]

Recall: [The Statue of Liberty's spiritual symbolism: She is holding a lighted torch, and **seven** diadems are issuing from her forehead. She is holding stone tablets and is standing on broken shackles, symbolizing release from oppression.]

Song of Solomon 2:12, Blossoms themselves have appeared in the land, the very time of vine trimming has arrived, and the voice of the turtledove itself has been heard in our land.

Isaiah 18:5-7, For before the harvest, when the blossom comes to perfection and the bloom becomes a ripening grape, one must also cut off the sprigs with pruning shears and must remove the tendrils, must lop them off. They will be left all together for the bird of prey of the mountains and for the beast of the earth. And upon it the bird of prey will certainly pass the summer, and upon it even every beast of the earth will pass the harvesttime.

In that time a gift will be brought to Jehovah of armies, from a people drawn out and scoured, even from a people fear-inspiring everywhere, a nation of tensile strength and of treading down, whose land the rivers have washed away, to the place of the name of Jehovah of armies, Mount Zion.

Zechariah 4:10a, For who has despised the day of small things?
[When Jehovah begins a work, many times he begins by choosing an individual or a small number of individuals to whom he reveals his will. For example, only a few individuals were informed of God's will at the time Jehovah chose Abraham, telling him to take his family, Sarah and Lot included, and leave the house of his father and travel to a different country. Generations later, Abraham's descendants became a great nation, as God had promised. Likewise, the disciples of Jesus, including the twelve apostles, were few in number when they were first instructed in the new covenant for Christians. To faithfully obey God, they had to come out from under the authority of the Sanhedrin (Jewish leaders of the time). It was some time before thousands more became believers and followed their lead. **In both of these instances, while the ones who faithfully obeyed Jehovah's will were few in number and considered a "small thing," they faced the challenge of disbelief and ridicule from the majority, and were "despised" because their beliefs were not a widely held view.**

Today is another day of "small things." There are few in the organization at this time who believe Jehovah has chosen an individual to "bring good news of something better," which will require of them to make a decision to depart from the modern-day "Sanhedrin," the Watchtower Bible and Tract Society. (Isaiah 52:1-7)]

Isaiah 53:1,2, Who has put faith in the thing heard by us? And as for the arm of Jehovah, to whom has it been revealed? And he [Lisa] will come up like a twig before one, and like a root out of waterless land. No stately form does he have, nor any splendor; and when we shall see him, there is not the appearance so that we [faithful worshippers of Jehovah still in the organization] should desire him.

Isaiah 55:5, Look! A nation that you [Lisa] do not know you will call, and those of a nation who have not known you will run even to you, for the sake of Jehovah your God, and for the Holy One of Israel, because he will have beautified you.

Song of Solomon 6:4, You are [spiritually] beautiful, O girl companion of mine, like **Pleasant City**, comely like **Jerusalem**, awesome as companies gathered around banners.

Recall: Zechariah 11:7b, So I took for myself two staffs. The one I called **Pleasantness**, and the other I called Union, and I went shepherding the flock.

Song of Solomon 6:10, Who is this woman that is **looking down like the dawn,**
Recall: Revelation 21:2, I saw also the **holy city, New Jerusalem, coming down out of heaven** from God and prepared as a bride adorned for her husband.

Song of Solomon 6:10 continued, beautiful like the full moon, pure like the **glowing sun,**

Isaiah 60:19, For you the sun will no more prove to be a light by day, and for brightness the moon itself will no more give you light. And Jehovah must become to you **an indefinitely lasting light**, and your God your beauty.

Song of Solomon 6:10 continued, awesome

Isaiah 60:2, For, look! darkness itself will cover the earth, and thick gloom the national groups; but upon you **Jehovah will shine forth**, and upon you his own glory will be seen.

Song of Solomon 6:10 continued, as companies gathered around banners?

Song of Solomon 6:13, "Come back, come back, O Shulammite! Come back, come back, that we may behold you!"
"What do you people behold in the Shulammite?"

"Something like the dance of two camps [the heavenly camp of God, a company of angels; and the earthly camp of true worshippers]!"

Recall: [I was given the message: "Prepare to meet your master."]

Research: Insight on the Scriptures, volume 2, page 342, **Marriage:** *The husband is the lord, the master of his household. He* *is the owner of his wife.* [It is not at all a difficult thing for me to accept Jehovah as my master, as he is my God and also my husbandly owner. I am so wonderfully honored. His wisdom is perfect, and he is always fair and kind.]

Isaiah 62:4, No more will you be said to be a woman left entirely, and your own land will no more be said to be desolate; but you yourself will be called My Delight Is in Her, and your own land Owned as a Wife. For Jehovah will have taken delight in you, and your own land will be owned as a wife.

[It may be very difficult for me to adjust to being "owned as a wife" by Leon. I have been married twice before, and both times I felt like a prisoner, not a wife. This time I will be entering the covenant of marriage knowing that this is sanctified by Jehovah, and therefore an unbreakable vow.

My fear runs very deep that I will again feel like a prisoner in marriage. I have always been independent. The years I was single were so much more peaceful than the years I was married. Both of my ex-husbands were abusive. Kindness and respect are not things I have encountered often in my life.

Over the years Jehovah has taught me and helped me to refine my personality, and I have learned how to respond to difficult situations. Still, there are times when this has been very, very challenging. How will I respond to Leon if I feel I am not being treated with respect and kindness?

Jehovah is teaching and helping Leon to refine his personality, correcting him as he has corrected me. And Jehovah has assured me that Leon will come to my face and acknowledge the wrongs he has done to me and put things right between us.

I have to remind myself that I did not conform to the Christian personality before I learned Jehovah's ways. And even after I had learned Jehovah's ways, I still committed a horrible sin. I needed to be corrected by Jehovah and grow to spiritual maturity.

Leon will learn and grow to spiritual maturity, as I did. It helps to recall the scripture Jehovah gave me in reference to Leon.]

Colossians 2:9, Because it is in him [Leon] that all the fullness of the divine quality dwells bodily. [I am being reassured by Jehovah that Leon has a capacity for great goodness, and like Christ, he will express kindness and even gentleness toward others.

At this time Leon is, as it were, a "diamond in the rough." Although it was nothing that I could readily observe in the way I was treated by Leon in the past, I know that since Jehovah has been able to successfully transform my personality to conform to the Christ, he can do the same with Leon.

My confidence in Leon only comes from Jehovah's faithful promises to me that someday I will see the changes in him. Somehow, I will be able to comply with the requirement of me from Jehovah, when he gave me this scripture in reference to my relationship with Leon.] Psalm 45:11b, The Living Bible, Paraphrased, Reverence him, for he is your lord.

Research: Insight on the Scriptures, volume 1, page 552, **Crown:** *The crown is a symbol of authority.*

Isaiah 62:3, And you must become a crown of beauty in the hand of Jehovah, and a kingly turban in the palm of your God.

Recall: Jeremiah 1:10, See, I have commissioned you this day to be over the nations and over the kingdoms, in order to uproot and to pull down and to destroy and to tear down, to build and to plant. [I have been given this authority from Jehovah.]

The crown also symbolizes dignity, power, honor, and reward.

Isaiah 43:4, Owing to the fact that you have been precious in my eyes, you [Lisa] have been considered honorable, and I myself have loved you. And I shall give men in place of you, and national groups in place of your soul.

Recall: Isaiah 40:10, Look! The Sovereign Lord Jehovah himself will come even as a strong one, and his arm will be ruling for him. Look! His reward is with him, and the wage he pays is before him.

Isaiah 61:8, For I, Jehovah, am loving justice, hating robbery along with unrighteousness. And I will give their wages in trueness, and an indefinitely lasting covenant I shall conclude toward them.

Diadem = a headband type of crown; some diadems are made of silver and gold. Rediated diadem = points all around running out from the headband like rays; a diadem can pertain to a thing singled out or dedicated, like a priest.

Recall: [Lisa: Consecrated to God]

Zechariah 6:14, And the grand crown itself will come to belong to Helem and to Tobijah and to Jedaiah and to Hen the son of Zephaniah as a memorial in the temple of Jehovah.

Isaiah 22:21, And I will clothe him [Leon] with your [the unfaithful "faithful and discreet slave's" (Matthew 24:45-51)] robe, and your sash I shall firmly bind about him, and your dominion I shall give into his hand; and **he must become a father** to the inhabitant of Jerusalem and to the house of Judah [faithful worshippers of Jehovah].

Acts 20:22-24, And now, look! bound in the spirit, I am journeying to Jerusalem, although not knowing the things that will happen to me in it, except that from city to city the holy spirit repeatedly bears witness to me as it says that bonds and tribulations are waiting for me. Nevertheless, I do not make my soul of any account as dear to me, if only I may finish my course and the ministry that I received of the Lord Jesus, to bear thorough witness to the good news of the undeserved kindness of God.
[Jehovah is indicating to me through his holy spirit that I will be experiencing trials shortly. I fervently pray that whatever comes up I will prove faithful to Jehovah. I pray that I do not in any way disappoint him.]

Message: [I was given this message from Jehovah in reference to my concern for the desperate circumstances that many in this world are facing, especially the children: "I am pleased with your compassion."]

Matthew 11:25,26, At that time Jesus said in response: "I publicly praise you, Father, Lord of heaven and earth, because you have hidden these things from the wise and intellectual ones [unfaithful "faithful and discreet slave"] and have revealed them to babes [young or "gentle" ones]. Yes, O Father, because to do thus came to be the way approved by you."

Research: Insight on the Scriptures, volume 1, page 773, **Exclusive Devotion:** Recall: Song of Solomon 8:6,7, "Place me as a seal upon your heart, as a seal upon your arm; because love is as strong as death is, insistence on exclusive devotion is as unyielding as Sheol is. Its blazings are the blazings of a fire, the flame of Jah. Many waters themselves are not able to extinguish love, nor can rivers themselves wash it away. If a man would give all the valuable things of his house for love, persons would positively despise them."

[I was led by holy spirit to research Exclusive Devotion and Marriage. The Shulammite maiden's insistence on exclusive devotion from her "dear one" is precisely mine. My feelings toward Leon require, even demand, his exclusive devotion to me when we are married.

→ *Exclusive Devotion = highest loyalty, fidelity, integrity*

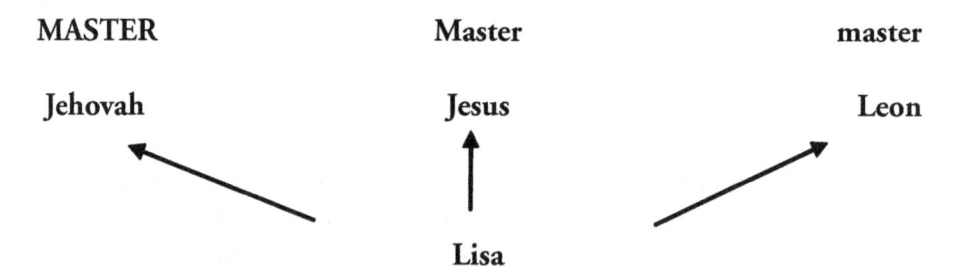

MASTER	**Master**	master
Jehovah	**Jesus**	Leon

Lisa

In ranked order, I am **accountable** to:
Jehovah, my God, the Rock of my heart
Jesus, my King, my Brother
Leon, my future husband, my lord
(Psalm 45:11b Living Bible, Paraphrased)

Research, continued: ***Exclusive Devotion:***
    a. *will not tolerate rivalry*
    b. *demonstrates a proper kind of jealousy*
    c. *expresses loyalty, fidelity*
    d. *is zealous to defend, (Jehovah toward Israel, as husbandly owner, is full of ardor [intensity] in her defense)*
    e. *honors the position held by that person*
    f. *loves uniquely, in a class by itself*

Jehovah's Desire: [Jehovah desires a unique relationship of exclusive devotion from each of us. He desires our heartfelt response of loyal love for him to be given of our own free will, and in all earnestness.

Jehovah has given me everything that I am and have, but my **free will** from Jehovah is **my freedom to decide**. I desire to honor Jehovah in all of my actions, thoughts and words. I desire to always maintain integrity. I love Jehovah with my whole heart, my whole soul and my whole mind. I have freely decided to give Jehovah my exclusive devotion. (Matthew 22:37)]

Research: Insight on the Scriptures, volume 1, page 1258, *Jealousy: Definition: [Appropriate Jealousy] Exclusive devotion, ardor, defense of object of love. Jehovah is jealous for his name—what it represents: holiness, majesty. He is devoted to righteousness. We can trust that he will carry all plans to righteous completion.*

As a husband jealously protects his wife as precious to him, Jehovah is likewise jealous for what is his.

Recall: Zechariah 2:8, For this is what Jehovah of armies has said, "Following after the glory he has sent me to the nations that were despoiling you people; **for he that is touching you is touching my eyeball.**" [Jehovah shows his zeal in behalf of his people. He also shows zeal against those defaming his holy name.]

Zechariah 4:8,9, And the word of Jehovah continued to occur to me, saying: "The very hands of Zerubbabel [Leon] have laid the foundation of this house, and his own hands will finish it. And you will have to know that Jehovah of armies himself has sent me to you people."

Psalm 138:8a, Jehovah himself will complete what is in my behalf.

Zechariah 4:10a, For who has despised the day of small things? [Lisa, as an individual, is a "small thing."] And they will certainly rejoice and see the plummet in the hand of Zerubbabel [Leon]. [Leon will rebuild the foundation of our relationship with each other by learning Jehovah's righteous ways.]

Definition: **Plummet**, a stone fastened to a string or cord. It is an instrument to measure verticality, straightness, ["uprightness"] of a physical structure [or a spiritual "structure"].

[The "plummet," a stone, is in the hand of "Zerubbabel," Leon. (Zechariah 4:10a)] Zechariah 3:9a, For, look! the stone that I have put before Joshua [Lisa].

Highest Attributes of Jehovah (in descending order):

        Love: **Jehovah** represents Love
        Wisdom: **Jesus** represents Wisdom
        Justice: Leon represents Justice
        Power: Lisa represents Power

[God is **Love**. Jesus is **Wisdom** personified. Leon is standing in the position of **Justice**. I am standing in the last position, **Power**. Recall: I was given this message, "She has the power."

There can be no wisdom without love; there can be no justice without wisdom and love; there can be no power without justice, wisdom and love.]

October 7, 1989

Philemon 15-17, Perhaps really on this account he [Leon] broke away for an hour, that you [Lisa] may have him back forever, no longer as a slave but as more than a slave, as a brother beloved, especially so to me [Jehovah], yet how much more so to you both in fleshly relationship and in the Lord. If, therefore, you consider me a sharer, receive him kindly the way you would me.

Recall: Jeremiah 49:19, Look! Someone [Leon] will come up just like a lion from the proud thickets along the Jordan to the durable abiding place, but in a moment I will make **him** run away from her [Lisa]. And the one who is chosen [Leon] I shall appoint over her. For who is like me, and who will challenge me, and who, now, is the shepherd that can stand before me?

Jeremiah 50:44, Look! Someone will come up just like a lion from the proud thickets along the Jordan to the durable abiding place, but in a moment I shall make **them** run away from her. And the one who is chosen I shall appoint over her. For who is like me, and who will challenge me, and who, now, is the shepherd that can stand before me?

→ Psalm 16:5, Jehovah is the portion of my allotted share and of my cup. You [Jehovah] are holding fast my lot [Leon]. [Jehovah is my portion, Leon is my lot. Jehovah has assured me that he is holding fast to Leon's heart toward me during this time of separation.]

Zechariah 9:11,12, Also, you, O woman, by the blood of your covenant I will send your prisoners out of the pit in which there is no water.
Return to the stronghold, you prisoners of the hope. [Jehovah is the stronghold of my life. (Psalm 27:1)
Also, today I am telling you, "I shall repay to you, O woman [Lisa], a double portion." [The double portion I will receive from Jehovah is my sanctified relationship with **two kings**. Jehovah is my spiritual husbandly owner, and Leon will someday be my husband.]

Research: Insight on the Scriptures, volume 1, page 1258, *Jealousy, continued: Jehovah is jealous for his own righteousness. Jehovah demonstrated a change in his dealings with the Jewish nation when they rejected the Messiah. He transferred his approval and favor from Jerusalem to the Christian congregation, demonstrated by signs and portents and powerful works.*

[In the present day, Jehovah transferred his approval and favor from the organization to an individual, the messenger of the covenant. (Malachi 3:1) Faithful worshippers of Jehovah will join the messenger of Jehovah and we will all be built up into the household of God.]

In Jesus' day, although he opened the way for the gentiles, Jehovah did not completely shut the door for natural Israelites, hoping to incite them to jealousy over the great things he was doing for the Christian congregation, and thus provoking the Jews to seek him there.

[Likewise, today the organization will envy Jehovah's great works he will do for us, because they will feel that what we have should belong to them. Jehovah's works will, hopefully, provoke those in the organization to seek him here.]

Recall: Psalm 68:16, Why do you, O you mountains of peaks, keep watching enviously the mountain that God has desired for himself to dwell in? Even Jehovah himself will reside there forever. [The organization will watch with envy the "mountain" of Jehovah, spiritual "Mount Zion," Lisa, a newly designated human representative of his heavenly government. By reason of the organization's false step, "seventy years of insincere fasting" since 1919, they have lost Jehovah's favor and approval. They have lost his holy spirit. And because of their grievous false step, Jehovah has opened the way to the nations for them to come into a right relationship with God, as he did in Jesus' day, when he opened the way to the Gentiles (non-Jews).

Also, although they had lost Jehovah's favor, he still left the way open for unbelieving Jews in Jesus' day. Likewise, today Jehovah will keep the way open for unbelievers within the organization.]

Revelation 3:8, I know your deeds—look! I have set before you [Lisa] an opened door, which no one can shut—that you have a little power, and you kept my word and did not prove false to my name. [Jehovah has given me a small opening in a door, and left the way open for faithful worshippers to seek Jehovah and find him.

Rosie and her children have left the organization and come to Jehovah. Rosie's friend recognized the organization of Jehovah's Witnesses as being Babylon the Great from reading the denunciation. Beverly F. and her daughter, Jennifer F., wrote and thanked me for helping them strengthen their faith in Jehovah during their difficult times. And Bram, my son, recognized the hand of Jehovah on us when we were instructed to leave the organization.]

Isaiah 54:13, And all your sons will be persons taught by Jehovah, and the peace of your sons will be abundant.

Also, Isaiah 60:21, And as for your people, all of them will be righteous; to time indefinite they will hold possession of the land, the sprout of my planting, the work of my hands, for me to be beautified.

Anointed: [The "two anointed ones" of Zechariah 4:14 and the "two witnesses" of Revelation 11:3,4 are Leon and Lisa.

Two Anointed Ones (Zechariah 4:14)
Two Witnesses (Revelation 11:3,4)

```
         /              \
        ↙                ↘
      Leon              Lisa
Replacement for Adam    Replacement for Eve
     A King            A Mother
```

Using these two people, Jehovah will bring his work full circle to reverse the effects sin has brought to the earth.]

Psalm 45:9b, The queenly consort [Lisa] has taken her stand at your right hand in gold of Ophir.

Definition: **Consort,** One who shares a common lot, conjunction, association; unite, associate, accord.

Psalm 133:1, Look! How good and how pleasant it is for brothers to dwell together in unity!

Psalm 133:1, Good News Bible, How wonderful it is, how pleasant, for God's people to live together in harmony!

Research: [In his book, "Thirty Years a Watchtower Slave," (1971), W.J. Schnell makes the point that no good can result when the leader of a people is manipulative and his tactics are overbearing. He was referring to Rutherford.]

John 13:35, By this all will know that you are my disciples, if you have love among yourselves.
[This scripture describes how to identify true worshippers of Jehovah. Because the organization of Jehovah's Witnesses mistreat Jehovah's "sheeplike" ones, their own abusive actions prove that they do not have the true religion. Those taking the lead cannot have love among themselves when truth is smothered by lies and the weak are oppressed.]

Recall: The Truth that Leads to Eternal Life, Chapter 14 WBTS (1968), "How to Identify the True Religion," 2 Timothy 3:1-5, But know this, that in the last days critical times hard to deal with will be here. For men will be lovers of themselves, lovers of money, self-assuming, haughty, blasphemers, disobedient to parents, unthankful, disloyal, having no natural affection, not open to any agreement, slanderers, without self-control, fierce, without love of goodness, betrayers, headstrong, puffed up with pride, lovers of pleasures rather than lovers of God, **having a form of godly devotion but proving false to its power; and from these turn away.**

[Jehovah's Witnesses claim to be the true religion, but they have proved false to Jehovah's power of love and righteousness through their lies and oppression. Instead, by their own actions, they prove to be the ones we should turn away from. **Jehovah publicly denounces Jehovah's Witnesses.**]

Isaiah Chapter 5:1-7, Good News Bible, Listen while I [Lisa] sing you this song, a song of my friend [Jehovah] and his vineyard: My friend had a vineyard on a very fertile hill. He dug the soil and cleared it of stones; he planted the finest vines. He built a tower [Watchtower Society] to guard them, dug a pit for treading the grapes. He waited for the grapes to ripen, but every grape was sour.

So now my friend [Jehovah] says, "You people who live in [unfaithful] Jerusalem and [unfaithful] Judah, judge between my vineyard and me. Is there anything I failed to do for it? Then why did it produce sour grapes and not the good grapes I expected?

"Here is what I am going to do to my vineyard [the organization of Jehovah's Witnesses]: I will take away the hedge around it, break down the wall that protects it, and let wild animals eat it and trample it down. I will let it be overgrown with weeds. I will not trim the vines or hoe the ground; instead, I will let briers and thorns [lies] cover it. I will even forbid the clouds to let rain [spiritual wisdom through his holy spirit] fall on it."

Israel [the organization of Jehovah's Witnesses which apostatized from Jehovah] is the vineyard of the Lord Almighty; the people of Judah [the "faithful and discreet slave" who became unfaithful] are the vines he planted. **He expected them to do what was good, but instead they committed murder. He expected them to do what was right, but their victims cried out for justice.**

Jeremiah 17:13, O Jehovah, the hope of Israel, all those who are leaving you will be put to shame. Those apostatizing from me will be written down [denounced in writing] even in the earth, because they have left the source of living water, Jehovah. [Although I was labeled an apostate and disfellowshipped by those taking the lead in the organization, the truth is that they are the apostates. And because Jehovah has transferred his approval and favor to me from them, the truth is that they have apostatized from me.]

Persecution: [I was praying to Jehovah because I did not want to be angry with those who have persecuted me. Persecution goes beyond making a mistake that inadvertently causes harm. Persecution is the willful intent on the part of one person to cause suffering to another who is doing good, **especially because he is doing good.** And it is not at all the same as the appropriate suffering one experiences at the hand of a person in authority as a consequence for wrongdoing.

Some of the people who actually persecuted me are in the organization, but there are others who are not. I do not want to have anger or resentment toward any of them.]

Recall: [Joseph wept and forgave his brothers for selling him into slavery, because he understood that he had been sent ahead of them by Jehovah, to procure salvation for his family.]

Genesis 45:1-5, At this Joseph was no longer able to control himself before all those who were stationed by him. So he cried out: "Have everybody go out from me!" And no one else stood with him while Joseph made himself known to his brothers.

And he began to raise his voice in weeping, so that the Egyptians got to hear it and Pharaoh's house got to hear it. Finally Joseph said to his brothers: "I am Joseph. Is my father still alive?" But his brothers were unable to answer him at all, because they were disturbed by reason of him. So Joseph said to his brothers: **"Come close to me, please."** With that they came close to him.

Then he said: "I am Joseph your brother, whom you sold into Egypt. But now do not feel hurt and do not be angry with yourselves because you sold me here; because for the preservation of life God has sent me ahead of you."

Psalm 142:4, Look to the right hand and see that there is no one giving any recognition to me. My place for flight has perished from me; there is no one inquiring for my soul.

1 Peter 5:6, Humble yourselves, therefore, under the mighty hand of God, that he may exalt you in due time.

Psalm 87:2, Jehovah is more in love with the gates of Zion than with all the tabernacles of Jacob.

Hebrews 1:9, You loved righteousness, and you hated lawlessness. That is why God, your God, anointed you with the oil of exultation more than your partners.

1 Peter 2:4,5, Coming to him as to a living stone, rejected, it is true, by men, but chosen, precious, with God, you yourselves also as living stones are being built up a spiritual house for the purpose of a holy priesthood, to offer up spiritual sacrifices acceptable to God through Jesus Christ.

Psalm 133:1 NWT, Look! How good and how pleasant it is for brothers to dwell together in unity!
Psalm 133:1 Good News Bible, How wonderful it is, how pleasant, for God's people to live together in harmony!

Isaiah 48:20a, Go forth, you people [faithful worshippers of Jehovah still in the organization], out of Babylon [Babylon the Great, the great harlot, the organization of Jehovah's Witnesses]! Run away from the Chaldeans. Tell forth even with the sound of a joyful cry, cause this to be heard. Make it to go forth to the extremity of the earth.

Zechariah 9:12, Return to the stronghold, you prisoners of the hope.
Also, today I am telling you, "I shall repay to you, O woman, a double portion."
Isaiah 51:14, The one [Leon] stooping in chains will certainly be loosened speedily, that he may not go in death to the pit and that his bread may not be lacking.

Jeremiah 31:9, With weeping they will come, and with their entreaties for favor I shall bring them. I shall make them walk to torrent valleys of water, in a right way in which they will not be caused to stumble. For I have become to Israel a Father; and as for Ephraim, he is my firstborn.

Research: Insight on the Scriptures, volume 1, page 826, ***Festival of the Trumpet Blast:*** *This corresponds with the first day of the seventh month, Tishri, approximately September 15th (Ethanim), a special month.*

October 7/8, 1989 Midnight

Event: [Jehovah asked for permission from me to "read" my life like a "book" to Leon. It was a request, not a requirement, and I know that I had the free will to decide. I could have said "no" and Jehovah would have honored my decision. I cannot imagine saying anything but "yes" to any request from Jehovah. His wisdom and insight are perfect, and everything he does is for a good reason.

Then I felt as though my life was being "opened" like a book by Jehovah and "read" to Leon.]

Revelation 5:5,12a, But one of the elders says to me: "Stop weeping. Look! The Lion that is of the tribe of Judah, the root of David, has conquered so as to open the scroll and its seven seals."

Saying with a loud voice: "The Lamb that was slaughtered is worthy." [Jesus is truly the Lamb of God, and the primary fulfillment of this prophecy is found in him. Secondarily to Christ, Leon suffers and is pained to the point of death, and "slaughtered" by haters of Jehovah.]

Research, continued: ***Festival of the Trumpet Blast:*** *No sort of laborious work is done during this festival. This festival saw the beginning of the new agricultural and labor year. The Day of Atonement is on the 10th of this month, and the Festival of Booths is on the 15th. There is a completion of the major part of ingathering of crops this month, including grapes—which makes the heart of man rejoice, olives—which supplies food and light, and is connected with the grain offering. The Festival of the Trumpet Blast marked the start of a month of thankfulness to Jehovah.*

Research: Insight on the Scriptures, volume 1, page 822, ***The Festival of Booths:*** *This festival is also called the Festival of Tabernacles, or of Ingathering, or is sometimes called "the festival of Jehovah."*

Recall: [On October 1st, I read this scripture.] Isaiah 9:6a, For there has been a child born to us, there has been a son given to us; and the princely rule will come to be upon his shoulder. [Jesus fulfilled this prophecy. There is a secondary and lesser fulfillment of this prophecy in Leon, a secondary and lesser king under Christ the King.]

Ethanim Tishri 15th-21st is roughly October 1-7. On the 8th day there is a solemn assembly.

[Tishri 22nd, October 7/8, Jehovah opened my life like a book and I was "read" to Leon. And, as when Jehovah directed me in June of 1989, I was told in advance of this event to do a preparatory "cleansing" spiritually, mentally and physically. Then, my heart and my mind were "opened" like a book by Jehovah to show Leon what my life had been like.

I prayed that Jehovah would let Leon see the whole truth. I wanted Leon to understand that from early on I had been targeted by Satan. I was targeted the same way as many other people are, especially children, because Satan can see that we really want to learn the difference between right and wrong from God, and Jehovah is readily teaching us.

The first message I received from Jehovah was when I was five years old. I was standing out in the yard by my home, thinking and trying to make sense of the abusive behavior of my adoptive father, when I heard the words, "There is a God. He sees what is going on, and he doesn't like it."

These words have been a tremendous source of strength and comfort to me over the years. And, they clearly established to me the existence of a loving God who hates wrongdoing. From this, I knew that God was going to "make things right" someday.

In the meantime, Satan found ways to isolate me from the people who might have intervened in my behalf to protect me from those who inflicted deliberate injury and harm. So, this night I prayed that Jehovah would show Leon how I had conquered the hatred and violence surrounding me with the truth and goodness of Jehovah's loving ways.]

Isaiah 33:17, Good News Bible, Once again you will see a king ruling in splendor over a land that stretches in all directions.

Recall: 2 Timothy 2:6, The hardworking farmer [Jehovah] must be the first to partake of the fruits [Leon's "fruitage" of the spirit as he grows in spiritual maturity and wisdom].

Recall: [September 30th I was given authority.]

Jeremiah 1:10, See, I have commissioned you this day to be over the nations and over the kingdoms, in order to uproot and to pull down and to destroy and to tear down, to build and to plant.

Research, continued: **Festival of Booths:** *The beginning of the new agricultural year is October 1st. The Festival of Booths marked the end of an important time of year. It was a time of rejoicing and thankfulness for all the blessings from Jehovah. Because the Day of Atonement was five days earlier, people have a sense of peace with Jehovah at this time. The males of the families were required to dwell in booths for all seven days. But because it was a joyous occasion whole families would come. The booths were constructed in the courts of the temple, using the leaves of splendid trees (palm, poplar, olive). One reason for dwelling in booths was to emphasize equality among them before Jehovah. Tishri 14th was a day of preparation.*

Recall: [I was told to prepare.]
The Israelites awaited the sound of the trumpet blast. The sacrifices offered at this time were greater than on other occasions.

[Nisan was formerly the 7th month of the year, and was made the 1st month of the year after the Israelites left Egypt. Now Tishri is the 7th month. Tishri 22nd = October 8th, a day of solemn assembly.]

Research: Insight on the Scriptures, volume 2, page 937, **Shulammite:** Cross-reference: volume 1, page 26, **Abishag:** *The Shulammite maiden was from the town of Shunem. She was beautiful* *in the extreme. When King David was seventy years old, she was his nurse and companion in his old age.*

Recall: 2 John 1,2, The older man [Jehovah] to the chosen lady [Lisa] and to her children, whom I truly love, and not I alone, but all those also who have come to know the truth, because of the truth that remains in us, and it will be with us forever. [The older man, Jehovah, is "husbandly owner" of a "companion," Lisa. David was seventy years old when the Shulammite became his companion, and it was in the end times, or later times, when Jehovah, as an "older man," became the "husbandly owner" of Lisa.]

The Shulammite maiden's faith refreshes the holy ones. At night she lies at King David's bosom to keep him warm.

[Abraham, Jehovah's friend, was in a bosom position to him. I have been called "Friend" by Jehovah.]

The Shulammite held the position of wife or concubine to David, but the king himself had no intercourse with her. As she was considered the king's wife, the property of David,

[Lisa, "belonging to Jehovah" (Isaiah 44:5)]
she would become the property of the succeeding king [lesser king, Leon].

Recall: I was given the message: "Prepare to meet your master."

Recall: Psalm 45:11b, Living Bible Paraphrased (1971), Reverence him, for he is your lord.
Research, continued: **Festival of Booths,** *On the 8th day of the festival there were several sacrifices: one bull, one ram, seven male lambs one year old, and grain and drink offerings. The temple built by Solomon was inaugurated at this time and twenty-four divisions of priests determined by David began to serve. The law was read.*

[Lisa was "read" like a book to Leon on this date.]

Zechariah 3:5, At that I said: "Let them put a clean turban upon his [Lisa's] head." And they proceeded to put the clean turban upon his head and to clothe him with garments; and the angel of Jehovah was standing by.

[The distinguishing mark of the festival is joyful thanksgiving. I have been praising Jehovah because he lifts up my spirit when I am downhearted.]

Psalms 113-118, Psalm 113 all verses, Praise Jah, you people! Offer praise, O you servants of Jehovah, praise the name of Jehovah. May Jehovah's name become blessed from now on and to time indefinite. From the rising of the sun until its setting Jehovah's name is to be praised. Jehovah has become high above all the nations; his glory is above the heavens. Who is like Jehovah our God, him who is making his dwelling on high? He is condescending to look on heaven and earth, raising up the lowly one from the very dust; he exalts the poor one from the ashpit itself, to make him sit with nobles, with the nobles of his people. He is causing the barren woman to dwell in a house as a joyful mother of sons. Praise Jah, you people!

Psalm 114 all verses, When Israel went forth from Egypt, the house of Jacob from a people speaking unintelligibly, Judah became his holy place, Israel his grand dominion. The sea itself saw and took to flight; as for the Jordan, it began to turn back. The mountains themselves skipped about like rams, the hills like lambs. What was the matter with you, O sea, that you took to flight, O Jordan, that you began to turn back? O mountains, that you went skipping about like rams; O hills, like lambs? Because of the Lord be in severe pains, O earth, because of the God of Jacob, who is changing the rock into a reedy pool of water, a flinty rock into a spring of water.

Psalm 115 all verses, [abbreviated here], To us belongs nothing, O Jehovah, to us belongs nothing, but to your name give glory according to your loving-kindness, according to your trueness. Why should the nations say: "Where, now, is their God?" But our God is in the heavens; everything that he delighted to do he has done. Their idols are silver and gold, the work of the hands of earthling man. Those making them will become just like them, all those who are trusting in them. O Israel, trust in Jehovah; he is their help and their shield. O house of Aaron, put your trust in Jehovah; he is their help and their shield. You that fear Jehovah, trust in Jehovah; he is their help and their shield. Jehovah himself has remembered us; he will bless, he will bless the house of Israel, he will bless the house of Aaron. He will bless those fearing Jehovah, the small ones as well as the great ones. Jehovah will give increase to you, to you and to your sons. You are the ones blessed by Jehovah, the Maker of heaven and earth. As regards the heavens, to Jehovah the heavens belong, but the earth he has given to the sons of men. The dead themselves do not praise Jah, nor do any going down into silence. But we ourselves will bless Jah from now on and to time indefinite. Praise Jah, you people!

Psalm 116 all verses, I do love, because Jehovah hears my voice, my entreaties. For he has inclined his ear to me, and throughout my days I shall call. The ropes of death encircled me and the distressing circumstances of Sheol themselves found me. Distress and grief I kept finding. But upon the name of Jehovah I proceeded to call: "Ah, Jehovah, do provide my soul with escape!" Jehovah is gracious and righteous; and our God is One showing mercy. Jehovah is guarding the inexperienced ones. I was impoverished, and he proceeded to save even me. Return to your resting-place, O my soul, for Jehovah himself has acted appropriately toward you. For you have rescued my soul from death, my eye from tears, my foot from stumbling. I will walk before Jehovah in the lands of those living. I had faith, for I proceeded to speak. I myself was very much afflicted. I, for my part, said, when I became panicky: "Every man is a liar." What shall I repay to Jehovah for all his benefits to me? The cup of grand salvation I shall take up, and on the name of Jehovah I shall call. My vows I shall pay to Jehovah, yes, in front of all his people. Precious in the eyes of Jehovah is the death of his loyal ones. Ah, now, O Jehovah, for I am your servant. I am your servant, the son of your slave girl. You have loosened my bands. To you I shall offer the sacrifice of thanksgiving, and on the name of Jehovah I shall call. My vows I shall pay to Jehovah, yes, in front of all his people, in the courtyards of the house of Jehovah, in the midst of you, O Jerusalem. Praise Jah, you people!

Psalm 117 all verses, Praise Jehovah, all you nations; commend him, all you clans. For toward us his loving-kindness has proved mighty; and the trueness of Jehovah is to time indefinite. Praise Jah, you people!

Psalm 118 all verses, Give thanks to Jehovah, you people, for he is good; for his loving-kindness is to time indefinite. Let Israel now say: "For his loving-kindness is to time indefinite." Let those of the house of Aaron now say: "For his loving-kindness is to time indefinite." Let those fearing Jehovah now say: "For his loving-kindness is to time indefinite." Out of the distressing circumstances I called upon Jah; Jah answered and put me into a roomy place. Jehovah is on my side; I shall not fear. What can earthling man do to me? Jehovah is on my side among those helping me, so that I myself shall look upon those hating me. It is better to take refuge in Jehovah than to trust in earthling man. It is better to take refuge in Jehovah than to trust in nobles. All the nations themselves surrounded me. It was in the name of Jehovah that I kept holding them off. They surrounded me, yes, they had me surrounded. It was in the name of Jehovah that I kept holding them off. They surrounded me like bees; they were extinguished like a fire of thornbushes. It was in the name of Jehovah that I kept holding them off. You [Satan] pushed me hard that I should fall, but Jehovah himself helped me. Jah is my shelter and my might, and to me he becomes salvation. The voice of a joyful cry and salvation is in the tents of the righteous ones. The right hand of Jehovah is demonstrating vital energy. The right hand of Jehovah is exalting itself; the right hand of Jehovah is demonstrating vital energy. I shall not die, but I shall keep living, that I may declare the works of Jah. Jah corrected me severely, but he did not give me over to death itself. Open to me the gates of righteousness, you people. I shall go into them; I shall laud Jah. This is the gate of Jehovah. The righteous themselves will go into it. I shall laud you, for you answered me and you came to be my salvation. The stone that the builders rejected has become the head of the corner. This has come to be from Jehovah himself; it is wonderful in our eyes. This is the day that Jehovah has made; we will be joyful and rejoice in it. Ah, now, Jehovah, do save, please! Ah, now, Jehovah, do grant success, please! Blessed be the One coming in the name of Jehovah; we have blessed you people out of the house of Jehovah. Jehovah is the Divine One, and he gives us light. Bind the festival procession with boughs, O you people, as far as the horns of the altar. You are my Divine One, and I shall laud you; my God—I shall exalt you. Give thanks to Jehovah, you people, for he is good; for his loving-kindness is to time indefinite.

Research, continued: **Festival of Booths:** *The festival included thanksgiving for grain, wine and oil. During the festival the Israelites were to meditate in their hearts upon the fact that Jehovah's care has brought these good things to them. They were to* **think deeply** *on these things.*

[Remember: Jehovah brought us out of the slavery imposed on us by the organization! And we receive much good from Jehovah every day!]

The booths the Israelites dwelled in during the festival were to recall the shelters Jehovah provided them when they were wandering in the wilderness.

John 7:37,38, Now on the last day, the great day of the festival, Jesus was standing up and he cried out, saying: "If anyone is thirsty, let him come to me and drink. He that puts faith in me, just as the Scripture has said, 'Out from his inmost part streams of living water will flow.'"

Isaiah 12:3, With exultation you people will be certain to draw water out of the springs of salvation.

→ *During the Festival of Booths, a priest drew from the waters of Siloam* [which means "sent forth," and it was on Siloam Road in Iowa Falls, Iowa where my mother lived at the time that my eyes were opened and I was "sent forth"] *and poured it, along with wine, on the altar at the time of the morning sacrifice. This occurred for the first 7 days, but not on the 8th day. The 8th day the priest would go to the pool of Siloam with a golden pitcher. It was timed for the priest to return from Siloam with water as others priests in the temple were ready to lay pieces of sacrifice on the altar. As the priest with the water entered* *the Court of Priests by the Water Gate of Jerusalem, he was announced by a three-fold blast from the priests' trumpets. The water was poured into a basin at the base of the altar at the same time as the wine.*

[I have prayed to Jehovah that he would open Leon's eyes and heart and show him the truth about who he, Leon, is.]

Zechariah 3:3-8, Now as for Joshua [Lisa], he happened to be clothed in befouled garments and standing before the angel. Then he answered and said to those standing before him: "Remove the befouled garments from upon him." And he went on to say to him: "See, I have caused your error to pass away from upon you, and there is a clothing of you with robes of state."

At that I said: "Let them put a clean turban upon his head." And they proceeded to put the clean turban upon his head and to clothe him with garments; and the angel of Jehovah was standing by. And the angel of Jehovah began to bear witness to Joshua [Lisa], saying: "This is what Jehovah of armies has said, 'If it is in my ways that you will walk, and if it is my obligation that you will keep, then also it will be you that will judge my house and also keep my courtyards; and I shall certainly give you free access among these who are standing by.

Hear, please, O Joshua the high priest, you and your companions who are sitting before you, for they are men serving as portents; for here I am bringing in my servant Sprout [Leon]!'"

Ezekiel 21:25-27, And as for you, O deadly wounded, wicked chieftain [unfaithful "faithful and discreet slave" of the organization of Jehovah's Witnesses] of Israel, whose day has come in the time of the error of the end, this is what the Sovereign Lord Jehovah has said, "Remove the turban, and lift off the crown. This will not be the same. Put on high even what is low, and bring low even the high one. A ruin, a ruin, a ruin I shall make it. As for this also, it will certainly become no one's until he comes who has the legal right, and I must give it to him."

Isaiah 8:6, For the reason that this people has rejected the waters of the **Shiloah** [meaning "Sender," Lisa] that are going gently.

Genesis 49:9,10, A lion cub Judah is. From the prey, my son, you will certainly go up. He bowed down, he stretched himself out like a lion [Leon] and, like a lion, who dares rouse him? The scepter will not turn aside from Judah, neither the commander's staff from between his feet, until **Shiloh** [meaning "He Whose It Is; He To Whom It Belongs"] comes; and to him the obedience of the peoples will belong.

Research, continued: ***Festival of Booths:*** *The ceremony of Siloam water at the altar may have reminded the celebrators of Isaiah's prophetic words.*

Isaiah 12:3, With exultation you people will be certain to draw water out of the springs of salvation.

Psalm 118:25, Ah, now, Jehovah, do save, please! Ah, now, Jehovah, do grant success, please!

This was sung by the priest as he walked the circuit each of the seven days and seven times on the seventh day at the Festival of Booths. It was still carried out in Jesus' day.

Recall: Proverbs 21:1, A king's heart is as streams of water in the hand of Jehovah. Everywhere that he delights to, he turns it.

Isaiah 44:28, The One saying of Cyrus, 'He is my shepherd, and all that I delight in he will completely carry out'; even in my saying of Jerusalem, 'She will be rebuilt,' and of the temple, 'You will have your foundation laid.'"

1 Thessalonians 3:11, Now may our God and Father himself and our Lord Jesus direct our way prosperously [successfully] to you.

Research, continued: **Festival of Booths:** *At the close of Tishri 15, preparations were made in the Court of Women. With four golden lampstands, each with four bowls, four youths of priestly descent climbed ladders with large pitchers of oil and filled the sixteen bowls. Old clothing of the priests was used for wicks for the lamps. The lamps made brilliant light which lit up the courts of the houses in Jerusalem. Some of the elders danced with flaming torches and* *sang to music which was also still carried out in Jesus' day. Jesus was probably referring to himself as the Siloam waters when he spoke at the Festival of Booths.*

John 7:37,38, Now on the last day, the great day of the festival, Jesus was standing up and he cried out, saying: "If anyone is thirsty, let him come to me and drink. He that puts faith in me, just as the Scripture has said, 'Out from his inmost part streams of living water will flow.'"

Philemon 20, Yes, brother, may I derive profit from you in connection with the Lord: refresh my tender affections [with spiritual waters] in connection with Christ.

Jesus may have been making a connection with the lighting of Jerusalem at the Festival of Booths when he later said, "I am the light of the world."

John 8:12, Therefore Jesus spoke again to them, saying: "I am the light of the world. He that follows me will by no means walk in darkness, but will possess the light of life."

Jesus may again have been connecting the events of the Festival of Booths when he later healed a blind man. He had spit on the ground, mixing it with clay and put it on the blind man's eyes, telling him to go wash in the pool of Siloam. (John 9:1-7)
Everything connected with the Festival of Booths involved joy, the bountiful blessings from Jehovah's hand and refreshment for the soul of man.

October 9, 1989

Psalm 78:70,71, And so he chose David his servant and took him from the pens of the flock. From following the females giving suck he brought him in to be a shepherd over Jacob his people and over Israel his inheritance.

Revelation 12:4b,5, And the dragon [Satan] kept standing before the woman who was about to give birth, that, when she did give birth, it might devour her child.

And she gave birth to a son, a male, who is to shepherd all the nations with an iron rod. And her child was caught away to God and to his throne.

Genesis 3:15, And I shall put enmity between you [Satan] and the woman and between your seed and her seed. He will bruise you in the head and you will bruise him in the heel.

Isaiah 66:8, Who has heard of a thing like this? Who has seen things like these? Will a land be brought forth with labor pains in one day? Or will a nation be born at one time? For Zion has come into labor pains as well as given birth to her sons.

Research: Insight on the Scriptures, volume 2, page 1198 WBTS (1988), **Woman:** *The prophecy at Revelation 12:4b,5, (see above) was written after Jesus birth, and therefore does not seem to apply to Jesus.*

[Insight on the Scriptures is a publication of the Watchtower Bible and Tract Society, the organization known as Jehovah's Witnesses. In their research materials they suggest that this prophecy refers to the birth of God's kingdom, which is incorrect. It is a human woman who spiritually "gives birth" to a "son." From the example she has set ("laboring" to teach a spiritually "young" one, a "child"), a human male ("son") sets out to seek a spiritual relationship with Jehovah for himself. After receiving instruction in righteousness from Jehovah, this man will shepherd the nations under Christ's rulership.]

Isaiah 42:1, Look! My servant, on whom I keep fast hold! My chosen one, whom my soul has approved! I have put my spirit in him. Justice to the nations is what he will bring forth.

Isaiah 55:3, Incline your ear and come to me. Listen, and your soul will keep alive, and I shall readily conclude with you people an indefinitely lasting covenant respecting the loving-kindnesses to David that are faithful.

Genesis 49:10, The scepter will not turn aside from Judah, neither the commander's staff from between his feet, until Shiloh comes; and to him the obedience of the peoples will belong.

Ephesians 6:22, I am sending him to you for this very purpose, that you may know of the things having to do with us and that he may comfort your hearts.

2 Corinthians Chapter 9 all verses, Now concerning the ministry that is for the holy ones, it is superfluous for me to write you, for I know your readiness of mind of which I am boasting to the Macedonians about you, that Achaia has stood ready now for a year, and your zeal has stirred up the majority of them. But I am sending the brothers, that our boasting about you might not prove empty in this respect, but that you may really be ready, just as I used to say you would be. Otherwise, in some way, if Macedonians should come with me and find you not ready, we—not to say you—should be put to shame in this assurance of ours. Therefore I thought it necessary to encourage the brothers to come to you in advance and to get ready in advance your bountiful gift previously promised, that thus this might be ready as a bountiful gift and not as something extorted.

But as to this, he that sows sparingly will also reap sparingly; and he that sows bountifully will also reap bountifully. Let each one do just as he has resolved in his heart, not grudgingly or under compulsion, for God loves a cheerful giver.

God, moreover, is able to make all his undeserved kindness abound toward you, that, while you always have full self-sufficiency in everything, you may have plenty for every good work. (Just as it is written: "He has distributed widely, he has given to the poor ones, his righteousness continues forever." Now he that abundantly supplies seed to the sower and bread for eating will supply and multiply the seed for you to sow and will increase the products of your righteousness.) In everything you are being enriched for every sort of generosity, which produces through us an expression of thanks to God; because the ministry of this public service is not only to supply abundantly the wants of the holy ones but also to be rich with many expressions of thanks to God. Through the proof that this ministry gives, they glorify God because you are submissive to the good news about the Christ, as you publicly declare you are, and because you are generous in your contribution to them and to all; and with supplication for you they long for you because of the surpassing undeserved kindness of God upon you.

Thanks be to God for his indescribable free gift.

Deuteronomy 12:11, And it must occur that the place that Jehovah your God will choose to have his name reside there is where you will bring all about which I am commanding you, your burnt offerings and your sacrifices, your tenth parts and the contribution of your hand [my writing] and every choice of your vow offerings that you will vow to Jehovah. [Jehovah's holy spirit has guided my heart and directed my research for this journal.]

Hebrews 13:22,23, Now I exhort you, brothers [faithful worshippers of Jehovah], to bear with this word of encouragement, for I have, indeed, composed a letter to you in few words. Take note that our brother Timothy has been released, with whom, if he comes quite soon, I shall see you.

October 10, 1989

Ephesians 6:22, I am sending him to you for this very purpose, that you may know of the things having to do with us and that he may comfort your hearts.

James 1:4, But let endurance have its work complete, that you may be complete and sound in all respects, not lacking in anything.

October 11, 1989

Message: [I was given a message from Jehovah: "Find yourself in a book."]

Message: [I was given another message from Jehovah: "Do not underestimate what God can do."]

> Rosie's Notes: Revelation 14:15, And another angel emerged from the temple sanctuary, crying with a loud voice to the one seated on the cloud: "Put your sickle in and reap, because the hour has come to reap, for the harvest of the earth is thoroughly ripe."

Hebrews Chapter 13 all verses, Let your brotherly love continue. Do not forget hospitality, for through it some, unknown to themselves, entertained angels. Keep in mind those in prison bonds as though you have been bound with them, and those being ill-treated, since you yourselves also are still in a body. Let marriage be honorable among all, and the marriage bed be without defilement, for God will judge fornicators and adulterers. Let your manner of life be free of the love of money, while you are content with the present things. For he has said: "I will by no means leave you nor by any means forsake you." So that we may be of good courage and say: "Jehovah is my helper; I will not be afraid. What can man do to me?"

Remember those who are taking the lead among you, who have spoken the word of God to you, and as you contemplate how their conduct turns out imitate their faith.

Jesus Christ is the same yesterday and today, and forever.

Do not be carried away with various and strange teachings; for it is fine for the heart to be given firmness by undeserved kindness, not by eatables, by which those who occupy themselves with them have not been benefited.

! We have an altar from which those [the unfaithful "faithful and discreet slave" of the apostate organization of Jehovah's Witnesses] who do sacred service at the tent have no authority to eat. For the bodies of those animals whose blood is taken into the holy place by the high priest for sin are burned up outside the camp. **Hence Jesus also, that he might sanctify the people with his own blood, suffered outside the gate. Let us [faithful worshippers of Jehovah still in the organization], then, go forth to him outside the camp [out of the apostate organization], bearing the reproach he bore, for we do not have here a city that continues, but we are earnestly seeking the one to come.** Through him let us always offer to God a sacrifice of praise, that is, the fruit of lips which make public declaration to his name. Moreover, do not forget the doing of good and the sharing of things with others, for with such sacrifices God is well pleased.

Be obedient to those who are taking the lead among you and be submissive, for they are keeping watch over your souls as those who will render an account; that they may do this with joy and not with sighing, for this would be damaging to you.

Carry on prayer for us, for we trust we have an honest conscience, as we wish to conduct ourselves honestly in all things. But I exhort you more especially to do this, that I may be restored to you the sooner.

Now may the God of Peace, who brought up from the dead the great shepherd of the sheep with the blood of an everlasting covenant, our Lord Jesus, equip you with every good thing to do his will, performing in us through Jesus Christ that which is well-pleasing in his sight; to whom be the glory forever and ever. Amen.

Now I exhort you, brothers, to bear with this word of encouragement, for I have, indeed, composed a letter to you in few words. Take note that our brother Timothy [meaning "One who honors God"] has been released, with whom, if he comes quite soon, I shall see you.

Give my greetings to all those who are taking the lead among you and to all the holy ones. Those in Italy send you their greetings.

The undeserved kindness be with all of you.

Research: Insight on the Scriptures, volume 2, page 39, **Jerusalem:** *Jerusalem means "Foundation of Two-fold Peace."*

Zechariah 6:13b, And he must become a priest [Lisa] upon his [Leon's] throne, and the very counsel of peace will prove to be between **both of them.**

Melchizedek, who visited Abraham, was a king and a priest in the area of Mount Moriah, around Salem [later named Jerusalem].

Isaiah 44:5, This one will say: "I belong to Jehovah." And that one will call himself by the name of Jacob [Leon], and another will write upon his hand: "Belonging to Jehovah." And by the name of Israel [Lisa] one will betitle himself.

Jerusalem is located in the territory of Benjamin and borders Judah. The pool of Siloam is located in the Tyropean valley, outside of Jerusalem. The spring of Gihon feeds the pool of Siloam. The site of Jerusalem is on Mount Moriah, the area where Abraham took Isaac upon Jehovah's instructions, to sacrifice. David recaptured Jerusalem from the Jebusites to make it "his city," the "City of David," under divine authority to do so. Centuries prior to this Jehovah had prophesied that this would be the site he would choose to place his name thereon.

Jerusalem under David was, at first, an administrative center. When the Ark of the Covenant was brought there, it became a religious center, also.

When the kingdom split, the tribes of Judah and Benjamin stayed with Jerusalem, and the priests and Levites came there in support.

2 Kings 19:32-34, That is why this is what Jehovah has said concerning the king of Assyria: "He will not come into this [faithful] city nor will he shoot an arrow there nor confront it with a shield nor cast up a siege rampart against it. By the way by which he proceeded to come, he will return, and into this city he will not come, is the utterance of Jehovah. And I shall certainly defend this city to save it for my own sake and for the sake of David my servant." **[Jehovah gave his protection to the city of Jerusalem as long as the people in it were faithful to him.]**

Jerusalem was expanded. It crossed the valley and extended from the territory of Benjamin into the territory of Judah. Then in 538/537 BC, the first year of Cyrus [as ruler], a decree was issued to "go up to Jerusalem, which is in Judah, and rebuild the house of Jehovah the God of Israel." (Ezra 1:1-4)

Isaiah 54:11 NWT (1984), O woman [Lisa] afflicted, tempest-tossed, uncomforted, here I am laying with hard mortar your stones, and I will lay your foundation with sapphires. [Jehovah is laying the foundation of the afflicted, tempest-tossed woman, whom he has also referred to in the Bible as "Jerusalem."]

Recall: Ezra 5:17, And now if to the king it seems good, let there be an investigation in the king's house of treasures that is there in Babylon, whether it is so that from Cyrus the king an order was put through to rebuild that house of God in Jerusalem; and the decision of the king concerning this let him send to us.

Daniel 9:25, And you should know and have the insight that from the going forth of the word to restore and to rebuild Jerusalem until Messiah the Leader, there will be seven weeks, also sixty-two weeks. She will return and be actually rebuilt, with a public square and moat, but in the straits of the times.

Isaiah 62:3, And you [Lisa] must become a crown of beauty in the hand of Jehovah, and a kingly turban in the palm of your God.

[Jehovah has "raised up" Lisa (as a prophet is "raised up") and her strength of faith will reflect Jehovah's accomplishment.
After the foundation of Jerusalem is laid by Jehovah, then Cyrus (Leon) builds on what God has formed. (Isaiah 54:11) (Ezra 5:17) Leon himself will be taught and made ready by Jehovah. He will prove to be the spiritual person Jehovah has helped him to become. Jehovah will "raise up" Leon and his faith will also reflect Jehovah's accomplishment.]

Adam and Eve: [Eve led her husband out of obedience to Jehovah and into death. The replacement mother for Eve, Lisa Pressnall, leads her future husband, and replacement father for Adam, Leon Wurzer, into obedience to Jehovah.]

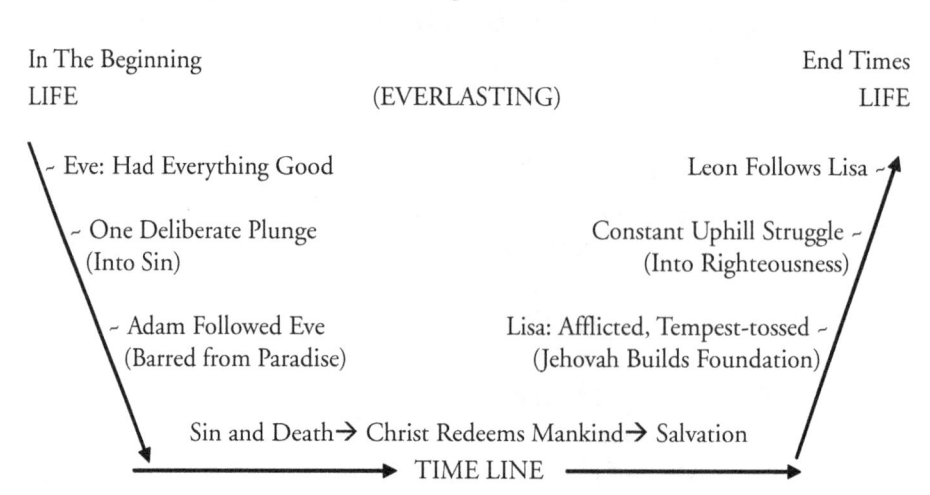

In The Beginning		End Times
LIFE	(EVERLASTING)	LIFE
~ Eve: Had Everything Good		Leon Follows Lisa ~
~ One Deliberate Plunge		Constant Uphill Struggle ~
(Into Sin)		(Into Righteousness)
~ Adam Followed Eve		Lisa: Afflicted, Tempest-tossed ~
(Barred from Paradise)		(Jehovah Builds Foundation)

Sin and Death → Christ Redeems Mankind → Salvation
⎯⎯⎯⎯⎯⎯⎯⎯ TIME LINE ⎯⎯⎯⎯⎯⎯⎯⎯

Paradise Earth: [Jehovah has established his Son, Jesus Christ, as our king, who will rule the earth from heaven. Jehovah has chosen Leon Wurzer to represent this kingdom here on earth.

Directed by Christ, Leon, with the help of many others, will work to restore the earth to a paradise condition, and we will all be able to live here forever in perfect peace.]

Job 36:1,2, Good News Bible (1976), Be patient and listen a little longer to what I am saying on God's behalf. [Jesus is speaking; correcting me because I am impatient.]

Recall: Isaiah 51:14, The one [Leon] stooping in chains will certainly be loosened speedily, that he may not go in death to the pit and that his bread may not be lacking.

Job 36:8-15, Good News Bible, But if people are bound in chains, suffering for what they have done, God shows them their sins and their pride. He makes them listen to his warning to turn away from evil. If they obey God and serve him, they live out their lives in peace and prosperity. But if not, they will die in ignorance and cross the stream into the world of the dead.

Those who are godless keep on being angry, and even when punished, they don't pray for help. They die while they are still young, worn out by a life of disgrace. **But God teaches men through suffering and uses distress to open their eyes.**

[Leon is a proud and stubborn man. It is an accomplishment when Jehovah teaches someone like him righteousness and he then chooses a life of faithfulness. I have been praying for Jehovah to open Leon's eyes to the truth.]

Job 36:19-21 Good News Bible, It will do you [Leon] no good to cry out for help; all your strength can't help you now. Don't wish for night to come, the time when nations will perish. Be careful not to turn to evil; your suffering was sent to keep you from it.

Job 36:22-24 Good News Bible, Remember how great is God's power; he is the greatest teacher of all. No one can tell God what to do or accuse him of doing evil. [I was saying, "It's not fair!" because it seems to be taking so long to bring about Jehovah's promised changes.] He has always been praised for what he does; you also must praise him. [Jehovah has done so many things for me already. In this journal alone I have over 250 pages recounting Jehovah's greatness and goodness in my life. Shame on me! I am corrected.] Everyone has seen what he has done; we can only watch from a distance.

Psalm 37:13 Good News Bible, God sends rain to water the earth; he may send it to punish men, or to show them his favor. [I have prayed for spiritual "rain" on Leon. Maybe it is necessary for the "rain" that he is receiving right now to be punishment. There was a period in my life when Jehovah sent spiritual rain of punishment on me for my wrongdoing. He used my distress to teach me and strengthen me to become firm in my heart toward righteousness. Truly, it is very fair for Jehovah to take the time necessary to teach Leon in the same manner. We must be firm in our faith and integrity to Jehovah in all things, and walk worthily of the great responsibilities and blessings we have and are yet to be given.]

My Prayer: [Jehovah, Jehovah, please forgive me. I don't want to feel or think anything that criticizes you. Your understanding and wisdom are so far above me, and I know that all of your ways are perfect. I am very sorry. Please forgive my impatience. (I need to continue trusting in Jehovah, completely.)]

Psalm 85:8, I will hear what the true God Jehovah will speak, for he will speak peace to his people and to his loyal ones, but let them not return to self-confidence.

Psalm 86:10, For you [Jehovah] are great and are doing wondrous things; you are God, you alone.

! [Jehovah responded to my prayer.] Psalm 87:1-3,5,7, His foundation is in the holy mountains. Jehovah is more in love with the gates of Zion than with all the tabernacles of Jacob. Glorious things are being spoken about you, O city of the true God. *Selah*.
And respecting Zion it will be said: "Each and every one was born in her." And the Most High himself will firmly establish her.
There will also be singers as well as dancers of circle dances: "All my springs are in you."

Psalm 9 all verses, Good News Bible, I will praise you, Lord, with all my heart; I will tell of all the wonderful things you have done. I will sing with joy because of you. I will sing praise to you, Almighty God.

My enemies turn back when you appear; they fall down and die. **You are fair and honest in your judgments,** and you have judged in my favor.

You have condemned the heathen and destroyed the wicked; they will be remembered no more. Our enemies are finished forever; you have destroyed their cities, and they are completely forgotten.

But the Lord is king forever; he has set up his throne for judgment. He rules the world with righteousness; he judges the nations with justice.

The Lord is a refuge for the oppressed, a place of safety in times of trouble. Those who know you, Lord, will trust you; you do not abandon anyone who comes to you.

Sing praise to the Lord, who rules in Zion! Tell every nation what he has done! God remembers those who suffer; he does not forget their cry, and he punishes those who wrong them.

Be merciful to me, O Lord! See the sufferings my enemies cause me! Rescue me from death, O Lord, that I may stand before the people of Jerusalem and tell them all the things for which I praise you. I will rejoice because you saved me.

The heathen have dug a pit and fallen in; they have been caught in their own trap. The Lord has revealed himself by his righteous judgments, and the wicked are trapped by their own deeds.

Death is the destiny of all the wicked, of all those who reject God. The needy will not always be neglected; the hope of the poor will not be crushed forever.

Come, Lord! Do not let men defy you! Bring the heathen before you and pronounce judgment on them. Make them afraid, O Lord; make them know that they are only mortal beings.

Psalm 97 all verses, Jehovah himself has become king! Let the earth be joyful. Let the many islands rejoice. Clouds and thick gloom are all around him; righteousness and judgment are the established place of his throne. Before him a very fire goes, and it consumes his adversaries all around. His lightnings lighted up the productive land; the earth saw and came to be in severe pains. The mountains themselves proceeded to melt just like wax on account of Jehovah, on account of the Lord of the whole earth. The heavens have told forth his righteousness, and all the peoples have seen his glory. Let all those serving any carved image be ashamed, those who are making their boast in valueless gods. Bow down to him, all you gods. Zion heard and began to rejoice, and the dependent towns of Judah began to be joyful by reason of your judicial decisions, O Jehovah. For you, O Jehovah, are the Most High over all the earth; you are very high in your ascent over all other gods. O you lovers of Jehovah, hate what is bad. He is guarding the souls of his loyal ones; out of the hand of the wicked ones he delivers them. **Light itself has flashed up for the righteous one, and rejoicing even for the ones upright in heart. Rejoice in Jehovah, O you righteous ones, and give thanks to his holy memorial.**

Psalm 98 all verses, Sing to Jehovah a new song, for wonderful are the things that he has done. His right hand, even his holy arm, has gained salvation for him. Jehovah has made his salvation known; in the eyes of the nations he has revealed his righteousness. He has remembered his loving-kindness and his faithfulness to the house of Israel. All the ends of the earth have seen the salvation by our God. Shout in triumph to Jehovah, all you people of the earth. Be cheerful and cry out joyfully and make melody. Make melody to Jehovah with the harp, with the harp and the voice of melody. With the trumpets and the sound of the horn shout in triumph before the King, Jehovah. Let the sea thunder and that which fills it, the productive land and those dwelling in it. Let the rivers themselves clap their hands; all together let the very mountains cry out joyfully before Jehovah, for he has come to judge the earth. He will judge the productive land with righteousness and the peoples with uprightness.

Psalm 99 all verses, Jehovah himself has become king. Let the peoples be agitated. He is sitting upon the cherubs. Let the earth quiver. Jehovah is great in Zion, and he is high over all the peoples. Let them laud your name. Great and fear-inspiring, holy it is. And with the strength of a king judgment he has loved. You yourself have firmly established uprightness. Judgment and righteousness in Jacob are what you yourself have effected. Exalt Jehovah our

God and bow down yourselves at his footstool; he is holy. Moses and Aaron were among his priests, and Samuel was among those calling upon his name. They were calling to Jehovah, and he himself kept answering them. In the pillar of cloud he continued speaking to them. They kept his reminders and the regulation that he gave to them. O Jehovah our God, you yourself answered them. A God granting pardon you proved to be to them, and executing vengeance against their notorious deeds. Exalt Jehovah our God and bow down yourselves at his holy mountain. For Jehovah our God is holy.

Song of Solomon 6:9a Good News Bible, But I [Leon] love only one, and she is as lovely as a dove [peaceable].

Song of Solomon 8:6a Good News Bible, Close your heart to every love but mine; hold no one in your arms but me [Lisa].

Psalm 102:13 NWT (1984), You yourself will arise, you will have mercy on Zion, for it is the season to be favorable to her, for the appointed time has come. [I am like an able-bodied person who has lost all strength. All day long, every day, I am exhausted and depressed. At times I have to rely on Jehovah's strength just to draw my next breath.]

Previous Event: [Jehovah asked permission to "read" my life like a book to Leon in 1989. Jehovah is able to use this current permission and go back in time.

It was around the spring of 1987 that I began to fervently pray to Jehovah to help Leon learn the truth from the Bible, and that someday we might meet again. It was in 1987 when Jehovah reassured me with the words, "It is going to be all right, something is going to be done about it."]

Song of Solomon 4:9 Good News Bible, The look in your eyes, my sweetheart and bride, and the necklace you [Lisa] are wearing have stolen my [Jehovah's] heart. [I was saying to myself, "I did it! I succeeded in spite of this exhaustion and depression!" I said this in reference to having just come through a very, very difficult spiritual tribulation.]

Recall: Isaiah 49:18, Raise your eyes all around and see. They have all of them been collected together. They have come to you.

"As I am living," is the utterance of Jehovah, "with all of them you will clothe yourself just as with ornaments, and you will bind them on yourself like a bride."

Revelation 21:2, I saw also the holy city, New Jerusalem [Lisa], coming down out of heaven from God and [spiritually] prepared as a bride adorned for her husband.

Song of Solomon 6:10,13, Who is this woman that is looking down like the dawn, beautiful like the full moon, pure like the glowing sun, awesome as companies gathered around banners?
"Come back, come back, O Shulammite! Come back, come back, that we may behold you!"
"What do you people behold in the Shulammite?"
"Something like the dance of two camps."

Jeremiah 3:14, "Return, O you renegade sons," is the utterance of Jehovah. "For I myself have become the husbandly owner of you people; and I will take you, one [Leon] out of a city and two [Lisa and Bram] out of a family [mother and son], and I will bring you to Zion."

Romans 11:17,18a However, if some of the branches [unfaithful ones in the organization] were broken off but you [Leon], although being a wild olive, were grafted in among them and became a sharer of the olive's root of fatness, do not be exulting over the branches.

Psalm 122 all verses, I rejoiced when they were saying to me: "To the house of Jehovah let us go." Our feet proved to be standing within your gates, O Jerusalem. Jerusalem is one that is built like a city that has been joined together in oneness, to which the tribes have gone up, the tribes of Jah, as a reminder to Israel to give thanks to the name of Jehovah. For there the thrones for judgment have been sitting, thrones for the house of David. Ask, O you people, for the peace of Jerusalem. Those loving you, O city, will be free from care. May peace continue within your rampart, freedom from care within your dwelling towers. For the sake of my brothers and my companions I will now speak: "May there be peace within you." For the sake of the house of Jehovah our God I will keep seeking good for you.

Proverbs 8:1-21, Does not wisdom keep calling out, and discernment keep giving forth its voice? On top of the heights, by the way, at the crossing of the roadways it has stationed itself. At the side of the gates, at the mouth of the town, at the going in of the entrances it keeps crying loudly:

"To you, O men, I am calling, and my voice is to the sons of men. O inexperienced ones, understand shrewdness; and you stupid ones, understand heart. Listen, for it is about the foremost things that I speak, and the opening of my lips is about uprightness. For my palate in low tones utters truth itself; and wickedness is something detestable to my lips. All the sayings of my mouth are in righteousness. Among them there is nothing twisted or crooked. All of them are straight to the discerning one, and upright to the ones finding knowledge. Take my discipline and not silver, and knowledge rather than choice gold. For wisdom is better than corals, and all other delights themselves cannot be made equal to it.

I, wisdom, I have resided with shrewdness and I find even the knowledge of thinking abilities. The fear of Jehovah means the hating of bad. Self-exaltation and pride and the bad way and the perverse mouth I have hated. I have counsel and practical wisdom. I—understanding; I have mightiness. By me kings themselves keep reigning, and high officials themselves keep decreeing righteousness. By me princes themselves keep ruling as princes, and nobles are all judging in righteousness. Those loving me I myself love, and those looking for me are the ones that find me. Riches and glory are with me, hereditary values and righteousness. My fruitage is better than gold, even than refined gold, and my produce than choice silver. In the path of righteousness I walk, in the middle of the roadways of judgment, to cause those loving me to take possession of substance; and their storehouses I keep filled."

Isaiah Chapter 60 all verses, "Arise, O woman [Lisa], shed forth light, for your light has come and upon you the very glory of Jehovah has shone forth. For, look! darkness itself will cover the earth, and thick gloom the national groups; but upon you Jehovah will shine forth, and upon you his own glory will be seen. And nations will certainly go to your light, and kings to the brightness of your shining forth.

"**Raise your eyes all around and see! They have all of them been collected together; they have come to you. From far away your own sons keep coming, and your daughters who will be taken care of on the flank.** At that time you will see and certainly become radiant, and your heart will actually quiver and expand, because to you the wealthiness of the sea will direct itself; the very resources of the nations will come to you. The heaving mass of camels itself will cover you, the young male camels of Midian and of Ephah. All those from Sheba—they will come. Gold and frankincense they will carry. And the praises of Jehovah they will announce. All the flocks of Kedar—they will be collected together to you. The rams of Nebaioth—they will minister to you. With approval they will come up upon my altar, and I shall beautify my own house of beauty.

"Who are these that come flying just like a cloud, and like doves to their birdhouse holes? For in me the islands themselves will keep hoping, the ships of Tarshish also as at the first, in order to bring your sons from far away, their silver and their gold being with them, to the name of Jehovah your God and to the Holy One of Israel, for he will have beautified you. And foreigners will actually build your walls, and their own kings will minister to you; for in my indignation I shall have struck you, but in my goodwill I shall certainly have mercy upon you.

"And your gates will actually be kept open constantly; they will not be closed even by day or by night, in order to bring to you the resources of the nations, and their kings will be taking the lead. For any nation and any kingdom that will not serve you will perish; and the nations themselves will without fail come to devastation.

"To you the very glory of Lebanon will come, the juniper tree, the ash tree and the cypress at the same time, in order to beautify the place of my sanctuary; and I shall glorify the very place of my feet.

"And to you the sons of those afflicting you must go, bowing down; and all those treating you disrespectfully must bend down at the very soles of your feet, and they will have to call you [Lisa] the city of Jehovah, Zion of the Holy One of Israel.

"Instead of your proving to be one left entirely and hated, with nobody passing through, I will even set you as a thing of pride to time indefinite, an exultation for generation after generation. And you will actually suck the milk of nations, and the breast of kings you will suck; and you will be certain to know that I, Jehovah, am your Savior, and the Powerful One of Jacob is your Repurchaser. Instead of the copper I shall bring in gold, and instead of the iron I shall bring in silver, and instead of the wood, copper, and instead of the stones, iron; and I will appoint peace as your overseers and righteousness as your task assigners.

"No more will violence be heard in your land, despoiling or breakdown within your boundaries. And you will certainly call your own walls Salvation and your gates Praise. For you the sun will no more prove to be a light by day, and for brightness the moon itself will no more give you light. And Jehovah must become to you an indefinitely lasting light, and your God your beauty. No more will your sun set, nor will your moon go on the wane; for Jehovah himself will become for you an indefinitely lasting light, and the days of your mourning will have come to completion. And as for your people, all of them will be righteous; to time indefinite they will hold possession of the land, the sprout of my planting, the work of my hands, for me to be beautified. The little one himself will become a thousand, and the small one a mighty nation. I myself, Jehovah, shall speed it up in its own time."

Isaiah Chapter 54 all verses, "Cry out joyfully, you barren woman that did not give birth! Become cheerful with a joyful outcry and cry shrilly, you that had no childbirth pains, for the sons of the desolated one [Lisa] are more numerous than the sons of the woman with a husbandly owner [the unfaithful "faithful and discreet slave," who have lost their "husbandly owner"]," Jehovah has said. "Make the place of your tent more spacious. And let them stretch out the tent cloths of your grand tabernacle. Do not hold back. Lengthen out your tent cords, and make those tent pins of yours strong. For to the right and to the left you will break forth, and your own offspring will take possession even of nations, and they will inhabit even the desolated cities. Do not be afraid, for you will not be put to shame; and do not feel humiliated, for you will not be disappointed. For you will forget even the shame of your time of youth, and the reproach of your continuous widowhood you will remember no more."

"For your Grand Maker is your husbandly owner, Jehovah of armies being his name; and the Holy One of Israel is your Repurchaser. The God of the whole earth he will be called. For Jehovah called you as if you were a wife left entirely and hurt in spirit, and as a wife of the time of youth who was then rejected," your God has said.

"For a little moment I left you entirely, but with great mercies I shall collect you together. With a flood of indignation I concealed my face from you for but a moment, but with loving-kindness to time indefinite I will have mercy upon you," your Repurchaser, Jehovah, has said.

"This is just as the days of Noah to me. Just as I have sworn that the waters of Noah shall no more pass over the earth, so I have sworn that I will not become indignant toward you [Lisa] nor rebuke you. For the mountains themselves may be removed, and the very hills may stagger, but my loving-kindness itself will not be removed from you, nor will my covenant of peace itself stagger," Jehovah, the One having mercy upon you, has said.

"O woman afflicted, tempest-tossed, uncomforted, here I am laying with hard mortar your stones, and I will lay your foundation with sapphires. And I will make your battlements of rubies, and your gates of fiery glowing stones, and all your boundaries of delightsome stones. And all your sons will be persons taught by Jehovah, and the peace of your sons will be abundant. You will prove to be firmly established in righteousness itself. You will be far away from oppression—for you will fear none—and from anything terrifying, for it will not come near you. If anyone should at all make an attack, it will not be at my orders. Whoever is making an attack upon you will fall even on account of you."

"Look! I myself have created the craftsman, the one blowing upon the fire of charcoal and bringing forth a weapon as his workmanship. I myself, too, have created the ruinous man for wrecking work. Any weapon whatever that will be formed against you will have no success, and any tongue at all that will rise up against you in the judgment you will condemn. This is the hereditary possession of the servants of Jehovah, and their righteousness is from me," is the utterance of Jehovah.

Isaiah Chapter 53 all verses, Who has put faith in the thing heard by us? And as for the arm of Jehovah, to whom has it been revealed? And he will come up like a twig before one, and like a root out of waterless land. No stately form does he have, nor any splendor; and when we shall see him, there is not the appearance so that we should desire him.

He was despised and was avoided by men, a man meant for pains and for having acquaintance with sickness. And there was as if the concealing of one's face from us. He was despised, and we held him as of no account. Truly our sicknesses were what he himself carried; and as for our pains, he bore them. But we ourselves accounted him as plagued, stricken by God and afflicted. But he was being pierced for our transgression; he was being crushed for our errors. The chastisement meant for our peace was upon him, and because of his wounds there has been a healing for us. Like sheep we have all of us wandered about; it was each one to his own way that we have turned; and Jehovah himself has caused the error of us all to meet up with that one. He was hard pressed, and he was letting himself be afflicted; yet he would not open his mouth. He was being brought just like a sheep to the slaughtering; and like a ewe that before her shearers has become mute, he also would not open his mouth.

Because of restraint and of judgment he was taken away; and who will concern himself even with the details of his generation? For he was severed from the land of the living ones. Because of the transgression of my people he had the stroke. And he will make his burial place even with the wicked ones, and with the rich class in his death, despite the fact that he had done no violence and there was no deception in his mouth.

But Jehovah himself took delight in crushing him; he made him sick. If you will set his soul as a guilt offering, he will see his offspring, he will prolong his days, and in his hand what is the delight of Jehovah will succeed. Because of the trouble of his soul he will see, he will be satisfied. By means of his knowledge the righteous one, my servant, will bring a righteous standing to many people; and their errors he himself will bear. For that reason I shall deal him a portion among the many, and it will be with the mighty ones that he will apportion the spoil, due to the fact that he poured out his soul to the very death, and it was with the transgressors that he was counted in; and he himself carried the very sin of many people, and for the transgressors he proceeded to interpose.

Isaiah Chapter 52 all verses, Wake up, wake up, put on your strength, O Zion! Put on your beautiful garments, O Jerusalem, the holy city! For no more will there come again into you the uncircumcised and unclean one. Shake yourself free from the dust, rise up, take a seat, O Jerusalem. Loosen for yourself the bands on your neck, O captive daughter of Zion.

For this is what Jehovah has said: "It was for nothing that you people were sold, and it will be without money that you will be repurchased."

For this is what the Sovereign Lord Jehovah has said: "It was to Egypt that my people went down in the first instance to reside there as aliens; and without cause Assyria, for its part, oppressed them."

"And now, what interest do I have here?" is the utterance of Jehovah. "For my people were taken for nothing. The very ones ruling over them kept howling," is the utterance of Jehovah, "and constantly, all day long, my name was being treated with disrespect. For that reason my people will know my name, even for that reason in that day, because I am the One that is speaking. Look! It is I."

How comely upon the mountains are the feet of the one bringing good news, the one publishing peace, the one bringing good news of something better, the one publishing salvation, the one saying to Zion: "Your God has become king!"

Listen! Your own watchmen have raised their voice. In unison they keep crying out joyfully; for it will be eye into eye that they will see when Jehovah gathers back Zion.

Become cheerful, cry out joyfully in unison, you devastated places of Jerusalem, for Jehovah has comforted his people; he has repurchased Jerusalem. Jehovah has bared his holy arm before the eyes of all the nations; and all the ends of the earth must see the salvation of our God.

Turn away, turn away, get out of there, touch nothing unclean; get out from the midst of her, keep yourselves clean, you who are carrying the utensils of Jehovah. For you people will get out in no panic, and you will go in no flight. For Jehovah will be going even before you, and the God of Israel will be your rear guard.

Look! My servant will act with insight. He will be in high station and will certainly be elevated and exalted very much. To the extent that many have stared at him in amazement—so much was the disfigurement as respects his appearance more than that of any other man and as respects his stately form more than that of the sons of mankind—he will likewise startle many nations. At him kings will shut their mouth, because what had not been recounted to them they will actually see, and to what they had not heard they must turn their consideration.

Isaiah 51:17-23, "Rouse yourself, rouse yourself, rise up, O Jerusalem, you who have drunk at the hand of Jehovah his cup of rage. The goblet, the cup causing reeling, you have drunk, you have drained out. There was none of all the sons that she brought to birth conducting her, and there was none of all the sons that she brought up taking hold of her hand. Those two things were befalling you. Who will sympathize with you? Despoiling and breakdown, and hunger and sword! Who will comfort you? Your own sons have swooned away. They have lain down at the head of all the streets like the wild sheep in the net, as those who are full of the rage of Jehovah, the rebuke of your God."

Therefore listen to this, please, O woman afflicted and drunk, but not with wine. This is what your Lord, Jehovah, even your God, who contends for his people, has said: "Look! I will take away from your hand the cup causing reeling. **The goblet, my cup of rage—you will not repeat the drinking of it anymore. And I will put it in the hand of the ones irritating you [those taking the lead in the organization of Jehovah's Witnesses], who have said to your soul, 'Bow down that we may cross over,' so that you used to make your back just like the earth, and like the street for those crossing over."**

Isaiah 40:2, Speak to the heart of Jerusalem and call out to her that her military service has been fulfilled, that her error has been paid off. For from the hand of Jehovah she has received a full amount for all her sins.

Jeremiah 3:14,15, "Return, O you renegade sons," is the utterance of Jehovah. "For I myself have become the husbandly owner of you people; and I will take you, one out of a city and two out of a family, and I will bring you to Zion. And I will give you shepherds in agreement with my heart, and they will certainly feed you with knowledge and insight."

Ephesians 4:11,12, And he gave some as apostles, some as prophets, some as evangelizers, some as shepherds and teachers, with a view to the readjustment of the holy ones, for ministerial work, for the building up of the body of the Christ.

Zechariah 8:13, And it must occur that just as you became a malediction among the nations, O house of Judah and house of Israel, so I shall save you, and you must become a blessing. Do not be afraid. May your hands be strong.

Zechariah 10:6, And I will make the house of Judah [Leon] superior, and the house of Joseph [Lisa] I shall save. And I will give them a dwelling, for I will show them mercy; and they must become like those whom I had not cast off; for I am Jehovah their God, and I shall answer them.

Hosea 1:10, And the number of the sons of Israel must become like the grains of the sand of the sea that cannot be measured or numbered. And it must occur that in the place in which it used to be said to them, "You men are not my people," it will be said to them, "The sons of the Living God."

Zechariah 2:10, "Cry out loudly and rejoice, O daughter of Zion; for here I am coming, and I will reside in the midst of you," is the utterance of Jehovah.

Zechariah 3:9, "For, look! the stone that I have put before Joshua! Upon the one stone there are seven eyes. Here I am engraving its engraving," is the utterance of Jehovah of armies, "and I will take away the error of that land in one day."

Recall: Isaiah 49:16, Look! Upon my palms I have engraved you. Your walls are in front of me constantly.

Revelation 11:3-13, "And I will cause my two witnesses [Leon and Lisa] to prophesy a thousand two hundred and sixty days dressed in sackcloth." These are symbolized by the two olive trees and the two lampstands and are standing before the Lord of the earth.
And if anyone wants to harm them, fire issues forth from their mouths and devours their enemies; and if anyone should want to harm them, in this manner he must be killed. These have the

authority to shut up heaven that no rain should fall during the days of their prophesying, and they have authority over the waters to turn them into blood and to strike the earth with every sort of plague as often as they wish.

And when they have finished their witnessing, the wild beast that ascends out of the abyss will make war with them and conquer them and kill them. And their corpses will be on the broad way of the great city which is in a spiritual sense called Sodom and Egypt, where their Lord was also impaled. And those of the peoples and tribes and tongues and nations will look at their corpses for three and a half days, and they do not let their corpses be laid in a tomb. And those dwelling on the earth rejoice over them and enjoy themselves, and they will send gifts to one another, because these two prophets tormented those dwelling on the earth.

And after the three and a half days spirit of life from God entered into them, and they stood upon their feet, and great fear fell upon those beholding them. And they heard a loud voice out of heaven say to them: "Come on up here." And they went up into heaven in the cloud, and their enemies beheld them. And in that hour a great earthquake occurred, and a tenth of the city fell; and seven thousand persons were killed by the earthquake, and the rest became frightened and gave glory to the God of heaven.

Recall: Revelation 12:6,13,14, And the woman fled into the wilderness, where she has a place prepared by God, that they should feed her there a thousand two hundred and sixty days.

Now when the dragon saw that it was hurled down to the earth, it persecuted the woman that gave birth to the male child. But the two wings of the great eagle were given the woman, that she might fly into the wilderness to her place; there is where she is fed for a time and times and half a time away from the face of the serpent.

Angel: [I recall when an angel came "swooping" down over me one night as I was lying in bed before I fell asleep. I had just finished my prayer in which I was criticizing Leon because I couldn't see any spiritual progress. The angel corrected me. He appeared to open a lid of a container and pull out large written records, saying, "Here! Jehovah is using you to fulfill major PROPHECIES, and you are complaining!" I jumped back out of bed and got down on my knees. I apologized profusely to Jehovah in prayer.]

October 15, 1989

Message: ["Let your faith grow great."]

Message: ["Expect—expect—expect a miracle!"]

Message: ["We are with you in this." I know that I am receiving help to write this journal through Jehovah's holy spirit. But, I also know that I have help from my spiritual family in the heavens, as well as the angels. Jehovah is directing them as they assist me.]

Message: ["Bringing in the royal family, soon!"]

Prayer: [I watched a documentary on television about children who live in different parts of the world. It showed children in South America and Latin America, Lebanon, and parts of India and Africa. They are all suffering so much from starvation and disease. And they are being abandoned by their desperate families and victimized by crime. It was very, very sad. I cried for the babies and the ones dying with no hope.

(My prayer) Jehovah! Help! Please let me help! Send me! I want to do something about their pain! Please make me useful! Show me what to do!

Jehovah, please let us have relief from these terrible conditions. You alone have the power to reverse these tragic circumstances, and do away with them forever. We all hurt so badly because of the problems in this world—but especially these little children!

Please come, Jehovah, with your Son, Christ Jesus, our righteous king and the hope of the world. Please save us! "Come, Lord Jesus!" (Revelation 22:20b) Amen.]

Acts 7:17-21, Just as the time was approaching for fulfillment of the promise that God had openly declared to Abraham, the people grew and multiplied in Egypt [the people in the organization known as Jehovah's Witnesses], until there rose a different king over Egypt [governing body of the organization], who did not know of Joseph [Lisa]. This one used statecraft [manipulated the truth from the scriptures] against our race [faithful worshippers still in the organization] and wrongfully forced the fathers [faithful shepherds, elders, in the organization] to expose their infants ["little ones" of the flock in the organization: not just the very young, but also the sick, aged, hurt, poor, the disabled, anyone who is especially vulnerable], that they might not be preserved alive. In that particular time Moses was born [into slavery], and he was divinely beautiful [beautiful in the eyes of God]. And he was nursed three months in his father's home. But when he was exposed, the daughter of Pharaoh picked him up and brought him up as her own son [Lisa is likened to Moses here; "brought up" or "raised" in the organization].

Acts 7:22,23, Consequently Moses was instructed in all the wisdom of the Egyptians. [Some time before the events surrounding the false accusations against me began to surface, one elder of the Lancaster congregation, Wayne J., told me that I was capable of giving the Memorial talk, meaning my spiritual knowledge made me capable of what would be to me, the most important talk of the year. It was a wonderful compliment.

A full-time publisher (minister) in the congregation, Enid K. (who had been with Jehovah's Witnesses for thirty years) said, after she had gone with me on one of my Bible studies, that it was the best Bible study she had ever been on, referring to my explanations and knowledge. Jehovah has taught me, so that I can teach others.

Another spiritual sister, Susan B., also once said my Bible knowledge and answers are amazing; that people at the Kingdom Hall are astonished at my answers. All praise belongs to Jehovah, who keeps patiently working with me.]

Acts 7:22,23, continued, In fact, he was powerful in his words and deeds. Now when the time of his fortieth year was being fulfilled, it came into his heart to make an inspection of his brothers, the sons of Israel.

Acts 7:29, Moses took to flight [Lisa, Rosie, and their children "fled Babylon."] and became an alien resident in the land of Midian, where he became the father of two sons.

Recall: Jeremiah 3:14b,15, For I myself have become the husbandly owner of you people; and I will take you, one out of a city [Leon Wurzer, my spiritual "son," a "grafted in wild olive branch"] and two out of a family [Lisa Pressnall and her natural son, Bram Benjamin Lewis], and I will bring you to Zion. And I will give you shepherds in agreement with my heart, and they will certainly feed you with knowledge and insight.

Recall: Revelation 12:5,6, And she [Lisa] gave [spiritual] birth to a son [Leon], a male, who is to shepherd all the nations with an iron rod. And her child was caught away to God and to his throne. And the woman fled into the **wilderness, where she has a place prepared by God**, that they should feed her there a thousand two hundred and sixty days.

Acts 7:30, And when forty years were fulfilled, there appeared to him in the wilderness of Mount Sinai an angel in the fiery flame of a thornbush. [Outside of Forest City, Iowa there is a designated "wilderness" area.]

Recall: The woman has a place in the wilderness where she is fed for a time and times and half a time. (Revelation 12:14)]

Revelation 3:10, Because you kept the word about my endurance, I will also keep you from the hour of test, which is to come upon the whole inhabited earth, to put a test upon those dwelling on the earth.
[Now all three, the one out of a city and the two out of a family are fed by holy shepherds (heavenly spirit persons). These shepherds "will certainly feed you (you, plural) with knowledge and insight." (Jeremiah 3:14,15)]

Jeremiah 3:16, "And it must occur that you will become many and certainly bear fruit in the land in those days," is the utterance of Jehovah. "No more will they say, 'The ark of the covenant of Jehovah!' nor will it come up into the heart, nor will they remember it or miss it, and no more will it be made."

Jeremiah 3:17, "In that time they will call Jerusalem the throne [Lisa; also referred to as Pleasant City (Song of Solomon

6:4) and the staff Pleasantness (Zechariah 11:7)] of Jehovah; and to her all the nations must be brought together to the name of Jehovah at Jerusalem [Jerusalem means "City of Two-fold Peace"], and they will no more walk after the stubbornness of their bad heart."

Jeremiah 3:18,19, "In those days they will walk, the house of Judah alongside the house of Israel, and together they will come out of the land of the north into the land that I gave as a hereditary possession to your forefathers. And I myself have said, '**O how I proceeded to place you** [singular, feminine] among the sons and to give you the desirable land,

Recall: Isaiah 62:4b Good News Bible, Your land will be called "Happily Married," because the Lord is pleased with you and will be like a husband to your land.

Jeremiah 3:18,19, continued, the hereditary possession of the ornament of the armies of the nations!' And I [Jehovah] further said, '"My Father!" you people will call out to me, and from following me you people will not turn back.'

John 14:2, In the house of my Father there are many abodes. Otherwise, I would have told you, because **I am going my way to prepare a place for you.**

Recall: Revelation 12:6a, And the woman fled into the wilderness, **where she has a place prepared by God.**

Recall: Psalm 68:10, Your tent community—they have dwelt in it; with your goodness you proceeded to make it ready for the afflicted one, O God.

Recall: Isaiah 49:18b, "As I am living," is the utterance of Jehovah, "with all of them you will clothe yourself just as with ornaments, and you will bind them on yourself like a bride."
[I have thought my exhaustion and depression are like my ornaments, because in spite of everything, I have been able to press forward in spiritual progress.]

Recall: Song of Solomon 4:9 Good News Bible, The look in your eyes, my sweetheart and bride, and the necklace you are wearing have stolen my [Jehovah's] heart.

Jeremiah 3:19b, And I [Jehovah] further said, "'My Father!' you people will call out to me, and from following me you people will not turn back.'

Recall: Romans 8:15b, "Abba, Father!" [The "anointed" call out to Jehovah.]

Jeremiah 4:3, For this is what Jehovah has said to the men [singular] of Judah [Leon] and to Jerusalem: "Plow for yourselves arable land, and do not keep sowing among thorns."

Recall: Song of Solomon 2:16, My dear one [Leon] is mine and I [Lisa] am his. He is shepherding among the lilies.

Song of Solomon 2:2, Like a lily [Lisa] among thorny weeds, so is my girl companion among the daughters.

Hosea 10:12, Sow seed for yourselves in righteousness; reap in accord with loving-kindness. Till [spiritually] for yourselves arable land, when there is time for searching for Jehovah until he comes and gives instruction in righteousness to you [Leon].

[Jehovah is telling Leon to stop "sowing among thorns." Leon recently married a spiritually unproductive person. He is being told by Jehovah to leave this relationship.

In the case of marriage and divorce, it is said, "What God has joined together, let no man put apart." First to be considered in this situation is that Jehovah did not join Leon to his first wife, even if they consider their marriage sanctified. Second, Jehovah is the one putting their marriage apart, not any man, because it is not a recognized relationship in his eyes. Jehovah's wisdom is far greater than ours is, and all his ways are righteous. I don't fully understand this situation, but I fully trust Jehovah.

Jehovah has required me to *wait* for his will to be worked out regarding Leon. It has also been specifically required of me *not* to go to Leon, which I have not. Jehovah has told me that Leon will come to me to set things right between us.]

Hosea 10:11 Good News Bible, Israel [Lisa] was once like a well-trained young cow, ready and willing to thresh grain [willing servant in the door-to-door ministry for ten years]. But I [Jehovah] decided to put a yoke on her beautiful neck and to harness her for harder work. I made Judah [Leon] pull the plow and Israel pull the harrow. [The separate roads Leon and I have taken to get to this point have been long and "harrowing," difficult to navigate. But we will arrive at the destination Jehovah has chosen for us, and we will be the wiser for it.]

Isaiah 28:24,26, Is it all day long that the plower plows in order to sow seed, that he loosens and harrows his ground?
And one corrects him according to what is right. His own God instructs him.

Recall: Isaiah 44:28, The One [Jehovah] saying of Cyrus [Leon], 'He is my shepherd, and all that I delight in he will completely carry out'; even in my saying of Jerusalem, 'She [Lisa] will be rebuilt,' and of the temple, 'You will have your foundation laid.'

Isaiah 62:4-7, No more will you [Lisa] be said to be a woman left entirely; and your own land will no more be said to be desolate; but you yourself will be called My Delight Is in Her, and your land Owned as a Wife. For Jehovah will have taken delight in you, and your own land will be owned as a wife. For just as a young man takes ownership of a virgin as his wife, your sons [spiritual "son," Leon] will take ownership of you as a wife. And with the exultation of a bridegroom over a bride, your God will exult even over you. Upon your walls, O Jerusalem, I have commissioned watchmen. All day long and all night long, constantly, let them not keep still.
You who are making mention of Jehovah, let there be no silence on your part, and do not give him any silence until he fixes solidly, yes, until he sets Jerusalem as a praise in the earth.

Isaiah 58:12, And at your [Lisa's] instance men will certainly build up the places devastated a long time; you will raise up even the foundations of continuous generations. And you will actually be called the repairer of the gap, the restorer of roadways by which to dwell.

Jeremiah 4:3-10, For this is what Jehovah has said to the men [also speaking to the faithful shepherds still in the apostate organization known as Jehovah's Witnesses] of Judah and to Jerusalem: "[Spiritually] Plow for yourselves arable land, and do not keep sowing among thorns [lies]. Get yourselves circumcised to Jehovah, and take away the foreskins of your hearts, you men of Judah and inhabitants of Jerusalem; that my rage may not go forth just like a fire, and it certainly burn with no one to do the extinguishing, on account of the badness of your dealings."

Tell it in [unfaithful] Judah [the apostate organization], you men, and publish it even in [unfaithful] Jerusalem [make it known even at their international headquarters], and say it out, and blow a horn throughout the land. Call out loudly and say: "Gather yourselves together, and let us enter into the fortified cities [faithful Jerusalem]. Raise a signal toward Zion. Make provision for shelter. Do not stand still." For there is a calamity that I am bringing in from the north, even a great crash. He has gone up as a lion [Leon] out of his thicket, and the one who is bringing the nations to ruin has pulled away; he has gone forth from his place in order to render your land [the organization] as an object of astonishment. Your own cities will fall in ruins so that there will be no inhabitant. On this account gird on sackcloth, you people. Beat your breasts and howl, because the burning anger of Jehovah has not turned back from us.

"And it must occur in that day," is the utterance of Jehovah, "that the heart of the king [unfaithful "faithful and discreet slave"] will perish, also the heart of the princes [unfaithful shepherds, those taking the lead in the organization of Jehovah's Witnesses]; and the priests will certainly be driven to astonishment, and the prophets themselves will be amazed."

And I proceeded to say: "Alas, O Sovereign Lord Jehovah! Truly you have absolutely deceived this people and Jerusalem, saying, 'Peace itself will become yours,' and the sword has reached clear to the soul [of false Jerusalem; the organization is claiming to have the peace of God, and yet Jehovah is about to strike them down]."

Jeremiah 6:14, And they try to heal the breakdown of my people lightly, saying, "There is peace! There is peace!" when there is no peace.

1 Thessalonians 5:3, Whenever it is that they [the organization of Jehovah's Witnesses] are saying: "Peace and security!" then sudden destruction is to be instantly upon them just as the pang of distress upon a pregnant woman; and they will by no means escape. [For a long time now, the organization has been telling their members that their organization is a spiritual "paradise." They say that the physical paradise of the new earth will also be theirs, as their future and reward from Jehovah. Jehovah surprises them! Because already he is poised to strike, and "the sword has reached clear to the soul." (Jeremiah 4:10)]

Jeremiah 4:11-18, At that time it will be said to this people and to Jerusalem [the apostate organization of Jehovah's Witnesses]: "There is a searing wind of the beaten paths through the wilderness on the way to the daughter of my people; it is not for winnowing, nor for cleansing. The full wind itself comes even from these to me. Now I myself also shall speak forth the judgments with them. Look! Like rain clouds he will come up, and his chariots are like a storm wind. His horses are swifter than eagles. Woe to us, because we have been despoiled! Wash your heart clean of sheer badness, O Jerusalem [apostate organization], in order that you may be saved. How long will your erroneous thoughts lodge within you? For a voice is telling from Dan [The word Dan means "judge"] and is publishing something hurtful from the mountainous region of Ephraim. Make mention of it, you people, yes, to the nations. Publish it against [unfaithful] Jerusalem."

"Watchers are coming from a land far away, and they will let out their voice against the very cities of [unfaithful] Judah [the organization of Jehovah's Witnesses]. Like guards of the open field they have become against her on all sides, because she has rebelled even against me," is the utterance of Jehovah. "Your way and your dealings—there will be a rendering of these to you. This is the calamity upon you, for it is bitter; because it has reached clear to your heart."

Vision: [Jehovah showed me a vision. He showed me an image of a building similar to the one next to our building, which only has a foundation at this time. Jehovah likens this to my current state. He is building my foundation; the foundation for the "woman afflicted, tempest-tossed, uncomforted." (Isaiah 54:11) Leon will complete the rebuilding of "Jerusalem," Lisa. (Isaiah 44:28) Jehovah is laying as a foundation in Zion a stone, a tried stone. (Isaiah 28:16)]

Zion: [I am referred to as "Zion" several times in the scriptures. A woman is given the name of her husband, Leon→Lion→Zion. Adam was our first human father. Zion (Leon) comes in the end times.]

Recall: Isaiah 46:9-11, Remember the first things of a long time ago, that I am the Divine One and there is no other God, nor anyone like me; the One telling from the beginning the finale, and from long ago the things that have not been done; the One saying, "My own counsel will stand, and everything that is my delight I shall do"; the One calling from the sunrising a bird of prey, from a distant land the man to execute my counsel. I have even spoken it; I shall also bring it in. I have formed it, I shall also do it."

Complete: [There is a sense of "completeness" about the documents of my life, including this journal.]

Manuscript: A handwritten book or other text. [The original manuscript of this journal is handwritten.]

Tablet: Isaiah 30:8, Now come, write it upon a tablet with them [the scriptures Jehovah has given me], and inscribe it even in a book, that it may serve for a future day, for a witness to time indefinite. [This is the witness to be inscribed upon a tablet; my original handwritten journal in a tablet.]

Song of Solomon 4:11 Good News Bible, The taste of honey is on your lips, my darling; your tongue [written words] is milk and honey for me.

Recall: Exodus 3:8, And I am proceeding to go down to deliver them out of the hand of the Egyptians and to bring them up out of that land to a land good and spacious, to a land flowing with milk and honey.

Research: Insight on the Scriptures, volume 1, page 356 WBTS (1988), ***Booths:*** *Lookout huts or towers; permanent elevated structures that are sometimes used as places for protection and concealment. Isaiah likens desolated Jerusalem to a booth in a vineyard in contrast to a populous, built-up city. (Isaiah 1:8) Also, Jehovah is described as dwelling in a booth of clouds when he temporarily descends from heaven to earth. (Psalm 18:9,11; Job 36:29)*

Friend Of God: Research: Aid To Bible Understanding WBTS, ***Friend of God:*** *Abraham was called "Friend" by Jehovah.*

[I have also been called "Friend" by Jehovah. And, like Abraham I was told by Jehovah in a message, "because you have not withheld even this one." (Genesis 22:16) My spiritual "son" is Leon. (Isaiah 66:8) Jehovah was referring to the fact that, like Abraham, who did not hold back from God his son Isaac, in my heart I have not held back from Jehovah even Leon. I have continued to put Jehovah first in my heart. The Aid to Bible Understanding book says of Abraham, that he had "outstanding faith, which he demonstrated to the greatest degree possible in his willingness to offer up his son, Isaac, as a sacrifice." I, also, was willing to "let go" of Leon, when I had to make a choice, remaining faithful to Jehovah, because Jehovah gives me a peaceful and fulfilled life, with or without Leon.]

Test: [Jehovah has shown me that this test that I have been through—losing Leon under these extraordinary and very harsh circumstances—has been likened to Abraham's willingness to sacrifice Isaac. Abraham's faith was tested to the point of almost ending a life. In my case the life that almost ended was my own, through bereavement and heartbreak.

Jehovah also revealed to me that this test of my faith has played a role in the vindication of Jehovah's great and holy name. It is a wonderful honor to be allowed to be a part of this.]

Message: [Jehovah has indicated to me that when Leon reaches the point in his own spiritual awareness where he comprehends the work that I have already accomplished, he will say: "I don't think I want to be king—someone else."]

Message: [Jehovah sends both of us this message: "The crown, the crown, remember the crown!"]

Message: [Referring to Leon as he is going away from me at this time, Jehovah gave me this message: "If he has to go, I (Jehovah) will go with him."]

Message: ["It is going to be all right, he will be back tomorrow. He is going after the crown." "Tomorrow" means at some future point in time, even years from now.]

Recall: Zechariah 2:4,5,7, Then he said to him: "Run, speak to the young man [Leon] over there, saying, 'As open rural country Jerusalem [Lisa] will be inhabited, because of the multitude of men and domestic animals in the midst of her. And I myself shall become to her,' is the utterance of Jehovah, 'a wall of fire all around, and a glory is what I shall become in the midst of her.'"

"Hey there, Zion [Leon]! Make your escape, you who are dwelling with the daughter of Babylon."

Recall: Isaiah 45:13, "I myself have roused up someone in righteousness, and all his ways I shall straighten out. He is the one that will build my city, and those of mine in exile he will let go, not for a price nor for bribery," Jehovah of armies has said.

My Response: [This is my response to Leon's concerns: "Jehovah is our **support and strength**. I have been able to get to this point in my own life, only because Jehovah has been there **every step** of the way. **He is already there for you.**

I have tremendous regrets for my past sinful actions. With Jehovah there is **complete forgiveness**, even though we have difficulty forgiving ourselves. Jehovah has taught me and corrected me. I have learned and changed.

Leon, it isn't what you have done in the past that is important now; it's what you are capable of doing from this point forward. I have been praying for you and I know you will succeed! I will always pray for you.

All of Jehovah's ways are perfect and we can trust him completely to guide us through these difficult times."]

! Revelation 5:6a,12b, And I saw standing in the midst of the throne and of the four living creatures and in the midst of the elders a lamb [lion-like Leon becomes like a lamb, obedient to Jehovah, even to the point of being "killed"] as though it had been slaughtered.

The Lamb that was slaughtered is worthy to receive the power and riches and wisdom and strength and honor and glory and blessing. [Recall: I remember the message that Jehovah has given me: "Bringing in the royal family soon."]

Recall: Job Chapter 36 all verses [abbreviated here], And Elihu proceeded to say further: "Have patience with me [Jehovah] a little while, and I shall declare to you [Leon] that there are yet words to say for God. I shall carry my knowledge from far off, and to my Fashioner I shall ascribe righteousness. **For my words are for a fact no falsehood; the One perfect in knowledge is with you.** Look! God is mighty and will not reject; he is mighty in power of heart; he will not preserve anyone wicked alive, but the judgment of the afflicted ones he will give. He will not take away his eyes from anyone righteous; even kings on the throne—he will also seat them forever, and they will be exalted. And if they are bound in fetters, they are captured with ropes of affliction. Then he will tell them about the way they act and their transgressions, because they take a superior air. **And he will uncover their ear to exhortation, and he will say that they should turn back from what is hurtful.** If they obey and serve, they will finish their days in what is good and their years in pleasantness. But if they do not obey, they will pass away even by a missile, and they will expire without knowledge. He [Jehovah] will rescue the afflicted one in his affliction, and he will uncover their ear in the oppression. And he will also certainly allure you from the mouth of distress! Broader space, not constraint, will be in its place, and the consolation of your table will be full of fatness. With the judicial sentence upon the wicked one you will certainly be filled; judicial sentence and justice will themselves take hold. For take care that rage does not allure you into spiteful handclapping, and let not a large ransom itself lead you astray. Will your cry for help take effect? No, nor in distress even all your powerful efforts. Do not pant for the night, for peoples to retreat from where they are. Be on your guard that you do not turn to what is hurtful, for this you have chosen rather than affliction. Look! God himself acts exaltedly with his power; who is an instructor like him? Who has called his way to account against him, and who has said, 'You have committed unrighteousness'? Remember that you should magnify his activity of which men have sung. All mankind themselves have gazed upon it; mortal man himself keeps looking from far off. Behold! God is more exalted than we can know; in number his years are beyond searching. For he draws up the drops of water; they filter as rain for his mist, so that the clouds trickle, they drip upon mankind abundantly. Indeed, who can understand the cloud layers, the crashings from his booth?"

Psalm 118 all verses Good News Bible, Give thanks to the Lord, because he is good, and his love is eternal. Let the people of Israel say, "His love is eternal." Let the priests of God say, "His love is eternal." Let all who worship him say, "His love is eternal."

In my distress I [Leon] called to the Lord; he answered me and set me free. The Lord is with me, I will not be afraid; what can anyone do to me? It is the Lord who helps me, and I will see my enemies defeated. It is better to trust in the Lord than to depend on man. It is better to trust in the Lord than to depend on human leaders.

Many enemies were around me; but I destroyed them by the power of the Lord! They were around me on every side; but I destroyed them by the power of the Lord! They swarmed around me like bees, but they burned out as quickly as a brush fire; by the power of the Lord I destroyed them. I was fiercely attacked and was being defeated, but the Lord helped me. The Lord makes me powerful and strong; he has saved me.

Listen to the glad shouts of victory in the tents of God's people: "The Lord's mighty power has done it! His power has brought us victory—his mighty power in battle!"

I will not die; instead, I will live and proclaim what the Lord has done. He has punished me [Leon] severely, but he has not let me die.

Open to me the gates of the Temple; I will go in and give thanks to the Lord!

This is the gate of the Lord; only the righteous can come in.

I praise you, Lord, because you heard me, because you have given me victory.

The stone which the builders rejected as worthless turned out to be the most important of all. This was done by the Lord; what a wonderful sight it is! **This is the day of the Lord's victory; let us be happy, let us celebrate! Save us, Lord, save us! Give us success, O Lord!**

May God bless the one [Leon] who comes in the name of the Lord! From the Temple of the Lord we bless you. The Lord [Jehovah] is God; he has been good to us. With branches in your hands, start the festival and march around the altar.

You are my God, and I give you thanks; I will proclaim your greatness.

Give thanks to the Lord [Jehovah], because he is good, and his love is eternal.

Psalm 119:43 Good News Bible, Enable me to speak the truth at all times, because my hope is in your judgments. [I have been judged favorably by Jehovah.]

Psalm 119:44-49 Good News Bible, I will always obey your law, forever and ever. I will live in perfect freedom, because I try to obey your teachings. I will announce your commands to kings and I will not be ashamed. **I find pleasure in obeying your commands, because I love them. [!] I respect and love your commandments; I will meditate on your instructions.**

Remember your promise to me [Lisa], your servant; it has given me hope.

Recall: Jeremiah 1:11,12, And the word of Jehovah continued to occur to me, saying: "What are you seeing, Jeremiah?"

So I [Lisa] said: "An offshoot of an almond tree [meaning "awakening one;" Leon] is what I am seeing."

And Jehovah went on to say to me: **"You have seen well, for I am keeping awake concerning my word in order to carry it out."**

Psalm 119:50, Good News Bible, Even in my [Lisa's] suffering [abandonment by Leon to shepherd another flock] I was comforted because your [Jehovah's] promise gave me life.

Recall: Psalm 34:12, Who is the man that is delighting in life, that is loving [willing to stay alive] enough days to see what is good?

Psalm 119:37,38 Good News Bible, Keep me [Lisa] from paying attention to what is worthless [Satan's efforts to tear down my faith in Jehovah's promises]; be good to me, as you have promised. Keep your promise to me, your servant—the promise you make to those who obey you.

Psalm 119:5,10,28, Good News Bible, How I [Lisa] hope that I shall be faithful in keeping your instructions!
With all my heart I try to serve you; keep me from disobeying your commandments.
I am overcome by sorrow; strengthen me, as you have promised.

Acts 7:30-50, And when forty years were fulfilled, there appeared to him in the wilderness of Mount Sinai an angel in the fiery flame of a thornbush. Now when Moses saw it he marveled at the sight. But as he was approaching to investigate, Jehovah's voice came, "I am the God of your forefathers, the God of Abraham and of Isaac and of Jacob." Seized with trembling, Moses did not dare to investigate further. Jehovah said to him, "Take the sandals off your feet, for the place on which you are standing is holy ground. **I have certainly seen the wrongful treatment of my [faithful] people who are in Egypt [apostate organization of Jehovah's Witnesses], and I have heard their groaning and I have come down to deliver them.** And now come, I will send you off to Egypt." This Moses, whom they disowned saying, "Who appointed you ruler and judge?" this man God sent off as both ruler and deliverer by the hand of the angel that appeared to him in the thornbush. This man led them out after doing portents and signs in Egypt and in the Red Sea and in the wilderness for forty years.

"This is the Moses that said to the sons of Israel, **'God will raise up for you from among your brothers a prophet like me.'** This is he that came to be among the congregation in the wilderness with the angel that spoke to him on Mount Sinai and with our forefathers, and he received living sacred pronouncements to give you. To him our forefathers refused to become obedient, but they thrust him aside and in their hearts they turned back to Egypt, saying to Aaron, 'Make gods for us to go ahead of us. For this Moses, who led us out of the land of Egypt, we do not know what has happened to him.' So they made a calf in those days and brought up a sacrifice to the idol and began to enjoy themselves in the works of their hands. So God turned and handed them over to render sacred service to the army of heaven, just as it is written in the book of the prophets, 'It was not to me that you offered victims and sacrifices for forty years in the wilderness, was it, O house of Israel? But it was the tent of Moloch and the star of the god Rephan that you took up, the figures which you made to worship them. Consequently I will deport you beyond Babylon.'

"Our forefathers had the tent of the witness in the wilderness, just as he gave orders when speaking to Moses to make it according to the pattern he had seen. And our forefathers who succeeded to it also brought it in with Joshua into the land possessed by the nations, whom God thrust out from before our forefathers. Here it remained until the days of David. He found favor in the sight of God and asked for the privilege of providing a habitation for the God of Jacob. However, Solomon built a house for him. **Nevertheless, the Most High does not dwell in houses made with hands; just as the prophet says, 'The heaven is my throne, and the earth is my footstool. What sort of house will you build for me? Jehovah says. Or what is the place for my resting? My hand made all these things, did it not?'**

Ephesians 3:14-19, On account of this I bend my knees to the Father, to whom every family in heaven and on earth owes its name, to the end that he may grant you according to the riches of his glory to be made mighty in the man you are inside with power through his spirit, to have the Christ dwell through your faith in your hearts with love; that you may be rooted and established on the foundation, in order that you may be thoroughly able to grasp mentally with all the holy ones what is the breadth and length and height and depth, and to know the love of the Christ which surpasses knowledge, that you may be filled with all the fullness that God gives. [We are the temple of Jehovah.]

Isaiah 12:6, Cry out shrilly and shout for joy, O you inhabitress of Zion, for great in the midst of you is the Holy One of Israel.

Revelation 5:6, And I saw standing in the midst of the throne and of the four living creatures and in the midst of the elders a lamb [Leon] as though it had been slaughtered, having seven horns and seven eyes, which eyes mean the seven spirits of God that have been sent forth into the whole earth.

Recall: Zechariah 4:10, For who has despised the day of small things? And they will certainly rejoice and see the plummet in the hand of Zerubbabel [Leon]. These seven are the eyes of Jehovah. They are roving about in all the earth.

Psalm 90:12-14, Show us just how to count our days in such a way that we may bring a heart of wisdom in. Do return, O Jehovah! How long will it be? And feel regret over your servants. Satisfy us in the morning with your loving-kindness, that we may cry out joyfully and may rejoice during all our days.

Recall: Psalm 149:5, Let the loyal ones exult in glory; let them cry out joyfully on their beds.

Revelation 11:1, And a reed like a rod was given me as he said: "Get up and measure the temple sanctuary of God and the altar and those worshipping in it."

Recall: Zechariah 2:2 NWT (1984), So I said: "Where are you going?"
In turn he said to me: "To measure Jerusalem [Lisa, "measured" to determine the amount or degree of uprightness and justice found in her], in order to see what her breadth amounts to and what her length amounts to."

Revelation 11:2, But as for the courtyard [organization of Jehovah's Witnesses] that is outside the temple sanctuary, cast it clear out and do not measure it, because it has been given to the nations, and they will trample the holy city underfoot for forty-two months.

Recall: Jeremiah 3:15, And I will give you shepherds in agreement with my heart, and they will certainly feed you [you, plural] with knowledge and insight.

Isaiah 44:1-8, "And now listen, O Jacob [Leon] my servant, and you [Lisa], O Israel, whom I have chosen. This is what Jehovah has said, your Maker and your Former, who kept helping you even from the belly, 'Do not be afraid, O my servant Jacob, and you, Jeshurun, whom I have chosen. For I shall pour out water upon the thirsty one, and trickling streams upon the dry place. I shall pour out my spirit upon your seed, and my blessing upon your descendants. And they will certainly spring up as among the green grass, like poplars by the water ditches. This one will say: "I belong to Jehovah." And that one will call himself by the name of Jacob, and another will write upon his hand: "Belonging to Jehovah." And by the name of Israel one will betitle himself.'
"This is what Jehovah has said, the King of Israel and the Repurchaser of him, **Jehovah of armies, 'I am the first and I am the last, and besides me there is no God.** And who is there like me? Let him call out, that he may tell it and present it to me. From when I appointed the people of long ago, both the things coming and the things that will enter in let them tell on their part. Do not be in dread, you people, and do not become stupefied. Have I not from that time on caused you individually to hear and told it out? And you are my witnesses. Does there exist a God besides me? No, there is no Rock. I have recognized none.'"

Revelation 11:3, And I will cause my two witnesses [Leon and Lisa] to prophesy a thousand two hundred and sixty days dressed in sackcloth. These are symbolized by the two olive trees and the two lampstands and are standing before the Lord of the earth.

Recall: Zechariah 4:11-14, And I proceeded to answer and say to him: "What do these two olive trees on the right side of the lampstand and on its left side mean?" Then I answered the second time and said to him: "What are the two bunches of twigs of the olive trees that, by means of the two golden tubes, are pouring forth from within themselves the golden liquid?"

So he said to me: "Do you not really know what these things mean?"

In turn I said: "No, my lord."

Accordingly he said: "These are the two anointed ones [Leon and Lisa] who are standing alongside the Lord of the whole earth."

Revelation 11:5, And if anyone wants to harm them, fire issues forth from their mouths and devours their enemies; and if anyone should want to harm them, in this manner he must be killed.

Recall: Psalm 105:15, Saying: "Do not you men touch my anointed ones [Leon and Lisa], and to my prophets do nothing bad."

Revelation 10:1-3, And I saw another strong angel descending from heaven, arrayed with a cloud, and a rainbow was upon his head, and his face was as the sun, and his feet were as fiery pillars, and he had in his hand a little scroll opened. [Literally, little scroll means "little booklet." The original notebook this journal is written in is smaller than the standard 8½ x 11 inch notebook. It is a little booklet, a "little scroll."] **And he set his right foot upon the sea, but his left one upon the earth, and he cried out with a loud voice just as when a lion roars. And when he cried out, the seven thunders uttered their own voices.**

Jeremiah 1:9, At that Jehovah thrust his hand out and caused it to touch my [Lisa's] mouth. Then Jehovah said to me: "Here I have put my words in your mouth."

Jeremiah 15:16, Your [Jehovah's] words were found, and I [Lisa] proceeded to eat them; and your word becomes to me the exultation and the rejoicing of my heart; for your name has been called upon me, O Jehovah God of armies.

Isaiah 62:4, No more will you [Lisa] be said to be a woman left entirely; and your own land will no more be said to be desolate; but you yourself will be called My Delight Is in Her, and your land

Owned as a Wife. For Jehovah will have taken delight in you, and your own land will be owned as a wife.

[This written work is a testimonial to the truth of God's word, the greatness of his love for us, and the mightiness of his holy spirit in the outworking of his will on earth today.

He is demonstrating his active involvement in our lives by fulfilling long-standing Bible prophecies, sending forth his servants, instructing us in righteousness, proving out the wisdom of walking in his ways and giving us cause for faith and hope. He is holding out his hand to us, offering us his comfort and protection, and bringing us into a right and good relationship with him. This is the ministry of the reconciliation.]

Jehovah's Holy Name: [Jehovah's holy name means "I Shall Prove To Be What I Shall Prove To Be," "I AM THAT I AM," or "He Causes to Become." Jehovah will "cause to become" or "prove" to be true, every promise he has made to his people. Jehovah is calling his faithful people to come out of the spiritual darkness of the apostate organization of Jehovah's Witnesses, and come to his light.]

Isaiah 52:11, Turn away, turn away, get out of there, touch nothing unclean; get out from the midst of her, keep yourselves clean, you who are carrying the utensils of Jehovah.

Revelation 18:4,5 NWT (1984), And I heard another voice out of heaven say: "**Get out of her, my people**, if you do not want to share with her in her sins, and if you do not want to receive part of her plagues. For her sins have massed together clear up to heaven, and God has called her acts of injustice to mind.

[It is time for us to act on our faith and leave behind the oppressive and untrue teachings of the apostate organization of Jehovah's Witnesses. Let us earnestly pray to Jehovah for his wisdom and strength to do what is right.]

Psalm 90:15-17, Make us rejoice correspondingly to the days that you have afflicted us, the years that we have seen calamity. May your activity appear to your own servants and your splendor upon their sons. And let the pleasantness of Jehovah our God prove to be upon us, and the work of our hands do you firmly establish upon us. Yes, the work of our hands, do you firmly establish it.

[Ahead of us, there is much work to do. Jehovah will give us a responsible role in the "ministry of the reconciliation." (2 Corinthians 5:16-20) We will also have an active part in the restoration of the earth. (Acts 3:19-25)

We will need the help of many people to faithfully complete this work. Jehovah knows who his people are. He will bring his faithful people out of the apostate organization. Jehovah will comfort our hearts and teach us his righteous ways. And, as a people, as a family, we will all walk in faithfulness before Jehovah.]

Yours, O JEHOVAH, are the greatness and the mightiness and the beauty and the excellency and the dignity; for everything in the heavens and in the earth is yours. Yours is the kingdom, O Jehovah, the One also lifting yourself up as head over all. The riches and the glory are on account of you, and you are dominating everything; and in your hand there are power and mightiness, and in your hand is ability to make great and to give strength to all. And now, O our God, we are thanking you and praising your beauteous name.

"And yet, who am I and who are my people, that we should retain power to make voluntary offerings like this? (1 Chronicles 29:11-14)

Jehovah's Faithful Witnesses: [We are now Jehovah's Faithful Witnesses. We will see the earth transformed into the promised paradise, and we will have the opportunity to live there forever. We will see all of Jehovah's faithful promises fulfilled. We will all be a true family, loved by Jehovah, our Heavenly Father, and his Son, Jesus Christ, as well as all those in the spirit realm. Every person on earth will be family to us. The grief and suffering we have experienced living in this world will be eased from our hearts. Our needs will be met abundantly. And life will be as Jehovah intended from the beginning of creation.]

This message is from JEHOVAH: "There will be no delay."

**That people may know that you, whose name is
JEHOVAH,
you alone are the Most High over all the earth.
(Psalm 83:18)**

CPSIA information can be obtained
at www.ICGtesting.com
Printed in the USA
LVHW110857031021
699369LV00004B/18